MUHAMMAD

For Malcolm
I take away fond memories
from Ashridge. Thank you.

25/5/84.

Also by Muhammad Zafrulla Khan

Islam: Its Meaning for Modern Man

MUHAMMAD
:Seal of the Prophets:

Muhammad Zafrulla Khan

ROUTLEDGE & KEGAN PAUL
London, Boston
and Henley

First published in 1980
by Routledge & Kegan Paul Ltd
39 Store Street,
London WC1E 7DD,
9 Park Street,
Boston, Mass. 02108, USA and
Broadway House,
Newtown Road,
Henley on Thames,
Oxon RG9 1EN

Set in 10/11 Phototronic Plantin by
Saildean Ltd., Surrey
and printed in Great Britain by
Redwood Burn Ltd
Trowbridge & Esher

British Library Cataloguing in Publication Data

Khan, Muhammad Zafrulla
Muhammad.
1. Muhammad, the prophet – Biography
297'.63   BP75   80-40570

ISBN 0 7100 0610 1

Contents

Preface

Muhammad, Prophet of Islam, peace be on him, has been described in the Holy Quran as an excellent exemplar (33:22). Also, he was commanded to announce: 'If you love Allah, follow me, Allah will then love you and forgive you your faults. Allah is Most-Forgiving, Ever-Merciful' (3:32).

This necessitated that his life should be lived in the light of day and that a full account of it should become available. It was also necessary that his life should be multi-faceted, in the sense that he should be called upon to fill a diversity of roles, and that he should fill those roles to perfection. Therefore, unlike all other Prophets, Muhammad was a historical figure. He was born in Mecca in 570 and lived through the first third of the seventh century. A full account of his life is available for study and research.

It is only lately that Western scholars have embarked upon an objective study of the life of the Prophet of Islam. With only two or three honourable exceptions, up to quite recent times, he was represented as an embodiment of all that was vicious and despicable. There is now genuine eager interest in the West both in Islam and its Prophet. Muhammad must be studied and judged as a prophet. He claimed to be a prophet who had been raised for the benefit of the whole of mankind, for all time. He was commanded to proclaim: 'O mankind, verily I am Allah's Messenger to you all' (7:159). In studying his life, certain factors must be kept in mind. Was the world in need of a comprehensive, universal divine message? Was the life of Muhammad, before he laid claim to prophethood, of such perfect purity as would indicate that he had been chosen and was being prepared for becoming the bearer of such a message? Did the message that he purported to bring contain guidance for the whole of mankind and was it suited to all their needs? Was it illustrated in his life and conduct? Did he succeed in conveying the message that was entrusted to him? Was he successful in initiating and in bringing about a moral and spiritual revolution in the lives of those who responded to his message?

The answers to these questions would help a seeker after truth to determine whether he was truly the divine instrument chosen for the regeneration of mankind through the ages.

The purpose of this volume is to institute a study of the life of Muhammad which should be illustrative of its diverse facets and should enable the reader to carry out an assessment of the extent to which it fulfilled the purposes for which he had been divinely appointed.

All references, unless otherwise specified, are to the Holy Quran.

Introduction

The study of a prophet's life is necessarily concerned not only with the physical but also with the moral and the spiritual; indeed, primarily with the moral and the spiritual as illustrated in the physical and the material.

Muhammad was a human being like the rest of us. He was commanded in the Holy Quran (18:111):

> Tell them: I am but a man like unto you; it is revealed to me that your God is One God. So let him who hopes to meet his Lord work righteousness and let him associate no one in the worship of his Lord.

An exemplar must be a man in all respects like his fellow men. A superhuman being cannot be an exemplar for human beings. His faculties, capacities, sentiments, reactions, reflexes, and all his values would be different from those of men. Even if he could understand men in every respect, men would not be able to understand, appraise and assess him completely. Thus, being a man like unto other men, Muhammad fulfilled the first and most essential condition of being an exemplar for other men. He was no different from them; he had similar faculties and capacities and he could understand them perfectly. So would they, if they tried, be able to understand him.

It may be said that a prophet is different from other men. This is true in a certain sense, but the difference is only one of degree, and not of kind. Every human being has a distinct personality and thus differs from his fellows in certain respects. His physical and mental characteristics and equipment may differ from those of the men with whom he associates and among whom he moves about. The only speciality of a prophet in respect of which he is distinguished from other men is that he enjoys an intense degree of communion with God. But even in that respect, those who believe in him and associate with him can share with him, to a greater or lesser degree, in such communion. They can understand him perfectly.

Did the Holy Prophet appear at a time when the world was in need of a universal and comprehensive spiritual guidance? It should be recalled that he was born in AD 570 and received the divine call in

1

610. He died in 632. History bears out that this was the darkest period of the Dark Ages. There was a faint glimmer of light, here and there, but on the whole, mankind was bereft almost entirely of spiritual light. The light and the guidance needed were supplied through Muhammad.

Pringle Kennedy has observed (*Arabian Society at the Time of Muhammad,* pp.8-10, 18-21):

> Muhammad was, to use a striking expression, the man of the hour. In order to understand his wonderful success, one must study the conditions of his times. Five and half centuries and more had elapsed when he was born since Jesus had come into the world. At that time, the old religions of Greece and Rome, and of the hundred and one states along the Mediterranean, had lost their vitality. In their place, Caesarism had come as a living cult. The worship of the state as personified by the reigning Caesar, such was the religion of the Roman Empire. Other religions might exist, it was true; but they had to permit this new cult by the side of them and predominant over them. But Caesarism failed to satisfy. The Eastern religions and superstitions (Egyptian, Syrian, Persian) appealed to many in the Roman world and found numerous votaries. The fatal fault of many of these creeds was that in many respects they were so ignoble. . . . When Christianity conquered Caesarism at the commencement of the fourth century, it, in its turn, became Caesarised. No longer was it the pure creed which had been taught some three centuries before. It had become largely de-spiritualised, ritualised, materialised. . . .
>
> How, in a few years, all this was changed, how, by 650 AD a great part of this world became a different world from what it had been before, is one of the most remarkable chapters in human history. . . . This wonderful change followed, if it was not mainly caused by, the life of one man, the Prophet of Mecca. . . . Whatever the opinion one may have of this extraordinary man, whether it be that of the devout Muslim who considers him the last and greatest herald of God's word, or of the fanatical Christian of former days, who considered him an emissary of the Evil One, or of certain modern Orientalists, who look on him rather as a politician than a saint, as an organiser of Asia in general and Arabia in particular, against Europe, rather than as a religious reformer; there can be no difference as to the immensity of the effect which his life has had on the history of the world. To those of us, to whom the man is everything, the milieu but little, he is the supreme instance of what can be done by one man. Even others, who hold that the conditions of time

and place, the surroundings of every sort, the capacity of receptivity of the human mind, have, more than an individual effort, brought about the great steps in the world's history, cannot well deny, that even if this step were to come, without Muhammad, it would have been indefinitely delayed.

In the fifth and sixth centuries, the civilised world stood on the verge of chaos. The old emotional cultures that had made civilisation possible, since they had given to man a sense of unity and of reverence for their rulers, had broken down, and nothing had been found adequate to take their place.... It seemed then that the great civilisation which had taken four thousand years to construct was on the verge of disintegration, and that mankind was likely to return to that condition of barbarism where every tribe and sect was against the next, and law and order were unknown.... The new sanctions created by Christianity were creating divisions and destruction instead of unity and order.... Civilisation like a gigantic tree whose foliage had over-reached the world... stood tottering... rotted to the core.... Was there any emotional culture that could be brought in to gather mankind once more to unity and to save civilisation?... It was among the Arabs that the man was born who was to unite the whole known world of the east and south (J. H. Denison, *Emotions as the Basis of Civilisation*, pp. 265-9).

Muhammad appeared on the scene at one of the darkest periods in all history, when all the civilisations, from Merovingian Gaul to India, were falling to ruin or were in a state of troubled gestation (L. Dermenghem, *The Life of Mahomet*, p. 171).

If the object of religion be the inculcation of morals, the diminution of evil, the promotion of human happiness, the expansion of the human intellect, if the performance of good works will avail in the great day when mankind shall be summoned to its final reckoning, it is neither irreverent nor unreasonable to admit that Muhammad was indeed an Apostle of God (S. P. Scott, *History of the Moorish Empire in Europe*, p. 126).

Philosopher, orator, apostle, legislator, warrior, conqueror of ideas, restorer of rational dogmas; the founder of twenty terrestrial empires and of one spiritual empire, that is Muhammad. As regards all standards by which human greatness may be measured, we may ask, is there any man greater than he?

(Lamartine, *History of Turkey,* p. 276).

The more one reflects on the history of Muhammad and of early Islam, the more one is amazed at the vastness of his achievement. Circumstances presented him with an opportunity such as few men have had, but the man was fully matched with the hour. Had it not been for his gifts as seer, statesman, and administrator and, behind these his trust in God and firm belief that God had sent him, a notable chapter in the history of mankind would have remained unwritten (W. Montgomery Watt, *Muhammad at Medina,* p. 336).

The condition of the world at the time of the advent of Muhammad has been summed up in the Holy Quran as: 'Corruption has appeared on land and sea in consequence of people's misdeeds' (30:42). This is amply borne out by the testimony that we have cited above. Thus, it is clear that the state of the world, at the time of the advent of the Holy Prophet, called loudly for universal and comprehensive divine guidance, to be set forth in God's words, and to be illustrated by a messenger whose life would be multi-faceted and who would serve as an exemplar for mankind. Such was Muhammad. Another very striking factor in his support is that no one else even remotely approaching his stature and his qualities appeared to guide mankind at the time of its greatest need. The conclusion is irresistible that he was beyond doubt the pre-determined instrument of God for the revival of mankind.

What of his origins and his background? Tradition, supported in a large measure by the Bible, has established that Muhammad was a descendant of Abraham, the great Patriarch, who is designated as the Friend of God in the Holy Quran (4:126), through his eldest son, Ishmael.

About a century and a half before the birth of Muhammad, Qusai, a descendant of Fihr, chief of Quraish, married the daughter of the Khuzaa chief of his time, as had done his ancestor Fihr before him. Khuzaa had been the wardens of the Ka'aba. Qusai was an active and intelligent youth who made himself useful to his father-in-law and was often employed by him as his deputy in the performance of the rites of the Ka'aba. When the Khuzaa chief died, Qusai attempted to assume the guardianship of the Temple. Khuzaa objected, claiming for their tribe the hereditary right to the post, and took up arms. Qusai called on his relatives for support and defeated Khuzaa in battle and drove them out. As a result of this successful operation, Quraish became the owners of the valley of Mecca and Khuzaa sank to a subordinate position.

Qusai was a man of remarkable character and intelligence. He persuaded Quraish to build houses in place of tents, grouped around the Ka'aba and in the narrow tributary valleys. The tribe consisted of thirty-six clans and had been in existence for several centuries. It appears, however, that only the more important clans, or those closely related to Qusai, built houses round the Ka'aba. The others lived farther away, probably in tents, while some may have remained nomadic in the desert.

As a settled community, Mecca attracted various types of individuals, not themselves of Quraish. When, in the sixth century, Quraish began to play a leading role in the oriental trade, some families grew rich and acquired retainers. They gathered around them slaves and domestic servants, guards to accompany the caravans, artisans, carpenters, sword-makers, weavers and workers in leather. A growing community also attracted fugitives, tribesmen who had fled from their tribes owing to blood-feuds and were glad to marry and to settle down in Mecca. An urban society began to grow, no longer confined to one tribe.

Qusai organised the pilgrimage to the Ka'aba. He divided his descendants into categories, to each of which he allotted specific duties. The custodianship of the Ka'aba he entrusted to his eldest son, Abdud Dar, and to that son's children. The annual pilgrimage lasted three days, during which large numbers of Arabs, from all over the peninsula, came to Mecca. Qusai decided that Quraish should provide the poor pilgrims with food and water during this period, for which purpose he collected a tax known as *rifada*. Though the religious rites of the pilgrimage lasted only three days, a series of fairs were held at various sites in the neighbourhood during the preceding weeks. As Quraish gradually changed from stockbreeders to merchants, these fairs offered them an opportunity to sell the articles brought by their caravans.

A remarkable reform introduced by Qusai was connected with the calendar. The Arab tribes had hitherto employed the lunar calendar, an easy system for the illiterate people in a country where the phases of the moon are rarely concealed by clouds. But the lunar year of twelve months is approximately eleven days shorter than the solar year. The pilgrimage was held in the twelfth month of the lunar year and moved back eleven days each year in respect of the solar year. Thus, in the course of thirty-three years, the pilgrimage moved completely round the calendar. Qusai decided that the best time to have the pilgrimage take place would be in the autumn. He accordingly persuaded the Arabs to accept an intercalary month every third year, in order to make the lunar year match with the solar year. The system was not quite accurate but was nevertheless a remarkable effort on the part of a primitive tribal chief in the deserts of Arabia.

Arab nomadic tribal chiefs have never exercised autocratic powers and tribal policy has always been discussed in public. Qusai gave these discussions a formal aspect by erecting a building immediately opposite the Ka'aba, called Dar-en-Nadwa, or House of Consultation.

Qusai died sometime between 450 and 460, bequeathing his position to his eldest son, Abdud Dar. In the second generation, the descendants of his second son, Abd Manaf, disputed the leadership with the descendants of Abdud Dar. A compromise was reached whereby the clan of Abdud Dar retained the guardianship of the Ka'aba and of the House of Consultation and the right to carry the tribal banner in war. The clan of Abd Manaf was given the duties of collecting the *rifada* tax, and of providing food and water for the pilgrims. A number of public duties were also distributed to branches of the family.

Quraish only became the capitalists of the oriental trade in the second half of the sixth century. During this period, certain clans, such as the descendants of Abd Manaf and of Makhzoom, became wealthy, while other families remained poor. The majority, however, acquired something of the commercial spirit and even the humblest inhabitants of Mecca would invest in trade whatever modest savings they could collect. Some would club together and would send one of their number with a caravan to trade with their money and share the profits on his return.

Thus the leading men of Mecca were not mere camel caravaners but capitalists. They went down in person to meet the Indian ships in Aden, purchased the articles and transported them first to Mecca, and then to Syria, Gaza or Egypt. In Damascus or in Egypt they bought goods of local manufacture and brought them back to Mecca, where they sold them to the Arab tribes at the fairs held in connection with the annual pilgrimage. A branch caravan route led from Mecca to the Lower Euphrates, passing south of the Nefood sand desert and gave the Meccans an additional commercial advantage. But the main trade route was that which bore the commerce of the east from Aden to Syria and to Egypt.

Of the sons of Abd Manaf, the eldest, Abd Shams, was extremely active in business and made a considerable fortune. Constantly preoccupied with his money-making ventures, he did not undertake any public duties in Mecca, owing to his frequent long absences on business journeys. As a result of his unwillingness to assume local responsibility, Hashim, the second son of Abd Manaf, undertook the family duties. He also had made a good deal of money and was well off. Installed in the office of entertaining the pilgrims, Hashim fulfilled it with princely munificence. He appealed to Quraish as his grand-father Qusai had done: 'Ye are the neighbours of God, and the keepers of His House. Pilgrims to the Temple are His guests; and it is meet that ye entertain them above all other guests. Ye are especially chosen unto this high dignity; wherefore honour His guests and refresh them. For, from distant cities, on their lean and jaded camels, they come unto you fatigued and harassed, with hair dishevelled and bodies covered with the dust and squalor of the way. Then invite them hospitably and furnish them with water in abundance.' Hashim set the example by a munificent provision, and Quraish were forward to contribute, every man according to his ability. Water, sufficient for the great assemblage, was collected in cisterns close by the Ka'aba, and at the stations on the route to Arafat. The distribution of food commenced upon the day on which the pilgrims set out for Mina and Arafat, and continued until they dispersed. During this period of five or six days, they were entertained with meat and bread, butter and barley, and with the favourite national repast of dates.

Thus Hashim supported the credit of Mecca. But his name is even more renowned for the splendid charity by which, in a time of famine, he relieved the necessities of his fellow citizens. Journeying to Syria, he purchased an immense stock of flour, and conveyed it upon camels to Mecca. The provisions were cooked, the camels slaughtered and roasted, and the whole divided among the citizens. Thus destitution and mourning were turned into mirth and plenty; and it was, as it were, the beginning of new life after the year of scarcity.

The foreign relations of Quraish were conducted by the sons of Abd Manaf. With the Roman authorities, and the Ghassanid prince, Hashim himself concluded a treaty; and he received from the Emperor a rescript authorising Quraish to travel through Syria in security. Abd Shams made a treaty with the Negus in pursuance of which Quraish traded with Abyssinia; Naufal and Muttalib entered into an alliance with the King of Persia, who allowed the merchants of Mecca to traffic in Iraq and Fars, and with the Kings of Himyar, who encouraged their commercial operations in the Yemen. Thus the affairs of Quraish prospered in every direction. Hashim established upon a uniform footing the mercantile expeditions of his people, so that every winter a caravan set out for the Yemen and Abyssinia, while in the summer a second caravan visited Gaza, Ancyra, and other Syrian marts.

The success and glory of Hashim exposed him to the envy of Umayya, the second son of his brother, Abd Shams. Umayya was rich, and he expended his wealth in a vain attempt to rival the splendour of Hashim's munificence. Quraish perceived the endeavour, and turned it into ridicule. Umayya was enraged and defied Hashim to a trial of superiority. Hashim was reluctant to enter into a contest, but consented at the urging of Quraish, with the stipulation that the vanquished party should lose fifty black-eyed camels, and be exiled from Mecca for ten years. A Khuza'ite soothsayer was appointed umpire; and, having heard the pretentions of both, pronounced

Hashim to be the victor. Hashim took the fifty camels, slaughtered them in the vale of Mecca, and fed with them all the people present. Umayya set out for Syria, and remained there for the period of his exile.

Hashim was advanced in years when, on a mercantile journey to the north, he visited Yathrab with a party of Quraish. As he traded there, he was attracted by the graceful figure of a female, who from an elevated position was directing her people beneath to buy and sell for her. Hashim inquired of the citizens whether she was single, and they answered that she had been married but was now divorced. They added that her dignity was so great amongst her people that she would not marry, unless it were stipulated that she should remain mistress of her own concerns, and have at pleasure the power of divorce. She was Selma, daughter of Amr of Banu Najjar, a clan of Khazraj. Hashim demanded her in marriage and she consented, for she was well aware of his renown and noble birth. She accompanied him to Mecca, but returned to Yathrab where she gave birth to a son, who remained with his mother at Yathrab.

Hashim died a few years after on a mercantile expedition to Gaza, and left his dignities to his brother, Muttalib. When Hashim's son had grown into boyhood, Muttalib set out for Yathrab to fetch him thence. On his return, as the inhabitants of Mecca saw him pass with a lad by his side they assumed that he had purchased a slave and exclaimed, 'Abdul Muttalib' ('Slave of Muttalib'). He explained that it was his nephew, the son of Hashim, but the name stuck and the boy, whose name was Shaiba, was thereafter known as Abdul Muttalib.

In due time Abdul Muttalib was installed by his uncle in possession of his father's property; but Naufal, another uncle, interposed, and violently deprived him of it. Abdul Muttalib, on reaching the age of discretion, appealed to his tribe for aid to resist this usurpation of his rights; but they declined to interfere. He then wrote to his maternal relatives at Yathrab, of whom, on receiving the intelligence, eighty mounted men started for Mecca. Abdul Muttalib went forth to meet them and invited them to his house; but their chief refused to alight until he had called Naufal to account. Proceeding straight away to the Holy House, he found him seated there among the chiefs of Quraish. Naufal arose to offer welcome but the stranger refused his welcome and, drawing his sword, declared that he would plunge it into him unless he forthwith reinstated the orphan in his rights. Naufal was daunted and agreed to the concession, which was then ratified by oath before the assembled Quraish.

Some years later, on the death of Muttalib, Abdul Muttalib succeeded to the office of entertaining the pilgrims. But for a long time he was destitute of power and influence, and, having at the time but one son to assist him in the assertion of his claims, he found it difficult to cope with the opposing factions of Quraish. It was during this period that he discovered the ancient well Zam zam. Finding it laborious to collect water for the pilgrims from the scattered wells of Mecca and to store it in cisterns by the Ka'aba, and perhaps aware by tradition of the existence of a well in the vicinity, he made a diligent search, and at last chanced upon the venerable masonry. It was a remnant of the palmy days when a rich and incessant stream of commerce flowed through Mecca. Centuries had elapsed since the trade had ceased, and with it had followed the decline of Mecca, and neglect of the well. In course of time, choked up, the remembrance of it had become so indistinct that even the site was now unknown.

As Abdul Muttalib, aided by his son Harith, continued digging deeper, he came upon the two golden gazelles, with the swords and suits of armour, buried there by the Jurhumite King more than three centuries before. Quraish, envying him these treasures, demanded a share and even asserted their right to the well itself, as the possession of their common ancestor Ishmael. Abdul Muttalib was not powerful enough to resist the claim; but he agreed to refer it to the decision of the arrows of Hubal, the god whose image was set up within the Ka'aba. Lots were cast, one for the Ka'aba and two for the respective claimants. The gazelles fell to the share of the Ka'aba, and the swords and suits of armour to that of Abdul Muttalib, while the arrows of Quraish drew blank. Acquiescing in the divine decree, they relinquished their pretensions to the well. Abdul Muttalib beat out the gazelles into plates of gold, and fixed them by way of ornament to the door of the Ka'aba. He hung up the swords before the door as a protection to the treasures within; but at the same time added a more effectual guard in the shape of a golden lock and key.

The plentiful flow of fresh water, soon apparent in the newly-discovered well, was a great triumph for Abdul Muttalib. All other wells in Mecca were deserted, and this alone was resorted to. From it Abdul Muttalib supplied the pilgrims, and the water itself soon shared the sanctity of the Ka'aba and its rites. The fame and influence of Abdul Muttalib now waxed greater and greater, a large family of powerful sons added to his dignity; he became, and continued to his death, the virtual chief of Mecca.

During his early troubles, while supported by an only son, Abdul Muttalib had felt so bitterly his weakness in contending with the large and influential families of his opponents, that he vowed that if Providence should grant him ten sons he would devote one of them to His service. Years rolled on, and the father at last found himself surrounded by the longed-for number, the sight of whom daily reminded him of his vow. He bade his sons accompany him to the Ka'aba, each was made to write his name upon a lot, and the lots were made over to the intendant of the Ka'aba, who cast them in the usual mode. The fatal arrow fell upon Abdullah, the youngest and best beloved. The vow must needs be fulfilled by the sacrifice of Abdullah. His daughters wept and clung around him and he was willingly persuaded to cast lots between Abdullah and ten camels, which was the current amount of blood money for one person. If the ransom was accepted, the father could spare his son without scruple. But the lot a second time fell upon Abdullah. Again, and with equal fortune, it was cast between him and twenty camels. At each successive trial, the anxious father added ten camels to the stake, but the lot still indicated that the blood of his youngest son was demanded. It was now the tenth throw, and the ransom had reached a hundred camels, when the lot at last fell upon them, and the father joyfully released Abdullah from his impending fate, and slaughtered the hundred camels between Safa and Marwa. The inhabitants of Mecca feasted upon them, and, Abdul Muttalib's family refusing to partake, the residue was left to the beasts and to the birds.

The prosperity and fame of Abdul Muttalib excited the envy of the house of Umayya, whose son, Harb, challenged his rival to a trial of their respective merits. The Abyssinian king declined to be the umpire, and the judgment was committed to one of Quraish, who declared that Abdul Muttalib was in every respect superior. Harb was deeply mortified, and abandoned the society of his opponent, whose companion he had previously been.

Abdul Muttalib gained an important accession of stability to his party by concluding a defensive league with Khuzaa, who were still inhabitants of Mecca. They came to him and represented that, as their quarters adjoined, such a treaty would be advantageous for both. Abdul Muttalib was not slow in perceiving this. With ten of his adherents he met Bani Khuzaa at the Ka'aba, and there they mutually pledged their faith. The treaty was reduced to writing, and was hung up in the Ka'aba. No one from the family of Umayya was present, or indeed knew of the transaction until it was thus published.

Chapter 1

:Early Years:

Abdul Muttalib, the son of Hashim, grandson of Abd Manaf, father of Abdullah and grandfather of Muhammad, was, in his time, the foremost chief of Mecca. In the year 570 occurred the memorable invasion of Mecca by Abraha, the Abyssinian viceroy of the Yemen. He had built a magnificent cathedral at San'a whither he sought to attract the worship of Arabia; and, thwarted in the attempt, vented his displeasure in organising an attack on Mecca with the purpose of destroying the Ka'aba. Upon this enterprise he set out with a considerable army. In its train was an elephant; a circumstance so singular for Arabia that the commander, his host, the invasion and the year, are still called by the epithet of the elephant. Arriving in the vicinity of Mecca, Abraha sent forward a body of troops to scour the valley and carry off what cattle they could find. They were successful in the raid, and, among the plunder, secured 200 camels belonging to Abdul Muttalib.

Abraha sent an embassy to Mecca carrying the message that he had no desire to do them injury. His only object was to demolish the Ka'aba; that done, he would retire without shedding the blood of any man. The citizens of Mecca had already resolved that it would be vain to oppose the invaders by force of arms; but they refused to allow the destruction of the Ka'aba on any terms. The embassy, however, prevailed on Abdul Muttalib to repair to the viceroy's camp, and there plead the cause of the Meccans. Abdul Muttalib was treated with great honour by Abraha, who, to win him over, restored his plundered camels, but could obtain no satisfactory answer from him regarding the Ka'aba. Abdul Muttalib returned to Mecca and Abraha made preparations to advance upon the city. Abdul Muttalib advised the Meccans to retire in a body to the hills and defiles about the city on the day before the expected attack. He himself repaired to the Ka'aba and, leaning upon the ring of the door of the Ka'aba, prayed aloud: 'Defend, O Lord, Thine own House, and suffer not the cross to triumph over the Ka'aba.' He then betook himself with the rest to the neighbouring heights and watched what the end might be. Meanwhile, a pestilential distemper broke out in the camp of the viceroy, with deadly pustules and blains. In confusion and dismay, the army commenced their retreat. Abandoned by their guides, the men

11

perished among the valleys and a flood swept multitudes into the sea. Scarcely any recovered who was smitten by the pestilence; and Abraha himself, a mass of malignant and putrid sores, died miserably on his return to San'a. This event is mentioned in the Holy Quran, where it is said (105:2-6):

> Dost thou not recall how thy Lord dealt with the People of the Elephant? Did He not destroy them and thus cause their design to miscarry? Then He sent upon their corpses swarms of birds, which beat them against hard lumps of clay, and thus made them like broken straw, left over.

The significance of this event is that the birth of the infant whom God intended to bring up under His care so that in due time he might become the recipient of the comprehensive and universal divine guidance for man, was approaching. Through him, the Ka'aba would be restored to the worship of the One True God, for which it had been originally built. God Almighty would, therefore, not suffer any harm to be done to the Ka'aba or to Mecca which were about to be honoured as just mentioned.

Some months previous to the invasion of Abraha, Abdul Muttalib had affianced his then youngest son, Abdullah, who was twenty-four years of age, to Amina, the niece of Wahb of Bani Zuhra, under whose guardianship she lived. The marriage took place, and not long after Abdullah left his wife, who was with child, and set out on a mercantile expedition to Syria. On his way back, he fell ill at Medina, and was left behind by the caravan with his father's maternal relatives. When Abdul Muttalib learnt of Abdullah's illness he despatched his eldest son, Harith, to take care of his brother. Arriving in Medina, Harith found that Abdullah had died about a month after the departure of the caravan. Amina was thus widowed only after a few months of her marriage before giving birth to her child. The child was born on 20 April 570. As soon as Abdul Muttalib was informed of the blessed event, he visited Amina, took the baby in his arms, went to the Ka'aba and, standing beside the Holy House, gave thanks to God. The child was called Muhammad, according to a dream of Amina. The word means 'one greatly praised'.

It was not the custom for the better class of women at Mecca to suckle their children. They procured nurses for them, or gave them out to nurse among the neighbouring desert tribes. The child thus developed a robust frame, and acquired the pure speech and free manners of the desert. The infant Muhammad, shortly after his birth, was made over to Thuweiba, the slave of his uncle Abu Lahab, who had lately suckled his baby uncle Hamzah. He was nursed by her for only a few days, but he retained in later life a lively recollection of her.

He periodically sent her clothes and other presents until the seventh year of the Hijra, when he received intimation of her death. He inquired after her son, his foster-brother, but he too was dead, and she had left no relatives.

When Thuweiba had nursed the child for some days, a party of Bani Sa'd, a clan of Hawazin, arrived at Mecca with ten women who offered themselves as nurses. They were soon provided with children, excepting Halima, who, somewhat reluctantly, took the infant orphan Muhammad, whose charge had been declined by the other women. Incidentally, Sa'd means 'fortunate', and indeed it was fortunate for Bani Sa'd that the child whom God had intended to be the greatest of His messengers, should be reared among them. Sixty years later, after the battle of Hunain, the prisoners taken from Bani Sa'd were released by the Holy Prophet as a matter of grace in memory of the days that he had spent among Bani Sa'd in his childhood.

Halima means 'the gentle one', and she proved a very gentle and affectionate foster-mother for her charge. At two years of age he was weaned and Halima took him to his home. His mother was delighted with his healthy and robust appearance and she asked Halima to take him back with her again to the desert, for she feared the unhealthy air of Mecca. Thus Halima returned with him to her tribe. He already looked like a child double his age. After another two years Halima again took the boy to his mother, who again persuaded her to take him back once more to the encampment of her tribe. She loved her foster-child and was happy that she had been able to keep him for so long. After one more year, she returned him to his mother and grandfather.

There can be no doubt that the constitution of Muhammad was rendered robust, and his character free and independent, by his five years among Bani Sa'd. Also his speech was formed upon one of the purest models of the language of Arabia.

Muhammad always retained a grateful impression of the kindness he had experienced as a child among Bani Sa'd. On one occasion, Halima visited him at Mecca after his marriage with Khadija. It was a year of drought in which many cattle had perished. Muhammad spoke to Khadija and she gave Halima a camel used to carrying a litter, and forty sheep with which she returned to her people.

Muhammad spent the sixth year of his life at Mecca with his mother, under the care of his grandfather. His mother then planned a visit to Medina and took him along with her to show him to the maternal relatives of his father. She was accompanied by her slave-girl, Um Aiman, who tended the child. They rode upon two camels. Arrived in Medina, she alighted at the house where her husband had died. The visit was of sufficient duration to imprint the scene and the society upon the memory of Muhammad, notwithstanding his tender age. In later days he used to recall things that happened on this occasion. Forty-seven years afterwards, when he entered Medina as a refugee, he recognised the place, and said: 'In this house I sported with Uneisa, a little girl of Medina; and with my cousins, I used to put to flight the birds that alighted upon the roof.' As he gazed upon the scene, he added: 'Here it was my mother lodged with me; in this place is the tomb of my father; and it was there, in that pond, that I learned to swim.'

After staying at Medina for about a month, Amina decided to return to Mecca, and set out in the same manner as she had come. When they reached a spot called Abwa, about half-way to Mecca, Amina fell ill and died; and was buried there. The little orphan was carried back to Mecca by Um Aiman, who, although only a girl, was a faithful nurse to the child, and continued to be his constant attendant.

It has been opined that the early loss of his mother imparted to the youthful Muhammad something of that pensive and meditative character by which he was afterwards distinguished. In his seventh year, he could appreciate the bereavement and feel the desolation of his orphan state. Many years later, during his journey from Medina to Hudaibiyya, he visited his mother's tomb by the way, and lifted up his voice and wept, and his companions also wept. When they asked him about it, he said: 'This is the grave of my mother; the Lord hath permitted me to visit it. So I called my mother to remembrance, and the tender memory of her overcame me and I wept.'

The charge of the orphan was now undertaken by Abdul Muttalib who had by this time reached the age of eighty. The child was treated by him with singular fondness. A rug used to be spread under the Ka'aba and on it the aged chief reclined in shelter from the heat of the sun. Around the carpet, but at a respectful distance, sat his sons. Little Muhammad was wont to run up close to his grandfather and take possession of his rug. His sons would seek to drive him off, but Abdul Muttalib would interpose, saying: 'Let my little son alone.' He would stroke him on the back and would be delighted to listen to his childish prattle. The boy was still under the care of his nurse, but he would often quit her and run into the apartment of his grandfather, even when he was alone or asleep.

The guardianship of Abdul Muttalib lasted but two years, for he died at the age of eighty-two. The orphan child felt the loss of his indulgent grandfather bitterly; as he followed the bier he was seen to weep, and when he grew up he retained a distinct remembrance of his death. The heart of Muhammad, in his tender years, was thus again sorely wounded, and the fresh bereavement was rendered more poignant by the dependent position in which it left him. The nobility of his grandfather's descent, the deference paid to him by everyone in

Mecca, and his splendid hospitality towards the pilgrims, in furnishing them with food and drink, must have been witnessed with satisfaction by the thoughtful child.

The events that Muhammad's father had died before his birth, that his mother died in his seventh year, and that his grandfather died a couple of years later, were not a series of coincidences of little significance. They were part of the divine design, so that he might develop early the qualities of self-reliance, reflection and steadfastness. Though repeatedly bereaved at a tender age, he had been well looked after, as he was under God's special care. We read in the Holy Quran about Moses: 'I surrounded thee with My love, so that thou mightest be reared under My care.... We delivered thee from sorrow and proved thee in diverse ways.... Then thou camest up to the standard, Moses, and I chose thee for Myself' (20:40-2). As with Moses, so with Muhammad. He was under the direct care of God even from before his birth and was being prepared, step by step, for the great responsibility that God intended to place upon his shoulders. He would be screened and sheltered from all harm, whether physical or moral, but would have to undergo all that was needed for the co-ordinated and balanced development of his personality.

The death of Abdul Muttalib left the children of Hashim without any powerful head, which enabled the other branch of Quraish, descended from Umayya, to gain ascendancy. Their chief at this time was Harb, who held the leadership in war and was followed by a numerous and powerful body of relations.

Of Abdul Muttalib's sons, Harith, the eldest, had died; and the chief of those who survived were Zubair and Abu Talib, both by the same mother as Abdullah, and Abu Lahab, Abbas and Hamzah. The last two were still very young. Zubair was the oldest, and to him Abdul Muttalib bequeathed his dignity and offices. Zubair left them to Abu Talib who, finding himself too poor to discharge the expensive and onerous obligations of providing for the pilgrims, waived the honour in favour of Abbas. But the family of Hashim had fallen from its high state and Abbas was able to retain only the giving of drink, while the furnishing of food passed into the hands of another branch. Abbas was rich, and his influential post, involving charge of the well Zam zam, was retained by him till it was confirmed to his family by the Holy Prophet on the fall of Mecca; but he never attained to a commanding position at Mecca. Abu Talib, on the other hand, possessed many noble qualities and won greater respect, but he too remained in the background. Thus, the prestige of the house of Hashim began to wane and the rival Umayyad branch rose to importance.

The dying Abdul Muttalib had consigned the guardianship of his orphan grandchild to Abu Talib, who discharged the trust kindly and faithfully. His fondness for his charge equalled that of Abdul

Muttalib. He made him sleep by his bed, eat by his side, and go with him wherever he walked abroad. This tender treatment was continued until his nephew emerged from childhood.

It was during this period that Abu Talib undertook a mercantile journey to Syria. He intended to leave the boy behind, for he was now twelve years of age and was able to take care of himself. But when the caravan was ready to depart and Abu Talib was about to mount, the boy, overcome by the prospect of so long a separation, clung to his uncle. Abu Talib was moved, and carried him along with the party. The expedition extended to Bosra, perhaps farther. It lasted for several months and afforded to young Muhammad opportunities of observation, which, it is supposed, he did not neglect.

Between the years 580 and 590 the valley of Mecca and its surrounding country were disturbed by one of those bloody feuds so frequently excited by the fiery pride and prolonged by the revengeful temper of Arab tribes. It was known as the Sacrilegious War as it began in one of the four sacred months in which fighting was prohibited. Several battles were fought between the rival tribes with varied success, and hostilities were prolonged for four years, when a truce was called. The dead were numbered up, and as twenty more had been killed of Hawazin than of Quraish, the latter agreed to pay the price of their blood, and for this purpose delivered hostages. One of these was Abu Sufyan, the famous antagonist of Muhammad in later days. In some of these conflicts the whole of Quraish and their allies were engaged. The descendants of Abd Shams were headed by Harb, son of Umayya, and took a distinguished part in the warfare. The children of Hashim were present also, under the command of Zubair, the eldest surviving son of Abdul Muttalib. In one of the battles Muhammad attended upon his uncles, but, though now near twenty years of age, he had not acquired love of arms. His efforts were confined to gathering up the arrows of the enemy as they fell and handing them to his uncles.

A confederacy for the suppression of violence and injustice, formed at Mecca shortly after the restoration of peace, aroused an enthusiasm in the mind of Muhammad which the martial exploits of the Sacrilegious War had failed to kindle. The honour of originating the movement is ascribed to Zubair, son of Abdul Muttalib. The descendants of Hashim and kindred families assembled together and took an oath that they would take the part of one oppressed and see his claim fulfilled so long as a drop of water remained in the ocean, or would satisfy it from their own resources. The league was useful, both as a restraint upon injustice, and, on some occasions, as a means of enforcing restitution. Muhammad used to say in later years: 'I would not exchange for the choicest camel in all Arabia the remembrance of being present at the oath which we took that we would stand by the oppressed.'

At one period of his youth Muhammad was employed, like other young men of his age, in tending the sheep and goats of Mecca upon the neighbouring hills and valleys. The hire received for this duty would, no doubt, have contributed to the support of his uncle, Abu Talib, and the occupation itself was congenial to his thoughtful and meditative character.

All the authorities agree in ascribing to the youth of Muhammad a modesty of deportment and purity of manners rare among the people of Mecca. He appears to have been specially safeguarded by divine grace. On one occasion, when he was engaged in his duty of tending sheep in company with a lad of Quraish, he asked him to look after his flock also, so that he could go into Mecca and divert himself there as other youths were wont to divert themselves by night. But no sooner had he reached the precincts of the city than a marriage feast engaged his attention, and he soon fell asleep. On another similar occasion he again fell asleep till morning on his way to the city. Thus he escaped temptation and sought no more after such diversions. It was quite in keeping with the character of Muhammad that he should have shrunk from the coarse and licentious practices of his youthful compatriots. Endowed with a refined mind and delicate taste, reserved and meditative, he lived much within himself, and the ponderings of his heart supplied occupation for leisure hours spent by others of a lower stamp in rude sports and profligacy. The fair character and honourable bearing of the unobtrusive youth won the approbation of his fellow citizens and by common consent he received the title Al-Amin, the Faithful.

Thus respected and honoured, Muhammad lived a quiet and retired life in the family of Abu Talib, who was prevented by limited means from occupying any prominent position in the society of Mecca. At last, finding his family increase faster than his ability to provide for them, Abu Talib bethought himself of setting his nephew, now of mature age, to earn a livelihood for himself. He approached Khadija, daughter of Khuweilid, who was a woman of means and was interested in mercantile enterprises. She agreed to employ his nephew to look after her merchandise in a caravan that was about to set out for the north. Muhammad prepared for the journey and, when the caravan was about to set out, his uncle commended him to the men of the company. Meisara, servant of Khadija, also travelled along with Muhammad in charge of her property. The caravan took the usual route to Syria which Muhammad had traversed with his uncle thirteen years before. In due time it reached Bosra, on the road to Damascus, about 60 miles to the east of the Jordan. The transactions of that busy mart, where the practised merchants of Syria sought to overreach the simple Arabs, were ill-suited to the taste and habits of Muhammad; yet his natural sagacity and shrewdness carried him prosperously through the undertaking. He returned from the barter with a balance more than usually in his favour.

When he had disposed of the merchandise and purchased for his mistress such things as she had need of, he retraced his steps in company with the caravan to his native valley. The mildness of his manners and his kind attention had won the heart of Meisara and, as they drew near to Mecca, he persuaded Muhammad to go in advance of the rest, and bear to his mistress first tidings of the successful traffic. Khadija was impressed by the mercantile success of Muhammad and also by his deportment and personality. She was of Quraish, distinguished by fortune as well as by birth. Her father, Khuweilid, was the grandson of Asad, and Asad was the grandson of Kosai. He had commanded a considerable section of Quraish in the Sacrilegious War. Khadija's substance, inherited and acquired from her former marriages, was considerable; and by means of hired agents she had increased it largely in mercantile speculations. To the blessing of affluence, she added the more important endowments of discretion, virtue and an affectionate heart; and, though now mellowed by a more than middle age, she retained a fair and attractive countenance. Several of the chief men of Quraish had sought her in marriage; but choosing to live on in dignified and independent widowhood, she had rejected all their offers. Her own impression of Muhammad was deepened by the praises of his fellow traveller, Meisara, and she resolved to make known her preference to Muhammad in a discreet and cautious way. The upshot was that with the approval of Abu Talib a marriage was arranged between Muhammad and Khadija.

Despite the disparity of age between them (Khadija was forty years of age and Muhammad was twenty-five) the union proved one of unusual tranquillity and happiness. It conferred upon Muhammad a faithful and affectionate companion and, in spite of her age, Khadija bore him several children. She, on her part, fully appreciated the noble genius and commanding mind of Muhammad, which his reserved and contemplative habit veiled from others but could not conceal from her. She continued to conduct the duties of her establishment and left him free to enjoy his leisure hours, undisturbed by care. Her house became his own and her bosom the safe receptacle of those longings after spiritual light which now began to agitate his soul.

Within the next ten or twelve years Khadija bore to Muhammad two sons and four daughters. The first born was named Qasim, and after him, according to Arabian custom, Muhammad became known as Abul Qasim. This son died at the age of two years. Meanwhile Zainab, the eldest daughter, was born; and after her, at intervals of one or two years, three other daughters, Ruqayya, Um Kulthum and Fatima. Last of all was born his second son, who died in infancy. Selma, maid of Safiya, Muhammad's aunt, officiated as midwife on these occasions, but Khadija nursed her children herself. Many years after Muhammad used to look back to this period of his life with fond remembrance. Indeed, so much did he dwell upon the mutual love of Khadija and himself that his wife Aisha declared herself more jealous of Khadija, whom she had never seen, than of all the other wives of the Holy Prophet.

At the time of his marriage with Khadija Muhammad was in the prime of manhood. Slightly above the middle size, his figure, though spare, was handsome and commanding; the chest broad and open; the bones and framework large, and the joints well-knit together. His neck was long and finely moulded. His head, unusually large, gave space for a broad and noble brow. The hair, thick, jet black and slightly curling, fell down over his ears. The eyebrows were arched and joined. His countenance was thin but ruddy. His large eyes, intensely black and piercing, received additional lustre from long, dark eyelashes. The nose was high and slightly aquiline, but fine, and at the end attenuated. The teeth were set apart. A long, black, thick beard, reaching to the breast, added manliness and presence. His expression was pensive and contemplative. His face beamed with intelligence. The skin was clear and soft; the only hair that met the eye was a fine thin line which ran down from his neck towards the navel. His broad back leaned slightly forward as he walked; and his step was hasty, yet short and decided, like that of one rapidly descending a declivity.

There was something unsettled in his eye, which refused to rest upon its object. When he turned towards anyone it was never partially, but with his whole body. Silent and reserved, he was in company distinguished by a graceful urbanity. His words were pregnant and laconic, but when it pleased him to unbend his speech was often humorous. At such seasons he entered with zest into the diversion of the moment, and now and then laughed heartily. But in general he listened to the conversation rather than joined in it.

Muhammad was a man of strong emotions, but they were so controlled by reason and discretion that they rarely appeared on the surface. When much excited, the vein between his eyebrows would mantle and violently swell across his ample forehead; yet he was cautious and circumspect. Generous and considerate towards his friends, he knew, by well-timed favour and attention, how to gain over even the disaffected and rivet them to his service. He did not pursue a foe after he had tendered submission. His commanding mien inspired the stranger with an undefined and indescribable awe; but on closer intimacy, apprehension and fear gave place to confidence and love.

Behind his quiet retiring exterior lay hid a high resolve, a singleness of purpose, a strength and fixedness of will, a sublime determination, destined to achieve the marvellous work of bowing towards himself the heart of the whole of Arabia as the heart of one man. Khadija was the first to perceive the noble and commanding qualities of her husband, and, with a child-like confidence, surrendered to him her soul, her will and faith.

It will be appreciated from the above, upon which all authorities are agreed, that Muhammad had been endowed by divine grace with all the qualities that would be needed for the discharge of the heavy responsibilities that God intended to lay upon him. This was not his own doing or that of anyone else. To a discerning eye, he would have been marked out as a person who was destined for a position of leadership from which to carry out a sublime purpose.

Muhammad was about thirty-five years of age when Quraish decided to rebuild the Ka'aba. A violent flood had shattered the Holy House; its walls showed ominous rents and it was feared lest it should fall. It was resolved that the walls of the Ka'aba should be raised and the roof should be covered. While it was being considered how this might best be done, a Greek ship was driven by bad weather upon the Red Sea shore not far off. When the news of this reached Mecca, the Quraish chieftain, Waleed, accompanied by a body of Quraish, proceeded to the wreck, purchased the timber of the broken ship, and engaged her captain, who was skilled in architecture, to assist in the rebuilding of the Ka'aba. The whole body of Quraish assisted in the operation, until the structure rose four or five feet above the foundations. At that stage, it became necessary to replace the Black Stone in position. Each of the four principal families of Quraish claimed the exclusive right of placing it in its proper place. The contention became hot, and bloodshed was apprehended. The building operation was suspended for four or five days and Quraish assembled again on the spot resolved to decide the difference amicably. It was agreed that the man who might chance to enter the court of the Ka'aba first by a particular gate should be chosen to decide the difference, or to place the stone in position himself. Muhammad happened to be that person. Seeing him, they all exclaimed: 'Here comes Al-Amin, we are content to abide by his decision.' Calm and self-possessed, Muhammad received the commission and at once resolved upon an expedient which should conciliate every one. Spreading his mantle upon the ground, he placed the stone on it, and said: 'Let one from each of your four divisions come forward, and raise a corner of this mantle.' Four chiefs stepped forward and, each holding a corner of the mantle, thus lifted the stone. When it had reached the proper height, Muhammad, with his own hands, guided it to its place. Everyone was satisfied and happy.

The walls of the Ka'aba were raised to a considerable height and were roofed over with fifteen rafters which rested upon six central pillars. The structure was surrounded by a small enclosure, of about fifty yards in diameter. The door for entering the Ka'aba was placed near the Black Stone on the eastern side, several feet above the ground. The building occupied somewhat less space than its dilapidated and roofless predecessor. The excluded area lay to the north-west, without the sacred walls, and is known as the Place of Ishmael.

In the meantime, Muhammad's family had grown. A sister of Khadija was married to Rabi', a descendant of Abd Shams, and had borne him a son who was named Abul Aas, who was now grown up and was respected for his uprightness and mercantile success. Khadija was fond of him, and looked upon him as her own son. Muhammad and she agreed to marry their eldest daughter, Zainab, who had just reached the age of womanhood, to Abul Aas. The union proved to be one of real affection. Somewhat later the two younger daughters, Ruqayya and Um Kulthum, were given in marriage to Utba and Utaiba, sons of Abu Lahab, uncle of Muhammad. Fatima, the youngest, was yet a child.

Shortly after the rebuilding of the Ka'aba, Muhammad comforted himself for the loss of his infant son, Qasim, by taking over the care and upbringing of Ali, son of his uncle, Abu Talib. A season of severe scarcity had been experienced, and Abu Talib was put to shifts for the support of his numerous family. Perceiving his difficulties, Muhammad repaired to his uncle, Abbas, and proposed to him that they should each take care of one of the sons of Abu Talib. Abbas agreed, and they went to Abu Talib who, on hearing them, gave them the choice of any two of his sons, excepting Akil and Talib. So Muhammad took Ali and Abbas took Jafar. Ali was then five or six years of age and remained ever after with Muhammad.

About that time, Muhammad admitted into his family another person unconnected with him by family ties, but of more equal age. This was Zaid, son of Haritha. His home had been among a tribe in the south of Syria. He was still a child when, journeying with his mother, the company was waylaid by a band of Arab marauders who carried him away captive and sold him into slavery. While yet a youth, he came into the ownership of Hakim bin Hizam, a nephew of Khadija, who presented him to his aunt shortly after her marriage to Muhammad. He was then about twenty years of age, small of stature, dark in complexion, with a short and depressed nose. He was an active and useful servant, and Muhammad conceived a strong affection for him. Khadija, perceiving this, made a present of him to Muhammad. His father searched long in vain for Zaid, and at last received tidings that Zaid was in Mecca. The father set out immediately to fetch him home. Arrived at Mecca, he offered a large payment for his ransom.

Muhammad summoned Zaid and left it in his option to go home or stay with him. He chose to stay. Delighted by his faithfulness, Muhammad took him to the Ka'aba, where he announced that Zaid was his son, and that they would inherit from each other. Zaid's father was contented with the situation and returned home glad at heart. Zaid, now a freedman, became known as Zaid bin Muhammad. By Muhammad's desire, he married his old attendant, Um Aiman. Though nearly double his age, she bore him a son called Usama.

Chapter 2

:The Divine Call:

Muhammad was now approaching his fortieth year. Always pensive, he had of late become even more thoughtful and retiring. Contemplation and reflection engaged his mind, and the moral debasement of his people pressed heavily on him. His soul was perplexed with uncertainty as to what was the right path to follow. Thus burdened, he frequently retired to seek relief in meditation amongst the solitary valleys and rocks near Mecca. His favourite resort was a cave in Mount Hira, a lofty conical hill two or three miles north of Mecca. Thither he would retire for days at a time, and Khadija sometimes accompanied him.

During this period he began to see dreams which were fulfilled according to their true import. This was an indication that he had now come up to the standard mentioned in 20:41 with reference to Moses. It was on a Monday in the last ten days of the blessed month of Ramadhan when he was occupied in worship in the cave that he suddenly perceived an unfamiliar presence before him. It addressed him and said, 'Recite', to which he replied: 'I am not able to recite'. Thereupon the presence seized him and, clasping him to its bosom, squeezed him hard and then, releasing him, directed him again, 'Recite', and received the same reply as the first time. This was repeated once more, as if the embrace had been intended each time to influence Muhammad's heart and to prepare him for the message that was to be delivered to him. After the third embrace, the presence released Muhammad and directed him: 'Recite in the name of thy Lord Who created. He created man from a clot of blood. Recite, for thy Lord is Most Beneficent, Who has taught by the pen, taught man that which he knew not' (96:2-6).

Thereafter the presence disappeared, leaving Muhammad much agitated and perplexed. His heart was beating fast and he did not understand the import of what had happened and what it portended. In that condition he left the cave and returned home all atremble and said to Khadija: 'Cover me up, cover me up.' Khadija, witnessing his agitation, became anxious and quickly covered him up. After a while, when his agitation had somewhat subsided, Muhammad related the whole of the incident to Khadija and said, 'I am afraid for myself', to which Khadija responded: 'Nay, be of good cheer. Surely, Allah will not humiliate thee. Thou dost carry out the obligations of kinship, thou art truthful, thou relievest people's burdens, thou possessest high moral qualities which have become rare, thou honourest thy guests and thou dost succour the distressed.'

This was Muhammad's first experience of verbal revelation. The import of the words revealed to him puts it absolutely beyond doubt that it was true revelation from God Almighty. The direction of the presence to Muhammad to 'recite' can also mean that he should read, and his response in that case could have meant 'I am unable to read'. It is a fact that Muhammad was unlettered and was not able to read or write. This is testified to by the Holy Quran, which has affirmed: 'Thou didst not recite any book before the revelation of the Quran, nor didst thou write one with thy right hand; in that case, those who reject it as a fabrication would have had further cause for doubt' (29:49).

But the direction 'Recite' conveyed to Muhammad that he was called upon to undertake a particular enterprise which would require him to convey a message to mankind, and his response was that he was not able to do so. The purpose of the repeated embraces was to influence and strengthen his heart so that he should be prepared to undertake the responsibility that God was about to place upon his shoulders.

Khadija took Muhammad to her cousin, Waraqa bin Naufal, who had discarded paganism and had become a Christian and had some knowledge of the Scriptures. He was now old and almost blind. Khadija asked him to hear what Muhammad had to say. Having heard him, he said, 'The angel who used to descend upon Moses has descended upon thee. Would that I were stronger and could survive till thy people will expel thee from thy home.' Muhammad was surprised and exclaimed, 'Will they indeed expel me?' Waraqa replied, 'There has been no messenger who has not been opposed by his people. If I survive till that time, I shall help thee with all my strength.' But he lived only a short time thereafter.

After his first experience of revelation, Muhammad received no further revelation for about six weeks. He passed this period in great perplexity and restlessness. He did not completely understand what had happened and what it might portend. Was it indeed a message from God or was it a secret urging of his own mind? This was a period of great anxiety for him. In the middle of this struggle in which his mind and soul were involved, he was one day walking from Hira to his home when he suddenly heard a voice, as if someone was speaking to him. He looked around him in all directions, but observed no one. He raised his eyes towards heaven and he beheld a grand chair suspended between heaven and earth on which was seated the same presence whom he had seen in the cave. He was greatly upset and hurried home, and arrived there he asked Khadija to cover him up, which she did. As soon as he lay down, he heard a majestic voice addressing him in the following words: 'O thou standing ready, wearing thy mantle, up and warn; and magnify thy Lord; and purify those around thee; and stamp out idolatry' (74:2-6).

Thereafter he began to receive revelation continuously. He had now been comforted, and he realised that he had been commissioned by God to call people to his Lord. Accordingly, he began to call people to the Unity of God and to condemn idol-worship. But he did not, at that stage, make any public announcement. He worked silently and confined his message only to those who were his close associates.

Did these two experiences of Muhammad constitute in truth his being commissioned by God, or were they in the nature of hallucinations, or the result of his imagination, or his invention? They could not possibly have been his invention, deliberate or unconscious, for if that had been so, he would not have behaved as he did immediately after his first experience in the cave and during the period of six weeks when there was a cessation of all revelation. He would have determined in his own mind what course he would follow after pretending that he had gone through the experience which he mentioned to his wife on reaching home from Hira. Nor would he have been perplexed and agitated during the period of the cessation of revelation.

It is equally utterly impossible that those experiences were the result of hallucination. Both messages are replete with wisdom and good sense and could not possibly have been induced by hallucination. Reflect for a moment on the grand prophecy contained in the very first word of the first message: 'Recite', or convey repeatedly. This was a clear indication that God intended to convey to him, through verbal revelation, that which would need to be repeatedly recited and to be conveyed far and wide. The fulfilment of this prophecy is conclusive proof that the experience was not the result of hallucination. Consider also the further grand disclosure that mankind was about to be admitted to profound and great truths which would be propagated widely through the agency of the pen; that the pen would become the instrument of spreading knowledge of every description widely among mankind. Is there any trace of hallucination in this? The matchless wisdom comprised in the revelations that were continuously vouchsafed to him thereafter also constitutes conclusive proof of the utter sanity and perfect sincerity of the recipient of those revelations.

The same considerations prove that the Holy Prophet, for such he was now, peace be on him, had not merely imagined those two experiences. The very fact that, throughout the rest of his life, he continued to be the constant recipient of revelation which comprised grand verities, knowledge of the unseen, assurances of help and success which were completely carried out, prophecies that were fulfilled to the letter and have continued to be fulfilled ever after, excludes any possibility that the revelation that the Holy Prophet claimed was constantly vouchsafed to him was only the product of his too lively imagination. We must, therefore, conclude that these experiences were the beginning of his prophethood, in which, from that moment onwards, he believed with the utmost sincerity, which belief continued to be strengthened and fostered every moment of his life till its end.

What was his mission? Briefly, it was the propagation of Islam, which means utter submission to God Almighty. The central pillar of Islam is the Unity of God, that is to say, that the Creator and Master of the universe is God, Who is One in His being and His attributes and has no associate. He is Eternal, Ever-Living. All that is in heaven or on earth is His creation and exists only through His support; therefore, all worship is due to Him and all deities beside Him that are worshipped by people are fiction and falsehood.

The Holy Prophet, peace be on him, taught further, that God Almighty had created the universe with the purpose that mankind should recognise Him and, becoming the manifestations of His attributes, should provide for their eternal welfare. For this purpose, God had divided human life into two parts, one the life of this world which is the period of action, and second, the life hereafter, which is the unending period of recompense. He appointed death as the dividing line between these two parts. He also stressed that God Almighty raises messengers and prophets for the guidance of mankind on the basis of knowledge vouchsafed to them by God. Such messengers and prophets had appeared among all people, in all regions and in all ages; and he too was a messenger of God.

These teachings were supplemented and expounded as the Holy Quran continued to be revealed till the whole structure of the faith was perfected. As his message was for all people and for all time, and he was endowed to perfection with all the excellences which had been bestowed in various degrees on previous prophets, he was appointed, by God Almighty, the Seal of the Prophets.

The first to believe in him was his wife, Khadija, who accepted him as true without any hesitation. Ali, who was at the time but ten years of age, and Zaid bin Haritha, the freedman of the Holy Prophet, were both members of his family. They also believed in him the moment he announced his mission. No express affirmation on their part was needed. Outside his family, Hazrat Abu Bakr, who was his most intimate friend, believed in him without question the moment he learnt of his claim.

Abu Bakr had long been associated with the Holy Prophet. He lived in the same quarter of the city as Khadija and thus the intimacy between him and the Holy Prophet was close and his attachment to him was now riveted by his implicit faith in the Holy Prophet, who said of him, on a later occasion, 'I never invited anyone to the faith who displayed not hesitation and perplexity excepting only Abu Bakr; who, when I had propounded Islam to him, tarried not, neither was perplexed.'

Abu Bakr was about two years younger than the Holy Prophet; short in stature, and of a small spare frame; the eyes deeply seated under a high projecting forehead. His complexion was fair, and face comely but thin, so that one could see the veins upon it. His nature was mild and sympathetic, but not incapable of firm purpose when important interests required. Impulse and passion rarely prompted his actions; he was guided by reason and calm conviction. Faithful and unvarying in his attachment to the Holy Prophet, he was known as Siddiq, the True.

Abu Bakr had a tender and compassionate heart. He was a diligent and successful merchant, and, being frugal and simple in his habits, possessed at the time of his conversion to Islam a capital of about 40,000 silver pieces. His generosity was rare and his charity unwearying. The greater part of his fortune was now devoted to the purchase of such unfortunate slaves as were persecuted for their attachment to the new faith; so that but 5,000 pieces were left when, twelve years later, he emigrated with the Holy Prophet to Medina. He was unusually familiar with the history of Quraish, who often referred to him for genealogical information. His judgment was sound and impartial, his conversation agreeable, and his demeanour affable and engaging. His society and advice were much sought after by Quraish, and he was popular throughout the city.

It is strong proof of the Holy Prophet's truth and sincerity that the earliest converts to Islam were not only of upright character, but his own bosom friends and people of his household; who, intimately acquainted with his private life, could not otherwise have failed to detect those discrepancies which have ever more or less existed between the professions of the hypocritical deceiver abroad and his actions at home. Abu Bakr's adherence to the Holy Prophet and his attachment to him were a source of comfort and strength for him. His influence was freely employed in the cause of Islam, and five of the earliest converts believed as the result of his persuasion and example.

Three of them were but striplings. Sa'd bin Abi Waqqas was in his sixteenth or seventeenth year. He was a nephew of Amina, mother of the Holy Prophet. Zubair, the nephew of Khadija and the son of the Holy Prophet's aunt, Safiya, was even younger; about the same age as Talha, a relative of Abu Bakr and a renowned warrior in later days.

The fourth convert was Uthman, son of Affan, who succeeded Umar as Khalifa; though he was of the Umayyad stock, on his mother's side he was the grandson of Abdul Muttalib. At this time Uthman was about thirty-five years of age. The Holy Prophet's daughter, Ruqayya, being now free from her connection with Utba, son of Abu Lahab, the Holy Prophet gave her in marriage to Uthman, and on her death some twelve years later, he gave his third daughter, Um Kulthum, in marriage to Uthman.

The fifth convert was Abdul Rahman, ten years younger than the Holy Prophet, a man of wealth and character. Abdul Rahman, Uthman, and Talha were, like Abu Bakr, merchants. On his first visit to the Holy Prophet, Abdul Rahman was accompanied by four companions who embraced Islam at the same time: Ubaidah, son of the Holy Prophet's uncle, Harith; Abu Salama; Abu Obaida, subsequently a warrior of note; and Uthman, son of Maz'un. The latter had already given up the drinking of liquor, and was with difficulty persuaded by the Holy Prophet to renounce the austerities of an ascetic life. His family were well inclined towards Islam, for two of his brothers, a son and some other relatives of his were among the early believers.

Other early converts included Abu Huzaifah bin Utbah of Banu Umayya, who became a martyr in the battle of Yamamah, fighting against Musailamah; Saeed bin Zaid of Banu Adi, brother-in-law of Umar, who died in the time of Muawiyah; and Arqam of Banu Makhzoom, in whose house the Holy Prophet later used to meet the Muslims and any visitors.

Then there were the two brothers, Abdullah and Ubaidullah, sons of Jahsh, who were cousins of the Holy Prophet, their mother being the sister of the Holy Prophet's father. They were not of Quraish. Zainab, who married the Holy Prophet later after her divorce by Zaid, was their sister. Ubaidullah was married to Um Habeebah, daughter of Abu Sufyan, who married the Holy Prophet after she became a widow.

Another notable Muslim of this period was Abdullah bin Masood. He was not of Quraish and belonged to Hudhail. He was a very poor man and after he became a Muslim he spent most of his time in the company of the Holy Prophet. He became a great scholar and jurist.

Then there was Abu Dhar Ghaffari. When he heard of the claim of the Holy Prophet he sent his brother to make enquiries. Not being satisfied with his report, he went to Mecca himself and, on meeting the Holy Prophet, embraced Islam. He was a man of great piety and of simple habits. He believed that it was not permissible to collect wealth, and this doctrine of his sometimes became the subject of controversy between him and the other Companions of the Holy Prophet.

Of the slaves and freedmen who believed in Islam at this stage, the most outstanding was Bilal bin Rabah, owned by Umayya bin Khalf who, on Bilal's becoming a Muslim, used to persecute him savagely.

He would take him out during the noon-day heat and make him lie down on the burning sand, would put hot pieces of stone on his chest and urge him to deny the Unity of God; but Bilal would continue to repeat 'Ahad, Ahad' ('One, One'). Abu Bakr took pity on him and purchased his freedom from Umayya. After the Migration to Medina, he was appointed the first muezzin by the Holy Prophet. After the latter's death Bilal gave up calling the Azan as it reminded him too poignantly of the beloved Prophet. After the fall of Damascus in the time of Hazrat Umar Bilal was persuaded to call the Azan once more, which he did and which plunged everyone present into a paroxysm of grief. Umar held him in such high esteem that when Bilal died Umar observed, 'Today the Muslims have been bereaved of their chief.'

Aamir bin Fuhairah was another slave whose freedom was procured by Abu Bakr and who became his servant. Khabbab bin Arat was a freedman who worked as a blacksmith in Mecca and had become an early convert to Islam.

The wives and children of these early believers were generally included along with them among the Muslims. Those who have been specially mentioned in this context are Asmaa, daughter of Abu Bakr; Fatima, daughter of Khattab, wife of Saeed bin Zaid; and Um Fazal, wife of Abbas, uncle of the Holy Prophet. Curiously, Abbas himself had not so far become a Muslim.

Of these early converts, Abu Bakr was the only one who possessed a standing and influence among Quraish. Leaving aside the slaves and freedmen, most of the Muslims were poor and of little account. Some of them, no doubt, were connected with respected families of Quraish, but a majority were youths who possessed no influence among their families. Those who were of ripe age were too poor to be held of any account. Thus the general impression among Quraish was that only the weak and the indigent had believed in Muhammad. This is another indication of the truth of Muhammad, as, in the beginning, a prophet is acknowledged only by the weak and the poor.

In the beginning, for about three years, the Holy Prophet carried on the propagation of his faith only privately. There was, during that time, no central place where the Muslims could meet together. The Holy Prophet received such seekers after truth who sought him out, in his own house or at some place outside the town. Not all the Muslims of that period knew each other intimately. At that time, Quraish generally confined their opposition to the new creed to derision and ridicule.

The practice of Islam in those days was confined to Prayer, which had not yet been established as regular Salat to be performed five times daily at appointed hours. The Muslims carried on worship in their own homes, or two or three or four of them together in one of the neighbouring defiles outside Mecca. It is related that, on one occasion, the Holy Prophet was engaged in worship along with Ali in a defile when Abu Talib came upon them. He had not so far heard of Islam. He watched the two together engaged in this new form of worship, and when they had finished he inquired from the Holy Prophet, 'Son of my brother, what is this new creed that you have taken up?' The Holy Prophet replied, 'Uncle, this is the religion of God which was the faith of Abraham,' and he invited Abu Talib to accept Islam. Abu Talib put him off, saying, 'I cannot give up the religion of my fathers.' But he told Ali, 'Son, adhere to Muhammad, for I am sure that he will not invite you to anything but good.'

About the same time, on one occasion, Sa'd bin Abi Waqqas and some Muslims were engaged in worship in a defile when some Quraish, happening to pass by them, admonished them against indulging in a new form of worship, which led to some controversy, but did not bring on a confrontation.

In the beginning of the fourth year of his ministry, the Holy Prophet received the revelation 'Declare openly that which thou art commanded to proclaim' (15:95), and shortly after was revealed the verse 'Warn thy nearest kinsmen' (26:125). In compliance with these directives, the Holy Prophet ascended to a height and called every one of the tribes of Quraish by its name. When they had collected together, he addressed them as follows: 'O Quraish, were I to tell you that a large host has collected together on the other side of this height and is preparing to attack you, would you believe me?' They responded: 'Surely, we would believe you as we have always found you truthful.' Upon this, he said: 'Then listen; I warn you that God's chastisement is approaching. Believe in God so that you may be safeguarded against it.' Hearing this, they burst out laughing. Abu Lahab said: 'Ruin seize thee. Didst thou call us only for this?' They then went their way laughing and joking.

The Holy Prophet then directed Ali to have a meal prepared and to invite the descendants of Abdul Muttalib to partake of it, so that the occasion might be utilised for conveying the divine message to them. About forty persons responded to the invitation. At the end of the meal, the Holy Prophet wanted to say something but again Abu Lahab made some observation which caused the guests to disperse.

Shortly after, the Holy Prophet directed Ali to prepare another meal and invited his relatives to it. On this occasion, he addressed them as follows: 'Descendants of Abdul Muttalib, I have brought you something, better than which no one has brought for his people. I call you to God. If you respond to my call, you will become the recipients of the best bounties of this life and the next. Which of you will be my helper in this enterprise?' There was dead silence, when suddenly Ali stood up and said: 'Though I am the weakest and the youngest of all those who are present here, I shall support you.' Thereupon, the Holy Prophet, addressing his guests, said: 'If you will hear and follow what this young one has said, you would do well.' On this there was general laughter and Abu Lahab said to his elder brother, Abu Talib: 'Now Muhammad directs you to follow your son.' The guests departed deriding and laughing at the Holy Prophet.

About this time the Holy Prophet felt the need of some place where the Muslims could gather together without hindrance, join together in divine worship and convey the message of Islam to whoever might come to them to learn about it. For this purpose, he chose the house of Arqam, an early convert to Islam, which was situated a short distance from the Holy Prophet's own dwelling, upon the gentle rise of Safa. Fronting the Ka'aba to the east, it was situated in a frequented position and pilgrims, in the prescribed course, must needs pass often by it. Thither were conducted any who exhibited an interest in Islam and there the Holy Prophet expounded to them his way more perfectly. On this account it became known among Muslims as the House of Islam. The Holy Prophet used this house as his centre for nearly three years. Umar was the last one to embrace Islam in this house. His adherence to Islam brought great strength to the Muslims, and thereafter they began to propagate their faith openly.

Of those who embraced Islam in Arqam's house, the better-known ones were the following.

1   Musa'b bin Umair, of Banu Abdud Dar. He was a handsome young man well-beloved by the other members of his family. He was sent to Medina as the missionary of Islam before Hijra.

2   Zaid bin Khattab, elder brother of Umar. He became a martyr in the battle of Yamamah. Umar was deeply grieved over his death. When he was Khalifa someone recited before him a very moving elegy that he had composed in memory of his own brother. Umar was deeply affected and observed, 'If I had possessed the faculty of composing such verses, I too would have composed a similar elegy in memory of my brother.' Upon this, the composer of the elegy submitted, 'Commander of the Faithful, had my brother died the blessed death of your brother, I would neither have mourned him nor composed an elegy in his memory.' Umar appreciated this observation deeply and said, 'No one has comforted me so well over my brother's death than you have by what you have said.' Thereafter, he ceased exhibiting his grief over his brother's death.

3   Abdullah bin Um Maktum, who was blind. He was related to Khadija, but was at the moment of little consideration. Yet he was a man of parts. He became remarkable for his knowledge of the Quran, and at Medina was repeatedly placed in positions of command.

4   Jafar bin Abi Talib, Ali's brother, and a cousin of the Holy

Prophet. It is reported that he resembled the Holy Prophet greatly, both in his features and in his moral qualities.

5-7 Ammar bin Yassar, his father and his mother, who belonged to the tribe of Mazhaj.

8 Suhaib bin Sanan, who is generally known as Suhaib Rumi (Byzantine). In fact he was not a Byzantine, but at a time when his father was the administrator of a certain region under the Iranian government he had been captured by the Byzantines and spent some time among them as their slave. He was later purchased and set free by Abdullah bin Jad'an Qarshi, who was a chieftain of Mecca. When he became a Muslim, the Holy Prophet observed, 'Suhaib is our first fruit from Byzantium.' At the time of Hijra Quraish would not let him depart for Medina. He had come to Mecca as a poor slave and was now well-to-do. He offered Quraish the whole of his property, which was considerable, if they would let him go. They agreed and he left for Medina. When the Holy Prophet learnt of this, he observed, 'Suhaib made a very profitable bargain.' He was close to Hazrat Umar when the latter was wounded fatally while leading the Salat, and Umar directed him to lead the Salat in his place. He also led the funeral prayer over Umar.

9 Abu Musa Ashari from Yemen. He recited the Holy Quran beautifully.

10 Umar bin Khattab, who later became the Second Successor of the Holy Prophet. His brother and some other members of his family had embraced Islam before him. He was one of those who felt that Muhammad's doctrine had become the source of great trouble among Quraish. He brooded over this and decided that the best way of dealing with this schism was to put an end to Muhammad. He set out with this design, but while he was on the way he learnt that his sister and his brother-in-law had embraced Islam. He proceeded to their house and arrived at a time when they were listening to a recitation of some verses of the Holy Quran by a Muslim. He was greatly upset and, drawing his sword, advanced upon his brother-in-law to make an end of him. His sister interposed herself between Umar and her husband and received an injury at the hands of Umar which drew blood. This made Umar pause, and in his mood of remorse over having accidentally wounded his sister, he asked to be shown the text of the verses which were being recited at the time of his arrival at the house. His sister told him that he should wash and purify himself before he could be allowed to peruse the text of the verses. He complied and, on reading the verses, was so deeply moved that he decided to go immediately and make his submission to the Holy Prophet, which he did. His conversion brought great satisfaction to the Holy Prophet and much cheered and encouraged the Muslims.

Now Islam began to be propagated openly in Mecca, at which

Quraish were much perturbed and began to consider measures the adoption of which should arrest its further progress. The opposition of Quraish to Islam was nothing surprising. At the emergence of every divine movement, opposition to it is always the normal reaction of those who are sought to be influenced by the movement. Indeed, a prophet is raised only when people have turned away from the straight path which God Almighty desires that they should follow. The prophet urges them to revert to that path, but their attachment to the ways to which they have become accustomed stands in the way, and they put themselves in opposition to the doctrine and teaching of the prophet. As the Holy Quran has said: 'Alas for My creatures! Whenever a Messenger comes to them, they deride him and make fun of him' (36:31).

It is a curious feature of such opposition that it is the more prominent people who are the most bitter in their opposition to a prophet. As the Holy Quran has said: 'Thus have We oriented the leading offenders of every town, with the result that they devise plots against Allah's Messengers' (6:124). The more exalted is the mission of a prophet, the greater is the opposition to him; as the Holy Prophet, peace be on him, was raised at a time when the world was sunk in the deepest spiritual darkness, he was bound to encounter greater opposition than any other prophet. The following were the principal causes of the opposition of Quraish to the Holy Prophet.

1   Quraish were devoted idol-worshippers and they held their idols in such honour that they could not endure to hear a single derogatory word about them. The Ka'aba, which had originally been built for the worship of the One True God, had, in the course of time, become studded with idols. As against this, the Unity of God Almighty was the basic doctrine of Islam. As the Holy Quran has admonished: 'Prostrate not yourselves before the sun, nor before the moon, but prostrate yourselves before Allah, Who created them' (41:38). Not only this, but their idols and their gods and their goddesses were described in the Holy Quran as the fuel of hell: 'Surely, you and that which you worship beside Allah, are destined to be the fuel of hell' (21:99). Such severe condemnation had greatly provoked Quraish who were united in their determination to wipe out Islam.

2   Aside from idol-worship, the customs and habits of the Arabs were sunk low. Adultery, liquor, gambling, plunder, murder and all sorts of illicit practices were rife among them. These were all condemned by Islam, and embracing Islam meant discarding all of them and adopting a new mode of life. Quraish were not at all ready to do that.

3   The Arabs were very sensitive with regard to the good name of their fathers and took pride in following in their footsteps, right or

wrong. As is said in the Holy Quran: 'When it is said to them: Follow that which Allah has sent down; their response is: Indeed not. We shall follow in the way of our fathers. But what if their fathers had no sense and were not rightly guided?' (2:171)

4   Quraish were a proud, arrogant people and did not consider anyone else their equal. Slaves were particularly looked down upon and were harshly treated. On the other hand, Islam sought to iron out all distinctions and to establish a universal brotherhood. It placed the master and the slave at the same level *vis-à-vis* God. This was anathema to the chieftains of Quraish.

5   There was a large number of wealthy and influential people among Quraish. The Holy Prophet, though he belonged to one of the principal families among Quraish, was neither wealthy nor was he counted among the leading personalities. The chiefs of Mecca were not prepared to follow someone who was not of equal status with them. That is why they said: 'Why has not this Quran been sent down to some great man of the two cities, Mecca or Taif?' (43:32)

6   The different tribes of Quraish were very jealous of each other, and, therefore, the tribes other than Banu Hashim resented that Banu Hashim should acquire prestige over them. Banu Umayya and Banu Makhzoom were particularly hostile towards Banu Hashim and that is why these two opposed Islam more bitterly than the rest of Quraish.

The leading opponents of Islam among Quraish were of three types. There were those who were not inspired by rancour and wished to behave well, but were not willing to follow the Holy Prophet, peace be on him, out of a sense of prestige, and also because they felt that Islam threatened their ancestral faith, habits and customs. Of the principal ones among them was Mut'am bin Adi of Banu Naufal. He was a confirmed pagan but generally behaved well towards the Holy Prophet. We shall see later that he took a leading part in terminating the boycott by Quraish of the Holy Prophet and the entire Banu Hashim; also on the return of the Holy Prophet from Taif, he very courageously extended his guarantee of protection to him so as to enable him to re-enter Mecca. Another one of the same type was Abul Bakhtari who was of Banu Asad; and a third one was Zubair bin Abu Umayya, brother of Um Salama, who later married the Holy Prophet.

In the second category were those leading men of Mecca whose opposition to Islam was characterised by a certain degree of mischief, though they did not enter upon active persecution. Of them was Utba bin Rabi'a of Banu Abd Shams. He was very wealthy and possessed great influence. In the battle of Badr when the Holy Prophet, peace be on him, espied him mounted on his red camel in the front of the enemy, he observed, 'If anyone from the enemy possesses some nobility of character, it is that rider of the red camel.' His brother Shaiba was of the same type. Both were killed in the battle of Badr by

Hamzah and Ali. Another was Waleed bin Mughirah, father of Khalid who subsequently won renown as a great Muslim general. He was the leading chieftain of Quraish, who esteemed him as their father. He died three months after Hijra by being accidentally pierced by an arrow. Another was Aas bin Wail Sahmi, the father of Amr bin Aas. He was also very rich and influential. He died a few weeks after Hijra in great agony from swollen feet.

The third type were bitter enemies of Islam and were bent upon wiping it out by every available means. They were in the majority and the bulk of Quraish were under their influence. The leading ones from among them who died infidels were, first, Umr bin Hisham of Banu Makhzoom. He was the bitterest and most rancorous enemy of Islam and the Muslims. He occupied a position of distinction among Quraish who referred to him as Abul Hikam ('father of wisdom'); but the Muslims retorted with naming him Abu Jahl ('father of stupidity'). He was killed in the battle of Badr by two Ansari striplings. Another one of the same ilk was Abu Lahab bin Abdul Muttalib, uncle of the Holy Prophet, peace be on him. He was Abu Jahl's match in his bitter enmity towards the Muslims and in their persecution. He did not march with Quraish to the battle of Badr, but sent a substitute. He fell ill and died shortly after. A third one was Uqbah bin Abi Mueet of Banu Umayya. He was extremely vicious and ill-natured. He was killed in the battle of Badr. Another one was Umayya bin Khalf of Banu Jamah, who was a rival of Abu Jahl in his persecution of the Muslims. He was killed in the battle of Badr. His brother, Ubayy bin Khalf, was of the same type. He died of an injury he received at the hands of the Holy Prophet, peace be on him, in the battle of Uhud. Then there was Nadhar bin Harith of Banu Abdud Dar, who was particularly bitter towards the Holy Prophet. He was captured in the battle of Badr and was executed on account of his previous crimes.

There were several others of the same type who subsequently embraced Islam, some of whom will be mentioned later on, on account of their zeal and devotion.

Once the hostility of Quraish was aroused, the Muslims were subjected to all manner of indignities, molestations and persecutions. Quraish were determined that the new doctrine must be crushed, and its followers forced to abandon it. By degrees the persecution grew hot. Those who were citizens for the most part escaped serious injuries, being protected as a point of honour by their families, though some of them were persecuted by the senior members of their own families. But the slaves and freedmen, who had no support, were exposed to much suffering.

In their opposition to the Holy Prophet, peace be on him, Quraish were hampered by the fact that he enjoyed the protection of his uncle

Abu Talib, and so long as that continued they could not raise their hands against him without the risk of arousing inter-tribal conflict. Therefore, their first design was to deprive the Holy Prophet of the support and protection of Abu Talib. For this purpose, they sent a delegation to Abu Talib to persuade him in a friendly manner to forbid his nephew carrying on propagation of Islam. The delegation was composed of, among others, Waleed bin Mughirah, Aas bin Wail, Utba bin Rabi'a, Abu Jahl and Abu Sufyan. They said to Abu Talib: 'You are honoured among us and we have come to request you to stop your nephew from carrying on with the propagation of his new doctrine. Should you be unable to do this, we would suggest that you should withdraw your guarantee of protection from him, and leave us to deal with him.' Abu Talib spoke to them very gently, and tried to reduce their sense of indignation against his nephew, and sent them back without giving them any kind of assurance.

As the cause of their indignation and anger continued to mount and their polytheism continued to be condemned in the Holy Quran in severe terms, they came back to Abu Talib, after a brief interval, and said to him: 'We are being castigated in ever harsher terms by Muhammad. We are described as foul, as an abomination, as the worst of mankind, as foolish and the progeny of Satan; our deities are condemned as the fuel of hell and our fathers are described as bereft of understanding. We cannot sit idle under such condemnation and cannot endure it any further. If you will not withdraw your guarantee of his protection, we would be left no choice but to stand up in opposition to you till one of the two parties is vanquished.' Abu Talib was much agitated and immediately sent for Muhammad. When he came, he spoke to him as follows: 'Son of my brother, my people have been gravely provoked by thy propaganda, and are bent upon thy destruction and also of mine. Thou hast called their wise ones foolish, have dubbed their fathers as the worst of mankind, have described their honoured deities as the fuel of hell, and have castigated the people as foul and an abomination. I counsel thee, as thy well-wisher, to stop this vilification and restrain thy tongue, for I have not the strength to oppose the whole of my people.' The Holy Prophet realised that Abu Talib's firmness in his support had been shaken and that he was likely to be deprived of this principal means of worldly support, but he exhibited no sign of anxiety and responded calmly: 'Uncle, this is not vilification, but appropriate description of fact; this is what I have been sent to do, that is to say, to call people to the straight path by exposing their errors. If I must face death in this cause, I am ready to submit to it gladly. My life is devoted to this cause and I cannot restrain myself from declaring the truth out of fear of death. Uncle, if you apprehend trouble on my account, you may withdraw your protection from me, but I shall not stop the propagation of that which is revealed to me. If these people were to place the sun on my right, and the moon on my left, I would not desist from doing my duty. I shall persist in it till God enables me to discharge it fully, or till I perish in the attempt.'

The Holy Prophet delivered himself of these sentiments with such sincerity and emotion that his face appeared to be shining. Having said his say he turned away, but Abu Talib called him back and, with tears in his eyes, said to him: 'Son of my brother, continue with the discharge of thy function; I shall support thee to the limit of my power so long as I am alive.'

Then Quraish had recourse to another stratagem. They again approached Abu Talib and brought with them a bright youth, Ammarah bin Waleed, who belonged to a noble family of Quraish, and said to Abu Talib: 'We have brought you Ammarah bin Waleed and you know that he is one of the best young men of Quraish. We propose that we shall hand over this youth to you and you may derive such benefit from him as you may wish. You may adopt him as your son, if you like; we are ready to surrender to you all our rights in him. We desire that in his place you may hand over Muhammad to us who has created great disorder among us by his attacks against our inherited faith, so that we might deal with him as we may wish. In this manner, a life will be rendered in place of a life and you will have no grievance.' Abu Talib responded to them: 'It is a preposterous proposal that I should adopt as my son one of your youths and should bring him up and provide for him, and in return I should hand over my son to you that you may kill him. I would never be a party to such an exchange.' On this Mut'am bin Adi said to Abu Talib: 'Your people have made every effort to settle this matter without giving rise to a conflict, but you do not seem inclined to accept any of their proposals.' To this Abu Talib retorted: 'I am not receiving fair treatment. Mut'am, I perceive that you are also inclined to support your people and to behave unfaithfully towards me. If your people persist in being unreasonable, I have nothing to say. You can do whatever you like.'

The leaders of Quraish then took counsel together and agreed that each tribe should coerce such of its members as had embraced Islam to repudiate it. They imagined that if this device proved successful Muhammad would be deserted by his companions, and, being left alone, would not be able to carry on his mission. When Abu Talib came to know of this, he too called together Banu Hashim and Banu Muttalib and, having apprised them of what he had learnt, proposed that they, on their side, should resolve to safeguard Muhammad in every respect. To this all present indicated their agreement, with the exception of Abu Lahab, who had become a determined and inveterate enemy of Islam. This device of Quraish obviated any inter-tribal conflict, but exposed individual Muslims to all manner of persecution at the hands of their respective fellow tribesmen. Attention may be drawn to some instances by way of illustration.

Uthman bin Affan was of Banu Umayya, and was a person of ripe age in easy circumstances. Yet, in pursuance of the measure resolved upon by Quraish, his uncle, Hakam bin Abil Aas, tied him up with ropes and administered a severe beating to him, which he bore with equanimity, without the least protest.

Zubair bin Awam belonged to Banu Asad and was a man of courage and determination. His uncle would roll him up inside a length of matting and would torture him with smoke in his efforts to persuade him to renounce Islam. He endured the torture cheerfully and continued to affirm that having recognised the truth, he would not denounce it.

Saeed bin Zaid, brother-in-law of Umar, was of Banu Adi and was respected in his circle. When Umar learnt that he had embraced Islam, he attacked him violently, and, in the process, caused injury to his own sister, which drew blood.

Abdullah bin Masood belonged to Hudhail. He was beaten up severely in the courtyard of the Ka'aba.

Abu Dhar Ghaffari was beaten up mercilessly and might have been killed if Abbas bin Abdul Muttalib had not intervened and rescued him from his assailants by reminding them that their victim was of Banu Ghaffar, who were settled along the Syrian trade route, and could block their trade caravans proceeding north.

These were instances of persons who were members of powerful tribes and to whom a certain degree of consideration was due. But the weak and those held in bondage were persecuted brutally and savagely. We have mentioned the case of Bilal bin Rabah, who was owned by Umayya bin Khalf and endured severe torture at his hands because he would not desert the Holy Prophet and persisted in his belief in the Unity of God. Abu Fakeeh was a slave of Safwan bin Umayya. He was mercilessly mistreated in the same way as Bilal; and so was Aamir bin Fuhairah, another slave, who was eventually purchased by Abu Bakr and set free. Thereafter he was employed by Abu Bakr in grazing his goats.

Labeenah was a female slave of Banu Adi who had embraced Islam. Before his own conversion to Islam Umar would beat her mercilessly, and when he became tired of beating her he would take breath and start beating her again. All she said in protest was, 'Umar, if you do not embrace Islam, God will not overlook your cruelty to me.'

Zunairah was a female slave of Banu Makhzoom. Abu Jahl beat her so cruelly that she lost her eyesight. He used to point to her and say, 'Had Islam been true, how could she have embraced it while we have failed to recognise its truth?'

Suhaib bin Sanan Rumi was no longer a slave and was comparatively well-off, but he was often beaten mercilessly by Quraish.

Khabbab bin Arat was a freedman who practised as a blacksmith. On one occasion he was seized and was forcibly held down on his back upon the burning charcoal of his own forge till the fire went out. He related this incident many years later to Hazrat Umar and exhibited his back which was studded with white patches left by his injuries.

Ammar, his father Yassar and his mother Samayyah, were most mercilessly and savagely tortured by Banu Makhzoom. On one occasion when they were being tormented the Holy Prophet happened to pass by, and, observing their pitiful condition, tried to comfort them with, 'Continue steadfast, family of Yassar, as your final resort is paradise.' In the end Yassar succumbed to his torture. His aged wife was so mercilessly wounded by Abu Jahl with a spear that she died on the spot. Ammar was also repeatedly tortured but survived.

The Holy Prophet himself, peace be on him, was to a large degree protected by the guarantee of Banu Hashim and Banu Muttalib to which reference has already been made. This guarantee was to some degree weakened by the bitter hostility of Abu Lahab and Quraish were contemplating measures against Banu Hashim and Banu Muttalib, though they had not yet taken any practical steps in that direction. They confined themselves to taunts, derision and molestation. On the approach of the annual pilgrimage, they gathered together in the house of Waleed bin Mughirah and put their heads together to decide how they should answer any inquirers after Muhammad and his doctrine on the occasion of the pilgrimage. Should they say that he was a soothsayer, or that he was insane, or that he was a misguided poet who was influencing people through his verses, or that he was a magician who was misleading people through the exercise of his magic? Waleed pointed out that none of these descriptions fitted Muhammad and that, therefore, their designation of him as belonging to any of these categories would not carry conviction. In the end, however, they agreed to represent him as a sorcerer who, through the influence of his sorcery, was breaking up families, separating sons from their fathers, brothers from their brothers, wives from their husbands. They started this propaganda in the pilgrimage season, directing it towards all the Arab tribes that resorted to Mecca in that season, and thus provoked great agitation against the Holy Prophet, peace be on him.

Quraish did not stop there. They constantly incited the mischievous elements among them to molest the Holy Prophet in every possible way. They followed him about and gave free rein to their tongues in uttering derisive and provocative slogans and phrases. His neighbours threw stones into his house, scattered thorns outside his door and put foul and evil-smelling substances inside the walls of his dwelling. On one occasion, someone threw the entrails of a goat into his house. He carried them out and exclaimed, 'Banu Abd Manaf, this is not the way of good neighbourliness.' On one occasion, when the Holy Prophet was engaged in Prayer and was in prostration in the courtyard of the Ka'aba, someone, at the instigation of Abu Jahl, placed the entrails of a camel over his shoulders. On hearing of this, one of his daughters came and removed them so that he should be able to get up.

About that time Quraish began calling him Mudhammam ('the reviled one') instead of Muhammad ('the praised one'). Someone mentioned this to the Holy Prophet, who smiled and observed, 'My name is Muhammad, and he who is Muhammad cannot be Mudhammam. Take note how God safeguards me against their abuse.'

On another occasion, when he was engaged in Prayer near the Ka'aba, Utba bin Abi Mueet stepped up to him and, winding a piece of cloth round his neck, began to squeeze it, whereby it became difficult for him to breathe. Abu Bakr, being apprised of this, came up running and rescued him, exclaiming: 'Would you kill a person for saying "Allah is my Lord"?'

On another occasion, when the Holy Prophet affirmed the Unity of God in the courtyard of the Ka'aba, some Quraish collected around him in a threatening attitude. His step-son, Harith bin Abi Hallah, came up running, seeking to guard him against any mischief that might be intended by Quraish. Someone from among Quraish drew his sword and killed Harith on the spot. In the confusion that ensued, it could not be determined who the assassin was.

The Muslims in Mecca were at this time facing great difficulties. The Holy Prophet did not mind being molested himself, but was anxious about the persecution to which the Muslims, particularly the weaker ones among them, were being subjected. He was well aware that this was a stage through which all those who adhered to the truth had to pass, and that such persecution served as a means of training them in the virtues of endurance and steadfastness. He told them that this had been the eternal way of God and it was the believers who triumphed in the end. On one occasion when he was sitting near the Ka'aba, Khabbab bin Arat and some other Muslims came to him and inquired: 'Messenger of Allah, seeing how the Muslims are persecuted by Quraish, why do you not call down the wrath of God upon Quraish?' Hearing this, the Holy Prophet was much agitated and admonished them: 'There were people before you who endured much greater hardships for the sake of their faith than those you have to endure. There were those whose flesh was wrenched away with iron pincers, so that their bones were exposed, but they remained steadfast. There were those whose bodies were sawn through, but they did not resile from their faith. Be certain that God will fulfil His design. A time is coming when a camel rider will journey from Syria to

Hadharmaut having no fear in his heart, save the fear of God. But you are impatient.'

On another occasion, Abdul Rahman bin Auf and some other Muslims came to him and submitted: 'Messenger of Allah, when we were pagans we were respected, and no one dared to raise hostile eyes at us. But since we have become Muslims, we have become weak and helpless and are held of no account. We have to endure the persecutions of the unbelievers in humility. Messenger of Allah, we would beg you to permit us to stand up to them.' To this he made answer: 'I have been commanded to forbear. I cannot permit you to fight your enemies.' With this they had to be content and to endure all persecution steadfastly.

Chapter 3

:Persecution:

When the sufferings and tribulations of the Muslims at the hands of Quraish reached their limit, the Holy Prophet directed that those of them who could afford it should migrate to Abyssinia across the Red Sea. He observed that the ruler of Abyssinia was just and did not permit anyone being wronged in his dominions. The title of the ruler of Abyssinia was Najashi. The capital of the country was Axum, which was close to modern Adowa. The Najashi of the time, whose name was As-hama, was a just, intelligent and powerful ruler. He was a Christian by faith and ruled over a vast domain. Under the direction of the Holy Prophet, eleven men and four women from among the Muslims migrated to Abyssinia. The better-known ones of them were: Usman bin Affan and his wife Ruqayya, daughter of the Holy Prophet; Abdul Rahman bin Auf; Zubair bin Awam; Abu Huzaifah bin Utba; Uthman bin Maz'un; Musa'b bin Umair; Abu Salama bin Abdul Asad and his wife Um Salama. All these were connected with powerful tribes of Quraish, which is an indication that even such people were not secure against the persecution of Quraish; and also that the weaker ones among the Muslims were so helpless that they could not undertake the journey.

When these emigrants arrived at the nearest port, they were fortunate in finding a trading vessel ready to leave for Abyssinia. They were all taken on board and the vessel set sail. When Quraish came to know of their migration they were much upset and sent some men after them in pursuit, but by the time they arrived at the coast the vessel had sailed away and they returned to Mecca frustrated. The Muslims, having arrived in Abyssinia, settled down in peace and in gratitude to God for having delivered them from the tyranny of Quraish.

It is related that they had been settled in their new home for only a short while when a rumour reached them that Quraish had all embraced Islam and that there was peace and quiet in Mecca. Hearing this, it is said, a majority of them set out on the return journey to Mecca. When they approached Mecca they discovered that the rumour had been without foundation. They were so perplexed that they did not know what to do. Some of them retraced their steps and went back to Abyssinia, and others entered Mecca secretly or under the protection of some influential powerful person. The migration and the alleged return took place in the fifth year of the prophethood of the Holy Prophet.

A careful appraisal of all the circumstances makes it very doubtful whether any such rumour had reached the migrants in Abyssinia and whether any of them had undertaken the return journey to Mecca. This incident has somehow been thought to be connected with another incident which is related in some *ahadith,* Bokhari's version of which is: 'On one occasion, the Holy Prophet, peace be on him, recited the verses of Sura Najm (Chapter 53) in the courtyard of the Ka'aba at a time when several of the chieftains of Quraish were also present and so were some Muslims. When he finished the recitation of the Sura, he fell down in prostration and all the Muslims and the disbelievers who were present also prostrated themselves.' The *hadith* does not mention why the disbelievers fell into prostration, but it appears that when the Holy Prophet recited, in a moving voice, the verses of the Sura which stressed the Unity of God and His Power and Might and His bounties and concluded with the warning: 'The Hour of Judgment is approaching, none but Allah can avert it. Do you then wonder at this announcement, and laugh at it, and do not weep, and continue preoccupied with vanities? Arise, and prostrate yourselves before Allah, and worship Him', the Holy Prophet and the Muslims immediately fell into prostration and Quraish were so moved by the scene and the whole atmosphere that they too, involuntarily, fell into prostration. This was nothing to be wondered at. Quraish were not atheists and acknowledged the existence of God. Thus, when, on the recitation of these majestic and glorious words, the Holy Prophet and the Muslims all went into prostration, Quraish were so overcome that they too went into prostration. But this was only a momentary reaction. After the prostration, Quraish were the same idol-worshippers as they had been before.

It is possible that Quraish, who were anxious to secure the return of the emigrants to Abyssinia, taking advantage of this involuntary action of theirs, may have started the rumour that Quraish had all embraced Islam and that Mecca had become a place of peace and security for the Muslims. It is also possible that when this rumour reached the Muslims in Abyssinia, they were greatly comforted and some of them immediately set out on the return journey to Mecca, but when they arrived near Mecca, they were undeceived and became perplexed.

Even if some of them had returned from Abyssinia, the greater number of these immediately went back. As the persecution of Muslims by Quraish was daily mounting, other Muslims, under the direction of the Holy Prophet, began to prepare secretly to follow them and joined them one by one. Thus the total number of emigrants to Abyssinia reached a hundred, of whom eighteen were women. Very few Muslims were left with the Holy Prophet in Mecca. This additional migration to Abyssinia is sometimes described as the second migration.

In this context, it is necessary to draw attention to an utterly unlikely and unfounded story which is related as the basis of the rumour which resulted in the return of some of the original migrants to Abyssinia. It is alleged that as the Holy Prophet, peace be on him, was eager that he might be vouchsafed some revelation which should prove effective in attracting Quraish to Islam and in removing their hostility towards it, when, during the course of his recitation of Sura Najm, he arrived at the verses 'Now, tell me about your goddesses, Lot and Uzza, and the third one, Manat, another of them', Satan, taking advantage of his eagerness, caused the following words to issue from his mouth: 'These are exalted personages and their intercession may be hoped for.' It is said that Quraish were greatly pleased on hearing such exaltation of their goddesses by the Holy Prophet, so that when he and the Muslims prostrated themselves at the end of the recitation of the Sura, they also prostrated along with them and thus an accord was established between the two sides. But that soon thereafter the Holy Prophet was made aware of his lapse and the offending verses were abrogated, and Quraish were disgruntled. As news of the accord had, however, been widely published, it reached Abyssinia also, and, learning of it, some of the migrants returned to Mecca.

This preposterous story is utterly without any foundation. According to the historians, the first migration to Abyssinia took place in the month of Rajjab of the fifth year of the prophethood, and the incident of the prostration took place in Ramadhan of that year and the return of some of the emigrants happened in Shawal of that year. Thus, there was only an interval of two or three months between the beginning of the migration and the return of some of the migrants, and the interval between the incident of the prostration and the return of the migrants was only a month. In the conditions that prevailed at that time, it was utterly impossible that the three journeys involved, that of the migrants from Mecca to Axum, that of someone who carried the news of the incident from Mecca to Axum and that of the migrants who, on learning of the alleged accord between Quraish and the Muslims, returned to Mecca, could have been accomplished within the brief period that elapsed between the start of the migration and the return of some of the migrants.

Further, the six authoritative compilations of *hadith*, namely, those of Bokhari, Muslim, Ibn Majah, Tirmidhi, Nasai, and Abu Daud, though they mention the recitation of Sura Najm and the prostration of Quraish, make no mention of the offending verses, nor do they make any reference to them in any other context. The great Imams of *hadith* like Allamah Aini, Qazi Ayadh and Allamah Novi, have rejected this story after discussing it in detail. Allamah Aini has concluded, 'There is no basis for it in fact or in reason.' Qazi Ayadh has observed, 'The story finds no support in the reports of cautious and intelligent narrators and is open to every type of criticism. None of its narrators has carried it to the Holy Prophet, peace be on him, or to any of his Companions.' Allamah Novi has written, 'Not a word of it is true on the basis of fact or from the angle of reason.'

Outstanding commentators like Imam Razi have described the story as false and nonsense. The most perceptive of the Sufis, Mohyuddin ibn Arabi, has said: 'There is not the least basis for it.' Tabari, the most authoritative biographer of the Holy Prophet, makes no mention of the offending verses.

A study of the Sura Najm itself is enough to refute the whole story. The offending verses do not fit in anywhere with the rest of it.

Above all, it is utterly inconsistent with the whole concept of Prophethood, and indeed with the righteousness of the Holy Prophet, peace be on him, that he could have been influenced by any Satanic incitement at any time. Reason rebels against the suggestion that a person who had in the whole of his previous life never bowed to an idol, who was emphatically commanded by God Almighty to condemn idol-worship unsparingly and to call mankind to the worship of the One True God, the very foundation stone of whose faith was the Unity of God, in support of which he was in constant conflict with his people, should have leaned towards idol-worship in order to please Quraish. Does the minutest study of his life reveal that he was ever inclined to make a compromise on doctrine with the disbelievers? He was expressly commanded (68:8-10):

> Surely, thy Lord knows best those who go astray from His way, and He knows best those who are rightly guided; so comply not with the wishes of those who reject the truth. They wish that thou shouldst be a little accommodating so that they may also be accommodating.

The Holy Quran excludes emphatically any idea of Satan being capable of influencing any righteous person, let alone a prophet or a messenger. For instance, it is said (16:40-4): Satan boasted:

> Lord, since Thou hast judged me as lost, I will make error appear attractive to them in this life and I will lead them all astray, excepting Thy chosen servants from among them. Allah said to him: This is the path which leads straight to Me. Surely, thou shalt have no power over My true servants, barring those

erring ones who choose to follow thee; and, surely hell is the rendezvous for them all.

Again, it is said: 'Shall I inform you on whom do Satans descend? They descend on every lying sinner' (26:222, 223).

In view of all this, is it possible to imagine that the Holy Prophet was liable, in any circumstances, to be influenced by Satan? Indeed, if such incitement of a prophet were at all possible, all prophethood and revelation would become doubtful and no reliance whatsoever could be placed on them, and the surest means of the guidance of mankind provided by God, of His grace and mercy, would be rendered futile.

Then, it may be asked, how did the story originate at all? Allamah Qastalani and Allamah Zarqani have offered an explanation which is supported by many research scholars. They have drawn attention to the fact that the disbelievers from among Quraish were in the habit of indulging in noisy interruptions of the recitation of the Holy Quran and tried to create confusion concerning its text, hoping thereby to frustrate and perplex the Muslims, as is said: 'The disbelievers say: "Listen not to this Quran, and interrupt its recital with noise creating confusion, perchance you may thus have the upper hand" ' (41:27). On this occasion also they made a similar attempt, and when the Holy Prophet mentioned the names of their goddesses, someone of them called out, 'These are exalted personages, whose intercession may be hoped for', so that some people may have been confused whether the Holy Prophet had himself uttered these words. This explanation is supported by the fact that Quraish, when performing a circuit of the Ka'aba, used to repeat the very formula 'These are exalted personages'. This explanation is supported by Mohyuddin ibn Arabi, Qazi Ayadh, Ibn Jarir, Imam Razi, and Hafiz ibn Hajar.

When Quraish found that the Muslims had found safe asylum in Abyssinia, they were much perturbed and cast about for means to have them expelled from that country. In the end, they selected two of their prominent men, Amr bin Aas and Abdullah bin Rabiyyah, to go as a delegation to Abyssinia for the achievement of their purpose. They prepared valuable gifts for Najashi and all his courtiers, which comprised mainly articles made from leather for which Arabia was then famous, and handed them over to their delegates. Arrived in Axum, Amr and Abdullah first established contact with the courtiers of Najashi and presented their gifts to them and by this means they gained access to Najashi, and, after presenting their gifts to him, submitted: 'Mighty King, some of our foolish people have abandoned their ancestral religion and have adopted a new faith which is opposed to your religion also. These people have created great disorder in our country, and now some of them have fled from our country and have taken refuge here. We request that you may be pleased to direct that they should be sent back to us.' Some of the courtiers supported their request, but Najashi, who was an intelligent ruler, refused to act unilaterally and said: 'These people have sought my protection. I will not decide anything without hearing them.' Thus the Muslim migrants were summoned and Najashi asked them what had they to say and what was the religion they had adopted. Jafar bin Abi Talib replied on behalf of the Muslims: 'Gracious King, we were an ignorant people, given to idol-worship, the eating of carrion, and to all manner of vices. We had no regard for ties of kinship, we misbehaved towards our neighbours, and the strong among us suppressed the weak. In this situation, God raised among us His Messenger whose noble descent, truth and integrity were well-known to all of us. He called us to the worship of the One True God, forbade idol-worship, inculcated truth, honesty and beneficence towards kindred. He urged us to behave well towards neighbours, forbade vice, falsehood, bloodshed, and devouring the substance of the orphan. We believed in him and followed him, on account of which our people turned against us, persecuted us, afflicted us and tormented us in diverse ways. They tried to wean us away from our faith by force. Thus, we were compelled to leave our home and to seek asylum in your country. We hope that under you we shall be safeguarded against tyranny.'

Najashi was impressed by what Jafar had said and asked him to recite to him somewhat of the revelation in which they had believed. Thereupon, Jafar recited the opening verses of Sura Maryam, hearing which Najashi was deeply moved and, with tears in his eyes, said: 'I perceive that these words and the words of Jesus have proceeded from the same Source of Light.' He told the delegation of Quraish to go back, and that he would not send the Muslims with them. He also returned their presents to them.

This set-back did not discourage the delegation of Quraish, who requested another audience of Najashi and on being granted it, submitted to him that the Muslims did not look upon Jesus with respect and were thus guilty of blasphemy. Najashi sent for them and asked them what was their belief concerning Jesus. Jafar replied that they believed that Jesus was a servant of Allah, and not God, but an exalted messenger of God, and was born of the Word of God which He had sent down upon Mary. On hearing this, Najashi picked up a straw from the floor and said, 'I do not regard Jesus greater than what you have told me even by the weight of this straw.' His remark upset the Christian clerics who were present, but Najashi did not pay any attention to them and the delegation of Quraish had to return disappointed.

While the migrants were still in Abyssinia, Najashi was involved in a battle with a rival. The migrants sent Zubair bin Awam across the Nile, to where the battle was being fought, to check up on the

situation and to report back to them whether their help might be
needed in any way; and in the meantime, they occupied themselves
with prayers for the victory of Najashi. Zubair returned within a few
days and told them that Najashi had been victorious.

The migrants continued to live in peace in Abyssinia for a long
while. A majority of them returned to Mecca about the time of the
Migration to Medina, and the rest returned to Medina at the time
when the Holy Prophet returned after his campaign against Khaibar.

When the Muslims migrated to Abyssinia, Abu Bakr also left
Mecca, intending to migrate, and headed towards the south. When he
arrived at Barkal Ghamad he met by chance Ibn Daghna, chief of
Qarah, who inquired from him whither he was bent. Abu Bakr replied
that his people had expelled him from Mecca and he intended to settle
at some place where he could worship God freely. Ibn Daghna said to
him, 'One like you should not be expelled, nor should he himself wish
to migrate. Come back to Mecca with me and worship God freely in
Mecca. I shall extend my protection to you.' Thus Abu Bakr was
persuaded to return to Mecca. Ibn Daghna reproved the leaders of
Quraish on making it difficult for people like Abu Bakr to live in
Mecca in freedom. Thereafter, Abu Bakr built a small mosque in the
courtyard of his house in which he performed his worship and recited
the Holy Quran. His recitation was made in a very moving tone and
his devotions began to interest and attract women, children and
simple-minded people. On this, Quraish complained to Ibn Daghna
that as Abu Bakr recited the Quran aloud, their women and children
and the weaker section of their people were attracted to his faith. He
should, therefore, tell Abu Bakr to stop making his recitation in an
audible voice. Ibn Daghna mentioned this to Abu Bakr, who told him
that he would not change his method, but that if Ibn Daghna was
being inconvenienced over it, he did not desire to continue under his
protection. God was sufficient for him as Protector. Thereafter Abu
Bakr was persecuted in diverse ways, but he remained steadfast as a
rock.

About the same time Islam and the Muslims were supported and
strengthened in Mecca by the adherence of two outstanding personalities, namely Hamzah bin Abdul Muttalib and Umar bin Khattab, to
Islam. We have mentioned earlier the conversion of the latter.

Hamzah was an uncle of the Holy Prophet, peace be on him, and
was very fond of him. He was accustomed to spending his day in
hunting. On returning to Mecca in the late afternoon he would
perform a circuit of the Ka'aba and would look in at the small parties
of Quraish who generally met in the courtyard of the Ka'aba at that
time of the day, and then return home. One day, on his return from
hunting, one of his maids said to him, 'Abul Hikam (Abu Jahl) has
just been reviling your nephew Muhammad, who did not say a word

in reply.' Hamzah was greatly agitated on hearing this and, after
performing a circuit of the Ka'aba, he advanced towards the party
among whom Abu Jahl was seated, struck him with force on the head
with his bow and said: 'I have just heard that you have been reviling
Muhammad. Now, listen. I also follow the religion of Muhammad,
and say the same as he says. If you consider yourself a brave man, now
is the time for you to speak up boldly.' The companions of Abu Jahl
stood up in his support and some grave incident might have ensued,
but Abu Jahl was affected by the bravery and daring of Hamzah and
restrained his companions, saying, 'There is reason for Hamzah to be
upset, for I have indeed been at fault.' Thus the matter went no
further.

In his agitation, Hamzah had uttered the words 'I too follow
Muhammad's religion' but when he reached home and his agitation
subsided, he began to reflect upon the situation with which he was
now faced. In the end, he decided to renounce paganism, and so he
went to the Holy Prophet and formally embraced Islam. On the same
day Abu Bakr proclaimed the Unity of God in the courtyard of the
Ka'aba openly. The Holy Prophet and some Muslims were also
present on the occasion. Quraish were greatly perturbed over the
daring of Abu Bakr and set upon him fiercely, and maltreated him so
mercilessly that when his fellow tribesmen intervened and carried him
to his house he was quite unconscious and his face was swollen. On
regaining consciousness his first words were directed towards discovering whether the Holy Prophet had been molested in any way.

When Umar's adherence to Islam became generally known,
Quraish were deeply agitated and encircled Umar's house. When
Umar emerged, he was surrounded by a large crowd, some of whom
might have offered violence to him, but just at that time, Aas bin
Wail, one of the great chiefs of Mecca, arrived on the scene and
inquired what had happened. He was told that Umar had become a
Muslim, upon which he observed, 'Even so, it is not necessary to raise
a tumult over it. I extend my protection to Umar.' The crowd then
dispersed. On account of the guarantee of Aas bin Wail, Umar was
left in peace, but he did not feel happy in this situation. So, after a few
days, he went to Aas bin Wail and told him that he did not need his
protection any longer. Thereafter he was often beaten and maltreated.

About the same time, Abdullah, son of Umar, who was quite young,
also became a Muslim. He grew up to be a great divine.

Quraish were alarmed at the adherence of Hamzah and Umar to
Islam. They took counsel together and sent Utba bin Rabi'a to talk to
the Holy Prophet, peace be on him, and to try to persuade him to stop
the propagation of Islam. Utba returned from his mission and
reported his failure, and Quraish felt that far from persuading the
Holy Prophet, he himself had been affected and influenced in his

favour. Shortly after, they met in the precincts of the Ka'aba and resolved that some of their chiefs should speak to the Holy Prophet. Accordingly, Waleed bin Mughirah, Aas bin Wail, Abu Jahl, Umayya bin Khalf, Utba, Shaiba, Abu Sufyan, Aswad bin Muttalib, Nadhar bin Harith, Abul Bakhtari and some others together in the courtyard of the Ka'aba and sent a message to the Holy Prophet that they were anxious to speak to him and he might come and hear what they had to say. He arrived immediately, and the substance of what they said to him was: 'Muhammad, you have been the cause of creating serious differences between sections of the people. You have condemned their ancestral religion, have reproved the leaders of the people, have described them as bereft of understanding, and have reviled their honoured gods. Thus, you have greatly humiliated and insulted the people. We are at a loss to decide how to deal with you. We do not know what you are seeking through all this propaganda. If your purpose is to gather wealth, we are willing to bestow upon you so much that you may be the wealthiest of us all. If you are seeking honour and status, we are willing to make you our chief. If you hanker after ruling power, we are even prepared to acknowledge you as our king. If all your agitation is due to some disease or disorder, we are prepared to provide for your proper treatment at our expense. If you can be made happy by marriage with a young woman, we can provide you with the best maiden among the Arabs.'

The Holy Prophet, peace be on him, listened patiently to their discourse, and when they had finished, said to them: 'Chiefs of Quraish, I desire none of these things and suffer from no disease or disorder. I am a messenger of God and have brought you His message. My heart is full of sympathy for you. If you listen to me and follow what I say, it will be entirely to your benefit, both here and hereafter. If you reject my message, I shall await the judgment of God with patience and steadfastness.'

The chiefs of Quraish then started a new line and said: 'If you insist upon our accepting you as a divine messenger, then let us come to some understanding about that. You know that our country is mostly desert and all that one observes in it are dry rocks and interminable sand-dunes. If you are truly a messenger of God, supplicate Him that there should be streams of water running in this country as they run in Syria and Iraq, and let these hillocks and dunes be levelled and become fertile arable land. If you can bring this about, we shall acknowledge you a messenger of God.' To this, the Holy Prophet responded: 'I am a messenger of God and my function is only to point out the way of truth and falsehood to/you and to expound to you that which would benefit you and that which would do you harm. I do affirm, however, that if you will respond to the call of God, He will, in due course, make you heirs of the bounties of this life as well as of the hereafter.'

Quraish retorted: 'If you are unable to do that which we have suggested, we would yet have believed in you if we had seen an angel descend upon you, or if you had dwelt in a palace and had at your disposal heaps of gold and silver. But you have none of these things available to you. We observe that you go about in the streets like us and seek your livelihood in the same manner as we do. Then what is that on account of which we might acknowledge you as a Messenger of God?' The Holy Prophet explained once more: 'I do not claim these things in the way that you desire. I can only repeat that if you will believe in me, then, according to the eternal way of God, you will surely partake of the bounties of this life and the next.'

Quraish began to lose patience, and challenged the Holy Prophet: 'If you can do none of these things, then bring upon us the chastisement with which you threaten us. Let a piece of heaven fall upon us; or let an angelic host confront us under the banner of God. It seems to us, indeed, that we cannot exist at the same time with you and your followers; either we shall survive, or you will survive.'

The Holy Prophet then withdrew with a sorrowful heart. On his departure, Abu Jahl announced in a passion: 'Chiefs of Quraish, you have seen that Muhammad has scornfully rejected all your suggestions and he is determined to continue in his turbulent course. I, therefore, swear that I shall not rest till I crush the head of Muhammad, and then let Banu Abd Manaf deal with me as they may wish.' The only ones of Banu Abd Manaf who were present on the occasion were those who did not belong to Banu Hashim or Banu Muttalib. Their response to Abu Jahl's challenge was: 'We have no objection. You can deal with Muhammad as you like.' Next day Abu Jahl took up his station on one side of the courtyard of the Ka'aba, having provided himself with a large piece of stone, and began to await the Holy Prophet, but when he arrived he was so overawed that he dared not make a move.

Some of Quraish announced that they were not unduly perturbed at the tumult that Muhammad had raised, as he had no surviving male issue and, after his death, his movement would peter out automatically. Thereupon, the Holy Prophet received the revelation (108:2-4):

> Surely, We have bestowed upon thee abundance of every kind of good. So be grateful to God, and as a token of thy gratitude, continue to spend thyself and all that belongs to thee in His cause. God Almighty will surely destroy all the progeny of thy enemies.

The pages of history bear eloquent witness to the glorious fulfilment of that part of the prophecy which related to the Holy Prophet, and the terrible chastisement that was imposed upon his enemies. The progeny of those who had predicted that his movement would peter out automatically all became the devoted followers of the Holy Prophet, and thus set their seal to the truth that the only one, out of not merely Quraish but all the tribes of Arabia, whose progeny has survived and flourished through the ages is Muhammad, the Messenger of Allah, on whom be peace.

Quraish were a prey to great agitation and did not know how to deal with the situation. In this state of uncertainty, Waleed bin Mughirah, Aas bin Wail and Umayya bin Khalf, having agreed upon a plan, approached the Holy Prophet and said to him, 'Our differences are widening and the strain between us is increasing. Is there no way of arriving at a settlement?' He inquired, 'Have you anything in mind?' They responded with, 'Let us adopt a common mode of worship. You should worship our idols along with God, and we shall worship God along with our idols. One benefit that might result from this accord is that the truth and righteousness of one side will affect the other side also.' The Holy Prophet smiled and observed, 'Your plan is utterly unacceptable. Believing in the Unity of God, how can I worship your idols also; and how can you, while worshipping your idols, worship the One True God also? These inconsistencies cannot be reconciled together.' A few days later, the Holy Prophet received the revelation (109:2-7):

> Proclaim: Hearken ye who disbelieve! I cannot worship those that you worship, nor can you worshipping them, worship the One True God. Thus it is not possible that I should at any time worship your idols, as it is also not possible that, worshipping your idols, you should worship the One True God; that is because you follow one religion and I follow another.

Having met with nothing but frustration, Quraish were much incensed, and at last resolved upon a complete boycott of the Holy Prophet, peace be on him, all Muslims, and all Banu Hashim and Banu Muttalib, unless the latter should renounce their guarantee of protection of the Holy Prophet. Accordingly, in Muharram of the seventh year of prophethood, an agreement was drawn up prohibiting intermarriage between Banu Hashim and Banu Muttalib on one side and the rest of Quraish on the other, forbidding any transaction between them and forbidding the supply of all provisions to them, till they should denounce Muhammad and hand him over to them. This agreement, to which Banu Kananah were also a party, having been reduced to writing, the chiefs of Quraish and Banu Kananah put their signatures or marks to it and it was suspended from one of the walls of the Ka'aba, as a great national pact. In pursuance of this pact, the Holy Prophet and all Banu Hashim and Banu Muttalib, with the sole exception of Abu Lahab, and all the Muslims, were compelled to retire to the quarter of Abu Talib in a narrow valley. The ban was put rigorously in force. The Hashimites soon found themselves cut off from all supply of corn and other necessaries of life. Quraish would sell them nothing; they were not strong enough to send forth a caravan of their own; if foreign merchants came, Quraish made them withhold their commodities from the besieged; and thus a great scarcity ensued which imposed terrible sufferings, particularly on women, children and old people. No one could venture forth from the Shi'b except in the season of pilgrimage, when, all enmities being hushed, the besieged were at liberty to join freely in the ceremonies. The failing stock of the Hashimites, replenished only by occasional and surreptitious ventures, reduced them to misery and distress. The wailing of the famished children within the Shi'b was audible outside. Many hearts were moved at the sight of such hardship, and mourned over the hostilities that gave them rise. Among these, and among the relatives of the isolated band, were some who ventured, in spite of threats, to introduce from time to time small quantities of provisions by stealth at night. Hakim, grandson of Khuweilid, used also, though the attempt was sometimes perilous, to carry supplies to his aunt, Khadija.

The sympathies of many were thus aroused by the sufferings of the besieged, but the cause of Islam did not make much progress during the period of this weary seclusion, which had its expected effect in cutting off the city from the personal influence of the Holy Prophet and his fellow Muslims. His efforts were of necessity confined to the members of his own clan, who, though not believing in his mission, were resolved to defend his person; and to strengthening the faith of those who believed in him.

The exemplary bearing of the Holy Prophet and his Companions under these trying circumstances, and the spirit of clanship that knit together all who had shut themselves up with him, must have secured in some degree the general countenance of the Hashimites, and may have added some few followers from their ranks. But the weary years of confinement dragged on with no important result. The time of pilgrimage alone afforded the Holy Prophet a wide field. That interval of universal amnesty was turned, as it had been before, to careful account in visiting and exhorting the various tribes that flocked to Mecca and the adjacent fairs. Thus the Holy Prophet visited the great assemblages at Okaz and other places, as well as the pilgrim encampments at Mecca and Mina. On these occasions he warned his countrymen against idolatry, invited them to worship and service of the One True God, and promised them prosperity and divine bounties here and hereafter if they would believe. No one responded to his call. Abu Lahab would dog his steps, proclaiming, 'Believe him not, he is a lying renegade.'

When the period of confinement had lengthened to nearly three years, the Holy Prophet said one day to Abu Talib that God had revealed to him that the agreement to which Quraish had subscribed against them had been so severely damaged by ants that of the writing only the name of Allah had remained legible. Thereupon Abu Talib went to the Ka'aba, where several Quraish were in conclave, and addressed them as follows: 'How long will you continue to conform to the conditions of your brutal agreement? My nephew has told me that God has wiped out the whole of the agreement except His own name. Let us examine the agreement to discover whether what my nephew has said is correct.' Some of those present endorsed what he had said and the original of the agreement was fetched and on examination it was found that with the exception of the name of God with which it began, the rest of the writing had become undecipherable. In consequence of this significant discovery, some of the chiefs of Quraish, Hisham bin Amr, Zaheer bin Abu Umayya, Mut'am bin Adi, Abul Bakhtari and Zamaa bin Aswad, felt that this cruel and unnatural agreement should be terminated. They went to other Quraish chiefs and one of them said to them: 'Chiefs of Quraish, do you consider it right that you should pass your days in comfort and your brethren should suffer misery and distress? Your pact is tyrannical and should now be terminated.' His companions supported him, but Abu Jahl protested, 'This pact will continue and no one can touch it.' Someone retorted, 'Oh no, it cannot continue. Even when it was written, we were not agreeable to it.' While this exchange was going on, Mut'am bin Adi seized the document and tore it up. Thereafter he and his companions proceeded to Shi'b Abu Talib with drawn swords and delivered the besieged.

It was during this period of confinement that a group of disbelievers of Mecca, on one of those occasions when the besieged were at liberty to move about, gathered round the Holy Prophet, peace be on him, and insisted on being shown some sign. It was night and the moon was full. The Holy Prophet pointed with his finger at the moon, and it appeared to those who were present that the moon had been split, so that half of it was visible on one side of the mountain and the other half on the other side of it. This event is described in the Holy Quran thus (54:2-4):

The Hour [of the ruin of Arab power] has drawn nigh and the moon is rent asunder. When they see a Sign they turn away and say, 'A powerful feat of magic!' They have rejected the truth and have followed their own fancies; but every divine decree will certainly be fulfilled.

This was a grand sign, which had some resemblance to a sign shown by Moses, but was much more awe-inspiring. The sign of Moses is mentioned in the Holy Quran as follows: 'We directed Moses, "Cast down thy rod," and lo, it appeared to swallow up all that the magicians had fabricated' (7:118).

Bokhari and Muslim have both described this event in their compilations as follows. The Meccans demanded that the Holy Prophet, peace be on him, should show them a sign. He showed them the moon divided into two sectors between which Mount Hira was visible.

This sign predicted that the ruin of Arab tribal power was approaching. The Arabs well understood that if a person saw the moon in his dream it signified Arab power, Arab rule or an Arab ruler. For instance, it is related in a well-known *hadith* that Aisha saw in a dream that three moons had, one after the other, fallen into her chamber. This dream was fulfilled in that the Holy Prophet, and after him Abu Bakr, and after him Umar, were each in their turn, when they died, buried in the chamber of Aisha.

Another significance of this event was that at the time of the display of this divine sign the fortunes of Islam, in the estimation of the worldly, were at the lowest ebb. The Holy Prophet and his small band of followers were shut up in a narrow valley where they were exposed to extreme privation and distress. They were helpless and, except during the pilgrimage season, they enjoyed no contact with the citizens of Mecca or anyone else. In this situation, God Almighty assured them that the time of the ruin of the power of their enemies was approaching, and that soon Islam would triumph.

Shortly after their deliverance from the Shi'b the Holy Prophet, peace be on him, suffered two grievous bereavements in the deaths of his wife Khadija and his uncle Abu Talib. There can be no doubt that these were hastened by their sufferings during their prolonged confinement in the Shi'b.

Abu Talib had been in the position of father to Muhammad, of whom he was very fond. The Holy Prophet also loved him deeply. In his last illness he visited him regularly and, when he perceived his uncle's end was approaching, tried to persuade him to subscribe to Islam. Abu Jahl and the others who were present entreated Abu Talib not to depart from the religion of his father, Abdul Muttalib. Thus his last words were, 'I die in the religion of Abdul Muttalib.' Abu Talib was more than eighty years of age when he died. The sacrifices to which he had exposed himself and his family for the sake of his nephew while yet incredulous of his mission stamp his character as singularly noble and unselfish. They afford at the same time strong proof of the truth and sincerity of the Holy Prophet. Abu Talib would not have acted thus for an interested deceiver; and he had ample means of scrutiny. When he had felt that life was ebbing he had summoned his brethren, the sons of Abdul Muttalib, around his bed and had commended his nephew to their care. Relieved of this trust, he died in peace. For forty years he had been Muhammad's faithful friend, the prop of his childhood, the guardian of his youth and, in later life, a very tower of defence. His unbelief had only made his influence the stronger. So long as he survived, his nephew needed not to fear violence or attack. There was no strong hand now to protect him from his foes.

The death of his faithful and devoted wife was a grievous loss for the Holy Prophet, peace be on him. For five and twenty years she had been his counsellor and support, and now his heart and home were desolate. His family, however, no longer needed maternal care. His three eldest daughters had all left him for their husbands' homes and the youngest, Fatima, was approaching womanhood. But for the Holy Prophet himself the loss of Khadija was hard to bear. Throughout the rest of his life he cherished her memory tenderly and often recalled her loyalty and devotion to him. She was sixty-five years of age when she died and was buried at Hujun. The Holy Prophet himself descended into her grave and smoothed out the resting place of her body. No funeral service was held, as a funeral service had not yet been established in Islam.

After the loss of these two devoted friends and companions the Holy Prophet, peace be on him, was exposed to severer molestation at the hands of Quraish. He was frequently affronted and insulted. On one occasion someone poured a quantity of dirt over his head when he was passing. On his arrival home one of his daughters, on observing his condition, quickly brought water and washed his head, sobbing bitterly while she did this. He comforted her with, 'Do not weep, dear daughter. Allah will safeguard thy father and all these troubles will be ended.' It was at this time that, at the instigation of Abu Jahl, Uqbah bin Abi Mueet heaped the entrails of a camel that had just been killed over his shoulders while he was in prostration in the courtyard of the Ka'aba. It was not till his daughter, Fatima, on learning of the incident, ran up to him and removed the foul burden from his shoulders that he was able to get up.

Chapter 4

:Steadfastness:

Having met with disappointment and frustration in every direction, the Holy Prophet, peace be on him, made up his mind to proceed to Taif and invite its people to Islam. Taif is a well-known city, distant about forty miles from Mecca to the south-east. It was the home of Banu Thaqeef. It was a rival city to Mecca and many influential and wealthy persons lived in it. Meccans also acknowledged its importance. This is affirmed by the Holy Quran, where it is said: 'They ask: Why was not this Quran sent down to some great man of the two cities, meaning Mecca or Taif?' (43:32)

In his journey to Taif, the Holy Prophet was accompanied by Zaid bin Haritha. He called on the leading men of the city, one after the other, but all of them rejected him and made fun of him. He stayed in Taif for about ten days. In the end, he called on the most prominent chief of the city, Abd Yaleel, and invited him to embrace Islam. He also rejected him and put him off with the cynical observation, 'If you are true, I dare not converse with you; if you are false, it is no use talking with you.' He advised him to leave the city as no one was ready to pay attention to him. Thereafter, he incited the rabble of the city to chase him out of the town. They started pelting him and Zaid with stones and went on reviling them for a distance of three miles beyond the city. Blood flowed from both legs of the Holy Prophet; and Zaid, endeavouring to shield him, was wounded in the head. The mob did not desist until they had chased them across the sandy plain to the foot of the surrounding hills. There, wearied and mortified, he took refuge in one of the numerous orchards, and rested under a vine. Hard by was a vineyard belonging to two Quraish, Utba and Shaiba, for the wealthy citizens of Mecca had gardens in the vale of Taif, as they have even today. Observing the condition of the Holy Prophet, and moved with compassion, they sent Addas, their servant, with a tray of grapes for his refreshment. The servant, a Christian slave from Nineveh, marvelled at the pious invocation with which the fruit was received by the weary travellers, 'In the name of the Lord', and a conversation ensued in which the Holy Prophet, learning from whence the servant came, made mention of the righteous Yunas, son of Mattai of Nineveh, a brother prophet like himself. Thereupon, Addas swore allegiance to the Holy Prophet, who must have been

57

solaced more by the humble devotion of the slave than by the welcome fruit and grateful shade. After a little, composed and reassured, the Holy Prophet betook himself to Prayer and made the following supplication: 'Lord, I make my complaint unto Thee of my helplessness and frailty, and my insignificance before mankind. Thou art Lord of the poor and feeble, and Thou art my Lord. Into whose hands wilt Thou abandon me? Into the hands of strangers that beset me round about, or of the enemy Thou hast given the mastery over me at home? If Thy wrath be not upon me, I have no concern; but rather Thy favour is the more wide unto me. I seek refuge in the light of Thy countenance. It is Thine to chase away the darkness, and to bestow peace, both in this world and the next; let not Thy wrath alight upon me, nor Thy indignation. It is Thine to show anger until Thou art pleased; and there is no other power nor any resource but in Thee.'

This supplication, made in a state of utter desolation and helplessness, is strong proof of the Holy Prophet's firm faith in God and in his own truth, sincerity and righteousness. Comforted by his supplication, he set out on his return to Mecca. He halted half way at Nakhla where he tarried for a few days. One night, when he was occupied with the recitation of the Holy Quran, a group of seven persons who belonged to Nasibain passed near him and heard his recitation, by which they were deeply affected. When they returned home, they communicated the substance of what they had heard to their people. This incident is mentioned in the Holy Quran at two places (46:30-3 and 72:2-20), where they are described as jinn, inasmuch as they had come by night and were strangers in the land. The Holy Prophet was informed of this incident through revelation.

He then resumed his journey towards Mecca, but before entering the city, where now he had no protector, he turned aside by a northward path to his ancient haunts on Mount Hira. From thence he sent twice to solicit the guardianship of certain influential chiefs of Quraish, but without success. At last he bethought him of Mut'am bin Adi; and sent him word requesting that he would bring him into the city under his protection. He assented, and having summoned his sons, bade them buckle on their armour and take their stand by the Ka'aba. Assured of his guarantee, the Holy Prophet and Zaid re-entered Mecca. When they had reached the Ka'aba, Mut'am stood upright on his camel and called aloud, 'O ye Quraish, verily I have given the pledge of protection unto Muhammad; therefore, let not anyone amongst you molest him.' The Holy Prophet then returned to his house guarded by Mut'am and his party.

Western writers have admired the Holy Prophet's journey to Taif as something lofty and heroic; a solitary man, despised and rejected by his own people, going boldly forth in the name of God, and summoning an idolatrous city to repent and support his mission, they opine, sheds a strong light on the intensity of his belief in the divine origin of his calling.

Though the Holy Prophet had been re-admitted to Mecca, he could not think of any fresh plan for the purpose of the propagation of his faith. By chance one day, Tufail bin Amr, a respected chief of Daus, who was also a poet, happened to arrive in Mecca. On hearing of his arrival, some Quraish, being apprehensive lest he should encounter Muhammad and become a Muslim, approached him and warned him not to be beguiled by him, as he was a sorcerer who, through his deceptive propaganda, brought about separation between brother and brother and between husband and wife. Tufail has related that Quraish admonished him so repeatedly that, believing in what they said, he became fearful, and, in order to safeguard himself against the wiles of Muhammad, he filled both his ears with cotton lest any word of the alleged sorcerer should penetrate to his mind and he might be involved in trouble. One day, he went early in the morning to the courtyard of the Ka'aba and noticed the Holy Prophet occupied in Prayer in a corner. The sight attracted him and he approached closer to the Holy Prophet. His ears were still filled with cotton, yet he could hear an odd word or two. He then reflected, 'After all, I am an intelligent person and can distinguish between right and wrong. What harm could I suffer if I were to listen to this person and determine whether he is in the right or not?' Upon this, he pulled out the cotton from his ears and threw it away and listened to the recitation of the Holy Quran by the Holy Prophet. When the latter had finished his supplications and began to walk away, Tufail came up to him and requested him to tell him something of his mission. The Holy Prophet recited a passage of the Holy Quran to him and called him to the Unity of God. He was so deeply affected that he immediately affirmed his faith in Islam. He then said to the Holy Prophet, 'I am respected in my tribe and they listen to me. I beg you to pray that God Almighty may guide them to Islam through me.' The Holy Prophet supplicated as he desired. When he arrived among his tribe, he explained to his wife and his father what had happened in Mecca and invited them to embrace Islam. They responded to his invitation and made their affirmations of Islam. Tufail then addressed himself to his tribe and invited them to Islam, but they rejected his invitation and adopted a hostile attitude. On this, Tufail returned to the Holy Prophet and told him that his people had refused to accept Islam and had become hostile and he requested that the Holy Prophet should curse them. The latter raised his hands in an attitude of Prayer and supplicated, 'Allah do Thou guide Daus.' He then directed Tufail to go back and continue to summon his people to Islam courteously and affectionately. He went back and continued his efforts as directed by the Holy Prophet and they bore fruit some years later. Tufail then migrated with seventy families of his tribe to Medina. This happened when the Holy Prophet was campaigning against Khaibar. Hazrat Abu Hurairah, who became a well known narrator of *hadith*, was of Daus and came to Medina with them.

The Holy Prophet, on his return from Taif, was leading a lonely life. He supplicated God Almighty that He should guide him in the matter of his marriage, so that he might choose rightly and wisely. A short while later he saw the angel Gabriel in his dream who presented him with a green silk kerchief and said, 'This is your wife in this world and the next.' The Holy Prophet observed that the kerchief bore a likeness of Aisha, daughter of Abu Bakr.

Sometime later, Khulah, daughter of Hakim and wife of Usman bin Maz'un, came to him and asked him, 'Messenger of Allah, why do you not marry?' He inquired, 'Whom shall I marry?' She submitted, 'If you wish, you can marry a virgin, and if you prefer, you can marry a widow.' He asked, 'Who are they?' Khulah submitted, 'The virgin is the daughter of your close friend, Abu Bakr; and the widow is Sudah, daughter of Zamaa and widow of Sakran bin Amr.' On this, the Holy Prophet asked her to find out about both. Accordingly, Khulah first approached Abu Bakr and his wife, Um Ruman, and mentioned the matter to them. They were surprised and wondered whether the match was permissible as Abu Bakr looked upon the Holy Prophet as his brother. On this being mentioned to the Holy Prophet, he pointed out that a spiritual relationship was no bar to marriage. Being apprised of this, Aisha's parents signified their assent with great pleasure. Thereafter, Khulah went to Sudah bint Zamaa and mentioned the proposal to her, whereupon she and her relations accepted it gladly. Thus the *nikah* of the Holy Prophet was performed, both with Sudah and with Aisha, in the month of Shawal of the tenth year of prophethood. The dower of the bride in each case was four hundred dirhems. Hazrat Sudah took up her residence with the Holy Prophet immediately, but as Aisha was only ten years of age at the time of her *nikah*, her wedding was postponed till after the Migration to Medina.

It might be permissible, in view of Western criticism of the concept of marriage in Islam, to offer some observations on the subject which might prove helpful in appreciating the attitude of Islam towards marriage. Islam considers married life as the norm and regards marriage essential for the complete fulfilment of life. It prohibits celibacy. Polygamy is permissible in certain situations, but on condition of equal treatment of the wives, without the least discrimination. A person who has any apprehension of not being able to conform to the strict standard required in that respect, is forbidden to marry more wives than one (4:4). The purpose of marriage is that the parties may be enabled to lead their lives at the highest level of righteousness. Islam does not permit self-indulgence and voluptuousness in marriage, and forbids unchastity. Husband and wife are required to assist each other in upholding the highest moral and spiritual values. A Muslim who fails to uphold that standard in marriage, whether monogamous or polygamous, falls seriously short of that which is required of him, and would fail to achieve beneficent fulfilment of life. Self-indulgence, in any form or shape, whether in marital relationship, or in eating or drinking, or in any other respect whatever, is inconsistent with the spirit of Islam.

The West is critical of Islam and the Muslims in respect of the attitude of both towards marriage and marital relationship. So far as Islam is concerned, Western criticism is based upon a total misconception of the spirit that Islam inculcates. So far as the Muslims are concerned, there are unfortunately many among them who fall short of the standard that Islam prescribes in this respect, as there are many who fall short in other respects, for instance those who indulge in liquor and gambling, etc. It is as unfair to ascribe the shortcomings of such Muslims to Islam, as it would be to ascribe the vicious immorality that is unfortunately so prevalent in the West today to Christianity.

So far as Judaism and Christianity are concerned, the righteous among them in earlier ages, for instance, all the Prophets of the Old Testament, married more wives than one, which is proof that polygamy is not inconsistent with the highest standard of spirituality. The truth is that in modern times the thinking of the West on these matters has been progressively vitiated, so much so that today almost all values in the West revolve around sex, which appears to be the principal preoccupation of men and women in all walks of life, so that the standards of Islam and the West in this respect may be contrasted by saying that Islam insists upon chastity and the upholding of moral and spiritual values, as against the Western preference for nominal monogamy and unchecked promiscuity.

When the Holy Prophet married Sudah bint Zamaa, she was a widow and of an advanced age. The principal motive of the Holy Prophet in marrying Sudah was to procure suitable female companionship and to provide protection and comfort for one who had suffered for the faith and deserved his compassion. In no single marriage of his was he inspired by any purely personal desire or motive. At the time when his *nikah* was performed with Aisha, she was only ten years of age. She was the daughter of his closest and most devoted friend; had been brought up from her birth in an atmosphere of piety and righteousness; her mind under the Holy Prophet's care could be moulded along lines of utmost beneficence; she could be instructed in an intimate relationship with regard to all that Islam required of a woman and could thus prove most helpful in guiding

Muslim women, both by precept and by example, along the ways of righteousness; and she could be expected to survive the Holy Prophet for a long period and to serve as a source of instruction for the whole Muslim community, as indeed it proved to be the case in fact. A great part of the knowledge of the ways and practice of the Holy Prophet, peace be on him, was handed down to future generations of Muslims through Aisha.

All his subsequent marriages were with widows or divorced women, and personal desire played no part in the motive behind any of those marriages. An insinuation to that effect has crept into some accounts of his marriage with his cousin, Zainab bint Jahsh, after she was divorced by Zaid bin Haritha. The circumstances, however, do not lend the least support to any such insinuation. The Holy Prophet had known Zainab, his first cousin, from the moment of her birth, and had he developed any fondness for her he could have married her at any time after Khadija's death. He had himself arranged her marriage with his freedman, Zaid bin Haritha, whom he loved as a son and whom he had adopted. When Zaid, despite the Holy Prophet's urging that he cleave to his wife, made up his mind to divorce her, the Holy Prophet felt himself under an obligation to provide her solace and comfort, but hesitated to offer her marriage as, according to Arab custom, marriage with a woman who had been married to one's adopted son was not considered lawful. He feared that such a marriage would draw hostile criticism upon him. While he was in that state of mind, he received divine assurance that adoption did not establish any legal relationship between the adopted son and the adoptive father, and that, therefore, his hesitation in offering marriage to Zainab should be laid aside. At the time of her marriage to the Holy Prophet, she was thirty-eight years of age, which for Arab women of the time was a period of advanced middle age. There was thus nothing in the circumstances attendant upon this marriage which could justify the reflection that it had been inspired by passion or desire. The subject is adverted to in the Holy Quran (33:38).

About the same time, the Holy Prophet, peace be on him, had experience of two very significant spiritual visions at the highest level. In one of these, he was conducted to Jerusalem where he encountered several of the past prophets and went through other spiritual experiences which constituted strong indications of the victory and supremacy of Islam. This spiritual journey is referred to in the Holy Quran in 17:2.

The other vision was one in which his spirit ascended to heaven, in the course of which ascent he also met some of the past prophets, and continued his ascent beyond them to the very precincts of the Divine. This experience of his is also described in the Holy Quran in some detail (53:8-19). During the course of this vision, the Holy Prophet traversed several spiritual stages and ultimately arrived at the highest pinnacle of spiritual glory.

At the mention of these experiences, his opponents derided him and made fun of him. With regard to his first vision, some of them who had been to Jerusalem put him questions concerning certain features of that city, and were surprised that he was able to describe them accurately. But even this did not serve to convince them that he was the recipient of divine revelation and was a true Messenger of God.

It was in the course of his second vision that the Salat was prescribed and was made obligatory to be performed five times a day, at appointed hours, in congregation. These times are: from the first flush of dawn till a few minutes before sunrise, for Fajar; from noon till mid-afternoon for Zuhr; from mid-afternoon till the decline of the light of the sun for Asr; from sunset till the end of twilight for Maghrib; and from the end of twilight till midnight for Isha.

Even as few as two worshippers make a congregation. But a single Muslim who has no opportunity of associating himself with another Muslim to form a congregation must nevertheless observe the Salat alone at its appointed hours. In certain contingencies, Zuhr and Asr may be joined together, and Maghrib and Isha may be similarly joined.

The postures of Salat are: Qiyam, during which the worshippers stand in a row with their arms folded in an attitude of the utmost humility; this is followed by Ruku, in which the worshippers bow down in even greater humility before their Lord; this is followed by two prostrations, one after the other, which are indicative of the uttermost humility of the worshippers before their Lord. These three postures constitute one *raka'a*, that is to say, one unit. At the end of two *raka'a*s, the worshippers continue their glorification of God and their supplications in a sitting position, which is called Qa'dah, and is indicative of serenity. The praise and glorification of the Divine and supplications to Him are prescribed for each posture and have to be repeated in Arabic, but it is permissible for the worshipper to supplement them with supplications in his vernacular. The worshippers must face towards the Ka'aba during the Salat. The Salat should preferably be performed inside a mosque behind the Imam (leader), but may be performed anywhere provided only that the place is clean. Before joining in the Salat a worshipper must wash his mouth, face, forearms and his feet.

The Salat is the principal form of worship in Islam. The Holy Prophet is reported to have said that the Salat is the spiritual ascension of the believer during which he holds communion with God. There is no doubt that if the Salat is offered with full concentration and in conformity to all the prescribed conditions, it becomes a means of achieving nearness to God. The Salat combines the body and the soul in divine worship which is in accord with the verity that there is an intimate relationship between the body and the soul in consequence of which each of them reacts to the condition of the other. During Salat both are united in the worship and glorification of God. The different postures are indicative not only of the humility of the body but also of the humility of the soul. The prescribed glorification of God for each posture is appropriate to that posture. For instance, during prostration the worshipper glorifies God in the terms 'Holy is my Lord, the Most High', whereby both the body and the soul feel and acknowledge their own extreme humility before the Lord.

In all worship, Islam insists upon the participation of the soul along with the body. Mere physical performance according to the prescribed procedure has no value and is strongly condemned. For instance, it is said: 'Woe unto those who pray but are unmindful of their Prayer, and pray only to be seen of people' (107:6,7). In the same way, concerning sacrifice, it is said (22:38):

> The flesh of the animals that you sacrifice reaches not Allah, nor their blood, it is your righteousness that reaches Him. Thus has He subjected them to you that you may glorify Allah for guiding you; and give glad tidings to those who carry out all commandments in their true spirit.

Regarding the fast, it is pointed out: 'O ye who believe, fasting is prescribed for you during a fixed number of days, as it was prescribed for those before you, so that you may safeguard yourselves against moral and spiritual ills' (2:184). The Holy Prophet said: 'He who does not give up uttering falsehood and misconduct abstains in vain from food and drink during the fast, as Allah does not require merely physical compliance from him.'

Thus it will be seen that Islam insists upon the body and the soul being joined together in all types of worship. Indeed, it not only insists upon spiritual as well as physical compliance, but assigns priority to spiritual compliance, for whenever physical compliance may be difficult or inconvenient, it may be modified or even dispensed with, but spiritual compliance must be carried out fully in all conditions and circumstances. The Islamic system of worship of the Divine in all its aspects is another strong proof that it was established under divine direction and was not prescribed by the Holy Prophet on his own.

During the last three years of the Holy Prophet's stay in Mecca, the prospect of the spread of Islam in Mecca was bleak and most discouraging. The hostility of Quraish and their persecution of the Holy Prophet and the Muslims was daily on the increase. His journey to Taif had been equally disappointing. The Holy Prophet was, however, assured of the ultimate triumph of Islam, and the revelations vouchsafed to him during this period contained strong indications of the approach of such triumph. He was, therefore, anxious that his striving in the cause of Allah and the propagation of Islam must not slacken. Consequently, he now turned his attention more and more towards the Arab tribes. The best way of conveying his message to them was to make an approach to them when they resorted to Mecca and Mina on the occasion of the pilgrimage, or when they gathered together on the occasion of certain festivals at Okaz, Majannah and Zul Majaz. In order to take full advantage of these opportunities, he started visiting them repeatedly. He was sometimes accompanied by Abu Bakr, or Ali, or Zaid bin Haritha. But, as has been mentioned earlier, Quraish continuously obstructed him in such efforts. For instance, his uncle Abu Lahab made it his business to follow him everywhere and to tell everyone not to pay any attention to him as he was a renegade, and was seeking to mislead them. When they found that his own near relations accounted him false, they shied away from him and sometimes ridiculed him and laughed at him. Abu Jahl also obstructed him in the same way. He would follow him, throw dirt upon him and warn people not to be beguiled by him, as he was seeking to wean them away from the worship of Lat and Uzza.

On one occasion, the Holy Prophet betook himself to the camp of Banu Aamir bin Sa's'a. Fortunately, none of Quraish had followed him on the occasion. He preached the Unity of God to them and sought their support for Islam. When he had finished, one of them, Buhairah bin Faras, called out, 'If I could get this man to support me, I could dominate the whole of Arabia', and then addressing the Holy Prophet, peace be on him, asked him, 'If we were to support you, so that you might prevail over your opponents, then after you pass away, would we have a share in government?' He replied, 'Kingdom is in the hands of God Almighty; He bestows it upon whomsoever He wills.' Buhairah exclaimed, 'You invite us to stand up in your support against the whole of Arabia, but when you triumph the fruits thereof would go to others. Begone. We have no need of you.'

In this manner, the Holy Prophet went round to different tribes, Banu Maharab, Fazarah, Ghassan, Marrah, Haneefah, Suldim, Abs, Kandah, Kalb, Harith, Azrah, Hadhramah and others, and called each of them to Islam, but they all rejected him. Banu Haneefah of Yamamah treated him harshly. Musailamah Kazzab, who later claimed prophethood, was the chief of Banu Haneefah.

This was a strange spectacle. The Messenger of God, whose message within a very few years thereafter found acceptance over wide areas of the earth, was seen making his solitary way to the tents of the chiefs of tribe after tribe and presenting God's message to each one of them, and entreating them to accept it as it portended great good for them; but every ingress was closed upon him and the response from every tent was 'Begone, we have no concern with you'. But he was not discouraged and from one tent he proceeded to another where he met with the same response.

In the meantime the revelation that was vouchsafed to him presented a wider and wider horizon to him and to his followers. They were invited to lift their eyes from the citizens to tribes, and from the tribes to the nation, and from the nation to the international situation. The two mightiest powers of the time were the Persians and the Byzantines. The dominions of both were close to Arabia. The Persian Empire was to the north-east of Arabia, and the Byzantine to the north-west. As their borders met in the north of Arabia, they had been at odds with each other at the time of which we are writing. For some time, the Persians had been pressing the Byzantines hard and had deprived them of a large part of their territory in what is today known as the Middle East.

Byzantium suffered another setback about the time of which we are writing. When news of this reached Mecca, Quraish, who favoured Persia and were not too well disposed towards Byzantium, interpreted the victory of Persia as a good augury that they would prevail over the Muslims and vanquish them as the Persians had vanquished the Byzantines. On this, the Holy Prophet, peace be on him, received the revelation (30:3-7):

> The Byzantines have been defeated in the land near-by, but after their defeat, they will be victorious within a few years; Allah's is the Supreme authority before and after, and the believers will rejoice on that day, with the help of Allah. He helps whom He pleases; He is the Mighty, the Ever-Merciful. This is the promise of Allah; He goes not back on His promise, but most people know it not.

This was a prophecy not only of the victory of the Byzantines within a few years, but also of the victory of the believers over their enemies about the same time, and thus it happened at the battle of Badr. The news of the victory of the Byzantines over the Persians was received about the same time, which delighted the Muslims. The receipt of this revelation predicting this double victory, at a time when the Holy Prophet, peace be on him, and the small company of believers in Mecca, were almost facing extinction in the estimation of Quraish, was both a source of reassurance for them, which strengthened their faith, and was another conclusive proof of the truth of the Holy Prophet.

The situation of the Byzantines at the time when this revelation was received was considered so hopeless by Quraish that one of them laid a wager with Abu Bakr that this prophecy would not be fulfilled. But all expectations of Quraish, both with regard to the Byzantines and the Muslims, were frustrated and disappointed by the subsequent victory of the Byzantines, and the decisive and shattering defeat of Quraish in the battle of Badr.

About the same time, the Holy Prophet was vouchsafed a revelation that indicated that he would have to migrate from Mecca, but that God Almighty would restore him to Mecca in triumph. The words of the revelation were: 'He Who has made the teaching of the Quran obligatory on thee, will most surely bring thee back to the place of resort' (28:86). This also was a double prophecy of grand import, which was fulfilled in an extraordinary manner.

The crushing defeat of mighty Quraish, arrogant and drunk with power, at the hands of a small straggly body of Muslims at Badr, which changed the whole course of human history, was an astounding event. This was also prophesied in a revelation vouchsafed to the Holy Prophet, about the same time, in Mecca, when the fortunes of the Muslims were at their lowest ebb. The words of this prophecy were (54:45-7):

> Do they boast: We are a strong host, well succoured? The host shall soon be routed, and they will turn their backs in flight. Aye, the Hour is their appointed time, and the Hour will be most grievous and most bitter.

Quraish heard these prophecies and ridiculed them, and laughed at the Holy Prophet and the Muslims, describing the revelations as the ravings of a madman. Having regard to the hopeless situation in which the Holy Prophet and his few Companions were placed at the time, and the constant frustration to which they were exposed, it is not surprising that Quraish should have accounted these revelations as the ravings of a madman. There was not the slightest indication in any direction that the Holy Prophet and the small body of believers would ever be delivered from the perils that confronted them in all directions. But they believed firmly that Allah, the All-Knowing and All-Powerful, having promised them deliverance and ultimate triumph, would most surely fulfil all His promises to the full.

A Western biographer of the Holy Prophet has observed (Sir William Muir, *The Life of Muhammad*, p.126):

> Muhammad thus holding his people at bay; waiting in the still expectation of victory; to outward appearance defenceless; and with his little band as it were in the lion's mouth; yet trusting in His Almighty Power Whose Messenger he believed himself to be, resolute and unmoved; presents a spectacle of sublimity

parallelled only by such scenes in the sacred records as that of
the Prophet of Israel when he complained to his Master: I, even
I only, am left. Nay, the spectacle is in one point of view even
more amazing. . . . It is this which brings if possible into still
bolder prominence the marvellous self-possession and enthusiasm which sustained Muhammad on his course. Say unto the unbelievers, such was the reiterated message from On High, Work ye
in your place. Wait in expectation; We too in expectancy are
waiting (11:123). And again: Say: Each of us awaiteth the issue;
wait therefore, hereafter shall ye surely know who they are that
have chosen the straight path, and who hath been guided aright
(20:136). Muhammad's bearing towards his followers, no less than
towards his opponents, exhibits the assurance of being the
vicegerent of God and the exponent of His will.

A ray of hope beamed in the north. At a distance of approximately
250 miles from Mecca was a town then known as Yathrab. Its
population was divided into two groups, Jews and pagans. There were
three principal tribes of Jews, Banu Qainuqa, Banu Nadhir and Banu
Quraidha. The pagans had two divisions, Aus and Khazraj. These two
were generally at loggerheads with each other. At the time of which
we are writing they were preparing for a fearful battle which became
known as the battle of Bu'ath. In that battle, many leading personalities on both sides perished.

As the Jews were an intellectual and religious people and were more
wealthy and more powerful than the Arab tribes, they were looked up
to by the latter. If any of them was desirous of having male issue, he
would make a vow that he would offer his first son to the Jews to be
brought up among them in their religion. Living in the proximity of
the Jews, Aus and Khazraj had acquired some glimmerings of
Scripture and prophethood. They had heard that the Jews, according
to their Scripture, were awaiting the advent of a prophet, under whose
leadership they would wipe out the pagans and would become a great
power.

While the Holy Prophet, peace be on him, was occupied with
visiting tribe after tribe, he came to know that a well-known
personality of Yathrab, Suwaib bin Thamat, had arrived in Mecca. He
was, on account of his bravery, noble descent and other good qualities,
known as Kamil (perfect), and was also by way of being a poet. The
Holy Prophet called on him and invited him to Islam. Having heard a
recitation from the Holy Quran, Suwaib expressed his appreciation of
it, and though he did not become a Muslim, he expressed his approval
of the Holy Prophet and did not deny him. After returning to
Yathrab, he soon perished in some local tumult. This was before the
battle of Bu'ath.

Shortly after, still before the battle of Bu'ath, the Holy Prophet, during his rounds on the occasion of the pilgrimage, espied a group of people who turned out to be of Aus, who had arrived in Mecca to procure help from Quraish against Khazraj. The Holy Prophet invited them to Islam, whereupon a young man named Ayas called out, 'By God, that to which this man calls us is better than that for which we have come here.' But the leader of the group took up a handful of gravel and threw it at Ayas, exclaiming, 'Shut up. We have not arrived here on such an errand.'

Sometime later, after the Battle of Bu'ath, in Rajab of the eleventh year of prophethood, the Holy Prophet encountered another small group from Yathrab, who were of Khazraj. He asked them courteously whether they would be willing to hear what he wished to say. On their signifying assent, he sat down among them, invited them to Islam and recited some verses of the Holy Quran. When he had finished, they looked at each other and expressed their readiness to accept Islam, lest the Jews should steal a march over them. There were six of them: (1) Abu Amamah, Asad bin Zararah of Banu Najjar, who was the foremost in signifying his acceptance of Islam; (2) Auf bin Harith, also of Banu Najjar, among whom Abdul Muttalib's father had been married; (3) Raf'e bin Malik of Banu Zareeq. The Holy Prophet bestowed upon him a copy of the Holy Quran which had so far been revealed; (4) Qutbah bin Aamir of Bani Salmah; (5) Uqbah bin Aamir of Bani Haram; (6) Jabir bin Abdullah bin Rayan of Bani Ubaid.

When parting from the Holy Prophet, they submitted that they had been much weakened by internecine conflicts and there were great differences among them, but on return home they would convey the message of Islam to their brethren, and it might be that Allah, the Exalted, may bring them all together through him; in which case, they would all combine in helping him. On their return home, Islam began to be preached in Yathrab.

In Mecca at this time, the Holy Prophet, peace be on him, and the Muslims were faced with the situation described by Sir William Muir, as set out above. After the Holy Prophet's encounter with the six first Muslims from Yathrab, he awaited some indication from them of how they were faring in their efforts to propagate Islam in their city. He wondered whether Yathrab would also reject him as Mecca and Taif had done, or whether God, of His grace, would open a way of deliverance for the Muslims through the spread of Islam in Yathrab. Thus, when the season of pilgrimage arrived, he issued forth eagerly from his home and arriving at Aqabah, in the direction of Mina, he looked about and suddenly discovered a small party from Yathrab, among whom were included five of the first Muslims who recognised him immediately and welcomed him eagerly and affectionately. This was a party of twelve, including the first five Muslims. The Holy Prophet withdrew with them into a defile where they told him that Islam was beginning to make progress in Yathrab and all twelve of them took the formal pledge of allegiance at his hands. The pledge affirmed that they would believe in the Unity of God, would not associate anyone with Him, would not commit theft, adultery, or murder, would not calumniate anyone, and would obey the Holy Prophet in all virtuous enterprises. The Holy Prophet told them that if they would adhere to their pledge sincerely, they would inherit paradise, but that if they exhibited any weakness they would be accountable for it to God. This pledge is known as the First Pledge of Aqabah.

Before departing from Mecca, they requested the Holy Prophet that someone may be sent with them who should instruct them in the teachings of Islam and should propagate Islam among their fellow tribesmen. He sent Mus'ab bin Umair of Abdud Dar, who was a very sincere young man, with them. Arriving in Yathrab, he took up his residence with Asad bin Zararah, who had been the first to accept Islam from among the people of Yathrab, and was a very sincere and influential person. As the Muslims in Yathrab by now formed a small community, the Holy Prophet, at the suggestion of Asad bin Zararah, directed Mus'ab to make a start with the Friday noon service. Thus the Muslims of Yathrab began to lead a communal life and by Allah's grace, Islam began to spread among Aus and Khazraj very rapidly. Sometimes a whole tribe accepted Islam on the same day, as happened in the case of Banu Abdul Ashhal, who were part of Aus. Their chief, S'ad bin Muaz, was also the chief of the whole of Aus. When Islam began to spread in Yathrab, S'ad resented it and considered how he could stop its progress. He was a first cousin of Asad bin Zararah, who had become a Muslim, and he hesitated to speak to him directly lest this should occasion some misunderstanding between them. He therefore requested another relative of his, Usyad bin Hudhair, to go and persuade Mus'ab to stop his missionary activities and also tell Asad that Mus'ab's activities were undesirable. Usyad also was a very influential chieftain among Banu Abdul Ashhal and at the suggestion of S'ad, he called on Mus'ab bin Umair and Asad bin Zararah and told Mus'ab in a tone of sharp rebuke that he should desist from his undesirable activities, for, otherwise, there would be trouble. Asad whispered to Mus'ab to deal gently with Usyad as he was a leading personage in his tribe. Mus'ab spoke respectfully and affectionately to Usyad and requested him to sit down and hear calmly what he might have to say to him before he made up his mind. Usyad considered the request reasonable and sat down. Mus'ab recited a few verses of the Holy Quran to him and expounded the Islamic doctrine very gently to him. Usyad was deeply affected and immediately embraced Islam. He then said that he had been sent by someone who was so much respected among his tribe that if he believed in Islam, the whole tribe would follow him. He said he would send him to them-immediately. S'ad bin Muaz arrived in a great passion and said to Asad, 'You are taking undue advantage of your relationship with me and that is not right.' Mus'ab made his approach to him in the same way as he had approached Usyad, and S'ad agreed to listen to him. Within a short time, S'ad also embraced Islam. Thereupon, S'ad and Usyad went together to their tribe and S'ad asked them, 'Bani Abdul Ashhal, how do you esteem me?' They affirmed unanimously, 'You are our chief and the son of a chief and we have complete trust in you.' Upon this, S'ad said to them, 'I shall have no connection with you till you believe in Allah and His Messenger.' He then proceeded to expound to them the doctrine and teachings of Islam, and before sunset, the entire tribe embraced Islam; and S'ad and Usyad broke up the idols of the tribe with their own hands. Both of them attained to a distinguished position among the Companions of the Holy Prophet, peace be on him, and S'ad acquired a standing among Ansar which Abu Bakr had acquired among the immigrants from Mecca. He was a most sincere and devoted Muslim and a great lover of the Holy Prophet. He was very intelligent and began to be counted among the topmost Companions. He died young and the Holy Prophet, peace be on him, truly observed, 'S'ad's death has moved even the throne of Rahman.'

Thus, Islam spread so rapidly among Aus and Khazraj that the Jews of Yathrab began to be apprehensive how the situation might develop. While the prospect in Yathrab for Islam and the Muslims appeared hopeful, in Mecca the Holy Prophet and the Muslims were passing their days in extreme discomfort and distress. Quraish, on learning of the progress of Islam in Yathrab, were roused to fierce enmity against the Muslims and made their lives miserable for them.

On the occasion of the pilgrimage in the thirteenth year of prophethood, several hundred of Aus and Khazraj came to Mecca; among them were seventy persons who had embraced Islam, or were ready to do so, and who had come to Mecca to meet the Holy Prophet, peace be on him. Mus'ab bin Umair was with them. His mother was a pagan, but was very fond of him. When she learnt of his arrival, she sent a message to him to go to her immediately, to which he sent back word that he would come and see her after he had paid his respects to the Holy Prophet. Thereafter, when he called on his mother he found her in a rage and greatly upset that he had not come to see her immediately. Mus'ab spoke gently to her and tried to persuade her to embrace Islam. She reacted very fiercely to his suggestion and signalled to her male relatives to seize Mus'ab and detain him, but he escaped.

The Holy Prophet, peace be on him, had been briefed by Mus'ab, and some of the Yathrab Muslims came to meet him secretly in ones and twos. The Holy Prophet sent a message that they should all meet him at midnight a few days later in the same spot where he had met some of them the previous year, so that he could speak to all of them in comparative privacy. He directed that they should not proceed to the rendezvous all together, or in large groups, but only in ones and twos, and taking precautions that their purpose should not become known. The Holy Prophet left his house shortly before midnight, and on the way took his uncle Abbas with him, who was still a pagan, but was very fond of him and was now the chief of Banu Hashim. On arrival at the rendezvous, where the Muslims of Yathrab had arrived as they had been instructed, Abbas opened the conversation with: 'Men of Khazraj, Muhammad is respected and loved among Banu Hashim, who have been the guarantors of his safety and have guarded him against all danger. He is now thinking of leaving Mecca and of going over to you. If you desire that he should go over to you, you will have to undertake to guard him against his enemies. If you are prepared to undertake this responsibility, well and good; but if not, you should say so frankly.' Braa bin Ma'roor, who was an aged and influential person among the Muslims of Yathrab, replied to him, 'Abbas, we have heard you, but we wish that the Messenger of Allah should also speak to us himself and tell us what responsibility he would wish us to undertake.' Thereupon the Holy Prophet, peace be on him, as was his practice, recited a few verses of the Holy Quran and made a brief exposition of the teachings of Islam and the obligations due to Allah and to one's fellow beings, and concluded with, 'As to myself, all I require of you is that if need arises you would behave towards me in the same manner as you would behave towards your near relations.' When he had finished, Braa bin Ma'roor took hold of his hand, according to Arab custom, and said: 'Messenger of Allah, we call to witness God Who has sent you with truth and righteousness, that we shall guard you as we guard our own lives. We have grown up under the shadow of swords. . . . ' He was interrupted by Abul Haitham bin Teehan, who said: 'Messenger of Allah, we have had close relations with the Jews of Yathrab since a long time. If we take up with you, those relations will be sundered. We are apprehensive lest when God bestows supremacy upon you you might leave us and return to Mecca and we may be left in an awkward situation.' The Holy Prophet smiled and said, 'No, no, that will not be. Your blood will be my blood, your friends will be my friends, your enemies will be my enemies.' On this, Abbas bin Ubadah turned to his companions and said, 'Do you realise what this covenant might involve? It means that you should now be ready to oppose all the whites and the blacks and should be prepared to make every sacrifice in this cause.' They responded, 'Yes, we realise this. But, Messenger of Allah, what shall we get in return for it?' He said, 'You will be admitted to the gardens of God's pleasure, which is the highest of all bounties.' They all affirmed, 'We are content with this bargain. Messenger of Allah, give us your hand.' He put forth his hand and the whole company of seventy devoted men took the pledge of allegiance at his hand. This became known as the Second Pledge of Aqabah.

At the end, the Holy Prophet, peace be on him, said to them: 'Moses had chosen twelve leaders from among his people who supervised them on behalf of Moses. In the same way I desire to appoint twelve leaders from among you who would supervise you. They will be like the disciples of Jesus for me, and will be responsible to me for their people. I would wish you to suggest some names to me for this purpose.' When the selection had been made, the Holy Prophet explained their duties to the designated leaders. They were:

1 Asad bin Zararah of Banu Najjar, who has already been mentioned. He started the Friday noon service in Yathrab. He was in the first rank of the Companions of the Holy Prophet. He died after the arrival of the Holy Prophet in Yathrab and before the battle of Badr.

2 Usyad bin Hudhair of Banu Abdul Ashhal. He has also been already mentioned. He is counted among the principal Companions. His father was the commander of Aus in the battle of Bu'ath. He was very sincere and possessed a keen intelligence. He died in the time of Umar.

3 Abul Haitham Malik bin Teehan, who has also been already mentioned. He was killed in the battle of Siffin, fighting on the side of Ali.

4 S'ad bin Ubadah of Banu Sa'edah, a branch of Khazraj. He was chief of Khazraj and was counted among the topmost Ansar. On the death of the Holy Prophet, peace be on him, some of the Ansar had put forward his name for the Khilafat. He died in the time of Umar.

5 Braa bin Ma'roor of Banu Salmah, a branch of Khazraj. He has also been mentioned already. He was very aged and much respected. He died before the arrival of the Holy Prophet in Yathrab.

6 Abdullah bin Rawaha of Banu Harith, a branch of Khazraj. He was a well-known poet and was a devoted believer. He died in the battle of Mutah, while commanding the Muslim forces.

7 Ubadah bin Thamat of Banu Auf, a branch of Khazraj. He was counted among the learned Companions. He died in the time of Uthman.

8 S'ad bin Rabi' of Banu Tha'labah, a branch of Khazraj. He was a very sincere and distinguished Companion. He became a martyr in the battle of Uhud.

9 Rafe' bin Malik of Banu Zareeq, a branch of Khazraj. He has been mentioned already. When he embraced Islam, the Holy Prophet

bestowed upon him a copy of the Quran which had been revealed up to that time. He became a martyr in the battle of Uhud.

10   Abdullah bin Amar of Banu Salamah, a branch of Khazraj. He became a martyr in the battle of Uhud. The Holy Prophet, peace be on him, sought to comfort his son, Jabir bin Abdullah, and told him that God had spoken to his father and had said to him, 'O My servant, I am pleased with thee. Ask Me for whatever thou might wish and thou wilt be bestowed it.' He submitted, 'Lord, my only wish is that I may be revived so that I may lay down my life again in the cause of Islam.' God affirmed, 'Were it not that I have determined that no one who has passed through death can go back, I would have granted thee thy wish.'

11   S'ad bin Khaithamah of Banu Haritha, a branch of Aus. He became a martyr in the battle of Badr. When he was about to go forth from his home, his father tried to persuade him to stay back and let him go forth. But he insisted and they agreed to cast lots. His name was indicated and he went forth.

12   Mundhar bin Amar of Banu Sa'edah, a branch of Khazraj. He had the temperament of a Sufi. He became a martyr in the incident of B'er Ma'oona.

The leaders having been appointed, the Holy Prophet's uncle, Abbas, admonished Ansar that in returning to their camp they should be very careful and should take every precaution that Quraish should not suspect that they had met the Holy Prophet, lest their proceedings of the night might become known and create difficulties. The Holy Prophet also directed them that they should return to their camp singly or two together. Abbas bin Nadhalah Ansari submitted, 'Messenger of Allah, we have no fear of anyone. If you will let us, we would attack Quraish in the morning and punish them for their persecution of the Muslims.' But he forbade any such design and told them to return silently to their camp, just as they had come. They slipped away accordingly and the Holy Prophet returned to Mecca with his uncle, Abbas.

Quraish heard a rumour that some secret conclave had been held during the night. Early in the morning, a delegation of Quraish arrived in the camp of the people from Yathrab and said to them: 'We have had good relations with you over a long period and we do not desire that anything should happen which might create any misunderstanding between us. We have heard that last night you have come to a secret understanding with Muhammad and we should like to know whether there is any truth in this.' As the main body of Aus and Khazraj were not aware of the secret meeting, they assured the delegation that nothing of the kind had taken place. Abdullah bin Ubayy was among them and he said, 'It is not possible that the people of Yathrab should embark on something important and I should not know about it.' The delegation went back satisfied and shortly after the men of Yathrab started on their return journey. Soon after they left Quraish received definite information of the secret meeting and they sent some people to pursue the men of Yathrab. They failed to come up with the main body, but they caught S'ad bin Ubadah who had fallen behind, and maltreated him severely. At last, Jubair bin Mut'am and Harith bin Harab, who knew S'ad, got wind of what was happening, and they arrived and rescued him.

When the men of Yathrab had returned home, the Holy Prophet, peace be on him, directed the Muslims in Mecca that those of them who could afford it should migrate to Yathrab. Accordingly, within a very short period, despite the opposition of Quraish, most of the Muslims in Mecca managed to migrate to Yathrab and many houses in Mecca were vacated. In the end only the Holy Prophet, Abu Bakr, Ali and the members of their families, and such weak and helpless people who could not afford to undertake the journey, or who were effectively prevented by Quraish from moving, were left in Mecca. As the emigrants arrived in Yathrab they were accommodated by Ansar in their homes as guests till the arrival of the Holy Prophet himself; whereafter, gradually, they were enabled to provide accommodation for themselves. The refugees from Mecca were entertained most gener-ously and warmheartedly by Ansar, and when the Holy Prophet himself arrived in Yathrab, the refugees expressed to him their deep appreciation of the kindness which Ansar had extended to them. This attitude of Ansar is commended highly in the Holy Quran (59:10).

When the greater part of the Muslims had departed from Mecca, Quraish began to be apprehensive that some development might take place in Yathrab which might become a source of anxiety for them. They also felt frustrated that those whom they had persecuted for so long were now out of their reach. They began to think of some means which might make them secure against any retaliatory action against them on the part of the Muslims from Yathrab. They felt that now that Muhammad was almost alone in Mecca, they should adopt some measure against him which might dispose of him finally. For this purpose their leading men gathered together in the Council House of Mecca and took counsel together. About a hundred of them were present on the occasion and there was also present among them an aged Shaikh from Nejd. After preliminary discussions, several plans were put forth. It was suggested that Muhammad may be chained up and abandoned in a cellar and thus starved to death. The Shaikh from Nejd pointed out that this plan was not likely to serve their purpose, as it was bound to become known to Banu Abd Manaf, who would rescue Muhammad and seek vengeance. Another suggestion was that Muhammad might be sent into exile, so that Quraish would have nothing further to do with him, and Mecca would become secure against his mischief. Again, the Shaikh from Nejd pointed out that Muhammad had a very persuasive and eloquent tongue. If he escaped from Mecca, he would beguile some tribe or other to lend him its support and he would stand up against Quraish to wreak vengeance upon them.

After a good deal of discussion, Abu Jahl said: 'I propose that we should select one young man from every tribe and arm the whole lot with swords. They should fall upon Muhammad as one man and despatch him. In this manner, the responsibility for his death would be shared by all tribes of Quraish. Banu Abd Manaf would not dare to fight with the whole of Quraish and would thus be reduced to accepting blood money for Muhammad, which we shall all provide.' This was agreed to. This nefarious plan is mentioned in the Holy Quran as follows: 'Call to mind the time, when the disbelievers plotted against thee that they might confine thee, or kill thee, or expel thee. They planned and Allah also planned, and Allah is the best of planners' (8:31).

God Almighty revealed their plan to the Holy Prophet, and directed him to migrate to Yathrab and not to spend even a single night more in Mecca. The Holy Prophet had been made aware by God much earlier that he should have one day to migrate from Mecca, and he was also shown in a vision the place to which he would have to migrate. It was a place of orchards and running springs. He described this vision later, and said that he had imagined that he would have to migrate to Yamamah or Hajar, but it turned out to be Yathrab.

Chapter 5

:Migration:

This was the turning point in the life of the Holy Prophet, peace be on him, and in the history of Islam and the world. The Holy Prophet was deeply attached to Mecca where he had been born and spent more than half a century of his life. Here he had married, and had children, and here he had received the divine command to wipe out idolatry and call mankind to the worship of One God. It is true that he and those who identified themselves with his cause had endured great hardships in Mecca for the sake of their faith. But they had been sustained by God's repeated assurances of support and ultimate triumph. They bore the severest persecution cheerfully and with steadfastness, and for all of them who had been left in Mecca after the two migrations to Abyssinia, the final departure from Mecca was a wrench. But God's will was their supreme law, and giving effect to it was their greatest pleasure.

Hitherto, the precepts of Islam had been few and simple but they had wrought a marvellous and mighty work. Never had man witnessed the like arousing of spiritual life, and faith that suffered sacrifice and took joyfully the sacrifice of all for the sake of conscience.

From time beyond memory, Mecca and the whole peninsula had been steeped in spiritual torpor. The people were sunk in superstition, cruelty and vice. It was common practice for the eldest son to take to wife his father's widows, whom he inherited with the rest of the estate. Pride and poverty had introduced among them the crime of female infanticide. Their religion was a gross idolatry; and their faith the dark superstitious dread of unseen beings whose goodwill they sought to propitiate and whose displeasure to avert, rather than belief in an over-ruling Providence. The life to come, and retribution of good and evil as motives of action were practically unknown.

Thirteen years before the Hijra, Mecca lay lifeless in this debased state. What a change had those thirteen years produced! A band of several hundred persons had rejected idolatry, adopted the worship of One God, and surrendered themselves implicitly to the guidance of divine revelation; praying to the Almighty with frequency and fervour, looking for pardon through His mercy, and striving to follow after good works, almsgiving, purity and justice. They now lived under a constant sense of the omnipotent power of God, and His providential care over the minutest of their concerns. In all the gifts of nature, in every relation of life, at each turn of their affairs, individual or public, they saw His hand. Above all, the new existence in which they exulted was regarded as the mark of His special grace. The Holy Prophet was the minister of life to them, the source, under God, of their newborn hopes; and to Him they yielded an implicit submission.

In so short a period Mecca had, from this wonderful movement, been rent into two factions which, unmindful of old landmarks of tribe and family, arrayed themselves in deadly opposition, one against the other. The believers bore persecution with a patient and tolerant spirit and a magnanimous forbearance. One hundred men and women, rather than abjure their precious faith, had abandoned home and sought refuge till the storm should be overpast in Abyssinian exile. Now again a still larger number, with the Holy Prophet himself, were migrating from their fondly-loved city with its Sacred House, to them the holiest spot on earth, and fleeing to Yathrab. There the same marvellous charm had, within two or three years, been preparing for them a brotherhood ready to defend the Holy Prophet and his followers with their blood. Jewish teaching had long sounded in the ears of the men of Yathrab; but it was not until they heard the spirit-stirring strains of the Holy Prophet that they too awoke from their slumber, and sprang suddenly into a new and earnest life.

Having received the divine direction to depart from Mecca, the Holy Prophet, peace be on him, emerged from his house in the fierce noon-day heat of the middle of June, with his face wrapped up against it, and went over to Abu Bakr's house and told him that he had been granted permission to emigrate. Abu Bakr enquired eagerly, 'Messenger of Allah, shall I accompany you?' On receiving this assurance, Abu Bakr shed tears of joy, and submitted, 'Messenger of Allah, in preparation for this day I have reared two dromedaries on the leaves of the acacia tree. I would beg you to accept one of them for yourself.' He offered to buy one of them and Abu Bakr had to submit to his condition. Food was prepared for the journey and Abu Bakr's elder daughter, Asmaa, tore her waist belt into two lengths with which she tied up the mouths of the two vessels into which water and victuals were packed. On this account she became known as 'she of two belts'. It was settled that the Holy Prophet and Abu Bakr would depart from Mecca the same night and take refuge in the cave Thaur. The Holy Prophet then returned home.

Early that night his house was besieged by young men drawn from different tribes of Quraish, with the design of doing away with him as soon as he should emerge from his house next morning. The Holy Prophet had with him certain deposits which individual Quraish had left with him. He handed these over to Ali and told him not to leave

Mecca before he had returned all of them to their owners. He then directed him to lie down on his mattress, and assured him that God would safeguard him against all harm. Ali lay down as directed and was wrapped up in the Holy Prophet's red mantle. The latter then slipped out of the house without being noticed by any of the besiegers, none of whom had expected him to depart from his house so early. He passed rapidly through the streets of Mecca and soon left the city behind, bending his course towards Thaur. He soon perceived Abu Bakr who was waiting for him and the two together climbed up to Thaur, a cave high up in the mountains three miles to the south of Mecca. Abu Bakr entered the cave first and cleaned it and invited the Holy Prophet to follow him.

The besiegers looked into the house at short intervals through the night and perceiving that his mattress was occupied, felt satisfied that he was inside the house. It was only at dawn that they discovered that he had left at some time during the night. In their frustration, they searched for him in Mecca but could find no trace of him. They rough-handled Ali but could discover nothing from him. They also went to the house of Abu Bakr and threatened his daughter, but could get no definite information from her.

When it became generally known that Muhammad had escaped, Quraish announced an award of a hundred camels, which was great wealth, for anyone who would bring Muhammad back to them, dead or alive. Several people scattered in all directions to look for him in the hope of winning the award. Leading Quraish summoned their best tracker and followed the tracks of the fugitives to the mouth of Thaur, where the tracker announced that the tracks did not proceed any further. One of them suggested that someone should enter the cave and see whether the fugitives had taken refuge in it. Another one ridiculed this suggestion, observing that no one in his senses would take refuge in the cave which was full of poisonous insects and reptiles.

Abu Bakr could hear their pursuers talking to each other outside the cave, and being much perturbed, whispered to the Holy Prophet, 'Messenger of Allah, Quraish have arrived so close that I can see their feet outside the cave. Were any of them to bend down and look into the cave, he might discern us inside.' The Holy Prophet sought to reassure him with, 'Be not anxious, Allah is with us. Abu Bakr, what do you think of two, with whom there is a third, even Allah?' Their pursuers returned to Mecca frustrated.

Before departing from his house, Abu Bakr had directed his son, Abdullah, who was a very intelligent young man, to keep track of the movements of Quraish and to make a daily report of them in the evening. He arrived every evening in the cave and spent the night with the fugitives. Abu Bakr had also arranged with his servant, Aamir bin

Fuhairah, who was in charge of his goats, to keep them supplied with
milk. Thus, they spent three nights in the cave. It had been arranged
with Abdullah bin Areeqat of Bani Dail, who was a trustworthy
person, was well-paid, and was an expert guide, that he should
accompany them in their journey. Abu Bakr had committed the two
dromedaries to his care and he had been directed to bring them to the
cave on the fourth evening. He arrived as he had been instructed and
the party of four, including Aamir bin Fuhairah, servant of Abu Bakr,
started on their journey to Yathrab. At the moment of departure the
Holy Prophet turned his face in the direction of Mecca and said,
'Mecca, thou art dearer to me than all other places; but thy people
would not let me dwell on in thee.'

As pursuit was still possible, the small company of travellers bore
west towards the coast and then continued north, parallel to the sea.
About mid-day, they made a halt in the shade of a rock, where Abu
Bakr succeeded in procuring a quantity of milk from a passing
goat-herd. After a brief rest they resumed their journey. A short while
later Abu Bakr warned the Holy Prophet that someone appeared to be
pursuing them, and was reassured by him that there was no cause for
alarm. The pursuer turned out to be one Suraqa bin Malik. His
version of the encounter was as follows: 'When the Holy Prophet
escaped from Mecca, Quraish announced that whoever brought
Muhammad or Abu Bakr, dead or alive, back to Mecca, would be
richly rewarded. Their proclamation was conveyed to us also. A little
later, I was sitting among my people, Banu Madhlaj, when one of
Quraish came to us and addressing me, said, "I have just espied some
people in the direction of the coast who are moving and I conceive
that they may be Muhammad and his companions." I felt that he was
probably right, but to put him off, I told him that they were some
people who had just passed near us. Shortly after, I slipped away and
mounting my horse, I took hold of a spear and departed silently from
the back of my house. I rode swiftly and soon came within sight of the
Holy Prophet and his companions. My horse stumbled, and I fell to
the ground, but I rose quickly and took an augury with divining
arrows. The indication was that I should not proceed with my design,
but I disregarded it, and mounting my horse I continued my pursuit
till I arrived so close to the party that I could hear the Holy Prophet
reciting something. I observed that he did not look in my direction
even once, but Abu Bakr looked back at me repeatedly. When I
advanced a little further, my horse stumbled again and his feet were
caught in the sand, and I fell down again. I got up and helped my
horse to free his feet from the sand. In his efforts to do so, a cloud of
sand was raised all around us. I again took an augury, with the same
result as before, whereupon I abandoned my design and called out
to the party in a conciliatory tone, on which they stopped. My

experience had convinced me that the star of the Holy Prophet was in the ascendant and that he would prevail in the end. Having approached close to them, I told them that Quraish had announced so much reward for killing them or for seizing them and taking them back to Mecca, and that I had started with this design but had now abandoned it. I offered some food to them, but they did not accept it. Only I was admonished not to make any mention of them to anyone else. I requested the Holy Prophet to give me a guarantee in writing. He directed Aamir bin Fuhairah to inscribe the writing on a piece of leather. When I was about to leave, the Holy Prophet said to me, "Suraqa, how will you feel when you will wear the bracelets of Chosroes?" I was surprised and inquired, "What! the bracelets of Chosroes bin Hormuz, Emperor of Iran?" He said, "Yes".' Suraqa embraced Islam after the fall of Mecca. During the time of Umar when Iran came under the domination of Muslims, the treasure of the Chosroes fell into their hands and was despatched to Medina as part of the spoils of war. Included among them were the gold bracelets of Chosroes which were encrusted with priceless jewels. Umar sent for Suraqa and told him to take the bracelets and put them on.

Shortly after parting from Suraqa, the party encountered Zubair bin Awam, who was returning to Mecca with a small party of Muslims after a trading journey to Syria. Zubair presented a suit of white garments to the Holy Prophet and another to Abu Bakr, and submitted that he would soon return from Mecca and join them in Yathrab. Of other people whom they encountered during the rest of their journey, many who knew Abu Bakr recognised him and inquired from him who was the person who was riding ahead of him. Abu Bakr would reply, 'He is the one who shows me the way,' meaning, that he was his spiritual preceptor, but the inquirers understood that he was some person whom Abu Bakr had taken with him as his guide.

After journeying for eight days the party approached Yathrab. The Muslims in Yathrab had learnt that the Holy Prophet had set out from Mecca on his way to Yathrab. For some days they had been coming out of Yathrab to welcome him, but after waiting for him through the forenoon they went back disappointed. On the day of his arrival, they had just returned to their homes when they heard a Jew, who was for some reason standing at a height, and who perceived the Holy Prophet and his companions approaching in the distance, call aloud, 'O ye Arabs, the one you have been awaiting is approaching.' On hearing this the Muslims were overjoyed, and, taking up their arms in a hurry, emerged from the city to welcome the illustrious traveller.

When Ansar had the first glimpse of the Holy Prophet, their joy knew no bounds. They felt that on them had been bestowed all the blessings of the here and the hereafter. Bokhari has reported Braa bin Aazib as saying that on no other occasion did he behold Ansar exhibiting such spontaneous joy as they did on the arrival of the Holy Prophet in Yathrab. Tirmidhi and Ibn Majah have reported Ans bin Malik as saying: 'The day the Holy Prophet arrived in Medina we perceived as if the city had been illumined, and on the day that he died it seemed to us that we had never seen Medina so dark.'

After greeting those who had come out to welcome him, the Holy Prophet did not proceed direct to the city, but veered a little to the right and arrived at Qaba, a suburb about a couple of miles from the city and a little higher from it. Some familes of Ansar, of whom the best known was the family of Amar bin Auf, had their residences in Qaba. At that time, their chief was Kulthum bin Hadam. The Ansar of Qaba welcomed the Holy Prophet very joyously and he chose to stay with Kulthum bin Hadam. The majority of the emigrants who had arrived before him had also been put up by Kulthum bin Hadam and other leading Ansar. It may be that the Holy Prophet chose to stop in Qaba for that reason. News of his arrival spread rapidly in Yathrab and the Muslims hurried joyfully to his residence to greet him. Some of them who had not had any opportunity of seeing the Holy Prophet before mistook Abu Bakr for him, as the latter, though somewhat younger than the Holy Prophet, looked older than him and there was nothing to indicate which of them was the Holy Prophet. After the Holy Prophet's arrival in Yathrab, the city became known as Medinaten Nabi ('City of the Prophet'), which was soon abbreviated to Medina.

Within three days of his arrival in Qaba, Ali also arrived from Mecca and joined the Holy Prophet. The first matter which the latter paid attention to was the building of a mosque at Qaba, of which he laid the foundation stone and which was constructed within a few days with the eager and diligent labour of his Companions who worked as builders and labourers. The Holy Prophet continued much attached to this mosque till the end of his life. After arrival in Medina he went every week to Qaba and led the Salat in the mosque there. Some divines have surmised that the words 'A mosque that was founded upon piety from the very first day, is surely more worthy that thou shouldst stand therein to lead the Prayer Service' (9:108) have reference to this mosque. The Muslims had built some mosques before the erection of this mosque, but this was the first mosque of which the foundation was laid by the Holy Prophet himself on the first day of his arrival in Qaba.

While he was still at Qaba, the Muslims of Medina began to speculate with whom would the Holy Prophet stay in Medina. Every family was eager to have the honour of being his hosts. When the Holy Prophet learnt of this, he intimated that he would stay with Banu Najjar to whom Selma, mother of his grandfather Abdul Muttalib, had belonged.

After a stay of more than ten days in Qaba, the Holy Prophet started towards the main city on Friday. He was accompanied by a large number of Ansar and Emigrants. He was riding a camel with Abu Bakr behind him. Progress was slow and the time of the noon Prayer arrived while they were on the way. The Holy Prophet stopped in the quarter of Banu Salam bin Auf and delivered a sermon and led the Friday Service. The Friday noon Service had already been instituted in Medina, but this was the first Friday Service in which the Holy Prophet participated himself.

After the Service, progress was resumed amidst shouts and songs of welcome. At every step the Holy Prophet was eagerly invited to stay with the Muslim whose house he was passing. He thanked everyone and continued his progress till his camel arrived in the quarter of Banu Najjar, where the men of the tribe were standing armed in rows to welcome him and the girls were singing songs of welcome from the roofs of the houses. Here again the question arose with whom would he stay. Everyone of the tribe was desirous that he should stay with him. Some of them, in their eagerness, would take hold of the halter of his camel. The Holy Prophet, peace be on him, directed, 'Leave my camel free, it is under divine direction.' It continued to advance and then sat down, but rose immediately and went a few steps forward and then returned and sat down on the spot where it had sat down first. On this, the Holy Prophet observed, 'Allah desires that this should be my dwelling place.' He then dismounted and inquired whose house was nearest. Abu Ayub Ansari came forward and submitted, 'Messenger of Allah, that is my house and that is my door. You are most welcome.' He responded, 'Well then, go and prepare some place for my stay.' Abu Ayub went and, having made his arrangements, returned within a few minutes and the Holy Prophet accompanied him into the house. It was a two-storey house and Abu Ayub suggested that the Holy Prophet should stay in the upper storey, but he preferred the ground floor so that people should have easy access to him. During the night Abu Ayub and his wife could get little sleep as they were disturbed by the idea that they were above the Holy Prophet, so next morning Abu Ayub respectfully insisted that the Holy Prophet should move to the upper storey and he yielded to his supplications. He continued to reside with Abu Ayub for several months till the construction of the mosque and his own quarters was completed. Abu Ayub took his food up to the Holy Prophet, and he and his wife subsisted on the leftovers. Often food was sent for the Holy Prophet by other Muslims, among whom the name S'ad bin Ubadah, chief of Khazraj, has been specially mentioned in biographies.

Um Saleem, a widow, was a devoted Muslim who had a ten-year-old son, Ans bin Malik. She brought him to the Holy Prophet and submitted, 'Messenger of Allah, I have brought my son to serve you and request that you may kindly bless him and accept him as your servant.' He thanked her and blessed the boy, who continued to serve him till his death. As Ans had opportunities of observing the Holy Prophet at close quarters, a large number of *ahadith* are narrated on his authority. He survived the Holy Prophet for more than eighty years and died in Basra when he was well over a hundred years of age. He often said that through the prayers of the Holy Prophet on his behalf he had been so much blessed in every respect as he could not have imagined.

A short while after his arrival in Medina, the Holy Prophet sent Zaid bin Haritha to Mecca to bring the members of his family and they all arrived safe within a few days. Along with them, Abdullah bin Abu Bakr arrived with the members of Abu Bakr's family.

In Medina also the first concern of the Holy Prophet was the construction of the mosque. The spot where his camel had sat down belonged to two Muslim boys, Sahl and Suhail, who were under the guardianship of Asad bin Zararah. It was a vacant site on which there were a few date trees and at one place the ruins of an old building. The Holy Prophet purchased this plot for the mosque and his own quarters for ten dinars (approximately six pounds sterling). The site was cleared of the trees and the ruins and was levelled and prepared for the building of the mosque. The Holy Prophet laid the foundation stone with Prayers and, as in the case of the mosque at Qaba, his Companions worked as builders and labourers. The Holy Prophet himself also occasionally shared in their work. The mosque was built of bricks and slabs of stone which were erected between wooden stakes. The roof was covered with the trunks and branches of date trees, and in the beginning the Holy Prophet delivered his sermon on Fridays leaning against one of these pillars. Some years later a pulpit was provided for him. To begin with the floor was unpaved, and as the roof leaked when it rained the floor became muddy. Therefore, some time later, the floor was paved with gravel. The mosque faced towards Jerusalem, but when the Qibla was, under divine direction, changed towards the Ka'aba, the mosque faced in that direction. The height of the mosque was 10 feet, its length 105 feet, and its width 90 feet. Since then it has been extended several times.

In one corner of the mosque a covered platform was prepared which was known as Suffah. This served as the resting place of indigent Emigrants, who had nowhere else to go to. This was their home and they became known as the Dwellers of Suffah. They enjoyed the company of the Holy Prophet most of the time, and occupied themselves with worship and the recitation of the Holy Quran. They had no permanent means of subsistence. The Holy Prophet looked after them, and shared with them whatever became available to himself and to members of his family. On occasion, the latter went without, and whatever was available was sent to the Dwellers of Suffah. Ansar also offered them hospitality, so far as they could afford it. Nevertheless, these people often faced starvation. This continued for several years till some of them began to find gainful occupation, and the national treasury could also afford to provide them with some relief.

The Holy Prophet's own quarter, a single chamber a few feet square, was adjacent to the mosque. One of its doors opened into the mosque through which he entered the mosque for prayer services, etc. When the number of his wives increased, a chamber was built for each of them, contiguous with the first chamber. Some of the Emigrants built their simple houses in the vicinity of the mosque.

This was the mosque of the Holy Prophet in Medina. As there was no public building where public affairs could be transacted and administered, the mosque served as headquarters for the administration. The Holy Prophet spent most of his time in the mosque. It was the place of consultation and also the place for the administration of justice. All directions were issued from the mosque. It also served as the public guest house. Later, when need arose, prisoners of war were also confined in the mosque. Sir William Muir has observed (*The Life of Muhammad*, p.177):

> Though rude in material, and insignificant in dimensions, the Mosque of Muhammad is glorious in the history of Islam. Here, the Prophet and his Companions spent most of their time; here, the daily service, with its oft-recurring prayers, was first publicly established; and here, the great congregation assembled every Friday, listening with reverence and awe to messages from Heaven. Here, the Prophet planned his victories; here, he received embassies from vanquished and contrite tribes; and from hence issued edicts which struck terror amongst the rebellious to the very outskirts of the peninsula. Hard by, in the apartment of Aisha, he breathed his last; and there, side by side with his first two Successors, he lies buried.

The construction of the mosque and its adjacent apartments was completed within about seven months, and the Holy Prophet, peace be on him, moved with his wife, Sudah, into her apartment. Those of the Emigrants who could not procure building plots in the vicinity of the mosque built their houses wherever they could procure a site, sometimes at quite a distance from the mosque, and some were able to procure houses from Ansar.

The times of Prayer services had been appointed, but there was yet no arrangement about the announcement that a Prayer service was about to be held. The worshippers came to the mosque for each

Prayer service according to their own estimate of the time of the service, but this was not satisfactory. When the mosque had been built it began to be felt that some suitable means should be adopted for calling the Muslims to Prayer services. A consultation was held and various suggestions were made, and in the end Umar advised that someone should be appointed to announce that the time of a service had arrived. The Holy Prophet, peace be on him, approved of this suggestion and directed Bilal to carry out this duty. Thereafter Bilal used to call out in a loud voice at the time of each Prayer that the service was about to be held, and the worshippers arrived in response to this call. The same announcement was made if it was desired to call the Muslims to the mosque for other purposes also. Some time later Abdullah bin Zaid Ansari was taught the Call to Prayer, which has since been in use, in his dream and he mentioned the dream to the Holy Prophet, who observed that this was a divine direction and told Abdullah to teach the Call to Bilal. When Bilal called the Azan for the first time Umar, on hearing it, hastened to the Holy Prophet and told him that he too had heard the same words in his dream. Thus was the current Azan established. No one will question that the Islamic Call to Prayer is the most blessed and most attractive way of calling people to divine worship. Five times a day, from every mosque around the globe, in every city and every village inhabited by Muslims, the announcement is made of the Unity of God and the Prophethood of Muhammad, peace be on him, along with a brief but comprehensive exposition of Islamic doctrine and teaching.

The Salat had been made obligatory while the Holy Prophet was still in Mecca, but except in the case of the Maghrib prayer service, which comprised three *raka'as,* the other services comprised only two *raka'as.* After the Migration to Medina the Holy Prophet, under divine direction, prescribed four *raka'as* for the three services other than Fajr and Maghrib, except that the old system continue in respect of services during a journey.

The Holy Prophet, peace be on him, laid the greatest stress, of all forms of worship, on the Salat. He observed that during the Salat a worshipper is in communion with his Maker. In his own case he was so fond of Salat that in addition to the five prescribed services he stood in Prayer for a long time in Tahajjud, after midnight, so that sometimes his feet would become swollen. He often observed that the Salat was the greatest comfort of his soul.

At this stage the Muslims in Medina belonged to two categories: those who had migrated to Medina from Mecca or some other place and were known as Emigrants; and those who belonged to Medina, and, because they had given refuge to the Holy Prophet and the Emigrants and had undertaken to help them, were known as Ansar ('Helpers'). The Emigrants were generally poor, as even those who had been well off in Mecca had left all their belongings when they migrated. Ansar entertained the Emigrants very hospitably and held back nothing from them. The Holy Prophet adopted a device to strengthen further the bond of brotherhood between Emigrants and Ansar. He called them together and established a special bond of brotherhood between one Emigrant and one Ansari, and in this way about ninety persons truly became pairs of brothers, one from Emigrants and one from Ansar. This bond of brotherhood proved in practice stronger than real brotherhood. Ansar offered to share their orchards with their Emigrant brothers, but as the latter were not trained in gardening or agriculture, Ansar were content to carry on with their gardening and horticulture, etc., but shared the produce equally with their Emigrant brethren. This system continued till gradually Emigrants built up their trade and businesses and acquired properties of their own, so that they could dispense with the help of Ansar. One instance may be cited by way of illustration.

Abdul Rahman bin Auf had established brotherhood with S'ad bin Rabi' Ansari. The latter made an inventory of the whole of his property and put it before Abdul Rahman and invited him to take half of everything. In his eagerness to share everything with this brother of his, he went so far as to suggest that he would divorce one of his two wives whom Abdul Rahman could marry after the lapse of the prescribed period of waiting. Abdul Rahman expressed his gratitude to S'ad and blessed him and told him that he was not in need of any of his property and all that he required was that S'ad might show him the way to the market place. He started in business in a small way and soon became a person of substance and ultimately became very wealthy. A short while after his arrival in Medina he married a young woman of Ansar, and when he told the Holy Prophet of his wedding he was asked what dower he had paid her. Abdul Rahman replied that he had paid his bride her dower in gold equal to a date stone, on which the Holy Prophet observed, 'You must arrange your wedding feast, even if it is limited to the meat of one goat.' This was an indication that already Abdul Rahman was able to afford a wedding feast on that modest scale.

In this system of brotherhood, it was also provided that on the death of an Ansari brother, his Emigrant brother would be entitled to a part of his inheritance. This system of brotherhood continued over a couple of years, till it was abrogated under divine direction.

This was a unique device which proved of great beneficence, over a crucial period, for the small but daily growing community of Muslims in Medina. Emigrants were not only provided with economic aid under it, but were consoled and comforted to a large degree in the strange and helpless condition in which they found themselves on arrival in Medina. They began to feel at home and a strong sentimental bond was forged between them and their brethren in Medina which welded them into one united community.

Thus, after the arrival of the Holy Prophet in Medina, its people were divided into the following groups:

1 Muslims, Emigrants and Ansar.
2 Those of Aus and Khazraj who had become nominally Muslims but did not truly believe in Islam and entertained secret designs against the Holy Prophet and the Muslims. They were the disaffected who were known as hypocrites.
3 Those of Aus and Khazraj who were still pagans, but were rapidly becoming Muslims, and who would be soon absorbed among them.
4 The Jews who were divided into three principal tribes, Banu Qainuqa, Banu Nadhir and Banu Quraidha.

This was a situation which was replete with dangerous possibilities in the future, and called for a strong measure of co-ordination and adjustment, more particularly as the very existence of the Muslims was bitterly resented and was seriously threatened by Quraish, who were busy designing measures to wipe out Islam and the Muslims. Therefore, as soon as the Holy Prophet was settled in Medina, he called together the representatives of the Emigrants, Aus and Khazraj, and the Jewish tribes for consultation and invited them to consider the desirability of establishing some system of mutual co-operation whereby risk of dissension might be obviated and the security of Medina might be provided for. After a thorough exchange of views, agreement was reached and was reduced to writing, of which the principal provisions may be summarised as follows:

1 The Muslims and Jews would deal with each other on the basis of sympathy and sincerity and would not indulge in any aggression or wrong against each other.
2 All sections of the people of Medina would enjoy complete religious freedom.
3 Everyone's life and property would be secure, and would be respected, subject to the maintenance of law and order.
4 All matters of difference would be submitted for decision to the Holy Prophet, and would be determined by him according to the laws and the customs of each section of the people of Medina.
5 No section would go forth to fight without the permission of the Holy Prophet.
6 In case of aggression against the Jews or the Muslims, both would combine in repelling the aggression.
7 In case of attack against Medina, all sections would combine in repelling it.
8 The Jews would not in any manner aid Quraish or provide refuge or comfort for them.

9 All sections would be responsible for their own upkeep and expenses.

10 Nothing in the agreement would afford immunity to a wrong-doer, or sinner or mischief-maker.

By virtue of this agreement, the relations between the Muslims and the Jews were duly regulated, and a basis for the governance of Medina was provided, whereunder each section would have complete freedom of religion, and complete autonomy with regard to its internal affairs, but would be knit into a central administrative system which would be presided over by the Holy Prophet.

At this time there were two outstanding personalities among the non-believing section of Aus and Khazraj. One was Abdullah bin Ubayy bin Salul, chief of Khazraj. He embraced Islam nominally after the battle of Badr, but continued hostile towards Islam and became the leader of the disaffected in Medina. The principal cause of his hostility was that before the advent of the Holy Prophet in Medina, Aus and Khazraj, who had suffered great loss of life and damage to property in consequence of their mutual dissensions which had culminated in the battle of Bu'ath, were eager to live at peace with each other and had decided to elect Abdullah bin Ubayy as their common ruler. It is related that a crown had already been prepared for him. The advent of the Holy Prophet in Medina frustrated that design. Abdullah bin Ubayy was sorely chagrined and thereafter always nurtured sentiments of hostility towards the Holy Prophet and the Muslims.

The other hostile personality was Abu Aamir, a chief of Aus. In his earlier years he had travelled to many countries, was inclined towards Christianity, but pretended to be a free religious teacher. He was known as a monk. On the advent of the Holy Prophet into Medina, he set himself up in opposition to him but was soon disgruntled and departed for Mecca along with a few of his followers. In the battle of Uhud he fought along with Quraish, while his son, Hanzalah, who was a devoted Muslim, became a martyr in the battle, fighting on the side of the Muslims. Abu Aamir continued in Mecca till its fall and then moved to Taif. When Taif also submitted to the Muslims, he moved to Syria to intrigue with the Byzantines against the Muslims, but was not able to achieve anything in that regard. When he was in Medina, he used to call the Holy Prophet the Exile and the Abandoned. In the end he died in Syria, an exile and abandoned.

The Holy Prophet had not been settled long in Medina when Abdullah bin Ubayy received a threatening letter from Quraish which said: 'You have given refuge to our man, and we swear by God that unless you repudiate him and fight him, or else expel him, we shall invade you with all our strength and put all your men to the sword and make ourselves masters of all your women.'

On receipt of this letter Abdullah and his supporters began preparations to fight the Holy Prophet, peace be on him. When he learnt of this, he went over immediately to Abdullah bin Ubayy and pointed out to him that for them to start fighting him would be to embark upon a suicidal enterprise, as they would be opposed by their own people who were devoted Muslims. He advised them to consider all the pros and cons before taking any step that they might regret when it was too late. They realised their mistake and held their peace. Quraish, having been frustrated in their design, then sent a similar letter to the Jews of Medina. They too held back. These were clear indications that Quraish were still bitterly hostile towards Islam and were bent upon wiping it out. If those who had given refuge to the Holy Prophet and the Muslims were threatened with wholesale slaughter and rapine, it may be imagined what their designs against the Muslims were.

Their letters to Abdullah bin Ubayy and the Jews were not merely sudden but passing ebullitions of their wrath; they were indications of their firm determination to destroy the Muslims. Some concept of their bitterness and venom may be formed from the following incidents. About that time, S'ad bin Muaz, chief of Aus, who was a devoted Muslim, went to Mecca to perform Umrah and stayed with his friend of olden days, Umayya bin Khalf, one of the chiefs of Quraish. Apprehending some untoward incident on the part of the Meccans, he requested his host to accompany him in his circuit of the Ka'aba, in order to obviate any such contingency. Umayya accompanied S'ad to the Ka'aba at noon when not many people were likely to be about. But it so happened that just at that time Abu Jahl also arrived and was outraged at seeing S'ad in the company of Umayya and inquired from the latter, 'Abu Safwan, who is your companion?' and received the reply, 'It is S'ad bin Muaz, chief of Aus.' Thereupon, Abu Jahl raged at S'ad: 'Do you people imagine that after giving shelter to that renegade you can perform the circuit of the Ka'aba in peace? Do you think that you have the strength to safeguard him and help him? I swear by God that had you not been accompanied by Abu Safwan, you could not have returned alive to your people.' S'ad was provoked to retort, 'If you obstruct us in approaching the Ka'aba, then be sure you will not be able to journey in security to Syria.' Umayya tried to soothe S'ad and asked him not to shout at Abul Hikam, to which S'ad retorted, 'Umayya, do keep out of this. I tell you I cannot forget the prophecy of the Holy Prophet that one day you will perish at the hands of the Muslims.' Umayya was much perturbed and when he returned home he related to his wife what he had heard from S'ad and said, 'I swear that I shall not go forth from Mecca against the Muslims.' But he went forth, albeit reluctantly, to the battle of Badr and was killed at Badr.

About the same time Waleed bin Mughirah, father of Khalid, fell ill, and when he perceived that his end was near he began to weep. Some of the chiefs of Mecca who were present with him were surprised and asked him why he wept. Waleed said, 'Think not that I weep for fear of death. I weep at the apprehension lest the faith of Muhammad might spread and his authority might extend to Mecca.' Abu Sufyan bin Harb sought to comfort him with, 'Grieve not. So long as we are alive, that cannot happen. We give you a guarantee.'

On their side, the Muslims in Medina were not unaware of the designs of Quraish. They had full trust in divine promises of security, but, naturally, they were fearful and anxious over the misery that might be inflicted upon them. In the beginning they were so apprehensive that they were not able to sleep much at night, not knowing when they might be attacked. The Holy Prophet, peace be on him, was most anxious as he bore the responsibility for the safety of the Muslims. It is recorded by Nasai that in his early days in Medina, the Holy Prophet slept but little at night. Bokhari and Muslim have recorded: 'Late one evening, the Holy Prophet said: "If one of our friends could keep watch for a time, I could have some sleep." As he said this, we heard the sound of weapons, on which he inquired: "Who is that?" The reply came: "Messenger of Allah, I am S'ad bin Waqqas. I have come to keep watch." Thereafter, the Holy Prophet slept for a while.'

The Holy Prophet was always on the alert. One night some noise was heard and people emerged from their homes, anxious to discover the cause of it. Some of them began to move in the direction from which the noise had been heard. They had not proceeded far when they saw the Holy Prophet coming from the opposite direction riding on the bare back of Abu Talha's horse, with his sword at his side. When he arrived near the assembled Muslims, he reassured them that he was returning after having investigated the cause of the noise and that he had not found anything to be anxious about. He must have been awake at the time when the noise was heard and had proceeded immediately in the direction of the noise.

Quraish were not content only with the letters that they had addressed to Abdullah bin Ubayy and the Jews of Medina. They carried on propaganda against the Muslims throughout the country, as far as they could reach, and as they enjoyed a degree of prestige on account of their guardianship of the Ka'aba, their hostile propaganda was turning all tribes against the Muslims. Their caravans carried their propaganda far and wide. All this intensified the anxiety of the Muslims in Medina. *Hadith* relates that all Arabia united in opposition to them and the Muslims went about armed during the day, and did not put their arms off even during the night. They wondered whether they would survive till such time when they might be able to sleep in peace at night, without any fear in their hearts except the fear of God. Their condition at the time is described in the Holy Quran as follows (8:27):

> Call to mind the time when you were few in numbers and were accounted weak in the land, and were afraid of being despoiled by people, and He provided you with shelter, and supported you with His help, and provided you with good things, that you may be grateful.

In Medina, the position of the Muslims at that time was, in some respects, even more precarious than it had been in Mecca, for in Mecca tribal custom and conventions afforded them, at least to those of them who belonged to some tribe or the other, a degree of security, but in Medina they were not only subject to the menace of Quraish but were also afraid of the devices and designs of the disaffected, and were not entirely reassured with regard to the attitude of the Jews.

In the first year after the Migration the first child born to an Emigrant was Abdullah bin Zubair, whose birth was an occasion of joy for the Emigrants. Zubair bin Awam, the father of the baby, was a first cousin of the Holy Prophet, and was married to Asmaa, the eldest daughter of Abu Bakr. She was the mother of the baby. Abdullah grew up a devoted and erudite Muslim who played an important role in the early history of Islam.

The Holy Prophet and the Muslims were grieved in that year by the death of two prominent leaders of Ansar, Kulthum bin Hadam, with whom the Holy Prophet had resided in Qaba, and Asad bin Zararah, who was one of the six men of Yathrab who became the first Muslims, a year prior even to the First Pledge of Aqabah. Mus'ab bin Umair, the first teacher of Islam in Medina, had resided with him, and he had also instituted congregational prayer and the Friday noon Service in Medina. He was, in addition, one of the twelve leaders of Ansar who had been appointed by the Holy Prophet immediately after the Second Pledge of Aqabah. On his death, Banu Najjar, whose leader he was, requested the Holy Prophet to appoint someone in his place. As there was no longer any need of tribal leaders, they were told that they did not need a leader any longer as the Holy Prophet himself was their leader.

Waleed bin Mughirah and Aas bin Wail, two influential chiefs of Quraish, also died in the same year. They were bitter enemies of Islam and were highly respected in Mecca. Their sons, Khalid bin Waleed and Amr bin Aas, embraced Islam within a few years and played a heroic part in the early history of Islam.

Chapter 6

:Regulation of Fighting:

In Medina the Muslims found themselves in a very precarious and unenviable situation. Their security was threatened not only by Quraish, who had put a price on the head of the Holy Prophet, peace be on him, and had followed this up by serving an ultimatum, through Abdullah bin Ubayy, that unless the Holy Prophet was expelled from Medina, they would invade Medina in full strength and slaughter all the men in it and enslave all the women; but they were not secure against the machinations of the disaffected in Medina, and had to be wary of the Jews. Quraish had declared war upon the Holy Prophet and the Muslims and all those who might support them. The state of war thus initiated continued over six years and was interrupted only by the Truce of Hudaibiyya in the sixth year. Less than two years later Quraish committed a glaring breach of the Truce and hostilities broke out again which were terminated only when the greater part of the peninsula had acknowledged the supremacy of the Islamic state and had submitted to it.

In view of the ultimatum of Quraish, the Muslims were accorded divine permission to take up arms in their defence and in the defence of their faith:

> Permission to fight is granted to those against whom war is made, because they have been wronged, and Allah indeed has the power to help them. They are those who have been driven out of their homes unjustly only because they affirmed: Our Lord is Allah. If Allah did not repel the aggression of some people by means of others, cloisters and churches and synagogues and mosques, wherein the name of Allah is oft commemorated, would surely be destroyed. Allah will surely help him who helps His cause; Allah is indeed Powerful, Mighty. If We establish these persecuted ones in the earth, they will observe Prayer and pay the Zakat, and enjoin good and forbid evil. With Allah rests the final issue of all affairs (22:40-2).

> If Allah were not to repel a section of mankind by another, the earth would be filled with disorder, but Allah is full of bounty towards all peoples (2:252).

It must be appreciated, however, that Islam regards war as an abnormal and destructive activity, to which recourse can be had only in the last resort. The Holy Quran describes war as a conflagration, and declares that it is God's purpose to put out such a conflagration whenever it erupts, meaning that when war becomes inevitable it should be so waged as to cause the least possible amount of damage to life and property; and that hostilities should be brought to a close as quickly as possible, as is said: 'Whenever they kindle a fire for war, Allah extinguishes it. They strive to create disorder in the earth and Allah loves not those who create disorder' (5:65).

Fighting is permissible only to repel or halt aggression. But even in the course of such fighting, Muslims are not permitted any trangression; as is said: 'Fight in the cause of Allah against those who fight against you, but do not transgress. Surely Allah loves not the transgressors' (2:191).

It is repeatedly stressed that the object of any fighting forced upon Muslims should be to put down aggression and persecution, for persecution is worse than killing. During the course of fighting, all customary restrictions and limitations must be observed except when the enemy fails to observe them; in which case Muslims may forego them also, but only to the extent to which the enemy dispenses with them (2:192). Should the enemy desist from the fighting, the Muslims should do likewise, for Allah is Most Forgiving, Merciful (2:193). When freedom from persecution is secured, fighting should be brought to an end, as is said: 'Fight them until there is no persecution, and religion is freely professed for the sake of Allah alone'; but even this is subject to the enemy continuing the fight, as is said: 'If they desist, then remember that no hostility is permitted except against the aggressors' (2:194).

Should war become unavoidable, every effort must be made to limit its mischief and horror and to bring hostilities to a close as early as possible. Savage practices like disfiguring the enemy dead and torturing prisoners of war, which were common in pre-Islamic Arabia, are prohibited altogether in Islam. With regard to customs and practices not in themselves barbaric or revolting, the principle laid down is that the Muslims might extend reciprocal treatment to the enemy, and might retaliate to the extent to which an injury or a wrong is inflicted upon them, but that the better part would be to endure and to forgive (16:127).

Permission to take up arms in defence was granted, but so far as numbers and material resources were concerned, the Muslims were at a fearful disadvantage *vis-à-vis* Quraish, who did not stand alone, but taking advantage of the prestige that they enjoyed as guardians of the Ka'aba and the influence that they exercised by virtue of their handling the trade between the east and the north and the north-west,

constantly incited the tribes against Islam and the Muslims. The latter
were only a small community in Medina, not more than a few
hundreds, and of material resources they possessed none. They were
in no position to take the field against an enemy as powerful as
Quraish. Indeed, they shrank from the prospect, as is said (2:217):

> Fighting is ordained for you, while it is repugnant to you. It
> may be that you dislike a thing which is good for you, and it
> may also be that you prefer a thing and it may be the worse for
> you. Allah knows all and you know not;

and again (4:78):

> Now that fighting has been prescribed for them, suddenly a
> section of them have begun to fear people as they should fear
> Allah or even more, and they say: Lord, why hast Thou
> prescribed fighting for us? Wouldst Thout not grant us respite
> yet awhile?

Fighting, under the conditions set out above, having been permitted
to Muslims, the Holy Prophet, peace be on him, had recourse to
certain measures which were designed to support and buttress the
security of the Muslims.

1   He undertook visits to neighbouring tribes in order to establish
treaty relations with them which should make Medina secure against
attacks by them. In this connection, he paid particular attention to
tribes which were settled along or near the caravan route to the north.
These were the tribes whose help to Quraish and whose hostility
towards the Muslims could spell great danger to the latter.

2   He started sending small scouting parties in different directions
from Medina so that information should be procured on the
movements and designs of Quraish and their allies, and Muslims
might not be taken by surprise by them. Another purpose in
despatching these parties was that there still were in and around
Mecca several persons who believed in Islam but could not profess it
openly out of fear of Quraish, nor could they migrate to Medina,
either because they were too poor or because Quraish would not let
them. It is with regard to such persons that it is said in the Holy
Quran (4:76):

> What keeps you from fighting in the cause of Allah and of the
> weak from among men, women and children who supplicate:
> Lord, deliver us from this town whose people are oppressors,
> and appoint for us from Thyself some friend, and appoint for us
> from Thyself some helper?

These persons could take advantage of the proximity of a scouting party and slip out of Mecca and join the scouting party, and thus be delivered from persecution. They could also travel among parties of Quraish to the north and finding a suitable opportunity could join a Muslim scouting party. For instance, the very first party that the Holy Prophet despatched under the leadership of Ubaidah bin Harith was confronted by a party of Quraish under the leadership of Ikramah bin Abu Jahl, out of whom Miqdad bin Amr and Utba bin Ghazwan, both Muslims, who had accompanied the party of Ikramah, left it and joined the Muslim scouting party.

3   One of the principal instruments that Quraish employed for the purpose of inciting tribes against Muslims was their trade caravans which proceeded to the north and then returned to Mecca and in the course of their journeys up and down set the tribes in the neighbourhood of Medina against the Muslims. This constituted a great danger for the Muslims. These caravans were accompanied by armed guards and their passing close to Medina in itself constituted a threat to the security of Medina. Besides, trade was the principal source of livelihood of Quraish and the most effective way of persuading Quraish to abandon their hostility towards Islam and the Muslims was to disrupt their trade and to deprive them of the benefits thereof.

This has always been recognised as a legitimate war activity. Everyone is familiar with the capture or destruction of enemy vessels, and of captured vessels and their cargo being treated as prize. Quraish were well aware that in the situation that they had themselves created, the obstruction of their caravans and the seizure of their goods by the Muslims was a legitimate and expected activity to which no objection could be taken. They never let any occasion pass without protest in which they felt they had been afforded a ground for grievance. Their failure to make any protest against the disruption of their trade confirms that this activity on the part of the Muslims was considered by them as legitimate.

Nevertheless, the Holy Prophet, peace be on him, insisted that the sole motive of anyone who joined in any expedition must be to uphold the Word of God and that everything else was incidental, pursuit of which should not influence anyone to participate in an expedition. Bokhari, Muslim, Abu Dawood, Tirmidhi and Nasai have reported that the Holy Prophet was asked: 'One person fights in order to display his bravery, another one fights out of a sense of family or tribal prestige, and a third one fights in order to show off; which of these can be considered as fighting in the cause of Allah?' He responded: 'None of them. Only that one can be deemed to be fighting in the cause of Allah who is inspired by the motive to put an end to the efforts of the disbelievers which they put forth for the suppression of Islam, and so that Islam should overcome these efforts of its enemies.'

Bokhari, Muslim and Abu Dawood have reported that the Holy Prophet directed: Do not be eager for confrontation with the enemy and seek peace and security from Allah. But when you happen to be confronted by the enemy, be steadfast.

4 When the Holy Prophet learnt that any tribe or clan was preparing to invade Medina, he would lead a force against it or despatch a force under the leadership of someone else to take suitable action to put an end to their intended aggression. Muslim, Abu Dawood and Tirmidhi have reported on the authority of Bareedah: 'The Holy Prophet's directions to the leader of an expedition used to be: "When you are confronted with the enemy, offer them the choice of three conditions. If they accept, then refrain from taking any action against them. First, call on them to embrace Islam. Should they agree, accept their offer and hold your hand from them. Next, invite them to migrate to Medina and tell them that if they do so they shall enjoy the same rights as the Emigrants and will have the same obligations as those of the Emigrants. Should they not be willing to migrate, tell them that they would be treated as Muslims but would not have the rights of the Emigrants as those can be acquired only by striving in the cause of Allah. If they reject your invitation to embrace Islam, call on them to submit to the Islamic state and agree to pay the tax. Should they accept, hold your hand and do not fight them. If they reject all your offers, then fight them in the name of Allah." '

Abu Dawood has reported on the authority of the father of Harith bin Muslim: 'The Holy Prophet, peace be on him, sent us on an expedition and when we arrived near our objective, I spurred my horse and went ahead of my companions. I encountered some men belonging to the tribe against whom we were marching and they adopted an attitude of humility, whereupon I invited them to accept Islam and they became Muslims. Some of my weak companions rebuked me that I had by my action deprived them of the expected spoils. On our return to Medina, the incident was reported to the Holy Prophet, peace be on him, and he sent for me and expressed his approval of what I had done, and said: "You have done extremely well. Allah has appointed such and such reward for you in respect of every one of that tribe. I shall dictate a certificate expressing my pleasure at your good action." He then dictated the certificate and put his seal to it.'

Abu Dawood and Tirmidhi have reported on the authority of Aasim bin Kaleeb who heard his father say that a man of Ansar stated: 'We were on a journey with the Messenger of Allah, peace be on him, when he set forth on a campaign and during the course of the journey we felt severe hunger and were much distressed as we had no provision with us. We caught some goats out of a flock and slaughtered them and started cooking the meat. Our cooking pots were bubbling when the Holy Prophet came up, and on learning what we had done, he upset our cooking pots with his bow and in anger, started to grind the pieces of meat into the dust under his feet, and exclaimed: "Plunder is no better than carrion." '

Dawood and Nasai have reported on the authority of Abu Hurairah that a person enquired from the Holy Prophet, peace be on him: 'What about one who goes forth in the cause of Allah, but also thinks that he will derive some worldly benefit too?' He said: 'Such a one will earn no merit,' and repeated this three times.

Muslim, Abu Dawood and Nasai have reported that the Holy Prophet said: 'Those who go forth in the cause of Allah and in consequence are awarded their share of the spoils, anticipate two-thirds of the reward which they would have been given in the hereafter, and only one-third remains for them in the hereafter. If there are no spoils, their reward in the hereafter remains entire.'

Abu Dawood relates: 'On one occasion when the Holy Prophet set forth on a campaign, an old Ansari, Ka'ab bin Ujra, provided a mount for a poor Companion, Wasilah bin Asq'a. After the campaign, Wasilah bin Asq'a came to Ka'ab bin Ujra and said to him: "God Almighty has bestowed these camels on me as my share of the spoils. Of these, you can take your share." Ka'ab replied: "May God bless these spoils for you. I did not provide you with a mount in order to share in the spoils. My motive was only to earn spiritual merit," and he refused to accept his share, which would have amounted to two-thirds.'

Nasai relates that one of the desert Arabs embraced Islam and accompanied the Holy Prophet, peace be on him, on a campaign. When some spoils were gained, the Holy Prophet set aside his share also. When he was told of this, he came to the Holy Prophet and submitted: 'Messenger of Allah, you have set aside a portion of the spoils as my share. I call God to witness that I had not become a Muslim for the sake of spoils. I had hoped that fighting in the cause of Allah an arrow might pierce my throat and I may be admitted to heaven,' on which the Holy Prophet observed: 'If this one truly desires such an end, God will bestow upon him what he seeks.' A short while later, there was some more fighting and he died as he had wished. The Holy Prophet observed, 'Allah has granted him his wish,' and he bestowed his cloak to serve as his shroud and prayed for him specially.

These incidents leave no room for any suspicion that the Companions of the Holy Prophet took part in fighting for the sake of spoils. It must be remembered that in those days there were no regular armies and no salaried soldiers. All were volunteers who provided their own arms and mounts and laid aside their normal occupations and activities during the period of a campaign. The only way of compensating them was by apportioning the spoils, if any, between them and allotting a share of the ransom of the prisoners of war to each of them.

It will be appreciated that with the Holy Prophet's advent in Medina, and in consequence of the pact that he entered into with the Arab and Jewish inhabitants of Medina, his responsibilities had been enormously increased, and though he did not in the least neglect his primary obligations as a Prophet in respect of the propagation of Islam and the instruction and training of the Muslims in the values of Islam, a great part of his time and attention was taken up by the multiplicity of the problems that bore upon the security of Medina. Indeed, the security of Medina was itself essential for the purpose of the propagation of Islam and the proper instruction and training of the Muslims. Quraish had within a very short time after his arrival in Medina started their hostile activities against the Muslims. A chief of Mecca, Karz bin Jabir Fahri, led a party of Quraish to within three miles of Medina and captured a number of camels belonging to the Muslims which were grazing in a pasture. When the Holy Prophet learnt of this foray he issued forth with a party of Emigrants in pursuit of the raiders, but they managed to make good their escape.

As soon as permission to take up arms against the aggression of Quraish had been received, the Holy Prophet set forth from Medina with a party of Emigrants in the direction of Mecca and arrived at Waddan where Banu Dhamarah, a clan of Banu Kananah, were settled. These people were thus collaterals of Quraish. The Holy Prophet spoke to the chief of Banu Dhamarah and settled the terms of a pact with him. The pact provided that Banu Dhamarah would maintain friendly relations with the Muslims, and would not aid or abet their enemies and would go to their help when called upon to do so. He undertook corresponding obligations on behalf of the Muslims in respect of Banu Dhamarah. The terms of the pact were reduced to writing and were subscribed to by both sides. After an absence of a fortnight, the Holy Prophet returned to Medina.

Shortly thereafter, the Holy Prophet despatched a scouting party of 60 camel-riding Emigrants under the leadership of Ubaidah bin Harith Matlabi. When this party arrived near Thaniyyatal Marrah, they suddenly found themselves in confrontation with 200 armed Quraish youths under the command of Ikramah bin Abu Jahl. A few arrows were shot by each party against the other and then the party of Quraish withdrew and the Muslims did not pursue them. It was on this occasion that Miqdad bin Amr and Utba bin Ghazwan, two Muslims, left the party of Ikramah and joined the Muslims.

In the same month, the Holy Prophet, peace be on him, despatched a party of 30 camel-rider Emigrants under the leadership of his uncle, Hamzah bin Abdul Muttalib, to the coastal district due east of

Medina. Hamzah and his party marched quickly, and, arriving in the territory called Ees, discovered Abu Jahl at the head of 300 mounted men ready to oppose them. Both sides arrayed themselves in battle order and hostilities were about to commence when the chief of the territory, Majdi bin Amr Juhni, who had good relations with both sides, intervened and a confrontation was avoided.

A few days later the Holy Prophet received some intimation of the movements of Quraish and set forth from Medina at the head of a party of Emigrants. He proceeded as far as Buat but not finding any party of Quraish returned to Medina.

Sometime later, again receiving some intimation of the movements of Quraish, the Holy Prophet, peace be on him, set forth with a party of Emigrants and, making several detours, arrived in the neighbourhood of Yenbo, on the coast. Again, there was no confrontation with Quraish, but the Holy Prophet made a pact with Banu Madlaj on the same terms which had been settled with Banu Dhamarah, and thereafter returned to Medina. In the course of that journey he despatched S'ad bin Abi Waqqas at the head of a party of eight Emigrants towards Khara to reconnoitre.

On one occasion the Holy Prophet, peace be on him, organised a scouting party of eight Emigrants drawn from various tribes of Quraish and appointed Abdullah bin Jahsh as their leader. In order to keep their objective secret, lest knowledge of it should reach Quraish, he did not disclose it even to the leader of the party, who was given his directions in a sealed cover, which he was instructed to open and read after having travelled for two days in the direction of Mecca. When Abdullah opened the cover in accordance with his instructions, he found that the Holy Prophet had directed: 'Proceed to Nakhlah, between Mecca and Taif, and there keep track of the movements of Quraish and inform me of them.' He was also directed that if any of his companions, on discovering the objective of the party, should be reluctant to continue with it, he should be permitted to return. Abdullah announced these directions to his companions and they all expressed their willingness cheerfully to carry out the directions. The party then proceeded towards Nakhlah. In the course of the journey the camel that S'ad bin Abi Waqqas and Utba bin Ghazwan had been riding strayed away and they went in search of it and were thus separated from their companions and were not able to rejoin them. The party arrived at Nakhlah and busied themselves as they had been directed. A few days later they encountered a small caravan of Quraish on its way from Taif to Mecca. The party consulted among themselves what course of action they should follow. One element in the situation was that the time was the end of one of the sacred months and they were not sure whether the month had ended or whether it was the last day of the month. If they let the caravan escape, it would soon enter within the boundary of the sanctuary around Mecca, where no action could be taken against it. In this situation, they attacked the four persons who were in charge of the caravan, of whom one, Amr bin Hadhrami, was killed, two were captured and the fourth escaped. The scouting party took over the merchandise of the caravan and made haste to return to Medina. When the Holy Prophet, peace be on him, was given an account of the incident, he was greatly displeased and observed, 'I had not directed you to fight in the sacred month,' and he refused to take his share of the spoils. Abdullah and his companions were much abashed and experienced deep remorse over their action. On their side, Quraish raised an outcry that the Muslims had dishonoured a sacred month. The man who was killed was a protégé of Utba bin Rabi'a, one of the chiefs of Mecca, and his death greatly provoked Quraish and still further stimulated their hostile designs against the Muslims. They sent two emissaries to Medina to secure the release of the two men who had been taken captive, but as S'ad bin Abi Waqqas and his companion Utba had not yet returned to Medina and the Holy Prophet was apprehensive that if they fell into the hands of Quraish they would not be spared, he refused the release of the captives, awaiting the return of S'ad and Utba. They arrived in Medina within a few days and the two captives were released on payment of ransom. But one of them, Hakam bin Kayan, had in the meantime embraced Islam and stayed on in Medina. The other returned to Mecca. A short while after this event the Holy Prophet received the revelation (2:218):

> They inquire from thee about fighting in the Sacred Month. Tell them: Fighting in it is a great evil; but to hinder people from the way of Allah and to deny Him, and to profane the Sanctity of the Sacred Mosque, and to expel its people therefrom, is a much greater evil in the estimation of Allah; and persecution is a worse evil than killing. They will not stop fighting you until they turn you back from your faith, if they can.

We are now approaching the time when the first pitched battle between the Muslims and Quraish was fought at Badr. Before entering upon an account of that famous battle, it might be helpful to set out briefly the policies, principles and tactics that the Holy Prophet followed in respect of his military and paramilitary activities, and which he directed the Muslims to observe:-

1 Where he had a choice, he preferred to set out on a Thursday, in the morning hours.
2 Before setting out, it was his practice to make suitable supplications to the Divine, along with the whole of his company.
3 He had established a fairly effective system of intelligence

concerning the movements of the enemy. Those entrusted with this duty were instructed that they should not report to him when he was among company. If he received some intelligence which occasioned anxiety, he did not make it public, and communicated it to only selected individuals.

4 When he set out on an expedition he did not normally announce his goal. On some occasions he would proceed for a few miles in a direction different from the direction of his goal and would then veer round to the direction of his goal.

5 At a short distance from Medina, he would make a halt and check up on everything. He set out finally after being satisfied that everything was in order.

6 On the occasion of important campaigns, the Holy Prophet called for volunteers and those who were prepared to accompany him arranged their own equipment and mounts. Anyone who was himself well-off might help another less favoured one in this respect. The Holy Prophet urged such aid and assistance and rendered it himself when he was able to do so.

7 Boys below fifteen years of age were not permitted to go to battle. Those who, out of their eagerness, sometimes slipped into the ranks of the volunteers were, if detected at the time of checking up, sent back.

8 A number of women generally accompanied the volunteers to help in arranging for food and to nurse the wounded and to take care of them. They also distributed water among the fighting men in the course of the battle. On certain occasions, women are known to have taken part in the fighting also.

9 The Holy Prophet took one or more of his wives with him on such journeys. They were selected by lot.

10 When the Holy Prophet received intimation that an enemy tribe was preparing to attack the Muslims, he forestalled their design in order to frustrate it. On such occasions he so contrived that the Muslim force should arrive unexpectedly at the enemy encampment or settlement. This method safeguarded the Muslims to a large degree, and, in many cases, it rendered fighting unnecessary and thus safeguarded the enemy also.

11 Whenever he despatched a force on such a campaign, he directed the commander that when the enemy were encountered, they should be invited to embrace Islam, and if they agreed they should be urged to migrate to Medina. If they became Muslims, but could not migrate, they were permitted to stay at home in peace. If the enemy rejected the invitation to accept Islam, they were invited to stop fighting the Muslims and to submit to the Islamic state. If they rejected all these offers, they should be fought.

12 When he despatched a force on a campaign, he admonished them: 'Muslims, go forth in the name of Allah, and fight in the cause of Allah. Do not defraud in the matter of the spoils, nor cheat the enemy. Do not mutilate the enemy dead nor kill women or children or monks or priests, nor those who have arrived at extreme old age. Always try to improve people's condition and behave benevolently towards them. Allah loves the benevolent.' In his time, Hazrat Abu Bakr used to add: 'Leave alone those who have dedicated their lives to the service of God and also that to which they are dedicated; do not cut down fruit trees, nor ruin an inhabited place.' All this was designed towards making war humane and to put an end to the inhuman practices that were current in Arabia before the advent of Islam.

13 Whenever the Holy Prophet despatched a party or a force, he appointed an *emir* (commander, or leader) over them. He directed that even if as few as three persons should set out on an errand, they should appoint one of themselves as their leader. He insisted on the rendering of full obedience to the *emir*. He said, 'Even if a stupid Negro slave is appointed *emir* over you, render him full obedience,' though he added that if the *emir* should require something to be done which was clearly opposed to a divine command or to a direction of his own, he should not be obeyed in that respect, but his authority must be upheld at all times.

14 In the course of a journey, when the Holy Prophet and his Companions had to ascend a height they glorified Allah in the words 'Allah is Most Great' and when they had to descend from a height, they glorified Allah in the words 'Holy is Allah'.

15 The Muslims were directed that during the course of a march, they should not make camp in a manner that might prove inconvenient for other people, nor should they march in a manner so as to block the way. He said in the course of a journey: He who does not safeguard the comfort of others in marching or camping would be deprived of his reward in respect of his *jihad*.

16 When the Holy Prophet encountered the enemy in the field of battle, he always supplicated the Divine before the commencement of the fighting.

17 He preferred fighting during the forenoon, and stopped fighting during the heat of the day and resumed it in the late afternoon.

18 Before a battle, he himself arranged his forces in battle order and resented any kind of irregularity or confusion.

19 An Islamic force generally carried two standards, one white which was rolled around a staff and was called Liwa; the second was generally black which floated from a staff and was called Raya. In battle, these standards were committed to the care of selected individuals.

20 The Holy Prophet appointed a password for his forces before a battle which helped to distinguish between friend and foe.

21 He disliked noise or confusion among the ranks and called for silent and diligent performance of duty.

22 Before a battle the Holy Prophet appointed *emirs* over different groups of his forces who were clearly instructed in their duties. In selecting these company commanders he kept in mind the consideration that the person selected for the command should be one esteemed among his group or company.

23 On special occasions, the Holy Prophet invited his Companions to take a special oath of allegiance and loyalty, as was done at Hudaibiyya, of which mention is made in the Holy Quran (48:19).

24 When the Holy Prophet was himself present, battle was not joined till he gave permission.

25 During the course of battle he issued special directions from time to time and announced them himself or directed someone with a powerful voice to go on announcing them.

26 Muslims were not permitted to run away from battle or to lay down their arms. They were commanded to prevail or to become martyrs. There was, however, permission to retreat as a manoeuvre (8:16,17). If due to some weakness anyone contravened this injunction the Holy Prophet was not wroth with any such, and gave them the benefit of the doubt that they might have retreated as a manoeuvre and encouraged them to be steadfast in future.

27 Muslims were forbidden to inflict an injury upon anyone's face. The Holy Prophet, peace be on him, observed that a Muslim should be most careful in inflicting an injury.

28 Muslims were under a strict injunction to take no prisoners, except in the course of regular fighting (8:28).

29 Prisoners of war were either released after the battle as an act of benevolence, or in return for ransom (47:5). Or else, they could ask for their ransom to be fixed which they could pay out of their earnings, in which case they were set at liberty so that they could earn their wages freely. Indeed, those to whom they were allotted were themselves urged to contribute towards the payment of their ransom, as an act of benevolence, as is said: 'Write out a deed of manumission for such of those under your control as desire it, if you see some good in them, and help them to secure their freedom with a portion of the wealth of Allah which He has bestowed upon you' (24:34).

30 Prisoners of war must be dealt with compassionately. Those taken prisoners in the battle of Badr testified to the extreme kindness with which their captors treated them.

31 Ransom was not insisted upon to be paid in cash. For instance, those of the prisoners taken in the battle of Badr who were literate were told that their ransom would be to teach a certain number of Muslim children to read and write.

32 Muslims were forbidden to pillage or plunder.

33 If anyone of the enemy declared his acceptance of Islam, even in the course of fighting, he was to be spared as no danger was apprehended any longer from him. In the course of fighting on one occasion an enemy combatant, when confronted with Usama bin Zaid, who was about to kill him, declared that he embraced Islam, but Usama killed him nevertheless. When this was reported to the Holy Prophet, he was greatly displeased and inquired from Usama, 'Why did you kill him after he had declared his acceptance of Islam?' Usama submitted, 'Messenger of Allah, he merely said so out of fear. He was not sincere.' The Holy Prophet retorted, 'Had you cut open his heart to make sure whether he was sincere or not?' The Holy Prophet went on repeating, 'How will you justify your action before Allah on the Day of Judgment?' Usama was so unhappy over the Holy Prophet's severe displeasure, that in relating the incident afterwards, he said, 'I wished that I had not been a Muslim before this event and had embraced Islam only after it, so that I should not have been the cause of such severe displeasure on the part of the Holy Prophet.' On the other hand, there are also instances in which the Holy Prophet himself did not accept the declaration of a person's embracing Islam if he was satisfied that he was making it only out of fear or temptation. A case is mentioned in Muslim that in a battle a prisoner was taken who belonged to a tribe who were allies of Banu Thaqeef. When the Holy Prophet passed near him he sought release by addressing him in the words, 'Muhammad, why am I being kept a prisoner? I accept Islam.' The Holy Prophet responded to him, 'Had you embraced Islam before you were taken captive, God would have accepted it of you and you would have achieved salvation, but not now.' In the end, he was exchanged in return for two Muslims who had been taken prisoners by Banu Thaqeef. There is not a single instance that any one was converted to Islam by being put in fear of death.

34 Muslims were enjoined strict fulfilment of their covenants and pledges. The Holy Prophet himself was most particular in this regard. On the occasion of the battle of Badr, Hudhaifah bin Yaman, having migrated from Mecca, joined the Holy Prophet and the Muslims just at the time when fighting was about to start. He submitted to the Holy Prophet that when he was about to leave Mecca, Quraish had made him promise that he would not take part in fighting against them. On learning this, the Holy

Prophet directed him to fulfil his promise and to refrain from joining in the battle. This is an illustration of the extreme strictness of the Holy Prophet in such matters, for a promise given under coercion would not legally be construed as binding. Hazrat Umar was so strict in these matters that in his time he announced that if a Muslim was guilty of cheating the enemy or of failing to carry out his pledged word to the enemy, he would be executed.

35   The bodies of those Muslims who became martyrs in battle were neither washed nor wrapped in a shroud. They were buried just as they had fallen.

36   In case of an emergency a number of martyrs were interred in a single grave. On such occasions, their bodies were lowered into the grave in the order of their degree of knowledge of the Holy Quran. Martyrs were buried on the field of battle.

37   The funeral service for martyrs was either held immediately after the battle, or if circumstances were not propitious, at some later time.

38   The Holy Prophet generally arranged that the enemy dead should be given decent burial by the Muslims.

39   In the time of the Holy Prophet, Muslim fighters were paid no salary.

40   On the occasion of the division of spoils, the commander first selected some article for himself as a memento, and thereafter, one fifth of the spoils was set aside as the share of Allah and His Messenger. The rest was divided equally between the fighters, those who were mounted receiving three times as much as those on foot. The personal belongings of an enemy who had been killed went to the Muslim fighter who killed him.

41   The one-fifth that was set aside for Allah and the Holy Prophet was administered at the discretion of the Holy Prophet. Part of it he distributed among his family and kindred, but the greater part was devoted towards fulfilling the collective needs of the community. The Holy Prophet observed on one occasion, 'I am forbidden to take even the equivalent of a single hair of a camel in excess of the one-fifth; the greater part of the one-fifth is also returned to you.'

42   In the field of battle the order of Salat was modified so that while the Imam led the service throughout, part of the fighting force joined in the service and then withdrew to make room for other parts, one after the other. In this manner, the greater part of the battle force continued to confront the enemy during the service (4:103).

43   After fasting had been prescribed, some of the Muslims observed the fast when they were on a journey and some did not.

Eventually, the Holy Prophet forbade the observing of the fast in the course of a journey.

44 By ancient custom among the Arabs, a spy was liable to be executed. The Holy Prophet maintained the penalty.

45 The Holy Prophet, peace be on him, forbade severely any interference with the emissary of the enemy or doing him any harm or inflicting any injury upon him. On one occasion, some emissaries of disbelievers came to him and spoke very impertinently to him. He was provoked, but observed, 'You are emissaries, and I am, therefore, not permitted to make a harsh retort to you.' On another occasion, an emissary came to him and after talking to him, he embraced Islam and submitted that he did not now wish to return to his people. The Holy Prophet observed, 'You are an emissary and must return to your people. I will be no party to any disloyalty. After you return to your people, you can come back if you so wish.' So he went back and after some time found the opportunity of coming back.

46 After the Hedjaz had been purified of all paganism, the Holy Prophet announced that if a pagan should wish to come to Medina as a seeker after truth, he would guarantee his security and safe return (9:6).

47 The Holy Prophet, peace be on him, was most particular with regard to the security and the rights of the pagans who established treaty relations with the Muslims. He observed, 'A Muslim who kills any covenanting pagan will not be permitted to perceive the breeze of paradise.' He also directed that a Muslim who should be guilty of killing a covenanting pagan by mistake must, in addition to paying his blood money to his heirs, also arrange to procure the freedom of a slave.

48 He also observed, 'I shall on the Day of Judgment seek justice on behalf of a covenanting pagan who is wronged or harmed in any way or is burdened beyond his capacity, or is deprived of something against his will.'

49 When the Holy Prophet went forth to battle, he did not stop for more than three days at the place of the fighting after he had achieved victory, so that the presence of the Muslim forces should not become a source of inconvenience or a burden for the local people.

50 Any motive other than the safeguarding of the faith and putting down any mischief against it was regarded as inconsistent with the purpose of *jihad*. The Holy Prophet, peace be on him, had announced that anyone who went forth to battle for the sake of spoils, or for the display of his bravery, or for any other worldly motive, disentitled himself to any spiritual reward.

In the time of the Holy Prophet, the Arab method of fighting a battle was that when the opposing forces had been drawn up in battle array, individual champions challenged their opposite numbers from among the enemy to single combat. After these combats, battle was joined on a large scale. Fighting was carried on on foot or on horseback, the latter was preferred on account of greater manoeuvrability. Camels were used as a facility for journeying or for the carriage of equipment and provisions. The weapons normally used were swords, spears and bows and arrows. Shields and armour and helmets were used for protection. Some tribes also employed a catapult for shooting stones at the enemy. The Holy Prophet also employed it during the siege of Taif.

In the midst of all these disturbances, the principal purpose of the advent of the Holy Prophet was not neglected. The Muslims were being instructed and trained progressively in all Islamic values. The five daily Prayers had been instituted in Mecca. In these Prayers, the Holy Prophet and the Muslims faced in the direction of Jerusalem. This practice continued for about eighteen months after the arrival of the Holy Prophet in Medina. He had from the beginning hoped that the Ka'aba might be appointed the Qibla (direction to be faced during Prayer), inasmuch as it was the first House that had been built for the worship of God, and the memories of Abraham and Ishmael were also attached to the Ka'aba. Mecca was also the birth place and the home of the Holy Prophet and the birth place of Islam. About a year and a half after the Holy Prophet's arrival in Medina, he received the revelation (2:143-5):

> Foolish people will say: What has caused the Muslims to turn away from the Qibla towards which they faced when in Prayer? Tell them: To Allah belongs the East and the West; He guides whom He pleases to the right path. . . . We did not appoint the Qibla which thou didst follow, except that We might distinguish him who follows the Messenger from him who turns away upon his heels, though this was indeed hard, save for those whom Allah had guided. . . . Surely, We see thy mind turning frequently to heaven in the matter of the Qibla; so We shall certainly make thee turn to the Qibla thou likest. Then turn thy face now towards the Sacred Mosque; and wheresoever you be, turn your faces towards it.

These verses directed the change of Qibla from Jerusalem to the Ka'aba in Mecca. They also explain the wisdom of Jerusalem having been appointed the Qibla for the Muslims in the beginning and its subsequent change to the Ka'aba. Jerusalem being the Qibla was a challenge to the pagans of Mecca, and in the early months after the Hijra, it continued to be a challenge to the pagans of Medina. When the latter had been absorbed among the Muslims, the need of that challenge came to an end and the Ka'aba was appointed the Qibla as a challenge to the Jews of Medina. Also, the change was a prophecy that Mecca would soon fall under the domination of the Muslims and the Ka'aba, being purified of idols, would be restored to the worship of the One True God. The Muslims were directed to concentrate their attention on the achievement of that purpose.

Of the forms of worship instituted by Islam for the purification and spiritual fulfilment of the Muslims, the Salat was instituted first and was followed by the observance of the fast during the month of Ramadhan, a short while after the arrival of the Holy Prophet in Medina, when he received the revelation (2:184-5):

> O ye who believe, fasting is prescribed for you during a fixed number of days, as it was prescribed for those before you, so that you may safeguard yourselves against moral and spiritual ills. But whoso from among you should be ailing, not being permanently incapacitated, or should be on a journey, shall complete the reckoning by observing the fast on a corresponding number of other days; and for those who find fasting a strain hard to bear as an expiation, the feeding of a poor person, if they can afford it. Whoso performs a good work with eager obedience, it is the better for him. If you had knowledge you would realise that it is better for you that you should fast.

The fast involves abstention from food and drink between the first flush of dawn till after sunset and abstention from marital intercourse during that period, throughout the month of Ramadhan. Though normal occupations and pursuits may be carried on during the month of Ramadhan, the emphasis should be on spiritual and moral exercises, like prayer, the remembrance of God, study of the Holy Quran and all forms of charity. The Holy Prophet laid emphasis on absolute purity, physical, moral and spiritual, throughout Ramadhan. He is reported as having said: 'Most unfortunate is the person who should be afforded the opportunity of observing the fast in its true spirit throughout the month of Ramadhan and should not thereby win forgiveness for all his previous sins and defaults. If a person who is observing the fast does not discard falsehood and chicane, he starves himself in vain as God sets no value on his going hungry and thirsty.'

He also warned against carrying anything to excess, even worship. He forbade people forming a habit of fasting continuously or for long periods. He admonished: 'You owe obligations to yourselves, to your wives and children, to your friends and neighbours, and should not neglect any of those obligations. The performing of those obligations according to the will and pleasure of God is also worship.'

The Holy Prophet directed that towards the end of Ramadhan every Muslim who can afford it should contribute seven pounds of wheat or barley or dates or grapes, to a collective charitable fund which should be distributed to the needy, the orphans, the widows, etc., so that it should be an atonement for any default which may have occurred in the observance of the fast, and should enable the poorer and needy sections of the community to participate cheerfully in the festival of the breaking of the fast at the end of the month of fasting. This festival was also instituted at the same time when the observation of the fast was made obligatory. This festival is celebrated joyously as an expression of gratitude to God for His having enabled His servants to observe the fast as prescribed by Him. On the day of the festival the Muslims, men and women, gather together in some open space and join together in an extra Prayer service so that both the body and the soul should participate in the celebration of the festival. There are two festivals which have been instituted in Islam. The second of them is celebrated on the day after the pilgrimage, when those who can afford it also sacrifice an animal to win the pleasure of Allah. With regard to these sacrifices, the Holy Quran has laid down (22:38):

Their flesh reaches not Allah, nor their blood, but it is your righteousness that reaches Him. Thus has He subjected these animals to you that you may glorify Allah for guiding you; and give glad tidings to those who carry out all commandments to the full.

Chapter 7

:Badr:

In the beginning of Ramadhan, it was generally known in Medina that a large trading caravan of Quraish was returning to Mecca from Syria under the leadership of Abu Sufyan. It was accompanied by about fifty armed guards. It was a richly-loaded caravan in which everyone of Quraish had invested his or her savings. It has been pointed out earlier that these caravans constituted a grave threat to the security of Medina and, therefore, on receiving intimation of the approach of the caravan, the Holy Prophet, peace be on him, despatched two Emigrants, Talha bin Ubaidullah and Saeed bin Zaid, to gather intelligence about the caravan and to report back. At the same time, he instructed his Companions that they should be ready to set forth to block the passage of the caravan to the south. On his side, Abu Sufyan, apprehending that his progress with the caravan might be blocked by the Muslims, sent a fast rider to Mecca to explain the situation to Quraish and bring an adequate force for the safeguarding of the caravan. He also veered somewhat to the west and began to travel fast with the caravan on a route closer to the sea. When his emissary arrived in Mecca he, according to Arab custom, began to behave wildly and started shouting: 'Men of Mecca, Muhammad and his Companions have set forth from Medina to attack your caravan. Make haste to gather a strong force for rescuing the caravan.' Hearing his cries of distress people began to assemble around the Ka'aba and leading Quraish harangued them and incited them to get ready to go forth against the Muslims and to destroy them. It was decided that a strong army should be got together for this enterprise and everyone who was capable of bearing arms should join it. If anyone was unable to do so for some unavoidable reason, he should provide a substitute in his place. The leaders of Quraish, with the exception of Abu Lahab and Umayya bin Khalf, declared themselves ready to proceed. Abu Lahab was afraid as his sister had seen in her dream only three days earlier that ruin was about to overtake Quraish, but he provided a substitute in his place. Umayya bin Khalf was afraid because of the prophecy of the Holy Prophet about his being slain which S'ad bin Muaz had mentioned to him earlier, but he was persuaded in the end to join the army that was to march north. Within three days, a well-armed and well-equipped force of more than a thousand warriors

became ready to set out from Mecca. Some of the Quraish leaders
were apprehensive lest Banu Bakr, a clan of Banu Kananah, with
whom their relations were not friendly, should take advantage of their
absence from Mecca and attack it. It so happened, however, that a
chief of Banu Kananah, Suraqa bin Malik bin Ja'tham, who happened
to be in Mecca, reassured them and guaranteed that no one of his
people would threaten the security of Mecca in any way. He himself
joined the Quraish army and accompanied it as far as Badr, but on
arrival there, when he saw the Muslim force, he left Quraish and
withdrew before the battle was joined. His conduct is referred to in
the Holy Quran as follows (8:49):

> Call to mind when Satan made the conduct of the disbelievers
> appear fair to them and assured them: No one shall prevail
> against you this day, and I will be your strong supporter. But
> when the two hosts came in sight of each other, he turned on his
> heels and announced: I am absolved of all obligation to you; I
> see that which you see not. I fear Allah.

Before setting out from Mecca, Quraish gathered around the
Ka'aba and supplicated: 'Lord, do Thou help out of the two parties
the one who is based on truth and is nobler and better in Thy
estimation than the other, and do Thou humiliate and disgrace the
other.' Thereafter, the Quraish host set forth from Mecca in great
pomp and panoply. They were accompanied by singing women who,
with the beating of drums and the singing of martial songs, incited the
men towards deeds of valour. Leaders of Quraish provided for the
host all the food that was needed during the journey. Nine or ten
camels were slaughtered every day for their meat. When this army
arrived at Jahfah, a little more than half-way to Badr, an emissary of
Abu Sufyan brought the news that the caravan had passed through the
danger zone safely and that it was not necessary for the Quraish force
to proceed any further. On hearing this, some of them counselled that
they should go back, but Abu Jahl and his party rejected the
suggestion violently and swore that they would proceed as far as Badr
and would hold a festival there for three days so that their prestige
may be established throughout the country and people should stand in
awe of them. Nevertheless, a small number went back, but the main
body went forward and arrived at Badr on the ninth day after setting
out from Mecca. They were a strong body of 1,000 well-armed
warriors. They had 700 camels and 100 horses. Most of them were in
armour and were well-armed.

In Medina, before the return of Talha bin Ubaidullah and Saeed
bin Zaid, the Holy Prophet received secret intimation, probably sent
by his uncle Abbas, that a strong army of Quraish had set out from

Mecca, but he did not disclose this information to anyone, except to a few of his very close Companions who were forbidden to mention it to anyone else. The Companions continued with their preparations to set forth against the caravan. Hitherto Ansar, who, according to the terms of the Second Pledge of Aqabah, had undertaken to safeguard the Holy Prophet in the event of an attack upon Medina, had not taken part in any scouting campaign; but on this occasion quite a number of them indicated their readiness to set forth. The Holy Prophet, while still in Medina, held a council and asked for advice from his Companions. Abu Bakr and Umar assured him of their utmost devotion, but he did not react to their declarations in any way, from which the leaders of Ansar gathered that he was waiting for them to declare their stand. Thereupon, S'ad bin Ubadah, chief of Khazraj, made a spirited declaration that they were ready to make whatever sacrifice may be needed in the cause of Allah. Thereafter, the Holy Prophet called for volunteers and a number of Emigrants and Ansar offered to set forth with him. But as the general impression was that the campaign was directed against the caravan, several of the Companions felt that it was not necessary for a large number to set forth on the venture. The selected Companions, who had been told by the Holy Prophet about the armed force of Quraish advancing from Mecca, were feeling uneasy whether in case of an encounter with the armed host they would be able to safeguard the Holy Prophet against all harm. They felt they were faced with a difficult and delicate situation, but perceiving that the Holy Prophet probably intended to go forward to meet the armed host, they responded to him as eagerly, and even more eagerly, than the rest.

The Holy Prophet set forth from Medina with a body of just over 300 Emigrants and Ansar on the twelfth day of Ramadhan. Of the principal Companions, those who were not able to accompany the Holy Prophet were Uthman bin Affan, whose wife Ruqayya, daughter of the Holy Prophet, was seriously ill, and he had been directed by the Holy Prophet to stay in Medina to look after her; S'ad bin Ubadah, chief of Khazraj, who was himself ailing and was unable to travel; Usyad bin Hudhair, chief of Aus, who was also prevented by some unavoidable difficulty; and Talha bin Ubaidullah and Saeed bin Zaid who had not yet returned from the errand on which they had been sent.

Setting out from Medina, the Holy Prophet made camp after a few miles and checked his forces. Some minors who had joined out of their eagerness to participate in the campaign were sent back. Umair bin Abi Waqqas, brother of S'ad, was also a minor and when he heard the direction of the Holy Prophet, he tried to conceal himself but was discovered and was told to go back, whereupon he began to cry. The Holy Prophet noticing his extraordinary eagerness, permitted him to remain. The Muslim force comprised a total of a little over 310, of

whom over 60 were Emigrants and the rest were all Ansar. They
lacked almost everything. They had only 70 camels and 2 horses,
which they shared between them turn by turn. The Holy Prophet
himself also took his turn, and when his Companions insisted that he
should be mounted all the time, he smiled and said, 'I am as much able
to walk as you and am not less eager than any of you to win spiritual
merit. Then why should I not walk in my turn?' There were only
seven men in armour and the equipment was both defective and
meagre.

Proceeding from Rauha when the Muslim force arrived at Zafran,
which was only one stage short of Badr, intimation was received that a
well-armed strong force of Quraish was advancing from Mecca. On
this, the Holy Prophet addressed his Companions, informed them of
the intimation that had been received and asked them what should be
done. Some of the Companions, being conscious of their weakness in
all respects, submitted that the better course would be to confront the
caravan, but the Holy Prophet did not approve of this suggestion. At
this, the principal Companions affirmed their devotion to the Holy
Prophet, and their total commitment to the cause of Allah in glowing
terms. For instance, Miqdad bin Amr submitted: 'Messenger of Allah,
we are not like the companions of Moses so that we should tell you,
"Go thou and thy God and fight the enemy, but here we shall sit." We
affirm, "Go forth wherever you wish, we shall be with you and shall
fight on your right and on your left and in front of you and behind
you."' The Holy Prophet was pleased with these assurances but
awaited some expression of view on behalf of Ansar. Perceiving this,
S'ad bin Muaz, chief of Aus, submitted: 'Messenger of Allah, it may
be that you are awaiting an expression of our view. We have believed
in you as a true Prophet of God and we have put our hands in your
hand in token of absolute commitment. Go wherever you determine,
we shall be with you. We call to witness Him Who has sent you with
Truth, that if you will command us to jump into the sea, we shall
jump into it and not one of us will hold back. God willing, you will
find us steadfast in battle. You will behold that from us which will
greatly please you.' The Holy Prophet was pleased and observed: 'Go
forward in the name of Allah and be glad that Allah has promised me
that we shall certainly prevail over one of these two bodies of Quraish
(the army or the caravan). I call God to witness that I am beholding
the actual spots where the leaders of the enemy will be cut down.' The
Companions were greatly reassured by these words and some of them
inquired: 'Messenger of Allah, if you had known of the advance of the
Quraish army, why did you not mention it to us in Medina, so that we
might have made some preparation for a confrontation in arms?' Even
now the Muslims did not know definitely whether they would be
confronted with the caravan or with the Quraish army.

The Holy Prophet, peace be on him, now began to advance rapidly towards Badr, and when he arrived close to it he asked Abu Bakr to ride behind him and the two went forward in advance of the Muslim force. Presently they encountered an old Bedouin from whom they gathered that the Quraish army had arrived near Badr. On learning this, the Holy Prophet rejoined his Companions and sent Ali, Zubair bin Awam and S'ad bin Abi Waqqas ahead to gather intelligence. When these entered the valley of Badr, they saw some Meccans collecting water from a spring. They took them by surprise and captured a Negro slave whom they brought back with them for questioning. The Holy Prophet was at the time engaged in Prayer and they started the interrogation of the slave. They asked him about the whereabouts of the caravan. He professed ignorance about the whereabouts of the caravan but said that Abul Hikam, Utba, Shaiba, Umayya and others were encamped on the other side of the valley. Those who were questioning him thought he was deliberately pretending ignorance of the whereabouts of the caravan and beat him and threatened him to force him to tell them the truth. He stuck to his story. The Holy Prophet then came up and forbade the Companions molesting the slave and questioned him in a gentle tone concerning the whereabouts of the Quraish army. He replied that the army was encamped behind the sand-dunes on the other side of the valley. On being asked the number, he replied that it was a large army but he did not know its exact strength. He was asked how many camels were daily slaughtered to provide meat for the army. He indicated ten. The Holy Prophet turned to his Companions and observed, 'The strength of the army is about one thousand.' He then inquired from the slave, 'Which of the leaders of Quraish are with the army?' He replied, 'Utba, Shaiba, Abul Hikam, Abul Bakhtari, Uqbah bin Abi Mueet, Hakeem bin Hizam, Nadhar bin Harith, Umayya bin Kalf, Suhail bin Amr, Naufal bin Khuweilid, Ta'eemah bin Adi, Zamaa bin Aswad are all there.' The Holy Prophet turned to his Companions and observed, 'Take note, Mecca has flung all the pieces of its liver before you.' This was a very wise observation as it changed the whole concept of the Muslims from confrontation with a strong well-armed force to the concept that God had brought the chiefs of Quraish out from Mecca to be destroyed at the hands of the Muslims.

Habib bin Mundhar submitted to the Holy Prophet that the spot chosen for the encampment of the Muslim force was not very suitable. He was asked whether he had any suggestion. He recommended that the Muslims should advance and should take possession of the spring of water nearest to Quraish, the water of which to his knowledge was both plentiful and pleasant. The Holy Prophet approved of the suggestion and the Muslims moved forward accordingly. The water of the spring was not as plentiful as was needed and also the new ground chosen for encampment was sandy and was not firm underfoot.

At the suggestion of S'ad bin Muaz a tent was set up for the Holy Prophet who retired into it for the night along with Abu Bakr. While the men in the Muslim camp were able to sleep by turn during the night, the Holy Prophet spent the whole night in supplication. By Allah's grace some rain fell during the night and the Muslims gathered a supply of water, and the rain also made the sand firm underfoot, while the ground under Quraish became muddy and their water became dirty.

The dawn came. It was Friday, 17th of Ramadhan, 14 March 623. After Fajr Prayer, the Holy Prophet delivered a brief address on *jihad*. When it began to be light, he started organising the Muslim force in battle array. One of them, Sawad, was standing out of line and the Holy Prophet indicated to him with his arrow to get into line, and by chance the arrow touched his chest, whereupon Sawad dared a protest: 'Messenger of Allah, you have been raised by God with truth and justice. But you have poked me with an arrow unjustly. I insist upon retribution.' The Companions were shocked, but the Holy Prophet told Sawad in a kindly tone, 'Well, Sawad, you may poke me with your arrow,' and he bared his chest before Sawad, who stepped forward and kissed the Holy Prophet's chest. He inquired, 'Sawad, why did you contrive this?' He replied, in a voice trembling with emotion, 'Messenger of Allah, we are facing the enemy and I know not whether I shall go back alive. I, therefore, wished that before my martyrdom I may touch your blessed body.'

About that time, Hudhaifah bin Yaman and Abu Jabal arrived and submitted that they had just come from Mecca and that when they were about to leave, Quraish had forbidden their egress and then permitted it only on condition that they would not take part in the fighting against them. The Holy Prophet told them, 'You must fulfil your promise. We seek help only from Allah and rely wholly on His succour.'

While the Holy Prophet was still occupied with the disposal of his force, the Quraish army began to move forward. At that stage, the Muslim force appeared to them even smaller than its actual number. They came forward with great aplomb. On observing them from a distance, the Holy Prophet supplicated: 'Lord, those people are advancing with great arrogance to wipe out the religion established by Thee. Do Thou of Thy grace, I beseech Thee, help Thy religion.' About this time a few men of Quraish advanced towards the spring of water which was under the control of the Muslims, who tried to stop them, but the Holy Prophet, peace be on him, directed that they should be permitted to drink from the spring in peace, which they did and returned to their ranks.

Now the forces faced each other in such order that the numbers of the Muslims appeared to Quraish double their actual strength, which disturbed Quraish, while the numbers of Quraish appeared to the Muslims smaller than their actual strength. Quraish deputed Umair bin Wahb to ride around the Muslim force and to make an estimate of their strength, and also discover whether there was any supporting force hidden behind them. Umair soon returned from his errand and reported his estimate of the numbers of the Muslim force and that there was no supporting force behind them; and added: 'Ye Quraish, calamities approach you, fraught with destruction. Their numbers are small, but death is astride upon the camels of Yathrab. Their only refuge is the sword. Not a man of them shall fall but in his stead one of ourselves will be slain; and when there shall have been slaughtered amongst us a number equal unto them, of what avail will life be to us after that?' Quraish were perturbed at Umair's words and Suraqa bin Malik was so overcome that he left them and went back. When someone tried to restrain him, he said, 'I see that which you do not.'

When Hakeem bin Hizam heard Umair's description of the Muslim force, he went to Utba bin Rabi'a and said to him, 'Utba, you are seeking retribution from Muhammad for the killing of Amr bin Hadhrami, who was your confederate. Would it not do if you were to pay his heirs his blood money and lead Quraish back to Mecca? This would redound to your great credit.' Utba expressed his willingness to follow this advice and added, 'Hakeem, after all the Muslims and we are closely related to each other. Would it be right that brother should raise his sword against brother and father against his son? Go to Abul Hikam and put your plan to him.' On his side, Utba mounted his camel and began to urge people that fighting between close relations was not called for, and that they should return to Mecca and leave Muhammad to his devices and let him settle with the other Arab tribes. He added, 'We shall see what happens. Besides, the fight in front of us is not easy. I am not a coward but those people appear to me eager to purchase death.' The Holy Prophet espied him from a distance and observed, 'If there is a spark of nobility in the host opposing us it is certainly in that rider of the red camel. If these people follow his advice, it would be to their good.'

When Hakeem bin Hizam approached Abu Jahl and mentioned his plan to him, he retorted sarcastically, 'Well, well, Utba now sees himself opposed to his relatives!' He then called to Aamir bin Hadhrami, brother of Amr, and said to him, 'Have you heard what your confederate Utba now says, and that at a time when we are in a position to wreak vengeance for the killing of your brother?' Aamir went into a paroxysm of rage and tearing off his clothes, according to Arab custom, began shouting, 'Woe to Amr, woe to Amr, he is not being avenged.' This created an uproar among the Quraish host and everyone became eager to fight. Abu Jahl's taunt had greatly provoked Utba and he came forward with his brother Shaiba and his son Waleed and challenged the Muslims to single combat. Some Ansar were about to respond to the challenge, when the Holy Prophet stopped them and told Hamzah bin Abdul Muttalib, Ali bin Abi Talib and Ubaidah bin Muttalib, who were his close relations, to go forward. According to Arab custom, each side identified itself and then Ubaidah confronted Waleed and Hamzah confronted Utba and Ali confronted Shaiba. Hamzah and Ali cut down their opponents almost immediately, but Ubaidah and Waleed exchanged several thrusts and in the end both fell down severely wounded. Upon this, Hamzah and Ali quickly despatched Waleed and carried Ubaidah back to their camp. He succumbed to his injuries during the journey back to Medina.

After these single combats, the Holy Prophet, peace be on him, returned to his tent, after directing the Muslims, 'Do not start the general fight till I order it; but if the other side should advance in force, shoot your arrows at them carefully and use your swords only for hand to hand fighting. There are some people among the opposing host who have joined them under coercion, but who bear no enmity towards us, like Abbas bin Abdul Muttalib. There are others to whom we owe gratitude for their kind treatment of us when we were being persecuted in Mecca, for instance, Abul Bakhtari. If a Muslim finds any of them at his mercy, he should spare him.'

In his tent, the Holy Prophet occupied himself with supplicating the Divine. Abu Bakr was with him in the tent and a company of Ansar, under the leadership of S'ad bin Muaz, stood at guard around the tent. Presently, shouts were heard which indicated that the Quraish army had begun the attack in force. The Holy Prophet continued his supplications and was heard to beseech, 'Allah, I remind Thee of Thy promise and beg Thee for its fulfilment. Lord, if Thou dost let this body of Muslims be destroyed today, Thy worship will be discarded altogether on the earth.' He continued his supplications in agony, standing up and falling into prostration, addressing his Lord as Ever-Living and Bestower of Life. Abu Bakr was much agitated at observing the agony of the Holy Prophet and tried to comfort him, but he continued his agonised supplications.

On the field, when the two hosts came face to face and the general fight broke out, Abu Jahl also supplicated, 'Lord, do Thou this day destroy in this field the party that has sundered the ties of kinship and has started an innovation in religion.' He is also reported as having supplicated, 'Lord, if the faith taught by Muhammad is true, do Thou send a rain of stones upon us or destroy us through some other painful torment.'

It was a most unequal contest. The Muslims were opposed by a well-armed, well-mounted host, more than three times their number, determined to wipe out Islam altogether, and they were well-equipped and well-nourished; while the Muslims were half-starved and, so far as resources went, could not have withstood the Meccans for more than a few minutes. But they were drunk with the glory of their faith in the Unity of God and the truth of the Holy Prophet. Their living faith had filled every one of them with an extraordinary power and they were performing feats of valour unmatched in human history. Everyone was eager to do more than anyone else and to sell his life dearly in the cause of Allah. Hamzah, Ali and Zubair created havoc in the ranks of the enemy. Abdul Rahman bin Auf has stated that when Quraish advanced in battle array, he looked to his right and left to see whether he was well supported, but was much perturbed on finding that on either side of him was an Ansar stripling. While he was revolving the situation in his mind, the youth on his right asked him in a whisper, 'Uncle, which of them is Abu Jahl, who persecuted the Holy Prophet in Mecca?' Before Abdul Rahman could reply to him, the youth on his left also made the same inquiry from him in a whisper. Abdul Rahman was nonplussed, but he pointed in the direction of Abu Jahl and instantly the two boys sped forward like arrows, and, within a few seconds, attacked Abu Jahl so suddenly that before he could put up his defence, or any of his close companions could intervene, he was lying wounded in the dust. His son, Ikramah, was with his father, but though he could not move in time to save him, he attacked Muaz, another assailant who was close to his father, and nearly severed his arm from his shoulder. As the mutilated limb hanging by the skin impeded his action, Muaz put his foot upon it, pulled it off, and went on his way fighting.

Despite such heroic deeds, the numbers of the enemy, their arms and their equipment appeared to furnish an impregnable barrier and for some time the issue of the battle continued in doubt. The Holy Prophet was still occupied with his supplications in mounting agony. After a long time, he stood up from his prostration and emerged from the tent reciting the divine promise that had been vouchsafed to him long before, while he was still in Mecca (54:45-7):

The hosts shall soon be routed, and they will turn their backs in flight; the context of which was: Do they boast: We are a strong host for the wreaking of vengeance? The hosts shall soon be routed, and they will turn their backs in flight. Aye, the Hour is their appointed time, and the Hour will be most grievous and most bitter.

He looked at the scene before him and saw that the battle was raging fiercely. He took up a handful of sand and gravel and, throwing it in the direction of the enemy, called out, 'May their faces be ruined,' and directed the Muslims to make a concerted attack. They closed their ranks and shouting 'God is Greatest' advanced in concert. Simultaneously a fierce gust of wind arose and sand and gravel began to fill the eyes, mouths and noses of the opposing host, so that they could not see clearly and were unable to manoeuvre. Also, they were facing the sun and this too obstructed their vision. The Muslims had the sun at their backs and took full advantage of the confusion into which the enemy ranks had been thrown. Very soon, Quraish were routed and rendered helpless. About seventy of them were killed and about the same number were taken prisoners. When those killed were identified, the terrible fulfilment of the divine design to cut off the roots of the disbelievers (8:8) became manifest. Almost all the principal personalities of Quraish were lying dead in the dust and a few who had escaped with their lives had been taken prisoners. At first, it was not known what happened to Abu Jahl, and Abdullah bin Masood was directed to go and see whether he was among the slain. Abdullah found him almost at his last breath and inquired from him, 'Are you Abu Jahl?' He replied, 'Have you today slain anyone of greater status than me?' Then he muttered, 'I wish I had not been killed by peasants' (meaning Ansar, who were not esteemed highly as warriors by Quraish). Then he inquired, 'Whose is the victory?' Abdullah replied, 'Of Allah and His Messenger.' Abu Jahl then ceased to breathe and gave up the ghost. Abdullah returned to the Holy Prophet and informed him of Abu Jahl's end.

During the fighting Abul Bakhtari had a companion seated on his camel behind him. A Muslim warrior came upon them and told Abul Bakhtari of the quarter given him by the Holy Prophet. He inquired whether his companion would be spared and was told the quarter did not extend to him, upon which Abdul Bakhtari exclaimed that he did not wish it said of him that he had abandoned his comrade through love of life. They were both killed.

Umayya bin Khalf and his son had not been able to escape, and Umayya implored Abdul Rahman bin Auf that for the sake of their ancient friendship, he might extend them his protection. Abdul Rahman was inclined to do so when Bilal, who had been the victim of Umayya's brutal persecution in Mecca, shouted to the Muslims that Umayya and his son should not be spared. Hearing Bilal's appeal, Muslim warriors crowded round them and Abdul Rahman, finding resistance impossible, bade them save their lives as best they could. Any defence was vain and they were both immediately despatched.

As soon as the Holy Prophet, peace be on him, had finished dealing with matters which demanded his immediate attention, he directed that the enemy dead should be buried together in one place. Accordingly, twenty-four of the most prominent of them were buried together in a large pit that had been dug for the purpose, and the rest were buried wherever they had fallen. When the burial had been completed, the Holy Prophet stood over the pit and, calling the names of the principal ones whose bodies had been lowered into the pit, exclaimed, 'Have ye found true that which your Lord did promise you? What my Lord promised me, that verily have I found to be true. Woe unto this people! You have rejected me, your Prophet! You cast me forth, and others gave me refuge; you fought against me, and others came to my help.' On this, Umar submitted, 'Messenger of Allah, do you speak to the dead?' 'Yea, verily,' replied the Holy Prophet, 'for now they well know that the promise of their Lord has fully come to pass.' At the moment when the corpse of Utba had been lowered into the pit a look of distress had overcast the countenance of his son, Abu Hudhaifa. The Holy Prophet turned kindly to him and said, 'Perhaps thou art distressed over thy father's fate?' 'Not so,' replied Abu Hudhaifa. 'Messenger of Allah, I do not doubt the justice of my father's fate; but I knew well his wise and generous heart and I had hoped that the Lord would have led him to the Faith. But now that I see him slain, and my hope destroyed, it is for that I grieve.' The Holy Prophet comforted Abu Hudhaifa and blessed him.

Of the Muslims, 14 had become martyrs, 6 Emigrants and 8 Ansar; among them the devoted stripling, Umair bin Abi Waqqas, who had obtained permission to remain among the fighters by beseeching the Holy Prophet with tears. A larger number had been wounded but that was not a distressing loss. The Holy Prophet and the Muslims stopped in the valley of Badr for three days after the battle. This time was spent in the burial of the Muslim martyrs and in taking care of the wounded and in collecting and sorting out the spoils. The prisoners taken, who numbered seventy, were secured and were committed to the custody of individual Muslims. The Holy Prophet directed that the prisoners should be dealt with gently and their needs and comfort should be looked after. One of them, Abu Aziz bin Umair, stated subsequently that the Ansar into whose custody he had been committed, provided him with bread, while they themselves subsisted on dates. On some occasions when they had only a small piece of bread, they gave it to him, and if out of a feeling of courtesy, he returned it to them, they insisted that he should eat it. Those prisoners who lacked adequate clothes were provided with what was needful in that respect. In this connection, Sir William Muir has observed (*Life of Muhammad*, pp.233-4):

In pursuance of Muhammad's command, and in accord with the passage [of the Holy Quran] already quoted, the Citizens, and such of the Refugees as had houses of their own, received the prisoners with kindness and consideration. Blessings on men of Medina, said one of these in later days, they made us ride, while they themselves walked on foot; they gave us wheaten bread to eat when there was little of it, contenting themselves with dates. It is not surprising, therefore, that some of the captives, yielding to these influences, declared themselves Believers, and to such their liberty was at once granted. The rest were kept for ransom. But it was long before Quraish could humble themselves to visit Medina for the purpose. The kindly treatment was thus prolonged, and left a favourable impression on the minds even of those who did not at once go over to Islam.

When the prisoners had been presented before the Holy Prophet, peace be on him, he said, 'If Mut'am bin Adi had been alive and had interceded on behalf of these prisoners, I would have set them free.' The Holy Prophet, no doubt, had in mind the kindness of Mut'am which he had exhibited towards the Holy Prophet and the Muslims when they were being severely persecuted in Mecca. He had been instrumental in terminating the prolonged boycott of the Muslims and the whole of Banu Hashim, and on the occasion of the Holy Prophet's return from Taif, had extended his protection to him.

Among the prisoners were several leading men of Quraish, like Nadhar bin Harith and Suhail bin Amr. Some of the prisoners were related closely to the Holy Prophet, for instance, his uncle Abbas bin Abdul Muttalib, his cousin Uqail bin Abi Talib who was a real brother of Ali, Abul Aas bin Rabi'i, his son-in-law, being the husband of his daughter Zainab. Out of the prisoners of war, Nadhar bin Harith, who had taken part in the murder of innocent Muslims in Mecca, including Harith bin Abi Hallah, foster brother of the Holy Prophet, was condemned to death on account of these offences. Subsequently, when the Holy Prophet heard the pathetic verses in which his sister had set forth an appeal for mercy being shown to her brother, he observed that if those verses had reached him in time he would have forgiven Nadhar.

Before setting out for Medina from the field of Badr, the Holy Prophet sent Zaid bin Haritha in advance to Medina to convey to the Muslims the news of the victory in the Battle of Badr, which greatly pleased the Muslims, though some of them who had not set forth with the Holy Prophet regretted their failure to do so. Shortly before the arrival of Zaid in Medina, Ruqayya, daughter of the Holy Prophet, wife of Uthman, who had been ill, had expired.

On arrival in Medina, the Holy Prophet, peace be on him, held a council to determine the disposal of the prisoners of war. According to Arab custom, prisoners of war were either slain or were condemned to permanent slavery. But the Holy Prophet was averse to such harsh measures. In the discussion that ensued Abu Bakr submitted that the prisoners should be released on payment of ransom as, after all, they were all related to the Muslims, and it was likely that in the course of time they might embrace Islam. Umar, who was made of sterner stuff, submitted that in the matter of faith no consideration was due to claims of kinship. The prisoners had by their conduct earned death as their recompense and should all be executed. He even suggested that each prisoner should be despatched by the Muslim related most closely to him. The Holy Prophet approved the view of Abu Bakr and decided in favour of the release of the prisoners on payment of ransom. His view was subsequently approved by Divine revelation to the effect: 'When you meet in battle those who have disbelieved, smite their necks; and after the slaughter fasten tight the bonds until the war lays aside its burdens. Then either release them as a favour, or in return for ransom' (47:5).

The ransom of each prisoner was determined on the basis of his means, the minimum 1,000 dirhems and the maximum 4,000 dirhems, and thus most of the prisoners were gradually released. Concerning Abbas bin Abdul Muttalib, Ansar represented that as he was their nephew they were willing to release him without ransom. But the Holy Prophet decided that Abbas could be released only on payment of ransom. He had been tied up in the Mosque and the Holy Prophet could not sleep because of his groaning on account of the tightness of his bonds. On this becoming known, those in whose custody he was loosened his bonds. When the Holy Prophet perceived this, he directed that no discrimination should be made in favour of Abbas and that if bonds were to be loosened, they should be loosened in the case of all prisoners.

Another prisoner was Abul Aas, son-in-law of the Holy Prophet. His wife, who was still in Mecca, sent some articles by way of ransom for her husband. These included a necklace that her mother, Khadija, had given her as part of her dowry. On seeing the necklace, the Holy Prophet was deeply moved and suggested that the articles sent by Zainab might be returned to her, to which his Companions immediately agreed. The Holy Prophet fixed the ransom of Abul Aas that on his return to Mecca, he should arrange to send Zainab to Medina, which he did. Shortly thereafter Abul Aas himself embraced Islam and migrated to Medina and thus the husband and wife were reunited. When Zainab was about to set out from Mecca some of Quraish tried to restrain her. On her insistence on departure, Habbar bin Aswad attacked her with his spear and the shock brought about her abortion. She was so deeply affected that she never recovered her normal health and in the end she died from the effects of the shock.

Those of the prisoners who were too poor to pay ransom were released as a matter of favour. Those of them who were literate were released on condition that they should teach reading and writing to ten Muslims. Zaid bin Thabet, who subsequently acted as the secretary of the Holy Prophet, was one of those who had learned reading and writing under this direction of the Holy Prophet.

One of the prisoners was Suhail bin Amr who was a leading personality of Quraish and was a great orator, who often delivered addresses against the Holy Prophet. Umar suggested that his front teeth should be extracted, so that he might be disabled from holding forth against the Holy Prophet. But the latter greatly disapproved of this suggestion and observed, 'Umar, how do you know that God may not place him in a position later which should be praiseworthy?' Suhail embraced Islam on the occasion of the fall of Mecca and after the death of the Holy Prophet, peace be on him, he delivered effective addresses which helped to confirm many people in their faith, and thus through Suhail's efforts they were safeguarded against apostasy. On one occasion in the time of Umar, Abu Sufyan and some other leading Quraish who had embraced Islam on the occasion of the fall of Mecca came to see Umar along with Suhail, and it so chanced that at the same time Bilal, Ammar and Suhaib, who were freedmen and were very poor but had embraced Islam in the early years, also arrived to see Umar. When the latter was informed of the people waiting to see him, he directed that Bilal and his companions may be shown in immediately. On hearing this, Abu Sufyan was much upset and said, 'I was preserved to experience such humiliation that ex-slaves should be admitted to meet the Khalifah ahead of me.' To this Suhail retorted, 'Then whose fault is it? The Holy Prophet called all of us to God. These people responded to his call immediately, but we held back. Then why should not they have priority over us?'

One of the prisoners was Waleed bin Waleed, who was the son of Waleed bin Mughirah, a chief of Quraish, and brother of Khalid bin Waleed. His ransom was fixed at 4,000 dirhems, which his brothers paid in, and Waleed was released and returned to Mecca. On arriving in Mecca Waleed declared himself a Muslim; whereupon his brothers were much upset and upbraided him, 'If you had made up your mind to embrace Islam, why did you pay the ransom?' Waleed replied, 'I postponed my declaration of the acceptance of Islam till after my ransom had been paid, lest it should be thought that I had become a Muslim in order to escape payment of my ransom.' Thereupon Waleed was taken into custody and began to be severely persecuted. But he remained steadfast, and after some time found an opportunity of escaping from Mecca and arrived in Medina.

At Mecca, the news of the defeat was received with consternation. Burning shame and thirst for revenge stifled for a time all outward expression of grief. 'Weep not for your slain,' was the counsel of Abu Sufyan, 'mourn not their loss, neither let the bard bewail their fate. If ye lament with elegies, it will ease your wrath and diminish your enmity towards Muhammad and his followers. Should that reach their ears, and they laugh at us, will not their scorn be worse than all? Haply the time may come and you may yet obtain your revenge. As for me, I will touch no oil, neither approach my wife, until I shall have gone forth again to fight with Muhammad.' It was this savage pride which so long prevented their sending to Medina for the ransom of their captive kinsmen.

A month elapsed thus and then they could refrain no longer. The wild cry of long-stifled grief burst forth at last from the whole city. In almost every house there were tears and wailing for the captive and the dead. This lasted an entire month. One house alone was silent. 'Why sheddest thou no tears,' said they to Hind, wife of Abu Sufyan, 'why weep not for thy father Utba, thine uncle also, and thy brother?' 'Nay,' replied Hind, 'I will not weep until ye again wage war with Muhammad and his fellows. If tears could wipe the grief from off my heart, I too would weep as ye; but it is not thus with Hind.' To mark her sullen sorrow, she forswore to use oil for her hair, or to go near the bed of Abu Sufyan, until an army should march forth against Medina.

The blind and aged Aswad had lost two sons and a grandson in the battle. Like the rest of Quraish, he sternly repressed his grief; but as days rolled on he longed to give vent to his feelings. One night, he heard the wild notes of a female wailing, and he said to his servant, 'Go see, it may be that Quraish have begun to wail for their dead; perchance I, too, may wail for my sons; for grief consumeth me within.' The servant returned, saying that it was the voice of a woman lamenting for her strayed camel. On this the old man gave way to a burst of beautiful and impassioned poetry: 'Doth she weep for her camel, and for it banish sleep from her eyes? Nay, if ye will weep, let us weep over Badr; weep for Uqail and for Harith the Lion of Lions.'

> There was much in the battle of Badr which Muhammad could represent as a special interposition of the Deity on his behalf. Not only was it a decisive victory gained over a force three times his own in number, but the slain on the enemy side included in a remarkable manner many of his most influential opponents. In addition to the chief men killed or made prisoners, Abu Lahab, who was not present in the battle, died a few days after the return of the fugitive army, as if the decree marking out the enemies of the Prophet was inevitable (Sir William Muir, *Life of Muhammad,* p.236).

The battle was productive of grave and lasting consequences both for the pagans and the Muslims. It was not only decisive and important in the history of Islam, but also proved an outstanding landmark in human history. That is why the Holy Quran describes it as the Day of Discrimination between falsehood and truth (8:42). It is true that after Badr there were several other battles fought between Quraish and the Muslims which involved much larger numbers on both sides and in which the Muslims were sometimes faced with great odds, but the spine of Quraish was broken in Badr which no surgical operation could thereafter repair permanently. The number of combatants killed on the side of Quraish was nothing remarkable in itself, what was remarkable was the quality and importance of those who had been slain. It was this that the Holy Quran has described as cutting off the root of the disbelievers (8:8). Of the leaders of Quraish the only one left, and that because he was not present in the battle, was Abu Sufyan, who ultimately became a Muslim on the fall of Mecca.

On the other side the Muslim position became visibly stronger in consequence of the victory at Badr which was strikingly decisive and utterly unexpected. It impressed the tribes of Arabia and considerably boosted the morale of the Muslims, whose faith was much strengthened and who began to feel confident and reassured. Another consequence was that the disaffected in Medina were restrained and curbed. The Muslims always looked upon it as a great national event. Those who had taken part in it from among them were ever after looked upon as possessing great distinction. On one occasion one of them committed a grave default and Umar urged that he should be punished as a traitor, but the Holy Prophet reminded him that the person concerned had fought in the battle of Badr and his default was, therefore, to be forborne. In the time of Umar when stipends were fixed for the Companions of the Holy Prophet, those who had participated in the battle of Badr were assigned a larger amount. They themselves also took just pride in their participation in the battle. As Sir William Muir has observed (*Life of Muhammad*, p.234):

> The significance of the Battle of Badr is also stamped by the exalted rank assigned to the famous Three Hundred. Their names were enrolled in the first rank of the Register of Umar, as entitled to the highest of all the princely dotations there recorded. They were, in fact, the peerage of Islam. Bring me hither the garment in which I went forth to Badr; for this end have I kept it laid up unto this day. So spake S'ad, the youthful convert, now about to die at four score years. Crowned with renown as the conqueror of Persia, the founder of Kufa, and the Viceroy of Iraq, his honours were cast into the shade by the glory of having been one of the heroes of Badr. In his eyes the garment of Badr was the highest badge of nobility, and in it would he be carried to his grave.

The prophecy set out in the Holy Quran (54:45-7) was fulfilled to the letter. Quraish were routed and turned their backs in flight. The hour of their destiny proved most grievous and most bitter.

So also was fulfilled the prophecy of Isaiah (21:13-17):

> The burden upon Arabia. In the forest of Arabia shall ye be lodged, O ye travelling companies of Dedanim. The inhabitants of the land of Tima brought water to him that was thirsty, they presented with their bread him that fled. For they fled from the swords, from the drawn swords, and from the bent bow, and from the grievousness of war. For thus has the Lord said unto me, Within a year, according to the years of an hireling, and all the glory of Kedar shall fail; and the residue of the number of archers, the mighty men of the children of Kedar, shall be diminished; for the Lord God of Israel has spoken it.

Yet, along with all these happy consequences for the Muslims, temporarily they became exposed to graver dangers, for naturally, in consequence of the tremendous shock of Badr, the hostility of Quraish towards the Muslims became much bitterer and more rancorous. The other tribes also, though they were impressed, yet they became apprehensive that if Islam and the Muslims were not soon vanquished they would become so strong that it would no longer be possible to put them down. Their hostile designs thus assumed a more practical and more dangerous aspect. The Jews of Medina, who had hoped that the confrontation at Badr would destroy the Muslims, felt frustrated and began to entertain hostile designs against the Muslims. Quraish, on their side, having received a severe check, began to think of having recourse to secret conspiracies against the Holy Prophet. The following incident may be cited as an illustration.

A few days after the battle, Umair bin Wahb and Safwan bin Umayya bin Khalf were mourning those slain at Badr in the courtyard of the Ka'aba, when Safwan suddenly turned to Umair and said, 'Life is no longer worth living.' Umair perceived his hint, and replied, 'I am ready to hazard my own life but the thought of my children and my unpaid debts restrains me. Were it not for that, I could go to Medina secretly and put an end to Muhammad. I have an excuse for my journey to Medina as my son is a prisoner there.' Safwan assured him, 'I shall be responsible for your debts and your children. You must go and carry through this design somehow.' Having agreed to this, Umair left Safwan and returned home, and having prepared a sword by boiling it in poison, set out from Mecca. When he arrived in Medina Umar saw him and became apprehensive. He went to the Holy Prophet and informed him that Umair had arrived, and intimated that he was apprehensive about him. The Holy Prophet directed him to bring Umair. Umar departed to fetch Umair and while on the way told some of the Companions that he was going to fetch Umair to meet the Holy Prophet but that he was apprehensive about him and they should go and sit with the Holy Prophet and remain on the alert. When Umar brought Umair, the Holy Prophet asked him to sit down next to him and inquired about his errand. Umair said, 'My son is a prisoner with you, I have come to obtain his release.' 'Then why this sword?' inquired the Holy Prophet, to which Umair replied, 'The sword is of no consequence. What did the swords do for us at Badr?' The Holy Prophet urged, 'Tell me your true purpose.' Umair repeated his previous reply, on which the Holy Prophet said, 'Well then, did you not conspire with Safwan in the courtyard of the Ka'aba?' Umair was dumbfounded, but persisted, 'I have not conspired about anything.' The Holy Prophet questioned, 'Have you not conspired to kill me? But remember, God will frustrate your design.' Umair fell silent and after some deep reflection, said, 'You are right. We did conspire as you have said. But it seems that God is with you, as there was no third person present when Safwan and I spoke to each other, and yet you have come to know of our design. Perhaps, God has brought this about to make me believe. I believe in you sincerely.' The Holy Prophet was pleased and addressing the Companions who were present said, 'Umair is now your brother. Instruct him in the teaching of Islam and release his son.' Umair remained for some time in Medina till he became fully instructed in the tenets of Islam, and became so devoted that he asked permission of the Holy Prophet to go to Mecca and to propagate Islam among the Meccans. He was granted permission and arriving in Mecca he persuaded several Quraish secretly to embrace Islam.

Though, after the battle of Badr, the pagan remnants of Aus and Khazraj rapidly embraced Islam and were absorbed among the Muslims, yet some of them who secretly entertained feelings of jealousy and rancour against the Holy Prophet and the Emigrants joined the disaffected and were always on the look-out for opportunities of damaging the cause of Islam and weakening the Muslims. Their leader was Abdullah bin Ubayy bin Salul, who ostensibly became a Muslim after the battle but continued to nurse his grievance against the Holy Prophet, and became a centre of disaffection against Islam and the Muslims.

Shortly after the battle of Badr, news was received that the Byzantines, who had for some years been under great pressure from the Iranians and had been continuously pushed back, had inflicted a severe defeat on the Iranians and had started recovering the territory which they had lost to them. This piece of news was a source of satisfaction to the Muslims, as their sympathies were with the Byzantines, while Quraish affected sympathy for the Iranians; and also because the victory of the Byzantines fulfilled the prophecy of the Holy Quran set out in 30:3-7.

Chapter 8

:Uhud:

It will be recalled that the ceremony of marriage between the Holy Prophet, peace be on him, and Aisha, younger daughter of Abu Bakr, had been performed in Mecca approximately three years before the Migration to Medina. The wedding took place two years after the Migration, when Aisha's age had approximated to fifteen years. Some historians have fallen into error with regard to her age at the time of the wedding. Thorough research has, however, established that at the time of the ceremony of marriage in Mecca, Aisha was between ten and eleven years of age, and that the wedding took place in Medina between four to five years after the ceremony of marriage. This puts beyond doubt that, at the time of the wedding, Aisha's age was at least fifteen years.

Aisha's mind and memory were extraordinary. Under the Holy Prophet's supervision, instruction and training, her faculties developed very rapidly, and as she observed the life of her illustrious husband very minutely and never forgot a single word that she heard from him, she performed a matchless service for the faith in the instruction and training of Muslim women in all aspects of the teachings of Islam. The greater part of the information that has become available about the daily life of the Holy Prophet is based on the reports of Aisha. She was esteemed most highly by the leading Companions of the Holy Prophet after his death, on account of her superior knowledge and understanding of the faith. Whenever they encountered any intellectual difficulty, they had recourse to Aisha, who always succeeded in resolving the difficulty for them. She survived the Holy Prophet for about forty years and died at the age of sixty-eight.

The battle of Badr added tremendously to the heavy burden of responsibility that the Holy Prophet already carried. The disaffected under the leadership of Abdullah bin Ubayy were a source of apprehension close to the Holy Prophet, their machinations had to be carefully watched and they had to be wisely and sympathetically dealt with.

The Jewish tribes and their adherents were another cause of continuous uneasiness. They had hoped that Islam, upon which they looked as a heresy, and the Muslims, would be either wiped out at

Badr or so weakened that nobody thereafter would pay any attention
to the Prophet and his message. But all their calculations were falsified
by the event and their hopes were frustrated. They began immediately
to intrigue with Quraish against the Muslims. Quraish were only too
ready to lend ear to the whisperings of the Jews, Thus, the Holy
Prophet, peace be on him, had need of even greater alertness than
before the battle of Badr.

In the following passages, Sir William Muir has set out an account
of the situation with which the Holy Prophet was faced at that time
(*Life of Muhammed,* pp.243-5):

Abu Sufyan, smarting under the defeat at Badr, and still bound
by his oath of abstinence, resolved by way of revenge, to beard
his enemies at their very doors. Setting out with two hundred
mounted followers, he took the eastern road skirting the
tableland of Nejd, and arriving by night at the settlement of
Bani Nadhir, one of the Jewish tribes living close to Medina.
Refused admittance by their chief, Huyay, Abu Sufyan repaired
to another leading man of the same tribe, who furnished him
with intelligence regarding Medina, and hospitably entertained
his party during the night. When the dawn was about to break,
the party moved stealthily forward, and fell upon the cornfields
and palm gardens two or three miles north east of the city. Some
of these, with their farm-houses, they burned to the ground, and
killed two of the cultivators. Then, holding his vow fulfilled,
Abu Sufyan hurried back to Mecca. Meanwhile, the alarm was
raised in Medina and Muhammad hastened, at the head of the
Citizens, in pursuit. To accelerate their flight, Quraish cast away
their wallets filled with meal (whence the name of the expedition), which were picked up by the pursuers. After an absence of
five days, Muhammad returned from the fruitless chase. Shortly
after, he celebrated the first festival of Idal-Adha.

During the summer and autumn, two or three expeditions
were undertaken against the tribes inhabiting the plain east of
Medina. These were of a minor interest in their immediate
results, but are significant of the widening circle of the struggle.
Juheina and other tribes on the sea-coast being already in the
interest of Muhammad, the Syrian trade by that route was now
absolutely barred. There remained the eastern route to Babylon-
ia. This passed through the territories of two powerful nomad
tribes, Suleim and Ghatafan, both allied to Quraish and
employed by them as carriers, They inhabited part of the great
plain of Najd in the centre of the peninsula. There Bani Suleim
had their headquarters in a fruitful plain, the seventh station
from Mecca on the caravan route which crossed the tableland to

the head of the Persian Gulf. Quraish now turned their eyes towards this territory, and entered into closer bonds with the tribes inhabiting it. Henceforth, the attitude of Suleim and Ghatafan, especially of the former, became actively hostile towards Muhammad. Incited by Quraish, and by the example of Abu Sufyan, they now projected a plundering attack upon Medina, a task in itself congenial with their predatory habits. Timely intelligence reached Medina that they had begun to assemble at Qarqarat al-Kudr; Muhammad, anticipating their design, hastened to surprise them at the head of two hundred men. On reaching the spot he found it deserted; but a herd of 500 camels, feeding under charge of a single boy, fell into his hands, and was divided as spoils of war. The boy was made captive, but afterwards, on professing faith in Muhammad, released.

A month later, Bani Ghatafan were again reported to be collecting troops in Nejd. Heading a strong force of 450 men, some mounted on horses, Muhammad himself proceeded to disperse them. In three or four marches, he reached the spot; but the enemy, having notice of his approach, had retired to the hills, and secured in fastnesses their families and cattle. One of them, who was met on the road, and employed as a guide, embraced Islam and was spared. In effecting this demonstration Muhammad was absent for seven days. In the autumn, he led another attack, at the head of three hundred followers, against Bani Suleim, who still maintained a threatening attitude. Arrived at their rendezvous, he found that the force had broken up. So, after staying unavailingly for some time to watch the autumn caravans of Quraish proceeding northwards, he returned without meeting the enemy.

The following month was marked by a more successful affair. Quraish, finding the sea-shore closely watched by Muhammad, dared not expose their merchandise to the perils of that route. They were reduced to great straits. If we sit still at home, they said, we shall be eating up our capital; how can we live, unless we keep up the winter and the summer caravans? We are shut out from the coast; let us try the eastern road by Iraq. Water is scarce upon this route, but the summer was now passed, and, moreover, a sufficient supply could be carried upon camels between the distant wells. Accordingly, they equipped a caravan to traverse the tableland of the central desert. It was headed by Safwan, and Quraish sent much property with him for barter, chiefly in vessels and bars of silver. An Arab guide promised to lead them by a way unknown to the followers of Muhammad; but intelligence of the rich venture and of the road which it was to take, reached the Prophet through an Arab who chanced to visit the Jews at Medina; whereupon Zaid was immediately despatched in pursuit with a hundred picked and well-mounted men. He came up with the caravan, and fell suddenly upon it. The leaders of Quraish fled, the rest were overpowered, and all the merchandise and silver were carried off, with one or two prisoners, to Medina. The booty was valued at 100,000 pieces; so that, after the appropriation of the Prophet's Fifth, 800 pieces fell to the lot of each soldier. The guide was brought to Muhammad, who promised him liberty if he would believe. He embraced Islam, and was set free. Zaid obtained great distinction in consequence, and thenceforward became a favourite commander.

It has been mentioned that shortly after his arrival in Medina, the Holy Prophet had made an agreement with the three principal Jewish tribes, Banu Qainuqa', Banu Nadhir and Banu Quraidha, which bound both sides to live together in peace and security, to maintain law and order in Medina and to co-operate with each other in the defence of Medina against any external attack. For a short while the Jews observed the terms of the agreement, at least they sought no opportunity of seeking a conflict with the Muslims. But when they observed that the Muslims were progressively gaining strength in Medina, they made up their minds to put a stop to this tendency. For this purpose they had recourse to every type of device. They tried to create dissension among the Muslims. For instance, on one occasion, when a large number of Aus and Khazraj were together and were in amicable converse with each other, some mischievous Jews appeared among them and somehow started a discussion of the Battle of Bu'ath, with the result that passions were aroused between Aus and Khazraj and both sides drew their swords. Fortunately, the Holy Prophet, peace be on him, received intimation of the situation and soon arrived on the scene with a party of Emigrants. He rebuked both sides for having reverted to pre-Islamic ways, forgetting the favour that God had bestowed upon them by making them brethren through Islam. Both sides were deeply moved by his words and, repenting of their misbehaviour, embraced each other with tears in their eyes.

> The Jews had not rested content with murmuring against Muhammad's rule, they sought to embarrass him by active sedition. One of their first attempts against Muhammad's regime was to stir up strife between the Refugees and Helpers (G. M. Draycott, *Mahomet*, p. 148).

The Jews, at first surprised to see the Qurashites beaten by a handful of peasants from Medina (Kaab bin Ashraf composed a melancholy song about the ruin of the patricians, these kings of Arabia), then decided that they need not come to a hasty conclusion because of the easy defeat of a troop of bourgeois without military training. They became alarmed at Muhammad's increasing authority; his prestige was heightened by the victory in which the people saw the confirmation of his prophetic mission. The Jews began to show their hostility to Islam openly (L. Dermenghem, *The Life of Mahomet*, p. 201).

After the battle of Badr, the Jews were greatly chagrined and began to give open expression to their feelings. Soon after the battle, the Holy Prophet called the leading men among the Jews together and inviting their attention to the battle as a clear Divine Sign, urged them to reflect on it and to accept his message and embrace Islam. To this, the Jews made the taunting retort: 'Muhammad, by slaying a few Quraish, you appear to have become arrogant. Quraish are not trained in the science of war. If you had been confronted by us, we would have shown you what fighting means.' Not content with provocative verbal challenges, they began to plan the assassination of the Holy Prophet himself. Apparently, this became generally known; for instance, when a devoted Muslim, Talha bin Braa, who was ill, felt that his end was approaching, he directed that if he died during the night the Holy Prophet should not be informed of his death till the morning lest he should decide to come out for his funeral prayers during the night and might be exposed to mortal danger on the part of the Jews. The Banu Qainuqa', the strongest and reputedly the bravest of the three principal Jewish tribes, took the lead in contravening the spirit of the agreement which they had made with the Holy Prophet. Ibn Hisham and Tabari have recorded: Banu Qainuqa' were the first of the Jews who broke the agreement between them and the Messenger of Allah. After the battle of Badr, they gave open expression to their frustration and jealousy and finally committed a breach of the agreement.

The Holy Prophet continued to admonish the Muslims to possess their souls in peace and not to furnish any occasion to the Jews to embark on any rash action. He himself was most anxious and careful that their feelings and sentiments should be duly respected. On one occasion, he rebuked a Muslim, who, being provoked by the observation of a Jew, designed to exalt Moses above all the Prophets, affirmed, somewhat fiercely, that it was the Holy Prophet who was most exalted among the Messengers of God. The Holy Prophet mentioned some superiority of Moses to assuage the feelings of the Jews. Despite this attitude of the Holy Prophet, the mischief of the Jews increased progressively and ultimately it was they who brought on the first conflict with the Muslims. It happened in this wise. A

Muslim woman went shopping to the shop of a Jew, and, while she was sitting occupied with selecting whatever she needed, some Jews who were also present in the shop started teasing her mischievously and the shopkeeper himself, taking advantage of her preoccupation with her shopping, pinned up the lower part of her skirt with her bodice. The woman, being annoyed at the attitude of those in the shop, stood up suddenly, intending to leave the shop, and in consequence of the shopkeeper's mischievous pinning up her skirt, the lower part of her body was exposed at which the shopkeeper and his companions burst out laughing. The outraged woman shrieked in great distress and called for help. A Muslim who was near rushed to her aid, and in the scuffle that ensued, the Jewish shopkeeper was killed, whereupon the Muslim was set upon and was immediately despatched. This drew the attention of Muslims and Jews in the vicinity of the shop and a delicate situation arose. When the Holy Prophet learnt of the incident, he went over and called together the leading men of Banu Qainuqa' and admonished them to fear God and mend their ways. They retorted arrogantly and repeated the challenge that he should lay no store by the victory at Badr as, in case of a conflict, they would show him what fighting meant.

The Holy Prophet felt that matters were coming to a head and, collecting a number of Muslims, he marched to the strongholds of Banu Qainuqa', who, instead of seeking a peaceful solution, appeared ready to fight. The Holy Prophet invested their strongholds and the siege continued for a fortnight. At the end of it, Banu Qainuqa', perceiving that they could no longer hold out, surrendered on condition that they, their families and their animals would be spared and the rest of their belongings would pass to the Muslims. The Holy Prophet accepted their terms, though, in terms of the agreement, the matter had to be settled according to Mosaic law, which was to the effect (Deuteronomy 20:10-14):

When thou comest nigh upon a city to fight against it, then proclaim peace unto it. And it shall be, if it make thee answer of peace, and open unto thee, that all the people that is found therein shall be tributaries unto thee, and they shall serve thee. And if it will make no peace with thee, but will make war against thee, then thou shalt besiege it. And when thy Lord thy God hath delivered it unto thine hands, thou shalt smite every male thereof with the edge of the sword; but the women, and the little ones, and the cattle, and all that is in the city, even all the spoil thereof, shalt thou take unto thyself; and thou shalt eat the spoil of thine enemies, which the Lord thy God hath given thee.

As this was the first default on the part of the Jews, the Holy

Prophet was not inclined to impose the extreme penalty upon them. On the other hand, it was no longer safe to let such a hostile and treacherous tribe continue in Medina to carry on its designs, particularly at a time when the disaffected, from among Aus and Khazraj, were bent upon mischief inside Medina, and the Muslims in Medina were also exposed all the time to external aggression on the part of hostile Arab tribes. In these circumstances, the expulsion of Banu Qainuqa' from Medina was the least penalty that was permissible. Indeed, it was too clement. The main purpose of the Holy Prophet was the security of Medina. Expulsion was not much of a punishment for any Arab tribe, especially when it does not own any land or orchard; as was the case with Banu Qainuqa'. They made their preparations to depart from Medina and to go and settle in Syria. The Holy Prophet appointed Ubadah bin Thamat, who was one of their confederates, to supervise the arrangements in connection with their departure. He accompanied them for several stages and returned to Medina when they were well on their way. They left behind only their arms and the instruments of their profession, which was that of goldsmith. It is reported that within a year of their exile, an epidemic broke out among them which destroyed the whole tribe.

The pre-emptive expeditions undertaken by the Holy Prophet, were not only conceived in wisdom for the safeguarding of the security of Muslims and of Medina, but also in beneficence towards his opponents. Altogether there were more than five dozen such expeditions, big and small, led by the Holy Prophet himself or under his directions, by Zaid or some other Companion of the Holy Prophet. There was little loss of life and very small other damage suffered by his opponents. As time passed and opposition to him and the Muslims spread over a larger and larger area, the expeditions had to be undertaken over longer and longer distances. The total loss of life suffered by the opponents of Islam in pitched battles between comparatively large forces as well as pre-emptive expeditions was 759 and by the Muslims 259. Military operations of one type or the other carried on during ten years, with an interval of about two years after the Truce of Hudaibiyya, involved only a total of 1,018 deaths. Yet, till quite recent times, the Holy Prophet has been represented by Western writers as a blood-thirsty fanatic who carried fire and sword over large areas in the attempt to impose his false creed upon unwilling people at the point of the sword. Nothing could be farther from the truth and from reality. It is true that very often in the course of these expeditions an individual or a group embraced Islam, and these were welcomed as brethren in the faith. As the only cause of hostility between the Muslims and their opponents was a difference of belief, anyone who professed belief in Islam thereby laid aside his hostility and was no longer an enemy and could not be treated as such.

What is relevant is that no one was at any time forced to believe. As has already been pointed out, there were instances in which the Holy Prophet rejected a profession of belief in Islam when he had reason to suspect that such profession was being made with an ulterior motive.

On this question of Islam having been spread by the sword, Thomas Carlyle has observed (*The Hero as Prophet*, p.61):

> The sword indeed: But where will you get your sword? Every new opinion has its starting precisely in a minority of one. In one man's head alone, there it dwells as yet. One man alone of the whole world believes it; there is one man against all men. That he take a sword, try to propagate with that, will do little for him. You must first get your sword! On the whole, a thing will propagate itself as it can. . . . In this great duel, Nature herself is umpire, and can do no wrong. The thing which is deepest-rooted in Nature, what we call truest, that thing and not the other will be found growing at last.

James Michener has said ('The Misunderstood Religion', *Reader's Digest*, June 1955, p. 88):

> No other religion in history spread so readily as Islam. The West has widely believed that this surge of religion was made possible by the sword. But no modern scholar accepts that idea, and the Quran is explicit in support of freedom of conscience.

> History makes it clear, however, that the legend of fanatical Muslims sweeping through the world and forcing Islam at the point of the sword upon conquered races, is one of the most fantastically absurd myths that historians have ever repeated (De L. O'Leary, *Islam at the Crossroads*, p. 8).

About this time the Holy Prophet's youngest daughter, Fatima, was married to his cousin, Ali bin Abi Talib. Within a year of her marriage she gave birth to a baby boy who was named Hassan by the Holy Prophet. A year later, she gave birth to a second boy who was named Husain. Those who claim descent from the Holy Prophet are descended from these two grandsons of his.

About the same time the Holy Prophet gave his third daughter, Um Kulthum, in marriage to Uthman bin Affan.

The exile of Banu Qainuqa' from Medina did not bring about any improvement in the relations between the remaining two principal Jewish tribes in Medina and the Muslims. On the contrary the Jews embarked upon greater and greater mischief and began to intrigue more extensively against the Muslims. The affair of Kaab bin Ashraf was only one link in this lengthening chain. Kaab was a Jew by creed but not by race. His father, Ashraf, was a clever and intelligent Arab of Banu Nadhan who came and settled in Medina and became a confederate of Banu Nadhir. Gradually, he acquired so much importance and influence that the chief of Banu Nadhir, Abu Rafe, bin Abi Haqeeq, gave his daughter in marriage to him. She gave birth to Kaab, who, as he grew up, acquired an even greater status than his father, so much so that in the end all the Jews in Arabia acclaimed him as their chief. He was a well built, handsome man, had acquired great wealth and was a poet of a high order. He was open-handed, and through his generosity exercised great influence over the Jewish divines and other notables. He was morally despicable and was a master of intrigue.

On the advent of the Holy Prophet, peace be on him, in Medina, Kaab bin Ashraf became a party to the agreement that the Holy Prophet had entered into with the Jews whereby it had been agreed that the parties would live in amity, peace and security, and would co-operate with each other in the defence of Medina. But Kaab, from the beginning, entertained sentiments of rancour and enmity towards the Holy Prophet and the Muslims and began to intrigue against them. He was much chagrined at the victory of the Muslims in the battle of Badr and began actively to plan the destruction of Islam and the Muslims. Up till then he had imagined that the religious zeal of the Muslims was only a temporary phase, and that gradually they would abandon Islam and revert to their ancestral creed. But the surprising victory of the Muslims in the battle of Badr, and the slaughter of almost all the leading personalities of Quraish in the battle, convinced him that Islam was not a casual phenomenon. His immediate reaction at the receipt of the news of the issue of the battle was one of incredulity. But when the news was confirmed, he was filled with apprehension and anger. He forthwith proceeded to Mecca and provoked Quraish with his speeches and his poetry and roused their wrath against the Muslims to boiling point. He took their leaders to the Ka'aba and put them on oath, their hands clutching the covering of the Ka'aba, that they would not rest till they had wiped out Islam and its founder from the face of the earth. Having achieved his purpose in Mecca, he travelled from tribe to tribe in the country and roused them against the Muslims. Returning to Medina, he began to address amorous and provocative verses to Muslim women, not sparing even the women of the family of the Holy Prophet. He gave wide publicity to his lewd poems. He then conspired to bring about the assassination of the Holy Prophet at a meal in his own house to which he intended to invite him along with some Jewish young men, who were to perpetrate the foul deed. But the Holy Prophet came to know of the design, which was thus frustrated. In this context, it must be remembered that the Holy Prophet, by virtue of the agreement which had been arrived at between the various tribes of Medina, was not only the spiritual leader of the Muslims, but was also the chief executive and chief magistrate of Medina. Thus everyone of these activities of Kaab amounted to treason and was punishable with death.

When the Holy Prophet was convinced of these various offences of Kaab, he determined that Kaab had earned the ultimate penalty several times over. In the atmosphere that prevailed in Medina at the time, any disciplinary action against Kaab was bound to start a dangerous civil war in Medina; and the Holy Prophet was anxious to avoid such a contingency at all costs. He, therefore, decided that Kaab would not be executed publicly, but silently without any fuss. He committed this enterprise to Muhammad bin Maslamah, a devoted Muslim of Aus, and directed him to consult the chief of Aus, S'ad bin Muaz, about the method of carrying it out. After consultation with S'ad, Muhammad bin Maslamah selected Abu Nailah, who was foster brother of Kaab, and two or three other Muslims, and proceeded to Kaab's residence where they made a tryst with him for that night for some plausible purpose, which they discussed with him. At night, when Kaab came to the tryst, they fell upon him and despatched him.

As regards the manner of the execution of Kaab, Stanley Lane-Pole has observed (*Studies in a Mosque*, p. 68):

> The reason is almost too obvious to need explanation. There were no police or law courts or even courts martial at Medina; some one of the followers of Muhammad must, therefore, be the executor of the sentence of death, and it was better that it should be done quietly, as the execution of a man openly before his clan would have caused a brawl and more bloodshed and retaliation, till the whole city had been mixed up in the quarrel.

When the news of the execution of Kaab became known in Medina, it occasioned great excitement in the city and the Jews called on the Holy Prophet and protested that their chief, Kaab bin Ashraf, had been assassinated in such and such a manner. The Holy Prophet heard what they had to say, and asked them whether they were aware of the offences of which Kaab had been guilty. He then reminded them of all the pernicious activities of Kaab, to which the delegation made no reply. The Holy Prophet then urged them that, at least in the future, they should agree to live in peace and in healthy co-operation and not to sow the seeds of enmity, intrigue and disorder. The Jews agreed to subscribe to a new covenant, guaranteeing mutual peace and security, discarding all mischief and disorder. This agreement was committed to the custody of Ali. There is no mention that thereafter the Jews ever charged the Muslims with any culpability in respect of the execution of Kaab bin Ashraf, for they knew and felt in their hearts that Kaab had richly earned his punishment.

Despite Abu Sufyan's raid against Medina, retreating from which the members of his party had to discard their wallets filled with meal, lest they should be overtaken by their Muslim pursuers, Quraish felt keenly the need of avenging the disaster and wiping out the disgrace that they had suffered at Badr. The profit made by the caravan led by Abu Sufyan, which had arrived safely in Mecca, had amounted to 50,000 dinars, and according to the decision taken by the leaders of Mecca immediately after the battle, was in deposit in the House of Consultation for the purpose of organising a force to march against the Muslims. This money was now taken out of deposit and preparations were started for getting together a large armed force for the execution of the design of Quraish. This resolve had been taken suddenly and preparations were pushed forward speedily. Quraish intended that they should take the Muslims by surprise. They were not, however, aware that the Holy Prophet had directed his uncle, Abbas bin Abdul Muttalib, who was sympathetic towards the Muslims, to stay on in Mecca and to keep him informed of the designs and movements of Quraish. Accordingly, Abbas despatched a fast rider of Banu Ghaffar to take a letter of his to the Holy Prophet, promising him a substantial reward if his letter was delivered within three days. When the courier arrived in Medina, the Holy Prophet was in Qaba and the courier delivered the letter to him there. The Holy Prophet immediately summoned his special scribe, Ubayy bin Kaab Ansari, and asked him to read out the letter to him, which he did. The letter contained the grave intimation that a strong army of Quraish was about to leave Mecca for Medina. The Holy Prophet told Ubayy bin Kaab that he should not divulge the intimation contained in the letter to anyone; and returning to Medina, despatched two of his Companions in the direction of Mecca to gather intelligence about the Quraish army. He also directed that a census should be taken of the Muslim population of Medina. This disclosed that the number of Muslims in Medina had by then reached 1,500.

Abu Sufyan led the Quraish army which numbered 3,000, of whom 700 were clad in mail. They had 200 horses, and 3,000 camels, and were well equipped in every way. They were accompanied by several women who included Hind, wife of Abu Sufyan, and the wives of Ikramah bin Abu Jahl, Safwan bin Umayya, Khalid bin Waleed and Amr bin Aas, and also the mother of Mus'ab bin Umair. The women, according to Arab custom, carried with them timbrels and other instruments of music to accompany their songs which were designed to rouse the warriors to heroic deeds.

When this force approached Medina, it veered to the north and stopped near Mount Uhud, close to a large pasture where the cattle of

Medina grazed and there were also some cultivated fields. Quraish captured the cattle and destroyed the tilth. The Holy Prophet, on being apprised of the approach of Quraish, sent Habib bin Mundhar to gather intelligence about the numbers and strength of the enemy, and told him that on return, he should communicate his intelligence to him in private. Habib slipped away and returned within a short time and submitted his report. This was Thursday evening and the advent of Quraish and their raid on the pasture had become generally known in Medina, and though the Muslims were not aware of the details about the Quraish army, the night was spent in great alarm. On Friday morning, the Holy Prophet held a consultation whether the attack of Quraish should be awaited in Medina or whether they should be fought outside. The Holy Prophet related a dream that he had seen the previous night, the details of which he interpreted as indicating that he would receive an injury himself, that the Muslims would suffer damage, that there would be carnage among the enemy, that a near relation of his would be killed, but that Medina would be safe. He therefore opined that the Muslims would be secure within Medina, but without it there was risk and danger. In this opinion the men of years and wisdom, both Emigrants and Ansar, concurred. Abdullah bin Ubayy, who had also been invited for consultation, strongly supported the view of the Holy Prophet. He added, 'Our city, O Prophet, is a virgin inviolate. Quitting it, we have ever suffered loss; remaining in it, we have beaten back every attack. Leave Quraish alone; if they remain, they will be in evil case. At length, frustrated in their design they will retire.' It was resolved accordingly to bring all outlying inhabitants within the walls, and, if Quraish should venture near, to drive them back by a galling discharge of arrows and stones from the walls and housetops.

This decision did not please the younger and more impetuous section of Ansar. 'Shall we sit quietly here,' they muttered, 'a laughing-stock for all Arabia, and look on in frustration while our possessions are ravaged all round? Disgrace will cleave to us ever after, and the enemy, emboldened, will repeat the insult. Nay, we should go forth and smite our foes, as was done at Badr.' Emigrants also sided with this party, and their ardour was so great that the Holy Prophet at last gave way, and announced his readiness to offer battle. Ascending the pulpit (the day was Friday) he stirred up the people, in his discourse, to fight courageously. 'If ye be steadfast,' he said, 'the Lord will grant you victory.' Then he commanded the men to make ready for the battle. The most part rejoiced at this, but some were grieved that the first decision had been set aside.

By the time the afternoon Prayer was ended the people had assembled in the court of the mosque, armed for battle. The Holy Prophet then retired with Abu Bakr and Umar to make ready. In a little while, he issued from his chamber clad in mail and helmet, his sword hanging from a leather girdle and shield slung over his shoulder. Ansar, seeing him thus accoutred, repented of their rash remonstrance and prayed that he would even now do as seemed good to him. But it was too late. 'I invited you to this,' he said, 'and ye would not. It becometh not a Prophet, when once he hath girded himself to the battle, to lay his armour down again until the Lord hath decided betwixt him and his enemies. Wait, therefore, on the Lord. Only be steadfast, and He will send you victory.'

The Holy Prophet called for three lances and fixed banners upon them. The one for Aus he committed to Usyad bin Hudhair, and the one for Khazraj to Habib bin Mundhar, and the one for Emigrants to Ali. Abdullah bin Um Maktum was appointed to command the city, and lead the public Prayers. The Holy Prophet mounted his horse and, surrounded by his followers, took the road to Uhud. There was but one other horse in the Muslim army. Arrived at an eminence, the Holy Prophet turned around and saw following, amid the palm plantations on the right, a rude and disorderly band of men, and being told that they were the Jewish confederates of Abdullah bin Ubayy, he commanded that they should go back to Medina. He then passed onwards to Sheikhein, half-way to Uhud, and having reviewed the force, and sent back some striplings unequal to the fight, there halted for the night. Abdullah bin Ubayy, with his followers, encamped near at hand; but, displeased at the rejection of his advice, and also at the unfriendly treatment of his Jewish friends, he kept sullenly aloof. The Holy Prophet passed the night with Bani Najjar, and a guard of devoted followers was stationed over him. Muhammad bin Maslamah patrolled the camp with fifty men.

At early dawn the Muslim army was in motion. In the dim morning light they marched, by the nearest path, through the intervening fields and gardens, and emerged upon the sandy plain beneath the peak of Uhud. The vicinity owes its verdure to a water-course, which carries off the drainage of the country lying to the south and east. The hill of Uhud, three miles distant from Medina, is a rugged and almost insulated off-shoot of the mountain range, projecting eastwards for three or four miles into the plain. The torrent, sometimes swollen so as to inundate the adjacent track, sweeps along its southern and western face and discharges its flood into the low basin lying beyond. Now dry, its course was marked only by deep sand and scattered stones. On the farther bank, upon a slightly sloping plain, bare and stony, the Holy Prophet halted the Muslim army. By this time dawn was breaking, and, although the columns of the enemy were in sight, the call for Morning Prayer was made by Bilal, and the whole army, led by the Holy Prophet, prostrated itself in worship. Abdullah bin Ubayy at this moment wheeled suddenly round and, deserting the

army with his 300 followers, took the road back to the city. To those
who sought to restrain him he replied that had it been a case of
fighting a straight battle he would not have shirked it, but as it was the
Muslims were bent upon self-destruction and he would have no part
in it. The Holy Prophet was thus left with but 700 followers, of whom
only 100 were clad in mail; but they were all true men, and, fighting in
the cause of God, they boldly faced a well-appointed enemy more
than four times their number. Advancing, they occupied the rising
ground in front; their rear was thus protected by the frowning heights
of Uhud, excepting on the left, where the rocks, receding, afforded the
enemy a dangerous opening, suited to the movements of their horse.
The Holy Prophet therefore posted on an adjoining eminence the
flower of Muslim archery, and gave their leader, Abdullah bin Jubair,
stringent orders in no possible contingency to quit the spot, but
steadily to check any attempt which Quraish might make to turn the
flank. 'Guard our rear,' he said, 'and stir not from this spot; if ye see us
pursuing the enemy and gathering spoils, join not with us; if we be
pursued and even worsted, do not venture to our aid.' Having thus
secured his rear, the Holy Prophet lined up his force in battle array
and appointed captains of different sections. At this stage he was
informed that the standard of Quraish was being borne by Talha, who
was of the family who were entitled, under the dispensation
established by Qusai bin Kalab, to be the standard-bearers of Quraish
in battle. On this, the Holy Prophet observed, 'We are better entitled
to conform to the family tradition,' and he took the banner of
Emigrants from Ali and committed it to Mus'ab bin Umair, who was
of the same family as Talha. He forbade his followers to engage the
enemy till he gave command, for he realised that the strength of his
position might be sacrificed by a premature advance. Having thus
disposed his force, he calmly awaited the enemy approach. The
Muslim force faced towards Medina.

Meanwhile, Abu Sufyan, as hereditary leader, brought up the
Meccan army; and, facing Uhud, marshalled it in front of the Muslim
line. The right wing was commanded by Khalid, the left by Ikramah,
son of Abu Jahl. Amr bin Aas commanded the Quraish horse and
Abdullah bin Rabiyya the archers. The women at first kept to the
front and beat their timbrels to shrill martial songs, but as the line
advanced they fell to the rear.

The battle opened by the inglorious advance of the exiled Abu
Aamir, who vainly expected his fellow citizens of Medina to fraternise
with him. He was received with a shower of stones and was forced
with his band of followers to retire, Talha crying out indignantly, 'Get
to the rear, ye slaves! Guard the camp, a fitting employment for you!'
Then, flourishing the Quraish banner, Talha advanced alone and
challenged the Muslims to single combat, shouting:

> The standard bearer hath the right
> To dye its shaft in blood
> Till it be broken in his hand.

Ali stepped forth and, rushing on Talha, with one blow of his sword brought him to the ground. Talha's brother, Uthman, who was in charge of the women, then ran forward and seized the banner which lay by the lifeless body. The women beat their timbrels loudly as they sang:

> Daughters of the brave are we,
> On carpets step we delicately;
> Boldly advance, and we embrace you!
> Turn back and we will shun you,
> Shun you with disdain.

Hamza responded to Uthman's challenge and, after a brief encounter, brought him also lifeless to the ground. Then striding proudly back to the Muslim ranks he shouted, 'I am the son of him who gave the pilgrims drink', meaning Abdul Muttalib who had held that office. One after another the family of Talha, two brothers and three sons, seized the standard; one after another, they fell in single combat.

At the commencement of the general action the Holy Prophet held up his sword and said, 'Who will take this sword, and give to it its due?' Several of his Companions, including Umar, Zubair and Ali, came forward one after another, but the Holy Prophet did not yield the sword to any of them, till Abu Dujana Ansari offered to take it and he gave it to him.

The result of single-combat encounters put the two armies on equality for the time. So long as it went on Quraish derived no advantage from their superior numbers, and the rapid destruction of their standard bearers carried dismay into their ranks. A general engagement ensued, and, pressed by the fierce ardour of the Muslims, the Meccan army began to waver. Their horse sought repeatedly to turn the left flank of the Muslims, but they were each time forced back by the galling archery of the little band which the Holy Prophet had posted there. The same daring contempt of danger was displayed as at Badr. The Meccan rank might be seen to quiver as Abu Dujana, distinguished by a red kerchief round his helmet, swept along the enemy's rank, and dealt death on every hand with the sword given him by the Holy Prophet. Hamzah, conspicuous with his ostrich feather; Ali, known by his long white plume, and Zubair in his bright yellow turban, carried confusion wherever they appeared.

But now the Muslims pressed their success too hotly. Their line lost form and order; and a portion, piercing the enemy ranks, fell to gathering the spoils. The archers, who had hitherto held the Meccan horse in check, saw from their height the tempting opportunity and, disregarding the strict injunction of the Holy Prophet as well as the earnest expostulations of their leader, hurried to the spoils. The ready eye of Khalid saw the chance, and he hastened to retrieve the day. Wheeling his cavalry round the Muslims' left, and sweeping from the rising ground the few remaining archers, he suddenly appeared in the rear of the Muslims and charged into their ranks. The surprise was fatal, and the discomfiture complete.

It might still have been possible to rally the Muslims had not a brave Quraish warrior, Abdullah bin Qami'a, attacked the Muslims' standard bearer, Mus'ab bin Umair, and severed his right hand with his sword. Mus'ab supported the standard with his left hand and advanced towards Ibn Qami'a who then severed his left hand also, whereafter Mus'ab folded both his arms round the standard and held it against his chest. Ibn Qami'a attacked him a third time and felled him to the ground. In the meantime, Wahshi, a Negro slave whom Jubair bin Mut'am had brought with him, promising him his freedom if he succeeded in killing Hamzah, who had killed Jubair's uncle, Ta'eemah bin Adi, in the battle of Badr, perceiving Hamzah passing near him, swung his javelin at him with unerring aim and brought him lifeless to the ground.

It was a moment of great peril for the Holy Prophet as well as the Muslims, some of whom, in their bewilderment, attacked each other and inflicted injuries upon their own people. Yaman, the father of Hudhaifa, was killed in this moment of peril and confusion by the Muslims despite Hudhaifa's shouts that they were attacking his father.

The Holy Prophet had been standing in the rear watching from a rising ground the first success when he narrowly escaped the sweeping charge of Khalid's horse. With the staff of followers who surrounded him, he joined in discharging arrows at the enemy till his bow was broken; then he betook himself to casting stones. One of Quraish pressed madly forward to cut him down, whom he pricked in the chest with the point of his spear. The injury was slight, but the man died subsequently of it. The enemy soon bore down upon him in strength and if a party of devoted followers (seven Ansar and seven Emigrants) had not rallied round the spot, he would have been in mortal peril. This small band performed unmatched feats of heroism inspired by their utter devotion to the Holy Prophet. Ali and Zubair, by their fierce attacks, repeatedly pushed back the enemy ranks that bore down upon the little group. Abu Talha Ansari broke three bows in shooting arrows at the enemy while he shielded the Holy Prophet against the arrows of the enemy. The Holy Prophet went on handing arrows to S'ad bin Waqqas and on one occasion encouraged him with the words

'Go on shooting your arrows, may my father and mother be your sacrifice.' Abu Dujana shielded the Holy Prophet with his own body, receiving all the arrows and stones aimed at his beloved master. His body was covered with multiple injuries, but he did not move an inch from his station lest any movement of his should expose some portion of the body of the Holy Prophet to the arrows of the enemy. Talha received so many arrows on his own body in his effort to shield the Holy Prophet that one of his hands was rendered permanently useless. Nevertheless when the attack was pressed this devoted band was sometimes pushed aside and the Holy Prophet was exposed to the missiles of his assailants. On one such occasion a stone aimed at him by Urbah bin Abi Waqqas, brother of Sa'd, struck his face, broke one of his teeth and cut open his lip. At another time a stone cast by Abdullah bin Shahab wounded his forehead; and a third time a stone directed at him by Ibn Qami'a struck his cheek and forced two rings of his helmet to be buried in his flesh.

Finally Ibn Qami'a pierced the line of the Muslims and, arriving close to the Holy Prophet, hit him in the side with his sword. The Holy Prophet escaped injury because of his double coat of mail, but the shock felled him down and Ibn Qami'a shouted that he had killed Muhammad. But Ali and Talha raised him up and the Muslims were much cheered that he was safe.

The degree of confusion among the Muslims about this time may be gauged from the fact that many of the Companions of the Holy Prophet, imagining that the Holy Prophet had been martyred, had withdrawn from the field and had thrown aside their arms. Umar was one of them. A group of them were sitting on one side when Ans bin Nadhar Ansari came upon them and asked them what were they doing there. They replied, 'The Holy Prophet having become a martyr, what purpose is there now in fighting?' Ans retorted, 'This is the time to fight so that we too should achieve martyrdom and, in any case, life is not worth living after him.' He then noticed S'ad bin Muaz and said to him, 'S'ad, I smell the fragrance of paradise issuing from yonder hill.' Saying this, he rushed into the enemy ranks and was killed fighting. After the battle, it was observed that his body bore the marks of eighty injuries and could not be identified till his sister identified him from one of his fingers.

Gradually the force of the battle subsided, as Quraish, imagining that the Holy Prophet had been slain, felt that their purpose had been achieved and they became occupied with looking after their dead and mutilating the corpses of the Muslims. Those who were still in the field now gathered round the Holy Prophet who, being supported by Talha and one or two others, climbed one of the cliffs of Uhud close behind and joined several of the Muslim army who had already found secure retreat there. The joy of the Muslims at finding the Holy

Uhud

Prophet alive was unbounded. Kaab bin Malik, who met him on the way, began to call aloud the good news, but the Holy Prophet motioned him to be silent. When the party found shelter in a cave, the first care of the Companions was to remove the helmet from the head of the Holy Prophet. Two of its rings were so firmly embedded in his cheek that Abu Obaida lost two teeth in the endeavour to extract them. The blood flowed copiously from his wounds. Ali ran to a hollow in the rock and brought some water in his shield. The Holy Prophet could not drink of it, but only rinsed his mouth. As the blood was being washed off his face, he remarked, 'How shall a people prosper that treat thus their Prophet who calleth them unto the Lord?' After a few moments, he supplicated, 'Allah, forgive my people, for they know not.' About this time, the Holy Prophet's daughter, Fatima, arrived from Medina and dressed the wound on her father's temple, stanching the blood with the ash of some burnt matting. The wound took more than a month to heal fully. Safiya, the Holy Prophet's aunt, was fondly attached to her brother Hamza, and the Holy Prophet, fearful of the effect which the sight of his mangled remains might have upon her, had desired her son, Zubair, to keep her aside till the body was buried, but she was not to be kept back. 'I will not go back', she cried, 'until I see him.' So the Holy Prophet led her to the spot, saying, 'Leave her to her grief alone.' She sat down with Fatima by the body, and both sobbed aloud. To comfort Safiya, he told her that her brother's name was already enrolled in Paradise as the Lion of God and of His Apostle. He spoke comfortingly also to the women of Medina, who were wailing over their dead. The grave being now ready, and the bodies laid out in order, he commanded that they should be buried by twos and threes in each grave.

In the meantime, the leaders of Quraish had been busy on the field of battle. They sought for the body of the Holy Prophet, and, not finding it, began to doubt his death. Many acts of barbarous mutilation were committed on the slain. Hind gloated over the body of Hamza. Tearing out his liver, she chewed it, fulfilling thus her savage vow, and she strung his nails and pieces of his skin together to bedeck her arms and legs. When Quraish had spent some time thus, and had disposed of their own dead, Abu Sufyan drew near to the foot of the hill, and, raising his voice, called out the names successively of the Holy Prophet, Abu Bakr and Umar. Receiving no reply (for the Holy Prophet enjoined silence) he cried again, 'Then all are slain, and we are rid of them.' Umar could contain himself no longer. 'Thou liest,' he exclaimed, 'they are all alive, thou enemy of God, and will requite thee yet.' Abu Sufyan, recognising Umar's voice, enquired, 'Tell me truly, Umar, is Muhammad alive?' 'Indeed he is alive and hears you,' replied Umar. 'I believe you in preference to Ibn Qami'a,' rejoined Abu Sufyan. 'Then this day shall be a return for Badr.

Fortunes alternate, even as the bucket.' He then called out glory to their idols, naming them one by one. The Holy Prophet directed Umar to reply, 'Glory to Allah. He is our Guardian and you have no guardian.' Abu Sufyan said, 'We shall meet after a year again at Badr.' 'Be it so,' answered Umar. With these words Abu Sufyan turned to go and the Meccan army began its homeward march.

Of the Muslims 70, 4 Emigrants and 66 Ansar, had laid down their lives on the field of battle. It was evident that the destruction of the greater part of the Muslim force was only averted by the foresight of the Holy Prophet in keeping a secure place of refuge in his rear. On the enemy's side, the loss was but 23.

It is surprising that though Quraish had vanquished the Muslims on this occasion and, if they had so wished, they could have pushed their victory further and could have attacked Medina itself, yet they decided to start on their return journey to Mecca. The Holy Prophet, out of abundant caution, sent S'ad bin Abi Waqqas after them to discover whether Quraish intended to invade Medina itself. He told him, 'If you find them riding their camels and leading their horses, you may conclude that they intend to return to Mecca and have no design against Medina; but if you find that they are mounted on their horses, then it is likely that they have some further design.' S'ad returned soon and informed the Holy Prophet that the Quraish army was headed towards Mecca.

The Holy Prophet had been much distressed by the barbarities committed by Quraish on the Muslim dead. The case of Hamza has been mentioned. The corpse of Abdullah bin Jahsh, cousin of the Holy Prophet, peace be on him, had been treated in a similar way. For a moment the Holy Prophet felt that Quraish should be repaid in their own coin, but he rejected the impulse and forbade forever mutilation of the enemy dead by Muslim warriors. While he was checking up on the Muslim dead, he deputed Ubayy bin Kaab Ansari to find out whether S'ad bin Rabi', a leading personality among Ansar, had been killed or was alive. Ubayy bin Kaab, after a thorough search, discovered S'ad at his last breath among a heap of Muslim dead. He was just able to send his greetings to the Holy Prophet in a low voice before he expired, with the message, 'May God Almighty bestow upon you, in a superlative degree, the reward which He bestows upon his Prophets in return for the devotion and sacrifices of their followers, and may He send comfort to your heart.' He also told Ubayy to convey his greetings to his brother-Muslims and to tell them that if the Holy Prophet suffered any pain while they were alive to safeguard him, they would be accountable for their default to God and no excuses would avail them. With these words he expired.

One of the martyrs of Uhud was Mus'ab bin Umair, who had been appointed by the Holy Prophet the first missionary of Islam in

Medina. Before he had become a Muslim he was accounted the best dressed and the most handsomely turned out young man in Mecca, who had been brought up in the lap of luxury. After he became a Muslim he adopted a most austere way of life. On one occasion when the Holy Prophet, peace be on him, noticed that the garment worn by Mus'ab bore several patches, his eyes became wet, recalling the manner of his earlier life. When Mus'ab's body was discovered he was clad only in one length of cloth which could not completely cover his body and the Holy Prophet directed that for burial his head should be covered by the cloth and his feet might be covered with wild grass.

The Holy Prophet began to move towards Medina about sunset. By this time, the Muslims in Medina, men and women, were streaming out in the direction of Uhud, all anxious to be reassured as to the Holy Prophet's safety. An Ansari woman, grief-stricken and bewildered, encountered the party among whom the Holy Prophet was riding towards Medina. She enquired from one of the party about the Holy Prophet and received the reply that her father, brother and husband had all become martyrs in the battle. She repeated her inquiry about the Holy Prophet and was told that he was safe and he was pointed out to her. On beholding him she said, 'All calamities are easy to endure, so long as you are safe.'

When the Holy Prophet entered the city he heard mournful wailings from most houses. He was deeply moved, and in order to comfort the mourners remarked 'My uncle Hamzah has also been martyred, yet no one mourns him.' The leaders of Ansar misconstrued this observation, as if the Holy Prophet was expressing his grief over the fact that there was no one to mourn Hamzah. They, therefore, told their women to stop mourning their dead and to proceed to the Holy Prophet's apartment and there mourn the death of Hamzah. They went and when the Holy Prophet heard their wailing, he inquired about the cause of it, and it was explained to him that the women of Ansar were mourning the death of Hamzah. He expressed appreciation of their devotion and affection and supplicated for God's favour upon them, but told them that Islam did not permit wailing and mourning of this type, and he forbade it for the Muslims.

A young Muslim, Jabir, whose father had become a martyr, came to the Holy Prophet who, perceiving his distress at the death of his father, said to him, 'Jabir, shall I tell you something that will please you?' Jabir submitted, 'Certainly, Messenger of Allah,' upon which the Holy Prophet told him, 'When your father, having been martyred, appeared before God Almighty, He spoke to him, face to face, and inquired, "What is your greatest wish?" Your father submitted, "Allah, I have been highly favoured, and all that I wish is that I should go back to the world and should lay down my life in the cause of the faith once more." God told him, "I would surely fulfil your desire, were it not that I have determined that no one who dies can go back to the world." Your father submitted, "Then let my brethren be told so that their eagerness for fighting in the cause of the faith may be further stimulated." ' It was on this occasion that the verse was revealed (3:170-1):

> Do not account those who are slain in the cause of Allah, as dead. Indeed, they are living in the presence of their Lord and are provided for. They are jubilant over that which Allah has bestowed upon them of His bounty.

S'ad bin Muaz, chief of Aus, brought his old mother to the Holy Prophet, and he condoled with her on the martyrdom of her son, Amr bin Muaz. She submitted, 'Messenger of Allah, so long as you are safe, we do not grieve over anything.'

R. V. C. Bodley has observed (*The Messenger*, p. 179):

> Muhammad did not admit defeat. Instead of letting his soldiers be fussed over by their womenfolk and give their versions of the fight, he fell them in. He was wounded himself, he was stiff, he was tired, he was fifty-six years old, but he put his legs across a horse and rode off as if he was pursuing a demoralised and routed enemy. It was masterly strategy, magnificent psychology, above anything any commander has ever conceived to revive the spirits of a shattered body of men. Neither did he relax or give ground when he arrived in Medina. On the contrary, he adopted a commanding, almost reproving, attitude.

G. M. Draycott has observed (*Mahomet*, p. 201):

> Reverses show the temper of heroes, and Muhammad is never more fully revealed than in the first gloomy days after Uhud, when he steadfastly set himself to retrieve what was lost, refusing to acknowledge that his position was impaired, impervious to the whispers that spoke of failure, supreme in his mighty asset of an impregnable faith.

Chapter 9

:Treachery:

The night following the Battle of Uhud was one of anxiety and unease for the Muslims of Medina. A sense of insecurity still prevailed, for Quraish might even yet return, and so the chief men again kept watch at the Holy Prophet's door. Before the dawn Prayers, the Holy Prophet received the intimation that the Quraish army had made camp at a distance of a few miles from Medina, and that a discussion was proceeding among the leaders on the desirability of attacking Medina. Some of them rebuked the others that they had neither killed Muhammad, nor enslaved Muslim women, nor plundered their homes and that they had thus missed a great opportunity that had come their way. They urged that they should go back, attack Medina and destroy the Muslims. Others argued that having established their superiority through their victory, they should be content with their triumph and should return to Mecca, lest by any further adventure they might risk their victory; for if they reverted to Medina, the Muslims would certainly fight them fiercely and would be joined by those of them who had not gone forth to Uhud. In the end, those who were eager for an attack against Medina appeared to have persuaded the rest and Quraish began to make preparations to march against Medina. When the Holy Prophet came to know of this development, he immediately directed that the Muslims should get ready to march forth against Quraish, but he laid down the condition that only those should go forth on this occasion who had been present at Uhud. Many of these had received injuries, but on hearing the command of the Holy Prophet, they all joined up cheerfully with their injuries bandaged, so that the general air appeared as if a victorious army had set forth in pursuit of a vanquished enemy. The Holy Prophet had dispatched two persons to gather intelligence about Quraish; their dead bodies were discovered at Hamral Asad, at a distance of eight miles from Medina. They had probably been slain by Quraish as spies. The Holy Prophet arranged for their burial and decided to camp for the night. He directed that fires might be lit all round, and, within a few minutes, 500 fires were kindled on adjoining heights, which gave the impression that the Holy Prophet had a large force under his command. About this time, a chief of Khuzaa, of the name of Ma'bad, called on the Holy Prophet and expressed his sympathy over those slain at

150

Uhud. Next morning, when he arrived at Rauha, he found the Quraish army making preparations to march against Medina. He went to Abu Sufyan and told him that he had just come from Hamral Asad where he had witnessed a formidable force in camp, who were much exasperated over their defeat at Uhud and were now eager to wreak vengeance on their enemies. Abu Sufyan was much impressed by what Ma'bad told him and abandoned the design to march on Medina and started with his army for Mecca. When the Holy Prophet learnt that Quraish were headed towards Mecca, he remarked that God had overawed them. He remained in camp at Hamral Asad for two or three days and returned to Medina after an absence of five days.

At Hamral Asad the Muslims made prisoner one of the enemy, the poet Abu Uzza, who had loitered behind the rest. He had been taken prisoner at Badr, and, having five daughters dependent on him, had been released on the promise that he would not again bear arms against the Holy Prophet. He now sought for mercy, but the Holy Prophet rejected his plea, observing, 'A believer may not be bitten twice from the same hole.' He was executed on account of his treachery.

Another Quraish, Mu'awiya bin Mughira, had been discovered in the vicinity of Medina on the night after the battle of Uhud. He begged Uthman bin Affan to intercede for him, and Uthman procured for him a three days' truce. Mu'awiya lingered on near Medina beyond the peiod of his truce, and having been discovered, was executed for having failed to observe the term of the truce.

Though the victory of Quraish in the battle of Uhud inflicted no great permanent loss on the Muslims, yet temporarily it proved awkward for them. They had lost seventy men, among them three or four leading personalities, and a very large number had received injuries; the Jews of Medina and the disaffected who had to some degree been cowed down by the victory at Badr were now revived in spirit, so much so that Abdullah bin Ubayy and his followers openly mocked at the Muslims and made fun of them; Quraish were much encouraged and felt that not only had they avenged their defeat at Badr, but that in future, whenever the occasion arose, they would be able to overcome the Muslims; Arab tribes also became more daring in their hostility towards the Muslims. All this, however, had a redeeming aspect also. The Muslims realised that they could never achieve success through acting contrary to the wishes and directions of the Holy Prophet. He had counselled them to oppose the enemy from inside Medina, but a section of them had insisted upon going forth to battle; he had issued strict instructions to the band of archers, who had been stationed in the pass at the rear of the Muslims, not to leave their post till they received directions to that effect, yet most of them had disobeyed the Holy Prophet's instructions at a crucial moment, which default of theirs had led to disaster. The Muslims thus learnt a salutary lesson of obedience to the Holy Prophet on all occasions to the minutest degree. Through Divine grace, the prejudice which the Muslims suffered as a result of their defeat at Uhud proved temporary and soon, under the wise, spirited and inspired guidance of the Holy Prophet, they began to march forward rapidly towards their goal.

S'ad bin Rabi' Ansari, whose death on the day of Uhud has been mentioned earlier, was a man of substance and occupied a distinguished position in his clan. He left him surviving no male issue, only his widow and two daughters. According to Arab custom, a widow and daughters received no part of the inheritance on the death of the head of the family, and in case there was no male issue, the inheritance went to his brothers or, in default of brothers, to his male collaterals. No law of inheritance had yet been established among the Muslims under divine command. Therefore on the death of S'ad his brother took possession of the whole of his property and his widow and daughters were left destitute. The widow, taking her two daughters with her, went to the Holy Prophet and explained their situation to him. He was deeply moved, but as he had so far received no divine instruction concerning inheritance, he told her to wait till some divine direction pertinent to her situation was vouchsafed. Not long after, verses 12-13 of Chapter 4 were revealed, regulating inheritance, whereby in the situation that had arisen the widow was held entitled to one-eighth of the inheritance, and the daughters to two-thirds of it, and the brother only to the small residue. Upon this, the Holy Prophet sent for S'ad's brother and directed him to hand over their respective shares to his brother's widow and his daughters, and to retain only his own share. He carried out the direction fully.

The Muslim law of inheritance, the greater part of which is set out in the verses cited above, was a great improvement on the Arab custom of inheritance, particularly so far as women are concerned. Altogether, in pre-Islamic Arabia, Arab custom bore hardly upon women, and Islam carried out a beneficent revolution in favour of women, into the details of which it is not necessary to enter here.

Another social reform of tremendous import was also instituted about this time. Liquor and gambling were resorted to by the Arabs on a very large scale, and they suffered from all their attendant evils. The Holy Prophet himself, peace be on him, had never indulged in any of these vices at any time, and some of his Companions had also abstained from them altogether. But as there had been so far no prohibition, many Muslims drank liquor, which sometimes led to very awkward situations. The first admonition that was revealed with regard to these two vices was: 'They ask thee concerning liquor and gambling. Tell them: There is great harm in both, and also some benefit for people, but their harm is greater than their benefit' (2:220). This was soon followed by: 'O ye who believe approach not Prayer when you are not in full possession of your faculties, until you realise the true import of your supplications' (4:44). Finally, soon after the battle of Uhud, the command was revealed: 'O ye who believe, liquor, gambling, idols and divining arrows are but abominations and Satanic devices. So turn wholly away from each one of them so that you may prosper' (5:91).

The Holy Prophet thereupon directed one of his Companions to proclaim the prohibition throughout Medina. Ans has related: 'I was at that time engaged in serving liquor to Abu Talha Ansari and some other Muslims. When we heard the voice of the announcer, Abu Talha asked me to find out what he was saying. I went out and discovered that he was proclaiming that liquor had been forbidden. When I returned to the company, I told them of the proclamation and Abu Talha directed me immediately to pour out all the liquor contained in the vessels, which I did. On that day, liquor ran on the side of the streets of Medina. The Holy Prophet interpreted the divine commandment as meaning that the smallest quantity of that of which a large quantity would inebriate had been forbidden.'

The setback that the Muslims suffered in the battle of Uhud encouraged the pagan Arab tribes to embark more daringly than before upon aggression against the Muslims. Only a short time had passed after the battle, while those who had been injured in the battle had not yet completely recovered from their wounds, when suddenly the Holy Prophet received intelligence that Tulaiha bin Khuweilid, chief of Banu Asad, and his brother Salamah bin Khuweilid, were busy urging their people to prepare for a march on Medina. The Holy Prophet immediately directed 150 fast-marching Muslims to proceed quickly under the leadership of Abu Salama bin Abdul Asad to disperse Banu Asad before they were able to set forth against the Muslims. Abu Salama advanced silently but rapidly with the force under his command and came up with Banu Asad at Qutan in central Arabia. As soon as Banu Asad saw the Muslims they scattered in all directions and no fighting ensued. Abu Salama returned to Medina with his force. He had been wounded in the battle of Uhud, and his injury had apparently healed, but under the stress of the rapid march the wound opened up again and, despite all possible treatment, it began to fester and in the end Abu Salama, who was a devout Muslim and was the foster-brother of the Holy Prophet, died of it. Tulaiha, the chief of Banu Asad, subsequently embraced Islam, but became an apostate and falsely claimed to be a prophet. He raised a force in his support, and after some time was defeated and left Arabia. Some time later he returned, repented and embraced Islam a second time and fought in several battles in the cause of Islam and eventually died a Muslim.

About the time when Banu Asad were preparing for the march against Medina, the Holy Prophet received the intelligence that Banu Lihyan were getting a large force ready at Ornah, a few miles from Mecca, under the incitement of their chief, Sufyan bin Khalid, for marching against Medina. The Holy Prophet, peace be on him, who was well aware of the strength and condition of the various Arab tribes, realised that Sufyan bin Khalid was at the bottom of the whole trouble, and that if he could be removed Banu Lihyan would not dare to invade Medina. He also knew that there was no other person among the tribe who could take his place and lead Banu Lihyan upon their contemplated expedition. He was apprehensive that if an armed force were despatched against Banu Lihyan the collision might, in the then circumstances, open wide the door of bloodshed. He therefore decided to send someone who might quietly put an end to Sufyan bin Khalid, who was the source of all the mischief. He selected Abdullah bin Anees Ansari for this purpose and warned him against the wiles of Sufyan, who was a resourceful mischief-maker. When Abdullah arrived in the camp of Banu Lihyan, he discovered that their preparations for the march upon Medina were proceeding apace, and he found an opportunity of putting an end to Sufyan during the night. When this became known, Banu Lihyan instituted the pursuit of Abdullah, but he managed to escape and, returning to Medina, reported the success of his enterprise to the Holy Prophet, who bestowed his own staff upon him as a memento of the great service that he had rendered. Abdullah cherished this blessed memento throughout the rest of his life, and, at the approach of his death, directed that it should be buried along with him.

The Holy Prophet was still receiving grave intelligence from all directions, but he apprehended the greatest danger from Quraish, who had been much encouraged by their victory at Uhud and were likely to embark upon some formidable project against the Muslims. In view of the danger that threatened from Mecca, the Holy Prophet directed a party of ten Companions of his to proceed quietly in the direction of Mecca, under the leadership of Aasim bin Thabit, and gather intelligence with regard to the designs and movements of Quraish. This party had not yet started on their errand when a few persons representing the tribes of Adhal and Qarah came to the Holy Prophet and submitted that many persons of their tribes were favourably inclined towards Islam and that the Holy Prophet might send some of his people with them to instruct their people in the tenets of Islam. The Holy Prophet was pleased at this welcome piece of news and directed the party, who had been made ready for gathering intelligence about Quraish, to accompany those people. It transpired afterwards that those pretended emissaries of their tribes had been promised a large number of camels as reward by Banu Lihyan, who had recourse to this stratagem for the purpose of avenging the execution of their chief, Sufyan bin Khalid, if they would beguile a number of Muslims to come out with them from Medina so that Banu Lihyan might slay them. When these treacherous emissaries of Adhal and Qarah arrived with the party of Muslims between Asfan and Mecca, they sent intimation to Banu Lihyan that they were proceeding in the direction of Mecca with ten Muslims who could be easily overwhelmed by Banu Lihyan. On receiving this intelligence, Banu Lihyan despatched a force of 200, half of whom were experts at shooting arrows, which overtook the party at Raji'. On seeing them, the party of Muslims climbed to the top of a dune and put themselves in a position of defence. The men of Banu Lihyan called out to them to come down from the height, assuring them that they would not be killed. Aasim replied that he could put no trust in their promise and would not get down. He raised his face towards heaven and supplicated, 'Lord, Thou seest the situation in which we are. Do Thou inform Thy Messenger of it.' They were overtaken by Banu Lihyan and seven of them died fighting. Banu Lihyan's purpose had been to catch them alive and so again they offered to spare the remaining three and to put them to no trouble if they would get down with them from the height. The three survivors were Khobaib bin Adi, Zaid bin Dathnah and Abdullah bin Taraq. They accepted the offer of Banu Lihyan, but, when they descended from the height, they were tied up securely with the bowstrings of their enemies, whereupon Abdullah bin Taraq protested that this was treachery, and that he had no longer any faith in their promise and would not go with them. He was beaten up and was dragged along for a short distance and was then slain. His body was thrown away, and Khobaib and Zaid were taken to Mecca where they were sold to Quraish. Khobaib was purchased by the sons of Harith bin Aamar bin Naufal, because he had killed their father in the battle of Badr; and Zaid was purchased by Safwan bin Umayya, whose father had also been killed at Badr.

While Khobaib and Zaid were in the custody of Quraish, Khobaib, on one occasion, borrowed a razor from the daughter of Harith, and it so happened that, at the same time, her small son approached Khobaib, who placed him affectionately on his knee. When the mother of the boy perceived that Khobaib had the razor in his hand she was terrified, but Khobaib reassured her that he had no intention of doing any harm to the boy. She had been so impressed by the good behaviour of Khobaib that she always said afterwards that she had never come across any other prisoner who was so well behaved as Khobaib. She also added that on one occasion she had seen that Khobaib had a bunch of grapes in his hand, from which he picked and ate the grapes, though in those days no grapes were procurable in

Mecca and Khobaib was secured in chains. She imagined that the bunch of grapes was a divine gift bestowed upon Khobaib.

After a few days Khobaib was taken out for execution. He asked permission for performing two *raka'as* of Prayer, and, permission being granted, he performed the Prayer in deep concentration and devotion, and when he finished he said, 'I was in a mood to continue for some time, but then I apprehended lest you should think that I was prolonging my Prayer in order to postpone the moment of my death.' He then bent forward, reciting the verses:

'As I am being slain while I am a Muslim,
I care not in which direction my body might fall;
All this is in the cause of Allah, and if He so wills,
He will be pleased to send down His blessings on my mutilated body.'

He had just finished when Uqba bin Harith cut him down.

Safwan bin Umayya took his prisoner, Zaid bin Dathnah, beyond the limits of the sanctuary, in the company of a number of leading personages of Quraish, and directed his slave, Nastas, to execute Zaid. Nastas advanced towards Zaid with his sword drawn and at that moment Abu Sufyan, who was among the spectators, went up to Zaid and asked him, 'Tell me truly, do you not wish that in your place Muhammad had been our prisoner and we should have executed him and you would thus have been saved to spend your days happily in the bosom of your family?' Zaid was outraged and retorted indignantly, 'What is it that you have said, Abu Sufyan? I call God to witness that I would not wish that I might be rescued in return for a thorn pricking the foot of the Messenger of Allah.' Abu Sufyan exclaimed involuntarily, 'By God, I have never seen anyone who is loved so devotedly as Muhammed is loved by his followers.' Nastas swiftly cut down Zaid.

It is related that when Quraish learnt that Aasim bin Thabit was among those who had been killed by Banu Lihyan at Raji', they, recalling that Aasim had, in the battle of Badr, killed a leading Quraish personage, sent chosen messengers to Raji', instructing them to bring back Aasim's head or a limb of his, so that their spirit of vengeance might be assuaged. It is also related that the mother of the one whom Aasim had killed had made a vow that she would drink wine in the skull of her son's killer. When the emissaries of Quraish arrived at Raji' they found that Aasim's corpse was completely covered by swarms of hornets and bees who could not be made to fly off despite their utmost efforts. In the end they returned to Mecca frustrated. Soon thereafter there was a storm which brought heavy rain, and Aasim's corpse was swept away by the fierce flood. It is written that when Aasim embraced Islam he had determined that he would abstain altogether from everything that was related to paganism, so that he would not even touch a pagan. When Umar learnt of his martyrdom and the safeguarding of his corpse by swarms of hornets and bees, he observed, 'God Almighty has regard even for the sentiments of His righteous servants.' In Aasim's case God safeguarded even his corpse from being touched by the pagans.

About the same time another tragic event took place on a larger scale. It has been mentioned that Banu Sulaim and Banu Ghatafan were settled in Nejd, which was a plateau in central Arabia, and were in league with Quraish against the Muslims. Through their mischievous activities and incitements, the whole of Nejd was being poisoned with enmity towards Islam. About the time when the tragedy of Raji' was enacted, Abu Braa Aamiri, who was a chief of Banu Aamir of central Arabia, came to see the Holy Prophet, peace be on him, who treated him with courtesy and kindness and expounded the teachings of Islam to him. He listened eagerly, and, though he did not embrace Islam, he requested the Holy Prophet to send a few Muslims with him who should expound Islam to the people of Nejd. He expressed the hope that the tribes of Nejd would not reject his message. The Holy Prophet expressed his distrust of the people of Nejd. Abu Braa assured him that there was no ground for apprehension and that he stood guarantee for the safety of his emissaries. The Holy Prophet believed his word and sent a company of seventy of his Companions to Nejd to carry the message of Islam to the Nejd tribes. It appears that at the time when Abu Braa visited the Holy Prophet, a few persons belonging to the tribes Ra'l and Zakwan, clans of Banu Sulaim, who had also presented themselves before the Holy Prophet, reinforced the request of Abu Braa. The party selected by the Holy Prophet for this mission were mostly Ansar and were well versed in the Holy Quran. They were poor people, who made their livelihood out of wood that they collected during the day in the forest and sold in Medina. They spent the greater part of the night in worship. When this party arrived at a well which was known as Be'r Ma'oona, one of them, Haram bin Milhan, maternal uncle of Ans bin Malik, went forward as an emissary of the Holy Prophet with the message of Islam to Aamir bin Tufail, nephew of Abu Braa, chief of the tribe Aamir. He was welcomed by Aamir bin Tufail and his companions, but when he sat down and felt at ease, and began to expound the teachings of Islam to those present, someone approached him from the back and killed him instantly with his spear. At the sudden attack, Haram bin Milhan cried out, 'God is Great. By the Lord of the Ka'aba, I have achieved my purpose.' Then Aamir bin Tufail urged Banu Aamir to attack the party of Muslims and kill them. But they refused to act in contravention of the guarantee of Abu Braa. He then took a party of Banu Ra'l and Banu Zakwan with him and advanced against the

Muslims, who, when they saw them, said that they had no quarrel with them. They had only arrived to carry out the Holy Prophet's directions, and had not come for the purpose of fighting. But their enemies paid no heed to what they said and proceeded to massacre them. Out of the Muslims who were then present on the spot, only one, Kaab bin Zaid, who was attacked and had been left for dead but who had not actually died, escaped with his life.

Two of the Muslims, Amr bin Umayya Dhamri and Mundhar bin Muhammad, had taken their camels for pasture and were not killed with the rest. When they returned, they apprehended from a distance what had happened, and consulted with each other what course they should adopt. Amr felt that they should escape and, returning to Medina, should inform the Holy Prophet of what had happened; but Mundhar did not agree with him and said that he would not run away from the place where their leader, Mundhar bin Amr, had become a martyr. He went to the spot and was killed fighting. Amr was taken prisoner and would have been executed, but when Aamir bin Tufail found that he was a Dhamri, he let him go, observing that his mother had made a vow to free a slave belonging to his tribe and that he would release him in fulfilment of his mother's vow. Thus, out of the seventy Muslims, only two, Amr bin Umayya Dhamri and Kaab bin Zaid, escaped with their lives.

Among the Muslims who were massacred at Be'r Ma'oona was the devoted freedman of Abu Bakr, Aamir bin Fuhairah, who was killed by Jabbar bin Salma, who later embraced Islam. He used to mention that he had been attracted to Islam by the last words of Aamir bin Fuhairah, which were 'By Allah, I have achieved my purpose'. Whenever Jabbar recalled this incident he wondered why Aamir, with his last breath, had uttered these words, and then he learnt that the Muslims considered laying down their lives in the cause of Allah as the greatest achievement. He was so deeply affected by this that, eventually, he embraced Islam in appreciation of this spirit of sacrifice.

The Holy Prophet learnt of the tragedies of Raji' and Be'r Ma'oona about the same time and was deeply grieved over them. The sudden tragic loss of about eighty devoted Companions of his, many of whom had committed the Holy Quran to memory, and all of whom were poor, humble and pious people, was a deeply distressing event. However, all he said was, 'To Allah we belong, and to Him shall we return'; to which he added, 'All this has come about in consequence of the suggestion of Abu Braa which had not appealed to me as I was mistrustful of the people of Nejd.' For a whole month, however, every morning during the dawn Prayer he supplicated in great agony for God's mercy, and that He might restrain the Banu Ra'l, Banu Zakwan, Banu 'Asabiyah and Banu Lihyan from continuing to shed the blood of innocent Muslims mercilessly and cruelly.

While Amr bin Umayya Dhamri was returning to Medina, he encountered two men of Banu Aamir who were returning from Medina after having made a pledge with the Holy Prophet. As Amr was not aware of this, he killed both of them in revenge for the tragedy of Be'r Ma'oona for which, in his view, Aamir bin Tufail, chief of Banu Aamir, had been responsible, though in fact, Banu Aamir had not participated in the tragedy. When Amr bin Umayya arrived in Medina, he narrated all the details of the tragedy of Be'r Ma'oona to the Holy Prophet and also mentioned the execution by him of the two men of Banu Aamir. The Holy Prophet rebuked him severely over what he had done and immediately arranged to send the blood-money for them to their heirs. As Banu Aamir were confederates of Banu Nadhir, and the latter were confederates of the Muslims, they were responsible for a proportionate share of the blood-money that had been paid by the Holy Prophet. Accordingly, the Holy Prophet went with some Companions to the settlement of Banu Nadhir and, putting the whole matter before them, demanded from them their share of the blood-money. The Banu Nadhir welcomed the Holy Prophet and requested him to wait so that they might collect the amount and pay it to him. The Holy Prophet and his Companions sat down in the shade of a wall, and the leaders of Banu Nadhir withdrew to one side, pretending that they would arrange to collect the amount which had to be paid to the Holy Prophet. Instead, however, they began to conspire that they should take advantage of this welcome opportunity and kill the Holy Prophet by someone mounting to the roof of the house against the wall of which the Holy Prophet was then sitting, and dropping a heavy stone on top of him. One of the Jews, Salam bin Mashkim, opposed this whole project and condemned it as treachery and a breach of their treaty with the Holy Prophet. But they did not listen to him, and, eventually, Amr bin Hajjash who was one of them carried a heavy stone to the top of the house, intending to drop it over the Holy Prophet. When he was about to carry out his foul design the Holy Prophet stood up suddenly and moved away, as if he had recalled something urgent that needed to be attended to immediately.

While both parties waited for him he returned to Medina, and after a short while his Companions who had been left behind became curious over his sudden departure and set out in search of him and, eventually, arrived in Medina. The Holy Prophet informed his Companions of the dangerous conspiracy that had been hatched by Banu Nadhir against his life, and sent for Muhammad bin Maslamah, of Aus, and directed him to go to Banu Nadhir and speak to them about the matter and tell them that as their mischief and their treachery had reached the extreme limit, it was not safe to permit them to continue in Medina and that it would be better for them to

leave Medina and to settle elsewhere. He was to allow them ten days
for their withdrawal from Medina. When Muhammad bin Maslamah
went and spoke to the leaders of Banu Nadhir, they told him
arrogantly to tell his master that they were not prepared to leave
Medina and that he was free to do whatever he wished. When their
reply was communicated to the Holy Prophet he observed involuntarily, 'God is Great; the Jews appear to be bent on fighting.' He
thereupon asked the Muslims to get ready, and with a company of his
followers he marched against Banu Nadhir.

An alternative version narrated by some of the historians is that,
sometime after the battle of Badr, though it is not specifically stated
how long after the battle, the chiefs of Quraish had sent a letter to
Banu Nadhir that they should expel Muhammad and his followers
from Medina, by force if necessary, else Quraish would take the field
against Banu Nadhir. Upon receipt of this letter Banu Nadhir held a
consultation and decided that the best way out of the situation would
be to kill Muhammad through some device, whereby he could be
persuaded to visit them and they could take advantage of the
opportunity to kill him. In pursuance of their device, they sent a
message to the Holy Prophet that they desired to arrange an exchange
of views between him and their divines and that if in consequence of
the exchange, his truth was established, they would believe in him.
They suggested that he should go to them accompanied by thirty
followers and that there would be thirty divines on their side to take
part in the exchange of views. In the meantime they arranged that
when the Holy Prophet should arrive the pseudo-divines, who would
have daggers hidden under their clothes, should find a suitable
opportunity to kill him. But a woman of Banu Nadhir sent word of
this design to an Ansari to whom she was related, and being informed
of it, the Holy Prophet, who was about to set out from his house,
cancelled his projected visit and told his followers to get ready, and
marched with a company of them against Banu Nadhir and besieged
their settlement. He sent a message to their leader that, in view of the
development that had taken place, he could not let them continue on
in Medina unless they made a new treaty with him assuring him that,
in future, they would not embark upon any treacherous design. But
they rejected his offer and thus a confrontation came about. Banu
Nadhir retired arrogantly behind their fortifications and a siege began.
The next day the Holy Prophet received intimation that Banu
Quraidhah were also bent upon mischief, upon which he marched at
the head of some of his Companions to the settlement of Banu
Quraidhah and set siege to it. Banu Quraidhah, finding that their
design had been discovered, were frightened, and offered to renew
their treaty with the Holy Prophet. He agreed and raised the siege,
whereafter he reverted to Banu Nadhir, who persisted in their

hostility, and a situation of confrontation arose. At this stage Abdullah bin Ubayy bin Salul sent a message to Banu Nadhir that they should not give way to the Muslims, and that he and his followers would lend them their active support and would fight on their behalf. But when fighting began Banu Nadhir looked in vain for support from Abdullah bin Ubayy and his followers. Banu Quraidhah also, though in sympathy with Banu Nadhir, did not come out openly in their support. Banu Nadhir had great confidence in the strength of their fortifications and were certain that the Muslims would not be able to do them any serious harm and would eventually get tired and lift the siege.

The confidence of Banu Nadhir appeared to be justified and though the siege continued for several days, it produced no change in their attitude. At last the Holy Prophet directed that some of the date trees of Banu Nadhir, which were outside their fortifications, may be cut down. These trees were of an inferior kind, the fruit of which was generally fed to animals and was not used for human consumption. The purpose of the Holy Prophet's direction was that Banu Nadhir, apprehending a large-scale destruction of their fruit trees, might become inclined to make terms, and thus a large number of human lives might be saved and peace and order might be restored at the sacrifice of a few inferior type of fruit trees. This served its purpose and by the time six date trees had been cut down Banu Nadhir, fearing large-scale damage, offered, after a siege lasting a fortnight, to open their gates on condition that they should be permitted to depart together with all their movables. This was what the Holy Prophet had himself offered them in the beginning, and as his sole purpose was the restoration of peace and security he accepted the offer, subject only to the condition that Banu Nadhir would not be permitted to take away their arms. This was agreed to, and the Holy Prophet appointed Muhammad bin Maslamah to supervise the departure of Banu Nadhir from Medina. Accordingly they departed with great pomp and show, with music playing and their camels loaded with all their movables. They had demolished their houses and carried away with them even the doors and lintels which were made of wood. Their arms and immovable properties, land and gardens, fell into the hands of Muslims, but as there had been little or no fighting these were not treated as spoils and the greater part of them were distributed among the poorer section of Emigrants who had hitherto been supported by their brethren of Ansar and thus, indirectly, Ansar also shared in these properties.

When Banu Nadhir were about to set out from Medina, some Ansar sought to detain those Ansar children, now grown up, who, in fulfilment of the vows of their parents, had been committed to the guardianship of members of Banu Nadhir and had been brought up in the Jewish faith. Banu Nadhir desired to take these young men with them. The Holy Prophet rejected the demand of Ansar as being opposed to the Divine command: 'There shall be no compulsion in matters of faith' (2:257). Two of Banu Nadhir, however, embraced Islam voluntarily and stayed on in Medina.

It had been understood that Banu Nadhir would depart from Medina and settle somewhere in the north beyond the boundaries of Arabia. Yet some of their leaders like Salam bin Abi Huqaiq, Kananah bin Rabi', Huyay bin Akhtab, and others, together with some of their followers, settled in the well known Jewish town, Khaibar, in the north of Hedjaz, where they were eagerly welcomed, and where they started conspiring against the Muslims, with dire results, as will be set out later.

It has been mentioned that, departing from Uhud, Abu Sufyan had challenged the Muslims to a trial of arms a year later at Badr and the Holy Prophet had announced acceptance of the challenge. When the time arrived, Abu Sufyan, while preparing to march to Badr, sent an emissary named Naeem, who belonged to a neutral tribe, to Medina, instructing him to try, by whatever means might be possible, to persuade the Muslims not to go forth to Badr. He went to Medina and spread exaggerated tales of the strength and preparations of Quraish and their eagerness for a trial of arms with the Muslims. His propaganda created a certain degree of restlessness among the weaker sections of the Muslims, who began to fear the prospect ahead. The Holy Prophet announced that he had accepted the challenge of Quraish and had promised to meet them at Badr, and would not fail to keep his promise, even though he may have to go forth alone and oppose the enemy with no support. This created a great stir among the Muslims who came forward in large numbers to go forth to Badr to meet Abu Sufyan's challenge. The Holy Prophet, peace be on him, set out from Medina at the head of 1,500 followers. On the other side Abu Sufyan marched out from Mecca with 2,000 followers. The Muslims arrived at Badr by the agreed date, but when Abu Sufyan learnt of the failure of the mission of his emissary, Naeem, he gave out that, as there was a severe famine and conditions were not propitious for a fight, they would return to Mecca and would prepare to invade Medina at a more suitable opportunity. As there was an annual fair at Badr at the time, the Muslims stopped for eight days at Badr and many of them took advantage of the fair to trade their goods on very favourable terms. At the end of the fair, as there was still no sign of Quraish, the Holy Prophet returned to Medina.

As the correspondence of the Holy Prophet was now expanding, he felt the need of a secretary who should be familiar with Hebrew, so that correspondence with the Jews might be facilitated, and no difficulty might be encountered with regard to the accurate phrasing

of agreements, covenants and treaties. He therefore directed his young
secretary, Zaid bin Thabet Ansari, who had acquired literacy in
Arabic under the tuition of the prisoners taken in the battle of Badr, to
learn Hebrew also. Zaid possessed a very keen intelligence and, with
diligent efforts, he acquired literacy in Hebrew within a fortnight.
Later, in the time of Abu Bakr, under his instructions, Zaid bin
Thabet compiled the Holy Quran in the form of a book.

By virtue of the covenant which had been drawn up between the
different sections of the people of Medina shortly after the arrival of
the Holy Prophet, peace be on him, he had, in effect, become the chief
executive and judicial authority in Medina. He decided such cases as
were submitted to him according to the law or the custom that
regulated the affairs of each section of the population. For instance, it
is related that towards the end of the fourth year of the Hijra, a case
was submitted to him in which a Jewish woman and a Jewish man
were charged with adultery. When the Holy Prophet determined that
the charge had been duly established, he inquired from the Jewish
divines what was the penalty for the offence under Mosaic law. They
submitted to him, falsely, hoping to mislead him and hold him up to
ridicule, that the penalty for adultery under Mosaic law was that the
faces of the persons guilty of the offence should be blackened and they
should be taken through the streets of the town riding a mount facing
backwards. It so happened that at that time Abdullah bin Salam, a
Jewish divine who had embraced Islam, was present, and he submitted
that the Holy Prophet was being falsely advised and that the penalty
for adultery, according to the Torah, was stoning to death. Thereupon
the Holy Prophet called for the Torah, and though the Jewish divines
still persisted in seeking to mislead him, Abdullah bin Salam clearly
demonstrated from the Torah that the penalty for adultery was as he
had advised the Holy Prophet, who determined accordingly.

About the same time, the aged mother of Ali, Fatima bint Asad,
died in Medina. This revered lady had been in the place of a mother to
the Holy Prophet, and had brought him up as one of her own children.
She had been very fond of him and he was deeply grieved at her death.
He gave his own shirt to serve as her shroud and himself made all
arrangements for her burial. He stood in the grave and lowered her
body into it while supplicating, 'May Allah reward thee for having
been a very good mother to me.' Of Abu Talib's children she was the
mother of four sons, Talib, Aqeel, Ja'far and Ali, and one daughter,
Um Hani.

So far all military operations undertaken by the Holy Prophet,
peace be on him, had been, directly or indirectly, of a defensive
character. The expeditions undertaken for the establishment of
peaceful relations with some of the Arab tribes fell into the same
category. Also, all these operations had been confined to the Hedjaz

and Nejd, that is to say to Central Arabia. In the fifth year of Hijra the scope of these operations began to be widened. The Holy Prophet received intimation that a large group of people, based on Dumatul Jandal, occupied themselves with robbing and looting travellers and caravans, and that there was some possibility that they might extend the scope of their disorderly marauding activities and might become a source of apprehension for the Muslims. There was, at the time, no serious danger apprehended from that quarter, but as one of the major purposes of the Holy Prophet's policy was the establishment of peace and security he urged his Companions that the state of affairs prevailing at and around Dumatul Jandal should be put an end to, and law and order should be restored in that part of the country. He set out at the head of 1,000 of his Companions, and arrived near Dumatul Jandal after a long and strenuous journey extending over a fortnight, but found that on learning about the approach of the Muslims, the mischievous elements had scattered, and though small parties were sent in search of them, no trace of them could be found. One of their shepherds was captured and he became a Muslim. After a stay of some days, the Holy Prophet returned to Medina with his Companions. This expedition put an end to the predatory activities of the local inhabitants of that region, and travellers and caravans proceeding through their territory were delivered from the peril to which they had hitherto been exposed. Also Islam, of which only the name had been known in those parts, was brought to the notice of the local inhabitants, who conceived some idea of the ways and habits of the Muslims. There were Christian settlements in the neighbourhood of Dumatul Jandal, but there is nothing to indicate that this expedition was directed against any of them.

During the Holy Prophet's absence from Medina the mother of S'ad bin Ubadah, chief of Khazraj, had died. On his return he went and prayed for her at her grave. S'ad submitted that before her death his mother had intended to give away something in charity but that she had not been able to carry her design into effect; and he inquired whether he could carry out her wish on her behalf. The Holy Prophet indicated that he could, and on S'ad's inquiry what would be the proper object of the charity, the Holy Prophet suggested that he might endow something of general benefit, like a well, or an orchard. S'ad complied with the Holy Prophet's suggestion.

In the same year, an eclipse of the moon was observed at Medina, and the Holy Prophet directed the Muslims to gather together for a prayer service which he led and which continued till the eclipse had ended. While the Muslims were so engaged, the Jews created an uproar by beating on their vessels, etc., under the mistaken notion that the moon had been bewitched by someone and that the noise they were making would dispel the witchery. It is a characteristic of Islam that it has not only wiped out all superstition, but on every superstitious occasion, it has enjoined worship and supplication which direct the attention of the Muslims to God Almighty as the Source of all power and every phenomenon and thus weed out all pagan notions. Prayer on the occasion of an eclipse serves to impress on the minds of the Muslims the verity that the true source of all light, whatever the instrument which is its apparent source, is God Almighty, and that on the occasion of any obstruction in the way of light, even though such obstruction takes place in the normal course of the working out of Divine law, they should turn their attention to God and contemplate His attributes. In this manner Islam has instituted the remembrance of God on every possible occasion in a Muslim's life, so that a Muslim should not, at any time, be neglectful of his Maker.

Mention has been made of the famine with which the people of Mecca were afflicted at the time when Abu Sufyan had marched from Mecca in pursuance of his challenge to meet the Muslims at Badr for a trial of arms. This famine occasioned great suffering, particularly to the poorer section of the inhabitants of Mecca. When the Holy Prophet learnt of the distress of Quraish, on account of the famine, he sent some silver, which might be used for providing relief for the indigent of Mecca. On another occasion of famine, it appears that Abu Sufyan had gone to the Holy Prophet and had requested him, on the basis of kinship, to pray that Meccans might be delivered from the affliction of famine. These incidents show that the attitude of Quraish towards the Holy Prophet was somewhat mixed. They were conscious of his innate goodness, piety and purity, but were inveterate enemies of his teachings which, they apprehended, spelled the ruin of their pagan beliefs and of their way of life.

Chapter 10

:Siege:

By the fifth year of the Hijar, the bitter hostility of Quraish towards Islam and the Muslims had assumed dangerous proportions. Their poisonous propaganda against Islam had set many Arab tribes of Hedjaz against the Muslims, so much so that even some of those who had hitherto maintained good relations with the Muslims, adopted a hostile attitude towards them. The lead was taken by Banu Mustalaq, a clan of the well-known Banu Khuzaa. Their chief, Harith bin Abi Dharar, visited several neighbouring tribes and induced them to join him in his hostile enterprise against the Muslims. When the Holy Prophet received intimation of this situation, he despatched Bareedah bin Haseeb to Banu Mustalaq to gather intelligence and to report back quickly. He returned soon and informed the Holy Prophet that Banu Mustalaq were indeed making large-scale preparations for the invasion of Medina. Thereupon the Holy Prophet announced his intention of leading a pre-emptive expedition against Banu Mustalaq and a large number of his Companions became ready to march with him, and so also a much larger number of the disaffected than had accompanied him on any previous occasion. This force had only thirty horses all told, and a larger number of camels, so that the members of the force had to take turns in riding. During the march a spy of Banu Mustalaq was captured and, on proof of his espionage, was executed. When Banu Mustalaq, who had designed a surprise attack against Medina, received intimation of the approach of the Muslim force, and learnt that their spy had been executed, they were perplexed and some of the tribes who had associated themselves with their project abandoned them and went home. The leaders of Banu Mustalaq, however, rallied their people and decided to offer battle to the Muslims. When the Holy Prophet arrived at Moraisi', near the coast and not far from the settlement of Banu Mustalaq, he made camp and having drawn up his force in battle array and having distributed the banners, he directed Umar to go forward towards Banu Mustalaq and to announce that if even at this stage they would abandon their hostility towards Islam, and would acknowledge the authority of the Holy Prophet, they would be left in peace and the Muslims would march back to Medina. The offer was arrogantly rejected and a confrontation became inevitable. Banu Mustalaq were the first to start shooting their arrows. At this the Holy Prophet commanded his followers to reply in like kind. Archery proceeded for some time and then the Holy Prophet directed a sudden attack which swept the opposing host off their feet, but the Muslims encircled them so effectively that the tribe was surrounded and was compelled to lay down its arms. The battle ended with the loss of ten of Banu Mustalaq and one Muslim.

After the battle, the Holy Prophet remained in camp at Moraisi' for a few days, towards the end of which an untoward incident threatened to assume dangerous proportions, but was rendered innocuous by the wise handling of the Holy Prophet. It so happened that a servant of Umar, of the name of Jahjah, went to the spring of Moraisi' to fetch water. At the same time Sinan, one of the confederates of Ansar, also arrived at the spring for the same purpose. An altercation ensued between these two ignorant persons in the course of which Jahjah inflicted an injury upon Sinan, who started shouting for Ansar to come to his help. Jahjah, on his side, began to shout for Emigrants to come to his help, in consequence of which several Ansar and Emigrants were attracted to the spot so that a confrontation threatened, and might have broken out had not a number of responsible persons on both sides arrived in time who reprimanded both sides and averted the threatened conflict. When the Holy Prophet was apprised of the incident he expressed his disapproval and observed that the incident had been a manifestation of the unruly spirit of pre-Islamic days. The incident was thus closed, and no more would have been thought of it, had not Abdullah bin Ubayy, the leader of the disaffected, unfortunately sought to revive it.

Abdullah bin Ubayy harangued his followers and concluded with, 'This ye have brought upon yourselves, by inviting these strangers to come amongst us. Now wait till we return to Medina; then the most honoured one among us shall surely expel the one meanest among us.' Zaid bin Arqam, a sincere young man, mentioned this utterance of Abdullah to his uncle, who reported it to the Holy Prophet. Umar, who was then in the company of the Holy Prophet, was outraged, and sought the Holy Prophet's leave to strike down the leader of the disaffected. But the Holy Prophet counselled forbearance, as he did not wish it said that he was keen on killing his own followers. He sent for Abdullah bin Ubayy and some of his associates and inquired from them what had happened. They swore that none of them had said anything like that which was attributed to them. Some Ansar urged that Zaid bin Arqam might have been mistaken. The Holy Prophet dismissed the whole affair, but Zaid's report was later confirmed by revelation. The Holy Prophet sent for Abdullah bin Ubayy and his associates and told them that Zaid's report had been confirmed, and then directed Umar to announce the immediate departure of the force

for Medina. It was high noon and the heat was intense, and though the
Holy Prophet generally avoided marching at that time of day, he
decided that in the circumstances it was best to start the march
immediately. Everyone became ready to set forth.

Usyad bin Hudhair, chief of Aus, was curious to discover the reason
for this unusual direction of the Holy Prophet. He went to him and
submitted, 'Messenger of Allah, you do not normally march at this
time of day. What has caused you to start the march at this time?' To
which the Holy Prophet replied, 'Usyad, have you not heard that
Abdullah bin Ubayy says that, arriving in Medina, the most honoured
one among us shall expel the meanest one among us?' Usyad
submitted, 'Messenger of Allah, you can certainly expel Abdullah
from Medina, for undoubtedly you are the most honoured among us,
and he is the meanest one. But, Messenger of Allah, you are aware that
before your arrival in Medina, Abdullah was highly esteemed among
his people and they were planning to make him their king. Your
arrival frustrated that project and he has since been full of envy
towards you. You need pay no attention to his nonsense, and may
extend him your forbearance.' Shortly after, Abdullah, son of
Abdullah bin Ubayy, who was a sincere Muslim, came to the Holy
Prophet much agitated, and submitted, 'Messenger of Allah, I have
heard that you intend to order the execution of my father on account
of his arrogance and mischief. If that is your decision, I would submit
that you should appoint me as my father's executioner and I would
immediately carry out your direction; but I would urge that you
should not appoint anyone else to carry out your direction, lest, out of
my weakness, I should thereafter bear a grudge against that person,
and thus incur the displeasure of God.' The Holy Prophet replied to
him, 'Have no fear. So long as your father remains with us, we shall
make our companionship pleasant unto him.' But the son was so
incensed against his father that when the Muslim force approached
Medina the son blocked the father's way and swore that he would not
let him proceed any further unless he confessed that the Holy Prophet
was the most honoured, and he, Abdullah bin Ubayy, the meanest of
the people of Medina. The father was thus compelled to confess as his
son required and it was only then that the son left him free to proceed.

The march started at noon and continued during the rest of the day
and throughout the night and during the morning hours of the next
day. When camp was made, everyone was so dead tired that they all
lay down immediately and slept for several hours. Thus, through the
wisdom of the Holy Prophet, the attention of the Muslims was
diverted from the unpleasant incident of the previous day and they
were safeguarded against the mischief that the disaffected had
contrived. Yet, no frustration served to discourage the disaffected.
Indeed, every frustration instigated them to embark upon greater

mischief and more serious disruptive designs. Thus, towards the end of this march another incident was sought to be ballooned out of proportion so as to become a source of serious trial for the Muslims. It became known as the Calumny, in which Aisha, the wife of the Holy Prophet, daughter of Abu Bakr, was involved. The true version of the affair may be presented in Aisha's own words as follows.

'It was the practice of the Holy Prophet that when he was about to set out on a journey he cast a lot to determine which of his wives should accompany him. On one such occasion, the lot put up my name and he took me with him. By that time, the discipline of the veil had been established. In the course of the journey, I would be seated inside the litter, which was lifted on to the back of the camel, and was removed and placed upon the ground when a halt was made. During this journey, when we were nearing Medina, the Holy Prophet directed that the march should start at night. On hearing the direction, I withdrew a certain distance in preparation for the march and when I returned, I missed my bracelet. I went back in search of it and was delayed a short while. In the meantime, those who had been appointed to lift my litter on to the back of the camel arrived and, assuming that I was inside the litter, lifted it on to the back of the camel and the march began. I was very slim at the time and my weight was very light, so that no one suspected that I might not be inside the litter. When I returned after recovering my bracelet, I found that the march had gone forward and no one been left behind. I was worried, but considered that I should remain on the spot, so that when my absence was discovered, someone might be sent back to fetch me. So I sat down and was soon overcome by sleep. It so happened that Safwan bin Mu'attal, whose duty was to follow in the wake of the Muslim force so as to bring up the rear and pick up anything that might have been forgotten and left behind, arrived towards the morning at the spot where I was lying asleep. As he had seen me before the veil had been imposed, he recognised me, and in great surprise ejaculated, "To Allah we belong, and to Him shall we return." His voice woke me up, and perceiving him, I immediately covered my face with my veil. He said nothing to me, but brought up his camel and made it sit down next to me and put one of his feet on each folded knee of the camel and I climbed on to its back. Safwan led the camel by its halter and we started in the direction of Medina till we arrived at the place where the Muslim force had made camp.

'Thereafter we arrived in Medina with the Holy Prophet, and it so happened that immediately after my return to Medina I fell ill and my illness lasted a month. During this period the calumny against me was noised about widely, but I had no notion of it. I did, however, notice that during the period of my illness the Holy Prophet did not extend to me the kindness and affection which I had been accustomed to receive from him, and this troubled me greatly. When he visited me, he greeted me in the usual manner and merely inquired, "How are you feeling now?" and then turned away. I was grieved at this, and my prolonged illness wore me out and rendered me very weak. One day I gathered from Um Mistah, who was distantly related to us, by chance, something about what was being said concerning me. I also learnt that her son, Mistah, was also one of those who slandered me. I was much distressed, and, in the stress of my grief, I forgot my illness. When the Holy Prophet came as usual and inquired, "How are you feeling now?" I sought his permission to retire for some days to my parents' house. He gave me permission, and I went home to them. My purpose in going home was to find out what was being said about me. I spoke to my mother and she sought to comfort me, saying, "Daughter, assuage thy grief, it often happens that when a man is married to more women than one, and he is fonder of one of them than of the others, scandal is multiplied about her." I then understood that scandal was being spread about me and I began to weep and spent the whole night in that condition.

'About that time, the Holy Prophet sought counsel with Ali bin Abi Talib and Usama bin Zaid. Usama said that he had never known anything but good about me. Ali was more cautious and said that the Holy Prophet might inquire from my maid, whereupon he sent for my maid Barairah and inquired from her whether she had noticed anything suspicious about me. She affirmed that she had never seen anything about me which might be open to objection, except that on account of my young age, I was sometimes careless about my domestic chores. The Holy Prophet had also inquired about me from his wife, Zainab bint Jahsh, who too affirmed that she esteemed me a good and pious woman.

'One day the Holy Prophet addressed the Muslims in the Mosque and, stating that some of them had disquieted him greatly about the members of his family, inquired whether there was anyone among them who could put an end to this scandal-mongering. He affirmed that he knew nothing at all about me, except that which was good, and that he also considered that the person who was being mentioned in this connection was a good man, who had never visited his house in his absence. Upon this, S'ad bin Muaz, chief of Aus, stood up and submitted, "Messenger of Allah, I shall put an end to this scandal. If the person who is responsible for noising it about belongs to my tribe, I deem him guilty of a capital offence and I shall immediately strike him down; if he is one of our brethren, Khazraj, I am prepared to act as you might direct." Upon this, S'ad bin Ubada, chief of Khazraj, protested against what S'ad bin Muaz had said about Khazraj and rebuked him. Usyad bin Hudhair, cousin of S'ad bin Muaz, supported his cousin and rebuked the Khazraj chief. But the Holy Prophet intervened and appeased the quarrel.

'About that time, when the Holy Prophet came to visit me, he sat down next to me and after reciting the Shahadah, said to me, "Aisha, you have heard what some people are saying about you. If you are innocent, I am hoping that God will proclaim your innocence; but if you are guilty of some default, you should seek forgiveness of God and turn to Him, for He accepts the repentance of a servant of His, who turns sincerely to Him, and has mercy on him." On hearing this from the Holy Prophet, my tears stopped and I asked my parents to reply on my behalf, but they said they did not know what they should say. I was a young girl and did not know the Holy Quran well, but, being disappointed with my parents, I said to the Holy Prophet, "I realise that you have been affected by what people have been saying, so that if I were to protest my innocence, you might doubt me, and if, despite my innocence, I were to confess myself guilty, you might believe me. I find myself in the situation of Joseph's father and say like him, 'It behoves me to be steadfast. It is Allah alone Whose help can avail against that which you assert, and Him I shall beseech for help' (12:19)." Saying this I turned over in my bed in the full certainty that as I was guiltless, God would soon proclaim my innocence. What I had in mind was that God would assure the Holy Prophet of my innocence through some dream or vision. I had no notion that revelation might be vouchsafed to the Holy Prophet in my behalf. But only a few moments later, while the Holy Prophet was still in our house, I observed perspiration over his face, from which I understood that he was receiving revelation. After a short while he smiled, and, turning to me, said, "Aisha, rejoice, for God has affirmed your innocence." My mother immediately urged me to thank the Holy Prophet, but my heart being caught in an upsurge of gratitude to God, I replied, "Why should I express my gratitude to him, I am deeply grateful to God Who has affirmed my innocence." The Holy Prophet had been vouchsafed the revelation which is set out in the Holy Quran in verses 12 to 21 of Sura Noor.

'When my innocence was established, my father, who used to support Mistah bin Athathah because of his poverty and his kinship, swore that as Mistah had been a party to the slander against me, he would not in future render him any help. But soon thereafter, the Holy Prophet received the revelation that Abu Bakr's resolve was not pleasing to God, upon which he resumed his support of Mistah and determined never to stop it.'

This scandal was a grave mischief which had been perpetrated by the disaffected, the principal one at the back of which was Abdullah bin Ubayy bin Salul. His purpose was not merely to attack the honour of a most pious and righteous woman, but to bring the Holy Prophet into contempt and to shake Muslim society to its foundations. The mean and wicked propaganda was carried on in such a manner that some sincere but simple Muslims were also caught in its wide net, among whom the names of the poet, Hassan bin Thabet, Hamnah bint Jahsh, sister of the Holy Prophet's wife, Zainab bint Jahsh, and Mistah bin Athathah, have been particularly mentioned. However, it is a great testimony to the high-mindedness of Aisha that she forgave all those who had been concerned in this affair and nursed no grievance against them. Whenever Hassan bin Thabet called on her thereafter, she received him graciously. It is related that, on one occasion, when he asked permission to present himself, a Muslim of the name of Masrooq, who was present, expressed his surprise to Aisha that she was prepared to let him come in. Aisha said to him, 'He is to be pitied; the poor man can no longer see, and I can also not forget that he used to compose verses in support of the Holy Prophet against his detractors.' She gave permission, and Hassan came in and sat down and recited some verses in praise of Aisha in which he mentioned that she was not given to speak ill of innocent women. On this, Aisha was amused and retorted, 'But what about you?'

Sir William Muir's summing up of the whole affair is: 'Little remark is needed regarding the character of Aisha. . . her life both before and after must lead us to believe her innocent of the charge' (*Life of Muhammad,* p. 304).

We now approach the maximum effort of Quraish and their confederates to wipe out Islam and destroy the Muslims. So far, Quraish and the principal tribes of Nejd, Ghatafan and Suleim, who were bitterly hostile towards the Muslims, had not yet combined their forces to achieve their purpose. A third element was now injected into the situation, namely, the leaders of Banu Nadhir, who had been expelled from Medina and had been welcomed at Khaibar. The most active of them were Salam bin Abi Huqaiq, Huyay bin Akhtab and Kananah bin Rabi'. They issued forth from Khaibar and first instigated Quraish to prepare themselves for a strong combined effort against the Muslims, and then went from tribe to tribe in Hedjaz and Nejd to procure their adherence to their design. They had little difficulty in winning over Ghatafan to the support of their cause, and their branches, Fararah, Murrah and Ashj'a, also agreed to go forth with them. Quraish and Ghatafan then procured the support of Banu Suleim and Banu Asad. The Jews succeeded in persuading their confederates, Banu Sa'd, to assist in their design. Quraish also had the support of their neighbouring tribes who were under their influence. Thus, with full preparation, this large host became ready to march against Medina like a fierce flood, with the firm determination to wipe out Islam altogether before returning from Medina. Their strength has been variously estimated at 10,000 to 20,000 warriors. Even if the lower figure is taken as correct, their number was larger than had ever faced an enemy at any time previously in the tribal wars of Arabia.

The overall command was vested in Abu Sufyan, who was also the commander of Quraish. Ghatafan were commanded by Ujainah bin Hathan Fazari, under whom each of the tribes had its own commander. Banu Suleim were commanded by Sufyan bin Abd Shams, and Banu Asad, by their chief Tulaihah bin Khuweilid. This great army was well equipped, well armed and well provisioned. It started its march towards Medina at the end of February or beginning of March 627.

It was not possible to keep the movements of such a large host secret, and also, the Holy Prophet's intelligence system was well organised, so that, as soon as this army began to move from Mecca, the Holy Prophet received intimation of it, and he summoned his Companions for consultation. Salman Farisi, who was a sincere Iranian Muslim and was knowledgeable in Iranian tactics and strategy, suggested that in the situation with which the Muslims were faced, the best way of securing themselves would be by digging a long and wide trench around that part of Medina which was unprotected and was vulnerable. This was a new idea altogether which had not been known among the Arabs, but the Holy Prophet, peace be on him, on learning that it was successfully followed in warfare among non-Arabs, decided to adopt it and commanded that a wide trench should be dug for the safeguarding of Medina along the side that was open and vulnerable. Under his own supervision, he had the lines of the trench marked out and allotted the digging of each length of fifteen feet to parties of ten Muslims. A friendly difference arose whether Salman himself, who was the originator of the idea of digging the trench, and, despite his age, was a strong and diligent man, should be allotted as an outsider to Emigrants, or, having arrived in Medina before the Hijra, should be counted among Ansar, as both were eager to obtain his co-operation. The matter was submitted to the Holy Prophet, and, after listening to both sides, he observed with a smile, 'Salman is neither Emigrant nor of Ansar; he is a member of my family and is one of us.' Thenceforward, Salman was always known as a member of the Holy Prophet's family.

Each party of ten divided their task among themselves and started the work of preparing the trench in right earnest. But the digging was not easy and the weather, being cold, added to the difficulties. Almost all the able-bodied Muslims had been drafted for the digging of the trench, and all other occupations were laid aside, so that those who were dependent upon their daily labour for their livelihood suffered great privation through hunger and lack of nourishment. The Holy Prophet stimulated the enthusiasm of the Muslims by himself carrying basket-loads of excavated earth, and joining in their songs, as at the building of the mosque:

O Lord, there is no happiness but that of the hereafter.
O Lord, have mercy on Ansar and Emigrants.

He also frequently repeated the following verses, covered as he was,
like the rest, with earth and dust:

O Lord, without Thee, we had not been guided!
We would neither have given alms, nor yet have prayed!
Send down upon us tranquillity, and in battle make our steps firm!
For they have risen up against us,
    and sought to pervert us, but we refused!
Yea, we refused.

As he repeated the last two words, he raised his voice high and loud.
With all the Muslims, he suffered the pangs of hunger as severely as
they.

On one occasion, a digging party encountered a piece of rock
embedded in the earth which could nohow be broken or moved by the
famished diggers. In the end, they approached the Holy Prophet and
mentioned their difficulty to him. He was in no better case than
themselves, yet he proceeded to the spot and, lifting a pick-axe, struck
the piece of rock pronouncing the name of Allah. The iron striking on
stone raised a spark, whereupon the Holy Prophet called out 'God is
Great' in a loud voice, and observed, 'I have been bestowed the keys
of the kingdom of Syria and have beheld the red-stone palaces of that
country.' His stroke had crushed a portion of the piece of rock. He
wielded the pick-axe a second time and struck the rock, again
pronouncing the name of Allah, and again a spark was struck from the
stone, on which he called out 'God is Great' and observed, 'Now I
have been bestowed the keys of Iran, and have beheld the white
palaces of Madaen.' This time a larger portion of the rock was
crushed. The same happened a third time, and when the spark was
struck, the Holy Prophet called out 'God is Great' and observed, 'This
time I have been bestowed the keys of Yemen, and I have beheld the
doors of San'a.' The rock was finally crushed and the broken pieces
were removed out of the way. The Holy Prophet's three visions that
he was vouchsafed were prophetic as presaging the future victories of
the Muslims and their prosperity, whereby the drooping spirits of the
Muslims were uplifted. The disaffected, when they heard an account
of these visions, jeered at them and scorned them as delusions
resulting from the extreme of hardship from which the Muslims were
suffering. Yet, in due time, all these prophetic visions were completely
fulfilled in the time of the Holy Prophet's successors.

About the same time, a devout Muslim, Jabir bin Abdullah,
observing the signs of starvation and weakness on the countenance of

the Holy Prophet, sought his permission to go home for a short while, and on arriving home, told his wife that the Holy Prophet was suffering the extreme of hunger, and inquired whether she had any food in the house. She said she had some barley flour and they had one goat. Jabir slaughtered the goat and kneaded the flour into dough and said to his wife, 'Now you prepare the food and I shall go and request the Holy Prophet to come and eat.' His wife warned him, 'Take care that you do not embarrass me by inviting a large number of people along with the Holy Prophet.' Jabir went and said to the Holy Prophet, almost in a whisper, 'Messenger of Allah, we have some meat and barley flour, and I have asked my wife to prepare a meal. I would request you to come with a few Companions and eat at our house.' The Holy Prophet inquired how much food there was, and Jabir told him. The Holy Prophet said, 'It is plenty', and then looking around him and raising his voice, called out, 'O ye company of Ansar and Emigrants, come along. Jabir has invited us to a meal. Let us go and eat.' Upon this a very large number, possibly a thousand or more, became ready to accompany him. He directed Jabir to hurry home and tell his wife that she should not take the cooking pot off the fire, nor to start baking bread before he arrived. Jabir went home quickly and informed his wife accordingly. She was greatly perplexed as the food was sufficient only for a few, and she was told that a huge throng was on the way. As soon as the Holy Prophet arrived, he said a Prayer over the cooking pot and the dough and said, 'Now start baking the bread.' When some of the bread was ready he started distributing the food, and people ate turn by turn in parties, and all ate their fill while the pot was still boiling and the dough had not all been used up.

In about a week's time through the continuous and diligent labour of the entire body of Muslims, the trench was completed, though everybody was exhausted. By that time, the combined forces of the Jews and the pagans in all their panoply were approaching Medina. Abu Sufyan at the head of his host first advanced towards Uhud, and finding it deserted, veered round towards that side of Medina from which an attack could be delivered effectively; but on approaching Medina, they were brought to a stand by the trench. Closely guarded all along by pickets on the city side, it formed a barrier which they could not pass. They were astonished and disconcerted at the new tactics of the Holy Prophet. Unable to come to close quarters, they made camp on the plain beyond, and contented themselves for some time with a distant discharge of archery.

Meanwhile Abu Sufyan succeeded in detaching Banu Quraidha, now the only remaining principal Jewish tribe in Medina, from their allegiance to the Holy Prophet. Huyay, the exiled leader of Banu Nadhir, now an ally of Quraish, sent by Abu Sufyan to the fortress of Banu Quraidha, was at first refused admittance. But perservering in his solicitations, and representing the overwhelming number of the confederate army as a surging sea, he at last persuaded Kaab, chief of Banu Quraidha, to relent. It was agreed that Banu Quraidha would assist Quraish, and that Huyay should retire into their fortress in case the allies marched back without inflicting a fatal blow upon Medina. Rumours of this defection reaching the Holy Prophet, he sent the two S'ads, chiefs of Aus and Khazraj, to ascertain the truth; and strictly charged them, if the result should prove unfavourable, to divulge it to none other but himself. They found Banu Quraidha in a sullen mood. 'Who is Muhammad,' said they, 'and who is the Apostle of God, that we should obey him? There is no bond or compact betwixt us and him.' After high words and threats, the messengers took their leave, and reported to the Holy Prophet that the temper of the Jews was worse even than he had feared.

Sir William Muir has recorded (*Life of Muhammad*, p. 309):

On the whole, my impression is that Banu Quraidha entered into some kind of league with the Jewish exile Huyay, making common cause with him, and promising to take part in following up any success on the part of Quraish – a promise which they were in the best position to fulfil – their fortress being, though at some distance from the city, on its undefended side.

On his side, the Holy Prophet had marched out of Medina at the head of 3,000 Muslims and had made camp between the trench and the city, keeping the hillock Sil'a at his back. He divided his men into small pickets which he posted along the trench and on the undefended sides of Medina, instructing them that they should remain alert all the time, throughout the day and night. The situation was one of great peril. The city was invested by thousands of well armed enemies watching for an opportunity to engage the Muslims in a decisive action and destroy them utterly. Inside the city, the Muslim women and children would be an easy prey for Banu Quraidha, hundreds of whose armed young men posed as formidable a threat as any well armed and disciplined army. Some of the weak Muslims were much perturbed and could not imagine what might transpire. The disaffected, and those whose minds were diseased, openly exclaimed: 'Allah and His Messenger have merely deluded us. A section of them asked leave of the Holy Prophet: Our houses are exposed. Their houses were not exposed, they merely sought an excuse to defect' (33:12-14).

But this time of peril also brought out the best on the part of the sincere believers. As the Holy Quran says: 'When the true believers saw the confederates, they said: Here is what Allah and His Messenger had promised us; Allah and His Messenger have been proved right.

The perilous situation only added to their faith and spirit of submission' (33:23). But the delicacy of the situation and the grave threat that it posed were recognised by all and caused much perturbation. As the Holy Quran has put it (33:11-12):

> Call to mind when the enemy came upon you from above you and from below you, and your eyes became distracted, and your hearts rose up to your throats, and some of you began to think unworthy thoughts about Allah. Then were the believers sorely tried, and were violently shaken.

In these circumstances, the Muslims did not know which way to turn. After the first two or three days, their continuous state of alertness exhausted them utterly. The enemy were aware of this and made repeated efforts to get across the trench at its weaker points; the defenders had to move continuously from one point to another wherever danger threatened, so that they could not concentrate their strength at any particular point. Besides, on account of the treachery of Banu Quraidha, it had become necessary to strengthen the pickets inside the city, so that women and children should not be exposed to any serious danger.

Sir William Muir has described part of this situation as follows (*Life of Muhammad*, pp. 310-11):

> The confederate host resolved if possible to storm the trench, and, having discovered a narrow and ill-guarded part, a general attack was made upon it. Spurring their horses, a few of them, led by Ikrama, son of Abu Jahl, cleared the ditch, and galloped vauntingly before the Muslim line. No sooner was this perceived than Ali with a guard of picked men moved out against them. These, by a rapid manoeuvre, gained the rear of Ikrama, and occupying the narrow point that he had crossed cut off retreat. At this moment Amr bin Abdood, an aged chief in the train of Ikrama, challenged his adversaries to single combat. Ali forthwith accepted the challenge, and the two stood man to man in the open plain. Amr, dismounting, maimed his horse, in token of his resolve to conquer or to die. They closed, and for a short time were hidden in a cloud of dust. But it was not long before the loud Tekbir, Great is the Lord, from Ali's lips, made known that he was the victor. The rest, taking advantage of the diversion, again spurred their horses across the trench and escaped, all excepting Naufal, who falling in the leap, was despatched by Zubair. His body was left in the trench. Quraish offered ten thousand dirhems for its removal. The Holy Prophet let them have it free.

Nothing further was attempted that day. But great preparations were made during the night; and next morning, Muhammad found the whole allied force drawn up against him. It required unceasing vigilance to frustrate their manoeuvres. Now they would threaten a general assault; now breaking up in divisions they would attack various posts in rapid and distracting succession; and at last, watching for their opportunity, they would mass their troops together on the least protected point, and, under cover of galling archery, attempt to force the trench. Once and again a dash was made at the city by such leaders of renown as Khalid and Amr, and the tent of Muhammad himself was at one moment in peril; but the brave Muslim front, and showers of arrows, drove the assailants back. This continued throughout the day; and, as the army of Muhammad was just sufficient to guard the line, there could be no relief. Even at night, Khalid's troops kept up the alarm, and rendered outposts at frequent intervals necessary. But the endeavours of the enemy were all without effect. The trench was never crossed in force; and during the whole affair, Muhammad lost only five men. The confederates had but three men killed. S'ad bin Muaz, chief of Aus, was wounded severely by an arrow in the shoulder.

Amr bin Abdood was a famous swordsman, and on account of his courage and bravery, was accounted the equal of a hundred warriors. He had been present in the battle of Badr, the experience of which had rendered him bitter and vengeful against the Muslims. He had called loudly for single combat in a very arrogant tone and Ali, with the permission of the Holy Prophet, went forward in answer to his challenge. The Holy Prophet gave him his own sword and uttered a prayer for him.

Approaching Amr, Ali said to him, 'I have heard that you have determined that if any Quraish makes two requests to you, you would comply with at least one of them.' Amr signified his confirmation, upon which Ali said, 'Then I ask you first that you embrace Islam and believing in the Holy Prophet earn divine favour.' Amr said he would not do that. Ali then said, 'If you do not grant my first request, my second request is that you should get ready to fight me.' In reply, Amr asked Ali to identify himself, and on his doing so, said, 'Nephew, you are young. I have no desire to shed your blood. Send someone from among your seniors to fight me.' Ali countered, 'You do not desire to shed my blood, but I have no hesitation in shedding your blood.' This retort infuriated Amr. He jumped from his horse and maimed it and, advancing like a fierce flame of fire towards Ali, struck him with his sword with such force that it cut through Ali's shield and wounded his forehead. Ali attacked him with such effect on his shoulder that his sword cut through his body and felled him down and he breathed his last within a minute or two.

However, this temporary success brought no relief to the Muslims who were progressively becoming weaker as the siege progressed. Their faith and devotion were unshaken, but their bodies were exhausted. The Holy Prophet, who himself fared no better, was deeply affected by the sufferings of the Muslims and took counsel with S'ad bin Muaz and S'ad bin Ubadah, chiefs of Ansar, on how the situation could be relieved. He suggested to them that one way might be to detach Ghatafan from Quraish by offering them a portion of the revenue of Medina. They inquired whether his suggestion was under divine direction. The Holy Prophet told them that he was asking their advice on what they considered was most expedient, and that no divine direction was involved, upon which they submitted that their counsel was that as they had not yielded anything of the kind to an enemy before they became Muslims, they should offer nothing to the enemy on this occasion except the sword. The Holy Prophet was much reassured by their steadfastness and did not press his suggestion.

The situation continued unrelieved and the Holy Prophet and the Muslims continued firm and steadfast, but under severe sufferings. Another factor in the situation which added to the anxieties of the Holy Prophet and his followers was the question of the security of women and children, particularly on such occasions when the enemy pressed hard to force the trench and all the Muslims were needed to withstand their onslaught and to repel them, and the only persons left to safeguard the women and children were such as were not capable of offering resistance to able-bodied and armed parties. On one occasion, the Jews sent a spy to assess the situation and report back to them. It so happened that at that time the only person who had been left to watch over the women and children was the poet Hassan bin Thabet, who, on account of the weakness of his heart, was not capable of fighting. When the women saw the Jewish spy prowling about, Safiya bint Abdul Muttalib, aunt of the Holy Prophet, told Hassan to kill the fellow as he was a spy and was obviously bent upon mischief. But Hassan felt helpless and Safiya herself went forward with a tent pole and killed the man. It was then decided that he should be beheaded and his head should be thrown in the direction on which the Jews were gathered in strength so that they might imagine that the women were well guarded. This ruse was successful, and the Jews went back to their strongholds.

On one occasion some of the Muslims came to the Holy Prophet and requested that he should make special supplications for relief and also teach them some prayers that they might offer up. He told them not to lose heart and to pray that God may be pleased to cover up their weaknesses, and strengthen their hearts and remove their anxieties. He himself supplicated, 'Allah, Revealer of commandments, Swift in calling to account, put the confederates to flight. Allah put them to flight, help us and shake them. O Thou that hearest the cry of the distressed and responds to the call of the afflicted, do Thou remove our anxiety, and our grief and our distress, for Thou seest in what situation my Companions and I are caught.'

By good fortune, about that time, No'eim bin Mas'ood who belonged to Ashj'a, a branch of Ghatafan, arrived in Medina. He was convinced of the truth of Islam though he had not yet proclaimed himself a Muslim. Having appraised the situation, he adopted a plan that succeeded in creating a rift between the confederates and the Jews. He went first to Banu Quraidha and pointed out to them that the interests of the allied army were diverse from theirs; before they compromised themselves irretrievably by joining in the attack on Medina, they should demand hostages from Quraish, as a guarantee against being in the last deserted and left in the power of the Holy Prophet. This appealed to them and they agreed to act upon his advice. He then went to the allied chiefs and cautioned them against the Jews, telling them that Banu Quraidha intended asking them for hostages and that they should be careful lest their hostages might be handed over to the Muslims. When Quraish sent to demand of Banu Quraidha the fulfilment of their engagement to join in a general attack upon the Muslims on the following day, they pleaded their Sabbath as a pretext against fighting on the morrow, and their fear of being deserted as a ground for demanding hostages. The allies, regarding this as a confirmation of No'eim's intelligence, were so fully persuaded of the treachery of Banu Quraidha that they began to fear an attack upon themselves from that quarter.

The confederate chiefs were already disheartened. After two days of vigorous fighting, they had not again attempted any general assault. The hopes entertained from another engagement, during which Banu Quraidha were to have fallen upon the city in the rear of the Muslims, were now changed into fear of hostilities from Banu Quraidha themselves. Forage was being obtained with the utmost difficulty; provisions were running short, and the camels and horses were dying daily in great numbers. Wearied and damped in spirit, the night set in upon them cold and tempestuous. Fierce winds and heavy rain beat mercilessly on the unprotected camp. The storm rose to a hurricane. Fires were extinguished, tents blown down, cooking vessels and other equipage overthrown. Cold and comfortless, Abu Sufyan suddenly resolved on an immediate march back. Hastily summoning the chiefs, he made known his decision. Break up the camp, he said, and march; as for myself, I am gone. With these words he leaped on his camel, so great was his impatience, while its forelegs were yet untied, and led the way back. Khalid with 200 horses brought up the rear, as a guard against pursuit. Quraish took the road by Uhud for Mecca and Banu Ghatafan retired to their desert haunts. Banu Quraidha thereupon made themselves secure in their strongholds and Huyay bin Akhtab, chief of Banu Nadhir, accompanied them. Thus before dawn the whole field was vacated and by a sudden and surprisingly unexpected turn in the fortunes of war the Muslims, who were apparently on the verge of being vanquished, became victorious.

During the night, when the allied camp was being vacated, the Holy Prophet called out, 'Is there anyone about?' But it was so cold and the Muslims who were close to the Holy Prophet were so exhausted by hunger and were in such fear that no one responded to his call, though he repeated it three times. At last he called Hudhaifah bin Yaman by name and he came and stood before him shivering with the cold. The Holy Prophet stroked his head with his hand and prayed for him, and said to him, 'Have no fear and be sure that God willing, you will be involved in no trouble. Slip quietly into the enemy camp, create no stir and do not interfere with anyone, and come back and report to me.' Hudhaifah has narrated: 'When I started, I felt that the cold had left me entirely and it seemed to me as if I was passing through a warm room, and I lost all my anxieties. The night was utterly dark and I slipped quietly and fearlessly into the enemy camp. I saw Abu Sufyan standing warming himself at a fire. I suddenly put an arrow to my bow and was about to shoot at him when I recalled the Holy Prophet's admonition that I was not to interfere with anyone. I was so close to Abu Sufyan that if I had shot my arrow at him, he could not have escaped. Abu Sufyan was urging his people to start on the march back. He mounted his camel while I was looking on and I returned to our camp. The Holy Prophet was then engaged in prayer; I waited till he had finished and made my report to him. He expressed his gratitude to God and said, "This has not happened through any power or effort of ours; it is only the grace of God which has vanquished the allied forces." ' Thereafter, the news of the flight of the pagans spread throughout the Muslim camp. It was probably on this occasion that the Holy Prophet observed, 'They will not now advance upon us for battle; it is we who shall advance against them.' Quraish were so disheartened after their flight that they did not dare to advance upon Medina ever after and the prediction of the Holy Prophet was fulfilled literally. When the allied forces had retired and it became clear that their march back was not a ruse, the Holy Prophet, peace be on him, directed the Muslims to break camp and marched them into the city.

The siege had lasted for three weeks, during which period the Muslims had suffered the extremes of distress and fear, which had been intensified by the treachery of Banu Quraidha. At the bottom of the whole trouble were the treacherous leaders of Banu Nadhir whom the Holy Prophet had mercifully permitted to withdraw from Medina.

It was through their incitement that all principal tribes of Hedjaz and central Arabia had joined together in their bitter enmity towards Islam to invade Medina and destroy the Muslims root and branch. It is certain that if on this occasion the allied forces could have contrived to enter Medina, not a single Muslim would have escaped alive, and the honour of no Muslim women would have been safe.

Badr, Uhud and the Confederate invasion were major efforts towards the wiping out of Islam and the ruin of Muslims. On each occasion, the disparity between the opposing hosts in respect of numbers, arms, provisions and means of transportation was striking, the odds being overwhelmingly in favour of Quraish and their allies. At Badr, 1,000 well armed and equipped Quraish were opposed by just over 300 half-famished and ill-armed Muslims. For a time during the actual fighting, the disparity told in favour of Quraish, but finally the decisive stage was short and sharp. In single combat, Quraish had lost three of their foremost leaders, and in the general fight, the flower of Quraish chivalry and bravery was laid in the dust. Quraish's arrogance and pride were humbled, and their spine was broken, never to be repaired and revived.

At Uhud, 3,000 well armed, well mounted and well accoutred Quraish warriors were opposed by 700 Muslims. Again, the advantage was overwhelmingly in favour of Quraish, and though they received a severe check at the start, disobedience of the Holy Prophet's strict instructions by the band of archers posted to guard the rear of the Muslims, ended in near disaster for the Muslims. If Quraish had pressed their advantage and invaded Medina, they might have achieved their purpose of destroying the Muslims.

The Confederate forces of Quraish and their allies numbered not less than 10,000. Only 3,000 Muslims were available for picketing the trench and the vulnerable parts of the city. During the greater part of the siege, the Muslims could be described as a force only in name. They were half-famished throughout and towards the end were absolutely spent and helpless. In the final stage they were caught and held between the upper and nether mill-stones of the allies and Banu Quraidha. They could not have survived this juxtaposition for longer than two or three days at the outside. Again, the dénouement was short and sharp. The fury of the forces of nature swept the allies away from the field, and they marched back in disorder and confusion, with their tails between their legs.

That disposed of Quraish and their allies. Banu Quraidha took to their strongholds, proud and arrogant in the certainty that their position was so strong and impregnable that the Muslims, in the condition in which they had been left by the prolonged siege, could do them no harm. The siege had been lifted, but the Muslims were by no means yet secure. The sequel to the siege had still to be worked out.

Even so does a fair and unbiased appraisal of the events of the five years beginning with the departure of the Holy Prophet, peace be on him, in the company of Abu Bakr, from Mecca, and ending with the ignominious flight of the Confederate armies, disclose that all that happened was only a series of chances which happened to turn in favour of the Muslims? Such a conclusion would be a gross misreading of history and would outrage reason and good sense. In the whole of human history, there has been no other period so brief as five years, so full of travail, trial and suffering, ending in the triumph of the weak over the strong, the humble over the arrogant, the God-fearing over the godless. In effect, it was the single personality of the Holy Prophet, peace be on him, burdened all the time with heavy responsibilities, and confronted continuously with situations brimful of problems, difficulties and perplexities, both internal and external, who, through the abounding grace and mercy of God, ministered to the welfare, not only of the Muslims alone but of the whole of the divergent communities of Medina, and safeguarded their security and laid firmly the foundations of a great world religion, strengthening at every step the faith of the Muslims, fostering their spirit of sacrifice, and instructing them in high spiritual and moral values and setting them a shining example in his own life in all the crises that crowded in upon him continuously.

Chapter 11

:Treason:

The Holy Prophet had scarcely had time to wash and change on his return home after the lifting of the siege, when he felt a strong urge, which he interpreted as a divine direction, to deal with the situation that had been created by the treachery and rebellion of Banu Quraidhah. He therefore announced that everyone should get ready to set forth towards the strongholds of Banu Quraidhah, and that the afternoon Prayer service would be held in camp. He sent Ali in advance at the head of a small detachment to reconnoitre. When Ali arrived at the strongholds of Banu Quraidhah, he found them in a truculent mood, and when he sought to speak to their leaders they abused the Holy Prophet and shamelessly held up his wives to ridicule.

Shortly after the departure of Ali and his men, the Holy Prophet set out himself riding a horse accompanied by a large number of Muslims. When he was approaching the strongholds of Banu Quraidhah, he was met by Ali who was waiting to receive him, and who suggested that the Holy Prophet should not proceed any further in person; the Muslims could resolve the situation between Banu Quraidhah and themselves. The Holy Prophet enquired from Ali whether his suggestion was prompted by any abuse of him by Banu Quraidhah. Ali replied in the affirmative, on which the Holy Prophet observed, 'Never mind, they persecuted Moses even more than they have persecuted me.' The Holy Prophet advanced with his followers and invested the strongholds of Banu Quraidhah.

In the beginning, the Jews behaved arrogantly and insolently. On one occasion, when a few Muslims had incautiously sat down in the shade of a wall of the stronghold, a Jewish woman cast down a heavy mill-stone upon them from the top of the wall, which killed one of the party, Khallad, and the others escaped. But as time passed they began to feel the privation and distress imposed upon them by the siege and began to cast about for means of relief. Their chief, Ka'ab bin Asad, made three proposals to them and told them to adopt whichever they pleased. He said, 'My first proposal is that we should all believe in the truth of Muhammad, as events have proved it and our scriptures support him. Once we embrace Islam, all controversy between us would cease.' His proposal was immediately and firmly rejected. He then said, 'My second proposal is that we should slaughter our women and children and then, without fear of consequences, take up our swords and go forth and fight the Muslims.' This proposal was also rejected as it was pointed out that after they had slaughtered their women and children, life would not be worth living. Finally, he said, 'My last proposal is that as this is the eve of Sabbath, and Muhammad and the Muslims would be unwary, believing themselves secure against any action on our part, we should emerge suddenly from our strongholds during the night and attack the Muslim force. If they are taken by surprise, we might repel them and put them to flight.' His people rejected this proposal also as they were afraid that they might incur divine wrath by dishonouring the Sabbath.

As their suffering and distress continued to mount, they thought of a device whereby they might be able to discover what the Holy Prophet had in mind concerning them, and they sent an emissary to the Holy Prophet requesting that Abu Lubaba bin Mundhar of Aus might be sent to them as that they might seek his advice. When he came to them, he was overcome by the pitious wailings of the Jewish children and the cries of the Jewish women, and in answer to the query whether Banu Quraidhah should offer to open their gates leaving their fate to be decided by the Holy Prophet, he nodded an affirmative, but, symbolically drawing his hand across his throat, intimated that they might fight to the last, as death was all they could expect. On retiring, he was greatly distressed that he had acted without any authority on the part of the Holy Prophet, and had been guilty of a grievous sin. So bitter was his remorse that he went and tied himself to a pillar in the mosque, occupying himself with supplication and seeking forgiveness. He continued in this condition till the Holy Prophet himself released him therefrom. His indiscretion became ultimately the cause of the ruin of Banu Quraidhah, who, instead of throwing themselves upon the mercy of the Holy Prophet, determined upon resistance to the bitter end.

At last when the siege had continued for about three weeks, Banu Quraidhah sent word to the Holy Prophet that they were prepared to abide by whatever might be determined by Sa'd bin Muaz, chief of Aus, who still suffered from the injury inflicted upon him by an arrow in the trench, and was under treatment in a tent pitched in the courtyard of the mosque under the directions of the Holy Prophet. Aus had been, in pre-Islamic days, confederates of Quraidhah, and they expected that Sa'd would deal leniently with them. The Holy Prophet signified his assent and Sa'd was summoned. He was conducted to the camp, supported on the back of a donkey. During his progress his tribesmen crowded round him with appeals for mercy for Banu Quraidhah. He answered not a word till he approached the scene, and then replied, 'Sa'd has been given the grace that he careth not, in the cause of God, for any reproach of the reproachful.'

In the meantime, three of Banu Quraidhah who had been convinced of the truth of Islam had declared themselves Muslims, and a fourth had been so ashamed of the treachery of his people that he had left them and had departed from Medina.

As Sa'd drew near, the Holy Prophet directed his Companions, 'Stand up to meet your chief, and assist him to dismount.' When Sa'd, having alighted, advanced towards the Holy Prophet, he told him, 'Banu Quraidhah have accepted you as an arbiter and have agreed to abide by your decision.' Sa'd turned himself to his people, who were still urging mercy upon him, and said, 'Will ye bind yourselves by the covenant of God that whatever I shall decide, ye will accept?' They assented. He then turned in the direction of the Holy Prophet and said, 'Does he who is present here also promise to abide by my decision?' The Holy Prophet replied, 'I promise.' Thereupon, Sa'd announced his judgment: 'The able-bodied males of Quraidhah shall be put to death, their women and children shall be made prisoners and the spoils shall be divided amongst the Muslims,' upon which the Holy Prophet observed, 'It appears that your judgment has been inspired by divine decree.' There can be no doubt that the situation had so developed that Sa'd's judgment was brought about by divine decree. Banu Quraidhah had requested that Abu Lubaba be sent to them, and he indicated something that was utterly without any basis, in consequence of which Banu Quraidhah had decided not to throw themselves upon the mercy of the Holy Prophet. At last, they had declared themselves ready to abide by the judgment of Sa'd, hoping that as chief of Aus, who had been their confederates, he would deal mercifully with them. On his side, Sa'd became determined that he would not let any ulterior consideration influence his judgment, which must conform to the will of God as he understood it. Before pronouncing his judgment, he secured the Holy Prophet's express promise to give full effect to it. All this could not have been mere chance. It was the Divine Will that the judgment should be left to Sa'd, and it was the Divine Will that moved Sa'd to pronounce the judgment that he did, which was in accord with Deuteronomy 20:10-14. It was also the Divine Will that this terrible judgment, which the treachery and rebellion of Banu Quraidhah had earned, should not be pronounced by the Holy Prophet himself, but that he should be bound to carry it through to the full.

The Holy Prophet directed that the able-bodied men of Banu Quraidhah should be separated from their women and children, and should be separately conducted to Medina. In the city they were lodged in separate houses and, under the direction of the Holy Prophet, were well looked after.

The attitude of the Jews towards the Holy Prophet and the Muslims had, from the beginning, been at the best suspicious and at the worst treacherous. Concerning the situation at the time of the investment of Medina by Quraish and their allies, E. Dermenghem has observed (*The Life of Mahomet*, p. 326):

> Quraish had allied themselves to the Bedouins and the Jews, and their formidable coalition was preparing to deal a decisive blow to Islam. The Banu Nadhir who had taken refuge at Khaibar incited their hosts against the new power that had risen threatening all anarchistic Arabia; they represented Muhammad as a tyrant waiting to put all the tribes into chains. The Bedouins of Tihama and Nejd joined Quraish in a body and the confederation had spies in the very heart of Medina amongst the Jews of Banu Quraidhah who desired, almost openly, the ruin of their burdensome ally.... The situation, if prolonged, might have become serious, the more so because Banu Quraidhah had allied themselves with the enemy.

Stanley Lane-Poole has observed (*Studies in a Mosque*, p. 68):

> Of the sentences on the three clans, that of exile, passed upon two of them, was clement enough. They were a turbulent set, always setting the people of Medina by the ears; and finally, a brawl followed by an insurrection resulted in the expulsion of one tribe; and insubordination, alliance with enemies and a suspicion of conspiracy against the Prophet's life, ended similarly for the second. Both tribes had violated the original treaty, and had endeavoured in every way to bring Muhammad and his religion to ridicule and destruction. The only question is whether their punishment was not too light. Of the third clan a fearful example was made, not by Muhammad, but by an arbiter appointed by themselves. When Quraish and their allies were besieging Medina and had well-nigh stormed the defences, this Jewish tribe entered into negotiations with the enemy, which were only circumvented by the diplomacy of the Prophet. When the besiegers had retired, Muhammad naturally demanded an explanation of the Jews. They resisted in their dogged way and were themselves besieged and compelled to surrender at discretion. Muhammad, however, consented to the appointing of a chief of a tribe allied to the Jews as the judge who should pronounce sentence upon them. This chief gave sentence that the men, in numbers some 600, should be killed, and the women and children enslaved; and the sentence was carried out. It was

a harsh, bloody sentence; but it must be remembered that the crime of these men was high treason against the State, during a time of siege; and one need not be surprised at the summary execution of a traitorous clan.

The next morning, the judgment of Sa'd bin Muaz was put into effect. The Holy Prophet directed that every sentenced person should be executed separately, and not within sight of others. When Huyay bin Akhtab, chief of Banu Nadhir, was being led to execution, observing the Holy Prophet, he said, 'Muhammad, I do not regret having opposed you, but the truth is that he who abandons God, is abandoned by God. No remedy is available against the decree of God. This is His command and His decree.'

When Ka'ab bin Asad, chief of Banu Quraidhah, was being conducted to the place of execution, the Holy Prophet urged him impliedly to the acceptance of Islam. He replied, 'Abu Qasim, I am held back from embracing Islam only by the consideration that if I were to do so, it might be said that I had been afraid of death. So let me die a Jew.'

Zubair bin Batia was a leading member of Banu Quraidhah, who had at one time done a favour to a Muslim, Thabet bin Qais, who pleaded with the Holy Prophet that Zubair may be spared, to which he agreed. Thabet carried the good news to Zubair. He said his life would be worth little to him while his wife and children were prisoners. Thabet went back to the Holy Prophet and mentioned to him what Zubair had said, whereupon he directed that Zubair's wife and children may be freed. When Thabet told Zubair of this further favour, he said, what would he and his wife and children subsist upon? Thabet again approached the Holy Prophet, who directed the restoration of his property to Zubair. When Thabet went to him with the news of this final concession, he inquired, 'How have our chief, Ka'ab bin Asad, and the chief of the Jews of Arabia, Huyay bin Akhtab fared?' Thabet told him that they had been executed, on which Zubair observed, 'When they have been executed, what shall I do with my life?'

Another Jew, Rifa'h, persuaded a Muslim lady to plead for his life with the Holy Prophet, who gave effect to her plea and directed that Rifa'h's life be spared. There were two or three other similar instances in which the Holy Prophet gave effect to a plea of mercy on behalf of a condemned person. In no single case did he reject such a plea. Someone reminded him that he had promised to give effect in full to the judgment of Sa'd bin Muaz, to which he replied that he was entitled to exercise the prerogative of mercy as the chief executive. This is an indication, that though he was bound to carry out Sa'd's judgment, his own inclination was towards mercy. Approximately 400 men of Banu Quraidhah were executed under the judgment of Sa'd bin Muaz and were given proper burial under the directions of the Holy Prophet.

The women and children of Banu Quraidhah were held prisoners in Medina. Some of them obtained their freedom by payment of ransom and some were freed by the Holy Prophet as a matter of grace. In the course of time, all of them became Muslims. The names of Atiyah Qurdhi, Abdur Rahman bin Zubair bin Bafia, Ka'ab bin Saleem and Muhammad bin Ka'ab, the last one a Muslim of note, are mentioned in this context by historians.

Though some Western writers like Stanley Lane-Poole and Margoliouth have not only justified the execution of Banu Quraidhah, but, in the words of Margoliouth, have pronounced it as inevitable and inescapable, yet several of them have criticised it in very harsh terms. For the benefit of such hostile critics, most of them Christians, and some of them Jews, a concrete instance might be cited from the Torah itself of the carrying into effect of the provisions in that behalf of Deuteronomy 20:10-14 (Numbers 31:6-12):

> And Moses sent them to the war a thousand of every tribe. . . and they warred against the Midianites, as the Lord commanded Moses; and they slew all the males, and they slew the kings of Midian, beside the rest of them that were slain; namely, Evi and Rekem and Zur, and Hur, and Raba, five kings of Midian; Balaam also the son of Beor they slew with the sword. And the children of Israel took all the women of Midian captive, and their little ones, and took the spoils of all their cattle, and all their flocks, and all their goods. And they burnt all their cities wherein they dwelt, and their goodly castles, with fire. And they took all the spoil, and all the prey, both of men and beasts. And they brought the captives and the prey, and the spoils unto Moses, and Eleazar the priest, and then to the congregation of the children of Israel, unto the camp at the plains of Moab, which are by Jordan near Jericho.

It has been mentioned that Sa'd bin Muaz, chief of Aus, had been wounded in one of the encounters during the siege of Medina by Quraish and their allies. After the lifting of the siege, the Holy Prophet had directed that he should be looked after in a tent in the courtyard of the mosque, where a Muslim lady of the name of Rafeidah, who was a trained nurse, was ministering to the wounded. Despite all her care, Sa'd's injury did not improve and the wound repeatedly burst open. It was in this condition that he was summoned to act as arbiter in the matter of Banu Quraidhah. In the discharge of this function, Sa'd had to endure considerable fatigue and hardship and his health deteriorated still further. In that condition he supplicated earnestly one night, 'Lord, Thou well knowest my eagerness to strive in the cause of Thy faith against the people who rejected Thy Prophet and expelled him from his home. Lord, I conceive that the armed struggle between Quraish and ourselves has come to an end. But if it is within Thy knowledge that there is to be still some further fighting with Quraish, I beg Thee to grant me enough time so that I might participate in such fighting. But if our fighting them has come to an end, I have no desire to live longer and do Thou permit me to die a martyr.' It is reported that the same night Sa'd's wound burst open and there was so much bleeding from it that some of the blood flowed out of the tent. Those who noticed it rushed into the tent and found that Sa'd was in extremity. He breathed his last shortly after.

The Holy Prophet was much grieved over Sa'd's death which was an irreplaceable loss for the Muslims. Sa'd had occupied the same position among Ansar which was occupied by Abu Bakr among Emigrants. His sincerity, his devotion, his sacrifices in the cause of Islam, and his love of the Holy Prophet were almost matchless. Every action and every movement of his demonstrated that the love of Islam and of the Holy Prophet was the nurture of his soul. As he was chief of his tribe, his example had been a great source of strength for Ansar. The Holy Prophet bore his great loss with his customary fortitude. He led the funeral prayer over him, helped to carry the bier to the graveyard, supervised the burial and returned only after the burial had been completed and he had prayed over the grave.

Later in the same year, an earthquake was felt in Medina, whereupon the Holy Prophet admonished the Muslims that earthquakes and other such natural manifestations should cause a Muslim to be alert in all respects and to concentrate his attention upon his relationship with God.

About the same time, the Holy Prophet fell from his horse and received injuries to his leg which necessitated his performing Salat in a sitting position.

By the end of the fifth year of the Hijra, the Muslims, having passed through all manner of trials and tribulations, and after suffering the extremes of distress and hardship, through the sheer grace of God became supreme in Medina, and therefore it might be said that at that time, a Muslim state had come into being. Islam has laid down only certain fundamental principles of statehood and has left the details to be worked out according to the needs and conditions of time, region, country and people.

The first fundamental principle is that there is perfect equality among people in matters of governance, and that authority for such governance is vested in the people, who should commit matters of administration into the hands of those best fitted to discharge them, as is said in the Holy Quran (4:59):

> Allah commands you to make over the trusts to those best fitted to discharge them and those who are entrusted with them should carry out their duties with equity and justice. Excellent indeed is that with which Allah admonishes you. Allah is All Hearing, All Seeing.

In this verse, governance has been described as a trust, and the implication is that the authority of governance is vested in the people who should entrust it to those most competent among them for the discharge of such trust. Those who are so trusted must discharge their trust equitably and justly. This is illustrated by a well known *hadith* comprised in the compilation of Muslim, in which it is narrated that Abu Dhar, one of the principal Companions of the Holy Prophet, having begged him to be appointed a governor, was told, 'Abu Dhar, you are a weak person; governance is a trust which, on the Day of Judgment, may prove to have been a source of humiliation and remorse, except in the case of a person who discharges all its obligations to the full.' In another *hadith* reported by Muslim it is narrated that the Holy Prophet said, 'I do not appoint to public office anyone who asks for it or is desirous of it.'

Another fundamental principle is that those entrusted with authority in public matters should exercise that authority in consultation with the people. For instance, among the characteristics of the believers it is mentioned, 'Those who hearken to their Lord, and observe Prayer and whose affairs are administered by mutual consultation, and who spend out of whatsoever We have bestowed upon them' (42:39). The Holy Prophet himself was directed: 'Take counsel with them in matters of administration, and when thou hast made up thy mind concerning a matter, put thy trust in Allah. Surely, Allah loves those who put their trust in Him' (3:160).

These are the two great and firm pillars on which an Islamic state is based. First, that the authority for governance is vested in the people, and that they should entrust that authority to those most competent among them for its discharge; and second, that he who is entrusted with such authority should discharge it equitably and with justice, in consultation with the people. Islam does not admit any hereditary right of governance, nor does it permit the exercise of public authority without consultation with the people. There is no room for dictatorship in Islam. Details with regard to the manner of electing or selecting the head of state, the procedure for consultation with the people or their representatives, the scope of such consultation and such like, are left to be worked out and established by the people according to their needs and circumstances in every age and in every region. There are many considerations that bear upon these matters into which it is not necessary, or even permissible, to enter in the course of a biography.

One further development that had now taken place was that Quraish ceased to be the principal centre of opposition to Islam in Arabia. Opposition had now become widespread throughout the country and the scope of the responsibilities of the Holy Prophet and the Muslims was correspondingly expanded. One consequence of the widening of the horizon in this matter was that the area of the authority of the Muslim state increased progressively and a large number of non-Muslims became subject to that authority. The basic direction in this context is (5:9):

> O ye who believe, be steadfast in the cause of Allah and be witnesses of justice to all concerned. Let not a people's hostility towards you incite you to act contrary to justice; adhere to justice in all situations, that is closest to righteousness. Be mindful of your duty to Allah; surely, Allah is aware of all that you do.

Any treaties and covenants made with, or pledges given to, any people, must be strictly adhered to: 'Fulfil every covenant, for you will be called to account for it' (17:35). So much is this obligation stressed and insisted upon that, though it is the duty of a Muslim state to assist Muslims in the matter of religion, this obligation is subject to any covenant or treaty entered into by a Muslim state with a non-Muslim state or people, as is said (8:37):

> You are under no obligation towards those who have believed but have not migrated, until they migrate. Nevertheless, if they seek your help in the matter of religion, it is incumbent on you to help them, except against a people between whom and yourselves there is a pact. Allah sees that which you do.

Concerning the non-Muslim subjects of a Muslim state, Bokhari has reported that the Holy Prophet said: 'He who kills any of those towards whom the Muslim state is under an obligation will be deprived of the breezes of heaven.' Abu Dawood has related that the Holy Prophet said: 'If a Muslim wrongs one towards whom the Islamic state has undertaken an obligation, or causes him loss, or requires from him that which is beyond his capacity, or takes from him something without his free consent, I shall demand justice for such non-Muslim against his Muslim wrong-doer on the Day of Judgment.' The Holy Quran goes further and prescribes: 'Allah does not forbid you to be benevolent and to act equitably towards those who have not fought you because of your religion, and who have not driven you forth from your homes. Surely, Allah loves those who are equitable' (60:9).

The sixth year of the Hijra was one of considerable activity. No important battle was fought, nor any great expedition undertaken. But small parties were constantly in motion, for the chastisement of hostile tribes, or the interception of caravans, or for the repulse of robbers and marauders. There were as many as seventeen such affairs during the year. They generally resulted in the dispersion of the enemy and the capture of flocks and herds; they also served to uphold the prestige of Islam.

In the very beginning of the year, the Holy Prophet received intimation of some hostile design on the part of the clan Qurta, a branch of Banu Bakr, who were settled at Dhariyyah in Nejd, seven days' journey from Medina. He despatched a light detachment of thirty mounted men under the command of Muhammad bin Maslamah Ansari to Nejd. Little opposition was encountered and the clan scattered, leaving their women and children behind. Muhammad bin Maslamah took no action against the women and children and, having captured a number of camels and goats, returned to Medina. On the way back, they captured one person on suspicion of hostility who did not disclose his identity to them. In fact, he was Thumamah bin Uthal of Yamamah, an influential chief of Banu Haneefah. He was bitterly hostile towards Islam and was always after slaying innocent Muslims. On one occasion, he conspired to kill an emissary of the Holy Prophet who had been sent to his part of the country. On another occasion he planned to kill the Holy Prophet himself. He realised, therefore, that if his captors came to know of his identity he would be severely dealt with. When the party arrived in Medina and Thumamah was brought before the Holy Prophet, he recognised him immediately and inquired from his captors whether they knew him. They confessed their ignorance and the Holy Prophet told them who he was. He directed that Thumamah should be well treated and sent him food from his own house.

The Holy Prophet gave orders that Thumamah should be confined in the mosque by being secured against a pillar of the mosque, so that he was able to watch the prayer services of the Muslims and all the other activities of the Holy Prophet and his Companions. Every morning the Holy Prophet went to him and inquired what did he have in mind. Thumamah replied, 'Muhammad, if you direct my execution, you would be justified as I have been guilty of grave offences against your people; but if you would extend benevolence to me, you would find me grateful. If you are willing to accept ransom, I am prepared to provide it.' On the third morning the Holy Prophet directed that Thumamah should be set free. As soon as he was released, he walked quickly out of the mosque, and those who were present imagined that he was returning home. But he went to a garden nearby, having washed and bathed, returned to the mosque and embraced Islam at the hands of the Holy Prophet. Thereafter he submitted, 'Messenger of Allah, there was a time when I entertained bitter enmity towards you and your faith and your city; but now you and your faith and your city are dearer to me than everything else.'

Sometime later, Thumamah submitted to the Holy Prophet, 'Messenger of Allah, when I was captured I was on my way to the Ka'aba for the performance of Umra. Now, what is your pleasure concerning me?' The Holy Prophet told him that he was free to proceed on his original errand, and gave him his blessings, and Thumamah left for Mecca. Having arrived in Mecca and performed the Umra he began to propagate Islam openly in Mecca. Quraish were outraged and seized him, and would have put an end to him but for the consideration that he was a chief of Yamamah and they had close commercial relations with Yamamah. So they rebuked him and let him go. When he was departing, he told Quraish that he would not let a grain of corn come to them from Yamamah unless the Holy Prophet permitted it. Arriving in Yamamah, he put his threat into effect and stopped the movement of the caravans of Quraish through Yamamah. As the greater part of the food supply of Mecca came from or through Yamamah, Quraish soon began to feel the pinch severely and they wrote to the Holy Prophet that, having regard to the kinship between them, he might be pleased to intervene and procure them relief from their distress. They followed this up by sending Abu Sufyan to Medina who described their distress to the Holy Prophet and sought his compassionate intervention, whereupon the Holy Prophet sent directions to Thumamah not to interfere with the movement of food supplies to Mecca, and the situation was thus relieved.

Thumamah continued the propagation of Islam zealously among his people and many of them were won over to Islam. Later, shortly after the death of the Holy Prophet when many of the Muslims in Yamamah turned away from Islam under the influence of Musaila-mah, the false claimant to Prophethood, Thumamah not only stood firm himself, but, through his devoted efforts, he held back many from submitting to Musailamah and helped them to adhere steadfastly to Islam. He rendered outstanding service to Islam during that crisis.

At one time Banu Tha'lbah, in their search for pasture, were tempted to advance beyond their usual limits in the direction of Medina. Herds of camels belonging to the Muslims had been sent out to graze in the same direction. They offered a tempting prize for a foray, and neighbouring tribes were suspected to be gathering for the purpose. Muhammad bin Maslamah was deputed by the Holy Prophet to visit the locality with ten followers and ascertain how matters stood. At Dhul Qassa, two or three days' distance from Medina, he was surrounded at night by overpowering numbers. After a short resistance, his men were all slain, and he himself was left for dead on the field. Someone who knew him, happening to pass that way, assisted him on his journey back to Medina. A body of forty well mounted fighters were despatched under Abu Obaida to chastise the offenders; but they had dispersed among the neighbouring heights, and beyond the capture of some flocks and household stuff, no reprisals were effected.

During the autumn of that year a well-freighted caravan from Mecca venturing to resume the sea-shore route to Syria was overpowered at 'Ees and was carried into Medina with a large store of silver and some of those who guarded it as prisoners. Among these was Abul Aas, son-in-law of the Holy Prophet. He was a nephew of Khadija and was a prosperous trader in Mecca. While declining to embrace Islam, he had equally resisted the bidding of Quraish to abandon his wife, Zainab, daughter of the Holy Prophet, and choose one of their daughters in her stead. 'I will not separate from my wife,' he said, 'neither do I desire any other woman from amongst your daughters.' The Holy Prophet much appreciated his faithfulness to Zainab. The attachment was mutual, for when the family migrated to Medina, Zainab remained behind at Mecca with her husband.

In the battle of Badr, Abul Aas had been amongst the captives, and when Quraish deputed men to ransom their prisoners, Zainab sent by their hands such property as she had for her husband's freedom. Among these things was a necklace which Khadija had given to her on her marriage. The Holy Prophet, seeing this touching memorial of Khadija, was deeply moved, and said to his Companions, 'If it seems right in your eyes, let my daughter's husband go free, and send these trinkets back.' All agreed, but as the condition of his freedom, the Holy Prophet required of Abul Aas that he should at once send Zainab to Medina. Accordingly, on his return to Mecca, he sent her away mounted on a camel-litter in charge of his brother Kinana. Certain of the baser sort, however, from amongst Quraish, went in pursuit, determined to bring her back. The first that appeared was Habbar, who struck her camel with his spear, and so affrighted Zainab as to bring on a miscarriage. Kinana at once made the camel sit down, and by the mere show of his bow and well-filled quiver, kept the pursuers at bay. Just then, Abu Sufyan came up and held parley with Kinana, 'Ye should not,' he said, 'have gone forth thus publicly, knowing the disaster we have so lately sustained at the hands of Muhammad. The open departure of his daughter would be regarded as proof of our weakness and humiliation. But it is no object of ours to keep back this woman from her father, or to retaliate our wrongs upon her. Return, therefore, for a little while to Mecca, and when this excitement shall have died away, then set out secretly.' His advice was followed, and some days after, Zainab, escorted by Zaid, who had been sent to fetch her, reached Medina in safety.

It was three or four years after this that Abul Aas was now again made prisoner with the caravan at 'Ees. As the party carrying him captive approached Medina, he contrived by night to have an interview with Zainab, who gave him the guarantee of her protection, upon which he rejoined the other prisoners. At morning Prayer she called aloud from her apartment that she had passed her word to Abul Aas. When prayers were ended, the Holy Prophet thus addressed the assembly; 'Ye have heard, as I have, the voice of my daughter. I call God to witness, that I knew nothing of her guarantee until this moment. But the pledge even of the least of us must needs be kept.' Thus saying, he retired to his daughter, and desired her to treat Abul Aas with honour, as a guest, but not to recognise him as her husband. Then sending for the captors of the caravan, he reminded them of his connection with Abul Aas, and said, 'If ye treat him well, and return his property unto him, it would be pleasing to me; but if not, the booty is yours which the Lord hath given unto your hands, and it is your right to keep it.' They all with one consent agreed to let the prisoner go free, and returned to him his property. This generosity, and the continued attachment of Zainab, so wrought on Abul Aas, that when he had adjusted his affairs at Mecca, he made profession of Islam and rejoined her at Medina. Their domestic happiness, however, was not of long duration, for Zainab died the following year from the illness caused by the attack of Habbar at Mecca.

About the same time Medina was early one morning startled by a cry of alarm from the adjoining height of Sal'a. The chieftain Oyeina, with a troop of Fezara horse, came down upon the plain of Ghaba, within a few miles of Medina, fell upon the camels of the Holy Prophet which were grazing there, drove them off, and having killed the keeper, carried off his wife. An Ansari, early on his way to the pasture lands, saw the marauding band and gave the alarm. A troop of horses were despatched at once in pursuit, and the Holy Prophet himself with some 600 men followed shortly after. The advance party hung daringly upon the rear of the marauders, slew several of them, and recovered half of the plundered camels. On the side of the Muslims only one man was killed. The Holy Prophet, with the main body, marched onwards as far as Dhu Qarad, in the direction of Khaibar; but by this time, the robbers were safe away in the desert. The wife of the keeper of the camels effected her escape on one of the plundered camels which she vowed to offer up as sacrifice of thanksgiving on reaching her home in safety. On mentioning her vow to the Holy Prophet, he rallied her on the ingratitude of seeking to slay the animal which had saved her life, and which was not hers to offer up. He bade her to go to her home in peace.

In the same year, Dihya was sent by the Holy Prophet on a mission to one of the governors of Syria. He was graciously received, and was presented with a dress of honour. On his way home, he was plundered of everything near Wadil Qura by the tribe of Judham. A neighbouring tribe, under treaty with the Holy Prophet, attacked the robbers, recovered the spoils, and restored his property to Dihya. On the news of the robbery reaching the Holy Prophet, he despatched Zaid with 500 men to chastise the delinquents. Marching by night and concealing themselves by day, they fell unexpectedly upon Judham, killed their leader and several others, and carried off some women and children, with all their herds and flocks. It so happened that the branch thus punished had, unknown to Zaid, just tendered submission to the Holy Prophet. Their chief hastened to Medina and appealed to the Holy Prophet against these proceedings and demanded justice. On the Holy Prophet repeatedly expressing his grief over the death of those who had been slain, the chief submitted that they were prepared to overlook their death as a result of misunderstanding, but that their prisoners should be released and their herds and flocks should be restored to them. The Holy Prophet acknowledged the justice of the demand and sent Ali to effect restoration. He met Zaid returning to Medina, and the prisoners and the booty were immediately surrendered to the chief.

Soon after, Abdul Rahman bin Auf was sent with 700 men on a second expedition to Dumatul Jandal, whence trouble was expected. He was first to gain over the people, if possible, and fight only in the last resort. But in no case, directed the Holy Prophet, shalt thou use deceit or perfidy, or kill any woman or child. On reaching Dumatul Jandal, Abdul Rahman summoned the tribes around to embrace Islam, and allowed them three days' grace. Within that period, Al-Asbagh, a Christian chief of Banu Kalb, gave his adherence, and many of the tribe followed his example. Others preferred to be tributaries, with the condition of being allowed to retain profession of the Christian faith. Abdul Rahman sent tidings of this success to the Holy Prophet, who in reply desired him to marry Tomadhir, daughter of the chief. Abdul Rahman accordingly married the lady, who bore him Abu Salamah, a famous jurist of after days.

It has been mentioned that a party of Banu Nadhir, after their exile, had settled down among their brethren at Khaibar. One of their leaders, Huyay bin Akhtab, had been executed along with Banu Quraidhah. But another of their leaders, Sallam bin Abu Huqaiq, generally known as Abu Rafe', was now the centre of their intrigues. He had taken a prominent part in the confederate force which had besieged Medina and was now busy in inciting Ghatafan and other tribes of Nejd to further depredations and aggression. Five men of Khazraj were appointed to carry out the execution of Abu Rafe', which they accomplished successfully. Abu Rafe"'s place among the Jews of Khaibar was taken by Usair bin Razam, who was not less bitterly opposed to Islam and the Muslims than Abu Rafe'. He now determined to carry into effect the designs of Abu Rafe' which he had not been able to accomplish. His very first action was to harangue the assembled Jews, informing them that he had determined upon certain new plans through which, with the help of Ghatafan and other tribes, he would accomplish the ruin of Islam and the Muslims. Thereafter, he started visiting Ghatafan and other tribes of Nejd and so provoked them that they began to prepare another expedition against Medina. When the Holy Prophet learnt of his activities, he sent Abdullah bin Rawaha with three Companions to Khaibar, to gather intelligence and return quickly. On their return they reported that what they had seen and heard left no doubt in their minds that the Jews were actively plotting against the Holy Prophet and the Muslims. About the same time, a non-Muslim, Kharajah bin Husail, happened to arrive in Medina from the direction of Khaibar and confirmed the report of Abdullah bin Rawaha. He said that he had left Usair making preparation to lead an attack against Medina. The Holy Prophet thereupon decided to make an effort to come to some understanding with Usair whereby all these conspiracies and alarums and excursions might be terminated and conditions of peace and security might be established. If Usair could be persuaded to abandon his mischievous activities directed against the Muslims, he could be acknowledged as the chief of Khaibar. With this in mind, he deputed Abdullah bin Rawaha and thirty Companions to proceed to Khaibar and to persuade Usair to come to Medina with a view of discussing such a possibility. When Abdullah's party arrived in Khaibar they called upon Usair to guarantee their security while they were in Khaibar; Usair agreed to do so on a mutual basis. During the conversation that ensued Abdullah explained that the Holy Prophet's purpose was to establish peace and security and to put an end to all fighting and hostility, and that the best way of achieving this was that he should himself proceed to Medina and talk directly to the Holy Prophet. If an understanding could be reached, the Holy Prophet would deal graciously with him and might recognise him as the chief of Khaibar. Usair expressed his approval of such a design and called together the leading personalities among the Jews of Khaibar for consultation. Most of them opposed the plan and in order to discourage Usair said that they did not expect that Muhammad would acknowledge him as chief of Khaibar. He told them that his own appraisal of the situation was that Muhammad was sick of the constant state of conflict and hostility and was anxious to put an end to it.

Thus Usair bin Razam agreed to accompany Abdullah bin Rawaha and his party to Medina and, on his side, selected an equal number of

Jews to accompany him to Medina. It is difficult to determine whether he had any secret design in his mind against Abdullah and his party, or whether he changed his mind after the two parties had set out from Khaibar on the journey to Medina. What happened is that when the parties arrived at Qarqarah, distant six miles from Khaibar, in the course of an apparently amicable conversation Usair stretched his hand towards the sword of Abdullah bin Unais Ansari who, apprehending mischief from him, spurred his mount forward and then veering round towards Usair called out to him, 'Enemy of God, have you determined upon treachery?' To which Usair made no reply. Abdullah repeated his question but Usair still remained silent and adopted an aggressive attitude. This was possibly a predetermined signal for the Jews to fall upon the Muslims and to destroy them. Swords were drawn on both sides and though the parties were equal in number and several of the Muslims were wounded, yet none of them was killed and they succeeded in disposing of all the Jews.

Abu Sufyan had since his frustrated flight from Medina after the siege felt greatly humiliated and thought that the best way of wiping out his disgrace would be to procure the assassination of the Holy Prophet through some device. He knew that the Holy Prophet went about freely in Medina, and spent the greater part of his day in the mosque or other places among his people, and that there was no one to guard him and that, therefore, anyone who had a murderous design against him could easily carry it into effect. He continued to brood over this and, having made up his mind, he one day incited a party of young men that one of them should carry out his design and thus rid the country of the source of all trouble. A few days later, a Bedouin youth came to Abu Sufyan and told him that he had come to know of his design and that he was prepared to carry it out if he was appointed for the purpose and was helped in achieving it. He said he was familiar with the route to Medina and that he had a sharp dagger which he knew how to conceal on his person so that no one would suspect that he was carrying it. He would, on finding a suitable opportunity, attack Muhammad, and having afflicted a mortal injury upon him, would escape and join some caravan so that the Muslims would not be able to trace him. Abu Sufyan approved of his design, provided him with a fast camel and needed provisions, and promised him a large reward on his return after accomplishing his mission. He warned him not to disclose his design to anyone.

This person travelling secretly by night arrived in Medina after six days, and finding that the Holy Prophet was at the time in the mosque of Bani Abdul Ashhal, immediately proceeded thither. As soon as the Holy Prophet perceived him among the people in the mosque, he said that this person was bent upon some mischief. Hearing this, he advanced rapidly towards the Holy Prophet but Usyad bin Hudhair, chief of Aus, seized him in his embrace, and in the struggle discovered the dagger which he had concealed on his person. When he had been overpowered and made secure the Holy Prophet asked him to tell him truly who he was and what was his purpose. He replied that he would disclose everything if his life was spared. He was assured that if he told the truth, he would be forgiven, whereupon he related the whole story from beginning to end and also mentioned what reward Abu Sufyan had promised him. He continued for some days in Medina and at the end voluntarily embraced Islam.

The Holy Prophet, having been alerted of Abu Sufyan's design, despatched Amr bin Umayya Dhamri and Salama bin Aslam to Mecca to gather whatever intelligence they could, and, if they found an opportunity to do away with Abu Sufyan, they might put an end to him. When they arrived in Mecca, their identity was discovered and they returned to Medina. On the way back, they encountered two Quraish spies and in the attempt to capture them one of them was killed in the scuffle and the other was brought captive to Medina.

These were dangerous times for the Muslims. Under the instigation of Quraish and the Jews, the whole country was aflame with enmity towards them. The enemies of Islam had, for the moment, abandoned any design of open attack against Medina but had adopted the policy of causing the utmost harm and damage to the Muslims by all secret and perfidious means. One of the links in this foul chain was the deceitful design of certain men of 'Ak and Urainah clans of Bedouins. Eight of them arrived in Medina and, professing love for and attachment to Islam, became Muslims. After some time, they represented to the Holy Prophet that the damp climate of Medina had upset their stomachs and spleens and that as they were not accustomed to city life and had lived in the open among animals they might be permitted to go and live somewhere outside Medina. The Holy Prophet told them to go and live among his herd of camels grazing in the plain south of Qaba, and drink of their milk. Following his advice, they soon recovered their strength, and suddenly, one day, attacked the keepers of the camels, and, having overpowered them, tortured them in diverse ways till they succumbed to the torment inflicted upon them. They then rounded up the camels and drove them away with them. One of the keepers, who had escaped, carried the tale of this tragedy to the Holy Prophet, whereupon a party of twenty was immediately despatched in their pursuit, who overtook them after they had traversed a short distance and, having secured them with ropes, brought them to the Holy Prophet, who in accordance with his practice, that in default of any revealed commandment with reference to any situation, he followed the Mosaic law, directed that they should be treated in the same way as they had treated their victims. The directions of the Mosaic law in this context may be gathered from the following: 'And if any mischief follow, then thou shalt give life for life, eye for eye, tooth for tooth, hand for hand, foot for foot, burning for burning, wound for wound, stripe for stripe' (Exodus, 21:23-5); and: 'If a man cause a blemish to his neighbour; as he hath done, so shall it be done to him; breach for breach, eye for eye, tooth for tooth: As he hath caused a blemish in a man, so shall it be done to him again' (Leviticus, 24:19-20). After this event, however, the Holy Prophet was vouchsafed the revelation: 'The recompense of an injury is a penalty in proportion thereto; but whoso forgives and effects a reform thereby has his reward with Allah' (42:41). Thereafter, as Bokhari has mentioned, the Holy Prophet urged benevolence and good treatment even of the enemy and utterly forbade mutilation.

Chapter 12

:Truce:

We now approach the most important event of the sixth year after the Hijra, which was pregnant with tremendous possibilities, and opened the way for the final triumph of Islam throughout Arabia. The Holy Prophet, and those who had emigrated with him, had not since seen their native city, or worshipped at the Holy House, or performed the Umra, which from childhood they had regarded as an essential part of their social and religious life. Since the change of the Qibla from Jerusalem to Mecca, the attention of the Holy Prophet and the Muslims had been concentrated on Mecca. They longed to revisit the scenes of their childhood and to perform the circuits of the Ka'aba. It so happened that about this time the Holy Prophet, peace be on him, saw in a vision that he was performing the circuits of the Ka'aba in the company of his followers. One of the four sacred months was approaching during which all fighting and conflict was, by established Arab custom, laid aside. The Holy Prophet communicated his vision to the Muslims and every one longed for its realisation. It foretold nothing of fighting or contest; the entrance was to be quiet and unopposed. If the Holy Prophet and the Uuslims approached at this time the Ka'aba in the peaceful garb of pilgrims, Quraish would be bound by every pledge of national faith to leave them unmolested. On the other hand, should Quraish oppose their entrance, the blame would rest with them; and even so, the strength of the pilgrim band would secure its safety. So soon as this was resolved upon, Emigrants and Ansar responded eagerly to the call, and made haste to prepare themselves for the journey. The Arab tribes around Medina who had entered into friendly relations with the Holy Prophet were also summoned, but few responded to the call.

When the arrangements for the journey were completed, the Holy Prophet mounted his camel, Qaswa, and led the cavalcade of 1,500 pilgrims to Dhul Haleefah, distant six miles from Medina and the first stage on the road to Mecca. Here a halt was made and the Holy Prophet directed that all of them should assume the pilgrims' garb and called out the Talbeeh ('Here am I, O Lord! Here am I!'). The sacrificial animals, seventy camels, were then set apart, ornaments were hung about their necks and a mark was affixed on their right sides. The Holy Prophet despatched a scout, Busr bin Sufyan of

Khuzaa, to proceed to Mecca and return with intelligence regarding the attitude of Quraish. A troop of twenty horse under the command of Abbad bin Bishr was directed to march in advance of the main body to give notice of danger. The pilgrims moved forward by ordinary stages. They carried no arms but such as are permitted by custom to a traveller, namely a sheathed sword, a bow and well-filled quiver. On this journey the Holy Prophet, peace be on him, was accompanied by his wife, Um Salama.

Tidings of the Holy Prophet's approach soon reached Mecca; and, notwithstanding the pious object and unwarlike attitude of the pilgrims, Quraish were greatly excited. Joined by the surrounding tribes, they were quickly under arms, and took up ground on the Medina road, resolved to perish rather than permit the Muslims to enter. A body of 200 horse, under Khalid and Ikramah bin Abu Jahl, was pushed forward in advance.

The Muslims had nearly reached Osfan, the second stage from Mecca, when the scout returned with the intelligence that Quraish were encamped at Dhu Towa, clothed in panthers' skins. Their wives and little ones were with them, and they had sworn to die rather than let the Muslims pass. Shortly after the Meccan cavalry came in sight, and the Muslim horse went forward to hold them in check. Further advance on the high road was now impossible, so the Holy Prophet called a halt and, having procured a guide, turned to the right by a route safe from the enemies' horses and after a fatiguing march through devious and rugged pathways reached Hudaibiyya, an open space on the verge of the sacred territory encircling Mecca. Here his camel stopped and, planting her forelegs firmly on the ground, refused to stir another step. 'She is weary,' said the people as they urged her forward. 'Nay,' observed the Holy Prophet, 'Qaswa is not weary, but the same hand restraineth her as aforetime held back the Elephant' – alluding to the invasion of Abraha. 'By the Lord,' he continued, 'no request of Quraish this day, for the honour of the Holy House, shall be denied by me.' He then urged his camel forward and it obeyed his gesture. He directed her to the extreme end of the open space and there alighted near some wells. It was, however, found that they were choked with sand and there was little or no water in them. The Holy Prophet took an arrow from his quiver and asked one of his followers to descend with it into a well and scrape away the obstructing sand. Abundance of water soon accumulated. The same night there was plentiful rain and all anxiety with regard to the supply of water was removed. On this the Holy Prophet observed that some of his followers had welcomed the morning with strengthened faith, and that others had rendered their faith doubtful. He who had said that God had sent down rain, by His grace and mercy, had adhered firmly to the reality of faith, but he who said that rain had descended under the

influence of such and such a planet affirmed his belief in the planet but
denied God. He thus instilled into the minds of his followers the
verity that though there was a system of cause and effect behind all
phenomena, yet faith in the Unity of God demanded that a believer
should overlook the intervening causes and sources and fix his
attention upon God Who is the Cause of all causes.

The road from Hudaibiyya led by a circuitous route to lower
Mecca. Quraish no sooner learned that the pilgrims had taken this
direction, than they fell back on the city for its defence, and began
sending deputations to ascertain the real intentions of the Muslims.
Hudaibiyya being only nine miles distant, the communications were
rapid and frequent. Budail bin Warqa, a chief of Khuzaa, a
neighbouring tribe, with a party of his people, was the first to arrive.
He acquainted the Holy Prophet with the excited state of Quraish, and
their resolve not to let the Muslims enter the city at any cost. The
Holy Prophet explained: 'We have not come to fight. Our only
purpose is to perform Umra. I regret that Quraish still entertain
warlike designs. I am even ready that they should stop fighting with
me and leave me free to deal with the others. If I am wiped out,
Quraish will have no further worry about me, but if God bestows
upon me victory over them and my faith becomes supreme, the
Meccans should have no hesitation in accepting me. However, if they
do not agree and insist upon continuation of war, then by Him in
Whose hands is my life, I shall not withdraw from this contest till I
lay down my life in this cause, or God bestows victory upon me.'
Budail was deeply moved by the Holy Prophet's words, and said that
if he was granted some time, he would go back to Mecca and try to
bring about an agreement. The Holy Prophet agreed and Budail and
his party returned to Mecca.

Arriving in Mecca Budail told Quraish that he had met the Holy
Prophet who had made a suggestion which he would like to mention
to them. On this some of the unduly excited and irresponsible of
Quraish declared that they were not prepared to listen to anything
from that person; but the serious-minded of them wished to hear what
Budail had to say. After listening to him, Urwah bin Masood, an
influential chief of Thaqeef, who happened to be in Mecca, stood up
and after obtaining the affirmation of Quraish that they had full trust
in him, said, 'In my opinion, Muhammad has made a good suggestion
and I think you should accept it. If you will let me, I would go to him
and try to carry the matter further.'

Having been encouraged by Quraish, Urwah came to the Holy
Prophet, who repeated to him what he had told Budail. Urwah was in
principle in agreement, but as an emissary of Quraish, he replied to
the Holy Prophet, 'Muhammad, if it comes to fighting and you
destroy your own people, you will be the first among the Arabs to

perpetrate such a grave wrong, but if Quraish overcome you all those who are with you will soon desert you.' At this, Abu Bakr started up and warmly resented the imputation. Urwah, not heeding him, became still more earnest in his speech and, according to the familiar Badawi custom, stretched forth his hand to take hold of the Holy Prophet's beard. 'Back!' cried a bystander, striking his arm. 'Hold thy hands from off the Prophet of God.' 'Who is this?' asked Urwah, surprised at the interposition of a red-haired ungainly youth whom he could not identify as he was wearing a helmet. 'It is thy nephew's son, Mughira bin Shu'bah. O ungrateful one,' he exclaimed, 'it is but as yesterday that I redeemed thy life.' These and other scenes at the interview struck Urwah with a deep sense of reverence and devotion of the Muslims towards the Holy Prophet; and this he endeavoured to impress upon Quraish when he carried back to them a message resembling that taken by Budail. But Quraish were firm. Whatever his intentions, the Prophet should not approach the city with any show of force, and thus humble them in the eyes of all Arabia. 'Tell him,' they said, 'that this year he must go back; but in the year following he may come, and having entered Mecca perform Umra.' Urwah told them, 'I have travelled much and have had the opportunity of being present before Caesar, Chosroes and Najashi, but I have not observed any one of them being accorded such honour and respect as I have witnessed the followers of Muhammad according him. My advice is that his suggestion is just and fair and you should accept it.'

Having heard Urwah's discourse, Halees bin Alqamah, a chief of Bani Kananah, offered to go and try to find a way of settlement. When the Holy Prophet saw him approaching from a distance, he said to his Companions, 'The person who is now coming to us belongs to a tribe who are impressed by a display of sacrificial animals. So collect your sacrificial animals and bring them forward so that he should realise for what purpose we have come.' Accordingly they drove their animals with shouts of 'God is Great' and brought them in front of the Quraish emissary. Witnessing this spectacle, he exclaimed 'Glory be to God, these people are pilgrims and they cannot be prevented from performing the circuits of the Ka'aba.' So he returned to Quraish and told them that he had seen the sacrificial animals of the Muslims which had convinced him that their only purpose was to perform Umra, and they should not be obstructed in the performance of this rite. But Quraish refused to listen to him, saying, 'Thou art a simple Arab of the desert, and knowest not the devices of other men.' Halees was enraged at this slight and swore that, if they continued to oppose the advance of Muhammad, he would retire with all his men. The threat alarmed Quraish. 'Have patience for a little while,' they said, 'until we can make such terms as are needful for our security.'

In the meantime, the Holy Prophet felt that some intelligent person

should be sent to Quraish who might put the Muslims' point of view
to them wisely and sympathetically. For this purpose he chose
Kharash bin Umayya of Khuzaa and provided him with one of his
own camels. When he arrived in Mecca the younger section of
Quraish were much excited and Ikramah bin Abu Jahl attacked his
camel and wounded it, and even threatened his life. But the older
section intervened and he returned to the Islamic camp. Not content
with this demonstration, a party of about fifty men was despatched by
Quraish to Hudaibiyya with instructions to watch around the Islamic
camp and to take advantage of any opportunity of inflicting damage
upon the Muslims. The Muslims, were, however, on the alert and the
whole party of Quraish was taken captive. But the Holy Prophet
directed that they should be released so that the pending negotiations
should not be disrupted. This incident is referred to in the Holy
Quran as follows: 'He it is Who held back their hands from you and
held back your hands from them in the Valley of Mecca, after He had
granted you victory over them' (48:25).

Thereafter the Holy Prophet thought of sending someone who
belonged to Mecca and was connected with a respectable family of
Quraish. He desired Umar to go as his emissary. Umar excused
himself on account of the personal enmity of Quraish towards him,
and also on the ground that he had no influential relative in the city
who could shield him from danger. He submitted that Uthman, who
belonged to one of the most powerful families in Mecca, would be a
fitter envoy. Uthman consented and the Holy Prophet provided him
with a written statement addressed to the leaders of Quraish in which
he explained his purpose and assured Quraish that they only intended
to perform Umra in peace, and having offered their sacrifices they
would return to Medina. He also instructed Uthman to try to make
contact with the poor Muslims in Mecca and to reassure them that
God would soon open some way for them and that they should
continue steadfast.

On entering the city, Uthman received the protection of a cousin,
and went straightway to Abu Sufyan and the other chiefs. 'We come,'
he told them, 'to visit the Holy House, and to honour it, and to
perform worship there. We have brought sacrificial animals with us
and after slaying them we shall depart in peace.' In confirmation he
produced the writing that the Holy Prophet had furnished him, which
was inspected with keen interest by the chiefs, but they adhered to
their resolve that the Muslims should not enter Mecca that year.
When Uthman sought to persuade them, they told him that he could,
if he chose, visit the Ka'aba and perform the circuits, but that they had
sworn that this year the Muslims could not enter the precincts of their
city. Uthman declined their offer to him and started to make ready to
return to the Muslim camp. A section of Quraish, thinking that they

might thereby obtain better terms, detained Uthman and his companions in Mecca. As his return was delayed, a rumour spread among the Muslims that the Meccans had murdered Uthman. Anxiety and alarm overspread the camp. The Holy Prophet himself began to suspect treachery; taking his stand under the shade of an acacia tree, and surrounded by the whole body of the pilgrims, he required a pledge from them of faithful service, and that they would stand by Uthman to the death. Everyone rushed forward enthusiastically to take the pledge. When all had taken the solemn oath, striking each one the palm of his hand on that of the Holy Prophet, he himself struck his own right hand upon his left, observing, 'This is the hand of Uthman; for if he had been here, he would not have lagged behind anyone in making this holy bargain, but he is at the time occupied with the work of God and His Messenger.' This pledge is known as the Covenant of the Pleasure of God. It is mentioned in the Holy Quran in the words: 'Allah was indeed well pleased with the believers when they swore allegiance to thee under the Tree, and He appreciated the surge of faith in their hearts and sent down tranquillity on them, and rewarded them with a victory near at hand' (48:19).

When Quraish learnt of this pledge, they became apprehensive and not only let Uthman and his companions depart, but determined to come to terms with the Muslims on condition that they should return to Medina on this occasion and perform Umra freely next year. On the other side, as the Holy Prophet had from the beginning been determined that he would not deny any request of Quraish for the honour of the Holy House, the prospects of an agreement began to be hopeful.

After some further interchange of messages Quraish deputed Suhail bin Amr, one of their leading chiefs, and other representatives with power to conclude a treaty of peace. When the Holy Prophet saw Suhail, he observed, 'There comes Suhail; now, if God so wills, the affair would be resolved.' (The root of the word Suhail is *sahl*, meaning easy.) When Suhail arrived with his companions, he said, 'We are ready to come to a settlement.' The Holy Prophet, peace be on him, said that he too was ready and summoned Ali to act as the scribe of the treaty, the purport of which was understood between the two sides, and the details of which would be put into shape during the writing of it. When Ali arrived, the Holy Prophet started dictating, and told him to write, 'In the name of Allah, Ar-Rahman, Ar-Rahim', to which Suhail immediately demurred, saying, 'We have no knowledge of Rahman; begin as is the Arab custom with: In Thy name, O Allah.' The Muslims were excited and insisted that the opening words should be as the Holy Prophet had dictated, but he told them there was no harm in adopting the suggestion of Suhail. The dictation proceeded: 'These are the conditions of peace between Muhammad the Messenger of God and. . .', 'Stop again,' interposed Suhail. 'If thou art what thou sayest, we would not have taken up arms against thee. Write, as the custom is, thine own name and thy father's name.' 'Write, then,' continued the Holy Prophet, 'between Muhammad son of Abdullah, and Suhail son of Amr,' whereupon Ali protested that having already inscribed the words Messenger of Allah, he felt it would be a sacrilege to rub out those words. The Holy Prophet thereupon himself rubbed out those words and the writing proceeded as Suhail had desired. The terms of the treaty were: 'War shall be suspended between Quraish and the Muslims for ten years. Whosoever wisheth to join Muhammad, or enter into treaty with him, shall have liberty to do so; and likewise, whosoever wisheth to join Quraish, or enter into treaty with them. If a man from among Quraish goeth over to Muhammad without the permission of his guardian, he shall be sent back to his guardian; but should any of the followers of Muhammad return to Quraish, they shall not be sent back. Muham- mad shall retire this year without entering the City. In the coming year, Muhammad may visit Mecca, he and his followers, for three days, during which Quraish shall retire and leave the City to them. But they may not enter it with any weapons, save those of the traveller, namely, to each a sheathed sword.'

While the treaty was being inscribed Suhail's son, Abu Jandal, wearing handcuffs and chains and bearing marks of injuries all over his body, staggered into the Muslim camp and told the Muslims that he had embraced Islam and was being kept in durance and tortured, as they could see from his chains and injuries. He begged that he should not be returned to Quraish as he would not be able to survive further torment. On his side Suhail demanded that he should be handed over into his custody. The Holy Prophet was deeply moved by the condition of Abu Jandal and pleaded with Suhail to let Abu Jandal remain with the Muslims, but despite the repeated pleas of the Holy Prophet, Suhail was adamant and his claim was admitted. As he was dragged away, the Holy Prophet said to Abu Jandal, 'Have patience and put thy trust in the Lord. He will work out for thee, and for others likeminded with thee, a way of deliverance. We are unable to help thee, as we have entered into an agreement with the Meccans, and we cannot go against our word.'

The Muslims were much agitated over this incident and Umar, being unable to restrain himself, approached the Holy Prophet and inquired, 'Are you not the Messenger of Allah?' To which he replied, 'Certainly.' Then Umar asked, 'Are we not based upon truth, and our enemies on falsehood?' To which the Holy Prophet replied, 'That is so.' 'Then why should we submit to such humiliation in the matter of our faith?' The Holy Prophet pointed out, 'Umar, I am the Messenger of Allah, and know what He desires. I cannot go against it, and He alone is my Helper.' Umar was still not satisfied and asked: 'Did you not tell us that we would perform the circuit of the House?' To which the Holy Prophet rejoined, 'Indeed I did, but did I also say that it would happen this very year?' Umar confessed that such had not been the case, on which the Holy Prophet counselled him, 'Then wait; you will, God willing, certainly enter Mecca and perform the circuit of the Ka'aba.' Still excited, Umar approached Abu Bakr and had a similar exchange with him. Abu Bakr admonished him, 'Umar, hold yourself in check, and do not let your grip on the stirrup of the Messenger of Allah be loosened, for by God, he to whom we have sworn allegiance is certainly true.' Umar subsequently confessed that, in his momentary excitement, he said all this to the Holy Prophet and to Abu Bakr, but was soon overtaken by remorse and sought to wash out this stain of weakness through prayer, and fasts and almsgiving and the freeing of slaves.

The inscribing of the treaty was completed and it was attested, on behalf of the Muslims, by Abu Bakr, Uthman, Abdul Rahman bin Auf, S'ad bin Abi Waqqas, and Abu Obaida. A copy was handed to Suhail bin Amr who returned with it to Mecca. The original was retained by the Holy Prophet.

After Suhail had departed, the Holy Prophet directed his Companions to slaughter their sacrificial animals, to have their heads shaved or close-cropped, and to prepare for the return journey to Medina. They were very gloomy over what they considered were the humiliating terms of the treaty and in their perplexity they paid no attention to the Holy Prophet's direction, though he repeated it two or three times, as if they had not even heard him. The Holy Prophet took their inaction to heart and retreated into his tent. Um Salama, who had witnessed all this from inside the tent, and who had noticed the signs of concern on his countenance, submitted, 'Messenger of Allah, do not be grieved. Your Companions are not disobedient, but are overborne by sorrow at the unequal terms of the treaty. I would venture to suggest that you need say nothing to them, but should slaughter your sacrificial animals and have your head shaved, so that, following your example, your Companions may do likewise.' The Holy Prophet approved of the suggestion and, emerging from his tent, proceeded to put it into effect. As the Muslims saw him thus occupied, they were jolted out of their mental lethargy and immediately started following his example which, thus, proved much more effective than his words.

These rites having been performed and the stay of the Muslims at Hudaibiyya having extended to nearly twenty days, the Holy Prophet directed the start of the march back to Medina. When the cavalcade arrived at Kara'l Ghamim, near Osfan, and had made camp for the night and settled down, the Holy Prophet summoned them and told them that a Sura had been revealed to him which was dearer to him than all else in the world. This Sura (48:2-4 and 28) comprised the tidings:

> Surely, We have granted thee a clear victory, so that Allah may open the way to cover up all thy shortcomings, past and future, and that He may complete His favour unto thee, and may guide thee along the right path for success. Surely, Allah will help thee with a mighty help. . . . Allah has in truth completely fulfilled for His Messenger the vision that He had vouchsafed him, namely, that you will surely enter the Sacred Mosque, if Allah so wills, in security, with your heads shaven or close-cropped and having no fear.

Umar and the Companions of the Holy Prophet were still much perplexed. Umar has related: 'During the course of the journey on the return from Hudaibiyya, I approached the Holy Prophet and accosted him, but he did not respond. I tried three times, but he remained silent. I was much grieved over his silence and admonished myself that the Holy Prophet's silence was an indication that I had ruined my soul. I withdrew myself from my fellows and was overcome by the fear that I might be condemned by God Almighty through some revelation vouchsafed to the Holy Prophet. While I was thus perplexed I heard someone call: "The Holy Prophet summons Umar bin Khattab." I imagined that my fear was about to be confirmed, and I hastened to the Holy Prophet and, having greeted him, sat down next to him. He told me that a Sura had just been revealed to him which was dearer to him than everything else in the world, and he then recited some verses of Sura Fateh. I submitted, "Messenger of Allah, is this treaty truly the victory of Islam?" He responded, "Most certainly this is a victory for us." '

On learning that some of the Companions were wondering whether their apparent frustration at Hudaibiyya was indeed a victory, the Holy Prophet admonished them, 'If you will reflect, this Truce is indeed a great victory for us. Quraish, who were committed to hostilities against us, have agreed to put an end to them and have made a covenant of peace with us. They have promised to open the gates of Mecca to us next year. We are returning in peace and security, safeguarded against the mischief of the Meccans and breathing the fragrance of further victories. Thus, this is a great victory. Have you forgotten Uhud and Ahzab when Quraish invaded you, and the earth, despite its vast expanse, was straitened for you, and your eyes became distracted, and your hearts rose up to your throats? Today the same Quraish have made a treaty of peace with you.' Upon this the Companions submitted, 'Messenger of Allah, we now understand and realise the truth. Our vision is limited, and we do not see as far as you are able to see. We now realise that this treaty is indeed a great victory for us.' Thereafter, the Holy Prophet and his company returned safely to Medina.

Sir William Muir's appraisal of the Treaty of Hudaibiyya is expressed thus (*Life of Muhammad*, p. 360):

> The people, led by the Vision to anticipate an unopposed visit to the Ka'aba, were crestfallen at the abortive result of their long journey. But, in truth, a great step had been gained by Muhammad. His political status, as an equal and independent Power, was acknowledged by the Treaty: The ten years' truce would afford opportunity and time for the new religion to expand, and to force its claims upon the conviction of Quraish; while conquest, material as well as spiritual, might be pursued on every other side. The stipulation that no one under the protection of a guardian should leave Quraish without his guardian's consent, though unpopular at Medina, was in accordance with the principles of Arabian society; and the Prophet had sufficient confidence in the loyalty of his own people and the superior attraction of Islam, to fear no ill effect from the counter clause that none should be delivered up who might desert his standard. Above all, it was a great and manifest success that free permission was conceded to visit Mecca in the following year, and for three days occupy the city undisturbed.

A short while after some Muslim women managed to escape from Mecca and arrived in Medina. The first of these was Um Kulthum, daughter of a pagan chief, Uqbah bin Abi Mueet, who had perished at Badr. On her mother's side she was closely related to Uthman bin Affan. She had the courage and endurance to travel from Mecca to Medina on foot, and on arrival at Medina she presented herself before the Holy Prophet and announced her acceptance of Islam. She was soon followed by her two brothers who claimed that she be handed over to them. They urged that though the words of the treaty specifically mentioned that every male *(rajul)* from among Quraish who might go over to the Holy Prophet must be returned to them, the purport of the treaty was general and applied to both men and women. In opposition to them Um Kulthum relied both on the language of the treaty and on the consideration that women were weak and occupied a subordinate position to men and that therefore returning a woman who had embraced Islam to Quraish would amount to imposing spiritual death upon her. She therefore urged that the exemption of women from the operation of the treaty was not only in accord with its language, but was reasonable, just and necessary. The Holy Prophet pronounced in favour of Um Kulthum and rejected the claim of her brothers. In this context, it must be remembered that Suhail bin Amr, envoy of Quraish at Hudaibiyya, had minutely scrutinised every word of the treaty before he agreed to it. Indeed, the terms of the treaty were expressed in the language proposed by him. The literal translation of this particular clause of the treaty, as reported by Bokhari, is: 'No one of our men, though he may belong to thy faith, shall come to thee, but that thou shalt be bound to return him to us.' It is thus clear that this clause of the treaty was specifically confined to men. This is easily understandable, as neither side contemplated that a woman would have the opportunity and the courage and the endurance to escape from Mecca to Medina and declare herself a Muslim. Another very strong factor in support of the position adopted by the Holy Prophet was that Quraish at no time raised the objection that in refusing to return women back to the custody of Quraish the Holy Prophet had been guilty of a breach of the terms of the treaty. Besides, it is a well recognised principle that a party making a claim under a treaty or engagement must establish its claim beyond doubt.

Some time later a young man, Abu Baseer Utbah bin Usyad Thaqafi, who was a resident of Mecca and was a confederate of Banu Zuhrah, embraced Islam and having escaped from Mecca arrived in Medina. Quraish sent after him two emissaries to Medina with the request that he should be returned to them. The Holy Prophet sent for Abu Baseer and told him to go back to Mecca. Abu Baseer urged that he was a Muslim, that he would be persecuted in Mecca and that Quraish would seek to force him to renounce Islam. The Holy Prophet said to him, 'We are under compulsion by virtue of the treaty that we have entered into, that we cannot permit you to remain with us. If you will be steadfast, seeking the pleasure of Allah, He will open some way for you. But we must conform to the terms of the treaty and you must go back to Mecca.' Abu Baseer, with great reluctance, started for Mecca with the emissaries of Quraish, terrified that he would be severely tormented by Quraish in order to force him to renounce Islam. When the party arrived at Dhul Haleefah, a few miles from Medina, he found an opportunity of doing away with the principal emissary of Quraish, and would have disposed of the other one also, but he escaped and arrived back at Medina ahead of Abu Baseer. He went straight to the mosque, where the Holy Prophet then was, and, in a terrified voice, blurted out, 'My companion has been killed and I too am in danger of my life.' The Holy Prophet sought to comfort him, and in the meantime Abu Baseer also arrived and submitted, 'Messenger of Allah, you returned me to Quraish and thus fulfilled your obligation, but God has delivered me from them and you are no longer responsible for me.' Upon this the Holy Prophet exclaimed, 'Woe unto his mother, he is likely to set ablaze the flames of war. Would that there were someone to restrain him.' From these words Abu Baseer realised that the Holy Prophet would, in any event, send him back to Mecca. So he slipped away quietly, and instead of returning to Mecca took up his position at Siefal Bahr, by the sea-shore on the caravan route to Syria. When this became known in Mecca, Abu Jandal and other young men who were convinced of the truth of Islam but dared not profess it openly in Mecca, gradually managed to slip out of Mecca and joined Abu Baseer, who was soon surrounded by more than seventy followers, all desperate as himself. They were now on their own and were not subject to the authority either of Quraish or of the Holy Prophet. They began to waylay every caravan from Mecca and spared no one. This confronted Quraish with a difficult and dangerous situation. They were at length so harassed by the activities of this group that they solicited the interference of the Holy Prophet, and, on condition that their activities were restrained, waived their right to have them delivered up as deserters. The Holy Prophet acceded to their request and wrote to Abu Baseer and Abu Jandal that as Quraish had voluntarily waived the relevant clause of the treaty, they should now go to Medina. When the Holy Prophet's emissary arrived in Siefal Bahr, Abu Baseer, who had been ill, was in extremity. He received the Holy Prophet's letter with great reverence and breathed his last while holding it in his hand. Abu Jandal and the rest of the group buried Abu Baseer in Siefal Bahr and then made their sorrowful way to Medina. It is worthy of observation that if Abu Baseer, on leaving Mecca, had not gone to Medina at all and had proceeded to Siefal Bahr, as he eventually did, Quraish could not have requested the Holy Prophet to direct him to return to Mecca, as his case would not have fallen within the terms of the Truce.

The Truce of Hudaibiyya was one of the most outstanding events in the life of the Holy Prophet. With it was terminated the struggle between him and Quraish which had extended over nineteen years, and had, after the Migration, assumed the character of an armed conflict. By virtue of the Truce, peace had at last been established, at least between Quraish and the Holy Prophet, and the major difficulty in the way of peaceful propagation of Islam had been removed. Thereafter, Islam began to spread rapidly in the greater part of Arabia. Some estimate of the rate of this progress might be made on the basis of the number of Muslims who were present with the Holy Prophet at Hudaibiyya, which was just short of 1,500, and the number that accompanied him two years later on the occasion of the Fall of Mecca, which was 10,000. This is eloquent testimony that the attraction and superiority of Islam lie in its spiritual power and not in armed conflict. The extreme anxiety of the Holy Prophet to secure a truce at Hudaibiyya and his acceptance of the obviously unequal terms of the treaty confirm his own commitment to peace and orderliness and his aversion to armed conflict.

The Holy Prophet, peace be on him, had now been largely set free to devote the greater part of his attention to the discharge of his major responsibility, which was to convey the universal message of Islam as widely as possible. He was commanded, 'O Messenger, proclaim widely that which has been sent down to thee from thy Lord; for if thou do it not, thou wilt not have conveyed His Message at all. Allah will safeguard thee against harm by the people' (5:68). This obligation was not confined to the Holy Prophet himself, but was laid upon the whole body of believers; as would appear from: 'You are the best people for you have been raised for the benefit of mankind; it is your duty to enjoin good, forbid evil and have firm faith in Allah' (3:111); and: 'Let there be from among you a party whose business it should be to invite to goodness, to enjoin equity and to forbid evil. It is they who shall prosper' (3:105). This obligation has to be discharged prudently and wisely, as is said: 'Call unto the way of thy Lord with wisdom and goodly exhortation, and contend with them on the basis of that which is best' (16:126). There is to be no compulsion whatever: 'There shall be no compulsion in religion, for guidance and error have been clearly distinguished' (2:257), and: 'Proclaim: This is the truth from your Lord; then let him who will, believe, and let him who will, disbelieve' (18:30).

The Divine Message that was committed to the Holy Prophet is meant for the whole of mankind: 'Proclaim, O Prophet: O mankind, verily I am Allah's Messenger to you all. To Him belongs the Kingdom of the heavens and the earth' (7:159).

Bokhari relates that the Holy Prophet said: 'I have been bestowed five bounties which distinguish me from previous Prophets. I have been helped with far-reaching prestige; the whole earth has been sanctified for me as a place of worship; the spoils of war have been made lawful for me; I have been permitted to intercede for people; all previous Prophets were raised for their respective people, and I have been raised for the whole of mankind.'

The law of Islam is universal, permanent and irrevocable; as is said: 'This day have I perfected your religion for your benefit, and have completed My favour unto you, and have chosen for you Islam as your faith' (5:4). It is narrated by Bokhari that on one occasion, some Jews said to Umar, with reference to this verse, 'Had this verse been revealed to us, we would have appointed the day of its revelation as a festival.' Umar replied, 'God Himself has appointed that day as a festival for us, for this verse was revealed to the Holy Prophet on the day of pilgrimage at Arafat, the following day being the Festival of Sacrifice.' Muslim has related that the Holy Prophet said, 'I am the last Prophet and my mosque is the last mosque,' meaning, that there would be no Prophet after him who might abrogate his Prophethood, nor would there be set up any place of worship, in which a new form of worship might be instituted.

As the Truce of Hudaibiyya had procured some respite for the Holy Prophet, therefore, soon after his return to Medina, he decided to address invitations to the rulers of countries in the proximity of Arabia in all directions to accept Islam. When he mentioned this project to his Companions and sought their counsel, he was advised that temporal rulers took no account of any communication addressed to them unless it bore the seal of the person sending the communication. Thereupon, the Holy Prophet had a silver signet prepared, bearing the words 'Muhammad, Messenger of Allah' so arranged that Allah was at the top, Messenger in the middle and Muhammad last. This signet was thereafter worn by the Holy Prophet till his death; it was then worn by Abu Bakr during the period of his Khalifat, and after him by Umar, and after him by Uthman, the Second and Third Successors of the Holy Prophet. It slipped off the finger of Uthman when he was sitting on the edge of a well called Arees and could not be recovered despite the utmost efforts to do so.

The Holy Prophet's invitations were sent to Heraclius, the Byzantine Emperor, the Iranian Emperor, the Viceroy of Egypt, the Chief of Yamamah, the Emperor of Abyssinia, the Governor of Ghassan, the Viceroy of Yemen and the Governor of Bahrain. They were not all despatched at one time, but were spread over a period of a few weeks. The very first one was addressed to Heraclius.

Ever since the Holy Prophet had received the Divine Call the Byzantine and Persian empires had been waging with each other a ceaseless deadly warfare. Until the year 621, unvarying success attended the Persians' arms. Syria, Egypt, and Asia Minor were overrun. Constantinople itself was threatened. At last Heraclius, the Byzantine Emperor, took matters seriously in hand and, shortly after the Holy Prophet's Migration from Mecca to Medina, started driving the invaders from their fastnesses in Asia Minor. During the three years in which Heraclius was retrieving the fortunes of the empire, the Holy Prophet was engaged in his struggle with Quraish. Then came the critical siege of Constantinople by the Persians, which preceded by little more than half a year the siege of Medina by Quraish and their allies. In 627, in his third campaign, Hercalius followed up his previous success, and at the close of the year achieved the decisive victory of Nineveh. In this action the forces of Persia were irretrievably broken. This event coincided with the Truce of Hudaibiyya. During the autumn, Heraclius, in fulfilment of his vow for the outstanding success which had just crowned his arms, performed on foot a pilgrimage from Emesa (Hims) to Jerusalem. Soon after his arrival there, his courtiers noticed one morning that the Emperor appeared to be seriously perturbed. On enquiry, he disclosed that the cause of his perturbation was that the previous night his study of the planets had revealed that a mighty king had arisen among the circumcised. He asked which were the people who practised circumcision, and was told that this was a custom of the Jews, but that the Jews, as the Emperor was aware, were not strong enough to pose any serious threat to the empire. About that time, the Governor of Ghassan sent intimation to Heraclius that an Arab of the name of Muhammad had claimed prophethood and that his influence was spreading, on which he directed an inquiry whether the Arabs practised circumcision; and on being told that they did, he exclaimed, 'Then he must be the king of those people.' A short while thereafter the Holy Prophet's letter addressed to Heraclius reached him.

The text of the Holy Prophet's letter was: 'In the name of Allah, Most Gracious, Ever Merciful. From Muhammad bin Abdullah, Messenger of Allah, to Heraclius, the Chief of Byzantium. Peace be on him who follows the guidance. I invite you to the acceptance of Islam. Be a Muslim and enter into the security of Allah. Be a Muslim and Allah will reward you doubly. If you turn away, you will bear the responsibility for your subjects. People of the Book! Let us agree upon one matter which is the same for you and for us, namely, that we worship none save Allah, and that we associate no partner with Him; and that some of us take not others for lords beside Allah. Then, if they turn away, say to them, "Bear ye witness that we have submitted wholly to Allah." '

The Holy Prophet committed this letter to Dihya Kalbi and instructed him to convey it to the Byzantine Emperor through the intermediary of the Governor of Ghassan. When Dihya, through this means, arrived in Jerusalem with the letter, he had to present it to the Emperor's nephew for its submission to the Emperor. When the nephew presented the letter to the Emperor, he directed him to open it and read it out to him, but as soon as he opened it and deciphered its first line he was upset and suggested that the letter should be turned down as the writer had been guilty of disrespect towards the Emperor as he had put his own name ahead of the Emperor's name in the letter, and instead of describing him as the Emperor of Byzantium, he had merely called him Chief of Byzantium. Heraclius waived aside his nephew's criticisms, and, taking the letter, directed that the bearer of the letter should be treated as a royal guest during the time that the letter was under his consideration. The Emperor also gave orders that search should be made for any compatriot of the writer of the letter who might be available and to arrange to present him before the Emperor. Bokhari has narrated on the authority of Ibn Abbas the following account in Abu Sufyan's words of what transpired as the result of the Emperor's direction: 'I had then gone to Syria with a few companions on a commercial errand. The time was after the Truce of Hudaibiyya. The Emperor's men searched for us and, taking us to Jerusalem, presented us before the Emperor, who was holding court wearing his crown and surrounded by his courtiers. He directed his interpreter to enquire from us which of us was most closely related to the claimant of prophethood. I submitted that I was his closest relative in that he was my cousin. The Emperor asked me to step forward and directed that my companions should stand behind me, and told the interpreter to warn my companions that he desired to put some questions to me concerning the person who claimed to be a prophet and that if I made any misstatement in answer to his questions, they should point this out to him. Thereafter, he asked me the following questions:

Emperor: What is the status of this claimant among his people?
Abu Sufyan: He belongs to a noble family among us.
Emperor: Has anyone among you made such a claim previously?
Abu Sufyan: No.
Emperor: Had you ever known him to tell a lie before he made his claim?
Abu Sufyan: No.
Emperor: Was there among his ancestors anyone who was a king?
Abu Sufyan: No.
Emperor: Are those who follow him from among your leading people, or are they weak and humble?
Abu Sufyan: They are weak and humble.
Emperor: Is their number increasing or diminishing?
Abu Sufyan: They are increasing.
Emperor: Has any of his followers resiled from his faith in disgust?
Abu Sufyan: No.
Emperor: Has he ever broken his pledge?
Abu Sufyan: No, but we have recently concluded an agreement with him concerning which we have some apprehension what it might lead to.
Emperor: Has there been any fighting between him and you?
Abu Sufyan: Yes.
Emperor: With what result?
Abu Sufyan: It has been like the ascending and descending of a bucket in a well. Sometimes he wins, and sometimes we win.
Emperor: What does he teach?
Abu Sufyan: He tells us to believe that God is One and that we should not associate anyone with Him. He forbids us to worship as our ancestors used to worship. He directs us to perform Salat, give alms, shun vice, fulfil our covenants and not to commit breach of trust.

Abu Sufyan has related that after this dialogue the Emperor explained to him, through the interpreter, the purpose of each of his questions and the conclusion that he had drawn from his answers, which was in each case in favour of the claimant. The Emperor added, 'I knew that a Prophet was about to be raised, but I did not imagine that he would be raised among you Arabs. If what you have told me is true, I consider that the time is not far when this man will obtain dominion over the soil which is under my feet. Were it possible for me, I would have gone to meet him, and if I had had this opportunity, I would have drawn comfort from washing his feet.'

Abu Sufyan has related that the Emperor then directed that the letter sent by the claimant to him should be read out. At the end of the reading comments were made from every direction and voices began to be raised, but that he and his companions did not know what was being said. They were directed to leave, and when they had come out, Abu Sufyan, addressing his companions, said to them, 'It seems to me that the star of Muhammad is in the ascendant inasmuch as the Byzantine Emperor seems to be afraid of him.'

Not long after, another letter couched in similar terms reached the court of Heraclius. It was addressed to Harith VII, prince of Bani Ghassan, who forwarded it to the Emperor, with an address from himself, soliciting permission to chastise the audacious writer. But Heraclius forbade the expedition and desired the attendance of Harith at Jerusalem.

Another letter of the Holy Prophet, peace be on him, was addressed to Chosroes Parvez bin Hormuz, Emperor of Iran, of the well-known Sassanid dynasty. Iran had long-standing relations with Arabia. Bahrain, in the east of Arabia, and Yemen in the west, were both part of the dominions of the Chosroes, and were administered by his governors. Another factor that engaged the interest of the Chosroes in the affairs of Arabia was that there were Jewish tribes who had been settled in Medina, Khaibar, Wadil Qura, etc. These Jewish tribes were opposed to the Byzantines on account of the hostility of the latter towards, and persecution of, Jews, but they had friendly relations with Iran. In the time of the Holy Prophet Jewish leaders often visited Iran and endeavoured, as far as they could, to set the Chosroes against the Holy Prophet.

The Holy Prophet's letter addressed to the Chosroes was carried by a devoted Companion of his, Abdullah bin Hudhaifa Sahmi, who was directed to approach first the Governor of Bahrain, Mundhar bin Sawi, and convey the letter to Chosroes through his mediation. This letter was also sealed like the one addressed to the Byzantine Emperor, and the text of it was: 'In the name of Allah, Most Gracious, Ever Merciful. From Muhammad, Messenger of Allah, to Chosroes, Chief of Iran. Peace be on him who follows the guidance, believes in Allah and His Messenger and bears witness that there is no one worthy of worship save Allah, the One, without associate, and that Muhammad is His Servant and Messenger. I invite you to the Call of Allah, as I am the Messenger of Allah to the whole of mankind, so that I may warn every living person and so that the truth may become clear and the judgment of God may overtake the disbelievers. I call upon you to accept Islam and thus make yourself secure. If you turn away, you will bear the responsibility for your subjects also.'

Abdullah bin Hudhaifa has related that when, on receiving permission, he presented the Holy Prophet's letter to the Chosroes, he directed his interpreter to read it out to him. On hearing it read out the Chosroes was outraged and, snatching the letter from the hand of the interpreter, tore it into bits, exclaiming, 'How dare a subject of mine address me in such words!' When the Holy Prophet, peace be on him, received the report of this incident, he observed, 'As regards these [meaning the Iranians], they will be broken to bits, and as regards those [meaning the Byzantines], they will be granted respite.' This pronouncement of the Holy Prophet was literally fulfilled regarding the empire of the Chosroes within a few years, but the empire of Byzantium, despite the loss of its eastern provinces, continued for centuries.

The Chosroes did not confine his wrath against the Holy Prophet to tearing his letter to bits, but directed his Governor of Yemen, Badhan, to despatch two strong emissaries to the Hedjaz who should apprehend this claimant of prophethood and produce him before the Chosroes. Accordingly Badhan selected one of his secretaries, Banweh, for this purpose, and despatched him to Medina, accompanied by a mounted guard, with a letter addressed to the Holy Prophet requiring him to accompany the two emissaries who would produce him before the Chosroes. When they arrived in Medina, they presented Badhan's letter to the Holy Prophet and counselled him to accompany them as directed in the letter, failing which the mighty Chosroes would ruin his country and his people. The Holy Prophet smiled, and then invited them, in a brief address, to embrace Islam and told them that they should stop for the night and that he would give his reply to the letter the next day. On their presenting themselves the next day, he told them, 'Convey to your master that my Master has slain his master last night.'

Banweh and his companion returned to Yemen and conveyed the message of the Holy Prophet to Badhan, who, on hearing it, exclaimed, 'If what he says comes about, he would indeed be a Prophet of God.' Not long after Badhan received a despatch from Sherweh, son of Chosroes Parvez, which contained the intimation that Sherweh had slain his father in the public interest on account of his tyranny and his merciless killing of the nobles of the empire. Badhan was instructed to obtain the allegiance of the people of Yemen to Sherweh, and was told that the directions sent by his father concerning an Arab personage were cancelled. On receipt of the despatch, Badhan involuntarily exclaimed, 'Muhammad's words have been proved true; it seems that he is a true Prophet of God and I believe in him.' He immediately wrote to the Holy Prophet conveying to him his adhesion to Islam.

The Holy Prophet's letter addressed to Muqauqis, the Viceroy of Egypt, subordinate to the Emperor of Byzantine, whose personal name was Juraij bin Meena, and who, like the people of Egypt, was a Copt and was of the Christian faith, was despatched by the hand of Hatab bin Abi Balta'h, who was a distinguished Companion of the Holy Prophet, and who had fought in the battle of Badr. The text of the letter was: 'In the name of Allah, Most Gracious, Ever Merciful, From Muhammad, Servant of Allah and His Messenger, to Muqauqis, Chief of the Copts. Peace be on him who follows the guidance. I invite you to the acceptance of the Call of Allah. Embrace Islam and be secure; Allah will reward you doubly. If you turn away, you will bear the responsibility of the Copts also. People of the Book! Let us agree upon one matter which is the same for you and for us, namely, that we worship Allah, and that we associate no partner with Him, and that some of us take not others for lords beside Allah. Then, if they turn away, say to them: "Bear ye witness that we have submitted wholly to Allah" (see p. 216).

When Hatab arrived in Alexandria and was granted access to Muqauqis and presented the Holy Prophet's letter to him, he read it and, addressing Hatab, said in a tone of raillery: 'If your master is truly a Prophet of God, then why did he not supplicate God that He might make me subordinate to him?' Hatab replied that Jesus also had not made such a supplication, and added, 'I advise you to take this letter seriously as in this country of yours there has been one who claimed that he was the lord and ruler of the world, but God seized him in such manner that he became an example for all subsequent generations. So I would beg you sincerely to take a lesson from what has happened to others and not to be the one to become a lesson for others.' Muqauqis then adopted a serious tone and said, 'We have already a faith, which we cannot discard unless we find a faith superior to it.' Hatab rejoined, 'Islam is a faith which relieves its followers from the need of any other faith; but it does not require you to discard faith in Jesus. Islam teaches faith in all the Prophets. As Moses had prophesied about the coming of Jesus, in the same way Jesus had prophesied about the advent of the Holy Prophet.'

In a later interview, when several high dignitaries of the church were also present, Muqauqis said to Hatab, 'I have heard that your Prophet was expelled from his home. Why did he not on that occasion supplicate that his enemies might be destroyed?' Hatab replied, 'The Holy Prophet was only compelled to leave his home, but Jesus was apprehended by the Jews and they attempted to put an end to him on the cross, yet he was not able to bring about the destruction of his enemies through supplication.' Muqauqis observed, 'You certainly are an intelligent person and have been chosen as an envoy by a wise man. I have reflected on what you have told me about your Prophet and I find that he has not taught anything ill nor forbidden anything good.' He then placed the Holy Prophet's letter in a small ivory box, sealed it and committed it to the custody of one of his female servants. He then sent for a scribe who knew Arabic and dictated the following letter: 'In the name of Allah, Most Gracious, Ever Merciful. To Muhammad bin Adbullah, from Muqauqis Chief of the Copts. Peace be on you. I have read your letter and have understood its contents, and that to which you have called me. I am aware that a Prophet is yet to arise; but I am of the opinion that he will appear in Syria. I have done honour to your envoy and I am sending you with him two damsels of high status among the Copts, and raiment and a mule for you to ride upon. Peace be with you.' He committed the letter to Hatab who conveyed it to the Holy Prophet.

Of the two damsels sent by Muqauqis, one was named Mary and the other was named Sireen. They were sisters. By the time they arrived in Medina they had embraced Islam under the instruction of Hatab. The Holy Prophet himself married Mary and gave her sister Sireen in marriage to the well-known Arab poet Hassan bin Thabet. From Mary a son was born to the Holy Prophet who was named Ibrahim. The mule was white and was named Duldul. The Holy Prophet rode it often. He was riding it during the battle of Hunain.

One very interesting particular concerning the letter addressed by the Holy Prophet to Muqauqis is that after the passage of centuries the original of the letter was discovered in 1858 by Monsieur Etienne Barthelemy, member of a French expedition, in a monastery in Egypt and is now carefully preserved in Constantinople. Several photographs of the letter have since been published. The first one was published in the well-known Egyptian newspaper *Al-Hilal* in November 1904; it is also reproduced at page 364 of Professor Margoliouth's book, *Muhammad and the Rise of Islam*, and also at page 198 of an Egyptian publication, *The Political History of Islam*, by Dr Hasan bin Ibrahim, Professor of History in the Islamic University of Cairo. Several non-Muslim scholars have confirmed that this is the original letter which the Holy Prophet had addressed to Muqauqis, Viceroy of Egypt. The text of this letter is in exact accord with the text mentioned in Islamic books of history and in compilations of *hadith*.

The Holy Prophet also addressed a letter to As'hama, Negus of

Abyssinia, who was already a great admirer of the Holy Prophet and held him in great honour and who had extended great kindness to the Muslims who had, under the Holy Prophet's direction, migrated to his country and were settled there. This letter was committed by the Holy Prophet to Amr bin Umayya Dhamri. Its text was as follows: 'In the name of Allah, Most Gracious, Ever Merciful. From Muhammad, Messenger of Allah, to the Negus, King of Abyssinia. Peace be on you. I praise Allah beside Whom there is no other worthy of worship, the King, the Most Holy, the Source of Peace, the Bestower of Security, the Protector. I bear witness that Jesus son of Mary was raised by the Word of Allah, which He sent to Mary. I call you to Allah, the One without associate, and to co-operation with me in obedience to Him and to following me, and to believing in that which has been revealed to me, for I am the Messenger of Allah and call you and your people to Allah, the Exalted. I have conveyed my message to you and have called you out of sincerity to the truth. Then respond to my sincere call. I have already sent my cousin Jafar and a party of Muslims to your country. Peace be on him who follows the guidance.'

When this letter was presented to the Negus he raised it to his eyes and, descending from his throne, announced, 'I bear witness that Muhammad is the Messenger of Allah.' He then called for a small ivory box and placed the letter in it, saying, 'So long as this letter is preserved under the care of our dynasty, the people of Abyssinia will continue to derive blessings from it.'

The Negus sent the following reply to the Holy Prophet: 'In the name of Allah, Most Gracious, Ever Merciful. To Muhammad, Messenger of Allah, from the Negus As'hama. Peace be on you, Messenger of Allah, and His mercy and His blessings. Allah, beside Whom there is no one worthy of worship, is He Who has guided me to Islam. Messenger of Allah, your letter has reached me. By the Lord of heaven and earth, Jesus, peace be on him, is not any more than you have mentioned, even by a particle. I have recognised that with which you have been sent to us. I bear witness that you are a true Messenger of Allah whose truth has been testified to. I make my pledge at the hand of your cousin and embrace Islam for the sake of Allah, Lord of the worlds. Peace be on you and the mercy of Allah and His blessings.'

This was the Negus who died in the ninth year of Hijra and for whom, on learning of his death, the Holy Prophet led a funeral service proclaiming that a righteous brother in Islam, the Negus of Abyssinia, had died and that his Muslim brethren should supplicate for the salvation of his soul. The Holy Prophet addressed a letter to his successor also, but he did not respond to his call and died a Christian.

The Holy Prophet had also sent a private letter to the Negus As'hama at the same time as the letter, the text of which has been set out above. In his private letter he had asked the Negus to perform his *nikah* with Um Habeebah, daughter of Abu Sufyan, who had been married to Ubaidullah bin Jahsh, cousin of the Holy Prophet, who had died in Abyssinia. He also requested the Negus that arrangements might be made for the return of Jafar and his companions to Medina. The Negus complied with both requests of the Holy Prophet.

The Holy Prophet addressed another letter to Haudha bin Ali, Chief of Bani Haneefa, a Christian tribe, in Yamamah. The letter was carried by Saleet bin Amr Qarshi who was very hospitably entertained by Haudha, was presented with change of raiment and provisions for his journey home. He was given a letter containing the following message to the Holy Prophet: 'Excellent and beautiful is the revelation to which you invite me. The Arabs revere my dignity. Grant unto me, after you, a share in the rule, and I will follow you.' When the Holy Prophet read the letter, he observed, 'Rule belongs to God; had this man asked of me but an unripe date, as his share in the land, I would not have given it to him.' Haudha died in the following year.

Chapter 13

:Victory:

The three principal Jewish tribes, Banu Qainuqa, Banu Nadhir and Banu Quraidha, had been settled in the oasis of Medina long before the Qayla (Aus and Khazraj) appeared on the scene. After their arrival the Jewish tribes continued for some time to occupy a position of dominance in the oasis. Even at the time of the Hijra their numbers exceeded those of the Arabs in the oasis. How the Jews came to be in Medina, and whether they were of Hebrew stock or were descendants of Arabs who had been converted to Judaism, is not clear. It is definite, however, that in course of time they had adopted many customs identical with those of their pagan Arab neighbours and intermarried with them, but they adhered to the Jewish religion and maintained their distinct existence.

The arrival of the Holy Prophet, peace be on him, in Medina was no more welcome to the Jews than it was to Abdullah bin Ubayy, Chief of Khazraj, who was shortly to be crowned King of Aus and Khazraj, a design that was frustrated by developments in Medina consequent on the arrival of the Holy Prophet. The Jews were expecting the advent of a Prophet, which had been foretold in Deuteronomy 18:18, but they believed firmly that the Prophet would be raised among the Jews and therefore could not reconcile themselves to the notion that he was raised among Arabs. They were thus both jealous and hostile and from the very beginning desired the discomfiture of the Holy Prophet. When Islam began to spread rapidly among Aus and Khazraj, the Jews were chagrined and became apprehensive that the stranger from Mecca might achieve a position of dominance in Medina. Nevertheless, they hoped that this tendency might soon be checked and arrested. When they received intimation that a strong, well-armed force was advancing from Mecca towards Medina, and that the Holy Prophet had gone out to meet and check it, the Jews flattered themselves with the hope that the Holy Prophet and the Muslims would meet their doom at the hands of Quraish. The utterly unexpected result of the battle came as a shock to them.

When, after the battle, the Holy Prophet perceived that Banu Qainuqa were taking up an aggressive attitude, he assembled them in their market and warned them in the following words: 'Beware lest Allah bring you the vengeance that He brought upon Quraish, and embrace Islam. You know that I am a Prophet who has been sent – you will find that in your books and in Allah's covenant with you.' The Jewish response to this appeal was a challenge. They said, 'Muhammad, you seem to think that we are like your people. Do not deceive yourself because you encountered a people with no knowledge of war and got the better of them; for, by God, if we fight you, you will find we are real men.' This reply seemed to foreclose chances of a peaceful accord. There is not the least doubt that at that period the three Jewish tribes, singly as well as collectively, were much stronger in every respect than the Holy Prophet's followers.

Subsequent developments have been set out in earlier chapters. It is clear that the Jews of Medina constantly incited Quraish, and later other tribes, towards aggressive action against the Muslims for the purpose of wiping out Islam altogether. The Holy Prophet bore patiently with them, but neither did his extreme clemency towards them, despite their misbehaviour, serve to persuade them to live at peace with the Muslims, nor did the harsh measure that he was compelled to adopt against Banu Quraidha serve as a warning. Khaibar, after the expulsion of Banu Nadhir from Medina, became the centre of Jewish intrigue. Leaders of Banu Nadhir were welcomed in Khaibar and Huyay bin Akhtab, chief of Banu Nadhir, became their principal leader. He was present with Banu Quraidha during their treasonable activities at the time of the siege of Medina and shared their fate after the siege was raised.

The Truce of Hudaibiyya deprived the Jews of their principal instrument, Quraish, whom they had so far employed as the spearhead of their nefarious designs against the Muslims. They also became apprehensive that unless they moved in adequate strength against the Muslims at an early date, the balance of strength might become adverse to them. They now relied upon the Ghatafan and other tribes of Nejd, with whom they had had friendly relations throughout, to carry out their purpose. When the Holy Prophet received intimation that the Jews of Khaibar and neighbouring Jewish settlements were actively planning aggression against the Muslims in concert with Ghatafan, he decided to move against Khaibar in the hope of coming to some settlement with them of the type that he had arrived at with Quraish. He assembled those who had accompanied him to Hudaibiyya and, taking precautions that their movement should not become known, accomplished the journey to Khaibar, distant less than a hundred miles, in three forced marches. So quick was the movement, and so complete the surprise, that the cultivators of Khaibar, issuing forth in the morning to their fields, suddenly found themselves confronted by a great force, and rushed back to the city in dismay. The rapidity of the approach cut off all hope of timely aid from Bani Ghatafan.

The vale of Khaibar was studded with villages and fortresses rudely
built but posted strongly on the rocks and eminences which here and
there rose from amidst date-groves and fields of corn. One by one,
before any opposition could be organised, these forts were attacked
and carried. From the villages first attacked, which were gained with
little loss, the Muslims proceeded to the strong fortress of Qamus.
Here the Jews, who now had time to rally round their chief, Kinana,
posted themselves in front of the citadel, resolved on a desperate
struggle. The first attempts to dislodge them having proved abortive,
the next morning the Holy Prophet placed his standard in Ali's hands
and the troops advanced. At this moment, a Jewish warrior, Marhab,
stepped forth from the Jewish line and challenged his adversaries to
single combat. Ali advanced against him, the combatants closed, and
Ali cleft the head of Marhab in two. His brother renewed the
challenge, and Zubair went forth and slew him. The Muslim line now
made a general advance, and, after a sharp conflict, drove back the
enemy. In this battle, Ali performed great feats of valour. Having lost
his shield, he seized the lintel of a door, which he wielded effectually
in its stead. The victory was decisive, for the Jews lost 93 men; while of
the Muslims, only 19 were killed throughout the whole campaign. The
citadel of Qamus surrendered on condition that the inhabitants should
be free to leave the country, but should give up all their property to
the victors. With the rest came forth Kinana, chief of Khaibar, and his
cousin. They were charged with breach of the compact because of
holding back the greater part of the treasure which had to be
delivered. They protested that they had not held back anything and
offered that if they were not telling the truth they would forfeit their
lives. The treasure was discovered, on information supplied by a Jew,
from a place where the two had concealed it. They paid the forfeit.

Zainab, sister of Marhab, had lost her husband as well as her father
and brothers in the battle and felt very bitter against the Holy
Prophet. Having ascertained that he fancied shoulder of lamb, she
dressed a kid with dainty garnishings and, having steeped the shoulder
in poison, sent the dish to the Holy Prophet for his evening repast.
Graciously accepting the gift, he took a piece of the shoulder for
himself and distributed portions to Abu Bakr and other friends,
including Bishr, who sat next to him. As he swallowed the first morsel,
the Holy Prophet called out, 'Surely, this shoulder has been poisoned,'
and he spat forth the mouthful. Bishr, who had eaten a portion, at
once changed colour and stirred neither hand nor foot until he died.
The Holy Prophet suffered excruciating pains and caused himself and
all those who had partaken of the dish with him to be freely cupped
between the shoulders. Zainab, put upon her defence, answered,
'Thou hast inflicted grievous injuries upon my people; thou hast slain
my father, my brothers and my husband. Therefore, I said within

myself, if he be a Prophet, he will reject the gift knowing that the kid is poisoned; but if he is a mere pretender, then we shall be rid of him, and the Jews will prosper again.' Her exculpatory statement was accepted and she was set free.

After the victory of Qamus the only remaining strongholds, Watih and Sulalim, were invested and, seeing no prospect of relief, capitulated, on condition that they would pay half the produce of their lands as a tax. They retained all their properties. Fadak, a Jewish settlement not far from Khaibar, profited by the example, and, having tendered a timely submission, was admitted to the same terms. On their march homeward the Muslims laid siege to the Jewish settlement Wadil Qura, which, after a resistance of one or two days, surrendered upon like conditions.

Of the spoils of Khaibar, a fifth was, as usual, set apart for the Holy Prophet's use and for distribution at will among his family and the destitute poor. The remaining four-fifths were sold by auction, and the proceeds, according to the prescribed rule, divided into shares, one for a foot soldier, and three for a horseman.

The villages and lands were disposed of in another way. One half, embracing all the places which surrendered without fighting, were reserved for the Holy Prophet, and constituted thereafter a species of Crown domain; the other half were allotted in freehold plots by the same rule as the personal booty. Even where the lands having been gained by fighting were apportioned as private property it was found expedient to leave the Jews in possession, on the same condition as with the public lands, namely surrendering half the produce. An appraiser was deputed yearly to assess the amount, to realise the rents, and bring them to Medina. So long as he was alive Abdullah bin Rawaha was charged with the performance of this duty. The Jews greatly esteemed his justice and impartiality in making the assessment.

On the way home the Holy Prophet had the pleasure of welcoming his cousin, Jafar, who, with some of the Migrants, had just returned from Abyssinia and had gone out to meet him. The Holy Prophet expressed great joy on meeting them; and the army, no less pleased, acceded cheerfully to his proposal that Jafar and his companions should share equally with them in the spoils of Khaibar.

During the autumn and winter of the seventh year of the Hijra several expeditions were despatched, under different leaders, in various directions. They were not attended by any important results, but served to extend the influence of the Holy Prophet and to bring him into relations with surrounding and even distant tribes.

The time came round when the Holy Prophet, according to treaty, might visit Mecca and perform Umra. Besides those who had accompanied him the previous year to Hudaibiyya, many others

joined the cavalcade which now numbered about 2,000 men. Muhammad bin Maslamah, with 100 horse, marched in advance of the
pilgrims. The sacrificial animals were sent forward to a spot in the
immediate vicinity of Mecca. Meanwhile Quraish, apprised of the
approach of the Muslims, according to agreement evacuated the city
in a body and, ascending the adjacent hills, watched for the coming of
the pilgrims. At last the cavalcade was seen emerging from the
northern valley. At its head was the Holy Prophet, seated on Qaswa;
Abdullah bin Rawaha, on foot in front, held the bridle; around on
every side were the chief Companions; and behind, in a long extended
line, came the rest of the pilgrims on camels and on foot. Seven years
had passed since the Emigrants last saw their native valley, and now
with quickened steps and long-repressed desire, they hastened
forward, and, as the Holy House came in view, raised high the
Talbeeh: 'Here am I, O Allah; here am I.' Still mounted on his camel,
the pilgrim mantle drawn under his right arm and thrown over the left
shoulder, the Holy Prophet approached the Ka'aba, touched the Black
Stone with his staff and made the seven circuits of the sacred spot,
with the people following. Just then Abdullah, as he led the Holy
Prophet's camel, recited, at the pitch of his voice, warlike and defiant
verses. He was admonished: 'Gently, son of Rawaha! Recite not this.
Say rather: "There is no god but the Lord alone! It is He that hath
upholden His Servant, and exalted His people! Alone hath He put to
flight the hosts of the Confederates." ' Abdullah proclaimed the words
accordingly, and people taking them up shouted them aloud as they
encircled the Ka'aba, till the mighty sound rang round the valley.

The circuits completed, the Holy Prophet, still upon his camel,
proceeded to the adjoining eminences of Safa and Marwa, and rode
seven times from one to the other, according to ancient custom. The
animals were sacrificed, and thus the ceremonies of Umra were
completed. On the morrow the Holy Prophet ascended into the inner
chamber of the Ka'aba and remained there till the hour of Prayer.
Bilal, mounting to the roof of the Ka'aba, summoned the pilgrims
with the usual call to midday Prayer. They gathered from every
quarter; and so, under the shadow of the Holy House, the Service was
led by the Holy Prophet in the same form as in the mosque of Medina.

Sir William Muir has observed *(Life of Muhammad,* p. 388):

It was surely a strange sight which at this time presented itself in
the vale of Mecca – a sight, one might almost say, unique in
history. The ancient city is for three days evacuated altogether
by its inhabitants, and every house deserted. As they retire, the
Exiles, many years banished from their birthplace, accompanied
by their allies, fill the valley, revisit the empty homes of their
childhood, and within the short allotted period fulfil the rites of

pilgrimage. The ousted citizens, with their families, climbing the heights around, take refuge under tents or rocks amongst the hills and glens; and, clustering on the overhanging peak of Abu Qobais, thence watch the movements of the visitors beneath, as with the Prophet at their head they perform the sacred rites – anxiously scanning every figure, if perchance to recognise among the worshippers some long-lost friend or relative. It was a scene rendered possible only by the throes that gave birth to Islam.

While at Mecca, the Holy Prophet lived in a tent of leather pitched for him near the Ka'aba. Yet he held friendly converse with several of the citizens and endeavoured to turn the present opportunity for conciliating the citizens of Mecca to the best effect, and not without success. But the time was short. Already the stipulated three days were ended, and he had entered on a fourth, when Suhail and Huweitib, chief men of Quraish, appeared and insisted that he and his followers withdraw from the city. The Holy Prophet gave immediate orders for departure and by nightfall not one of the pilgrims was left behind.

Not long after, Khalid bin Waleed, the Quraish commander who had turned the rear of the Muslims in the battle of Uhud, repaired to Medina, and gave in his adhesion to the cause of Islam. Two others followed him. One, his friend, the equally famous Amr, of versatile ability and weighty in counsel, who had been employed by Quraish in their embassy to Abyssinia. The other was Uthman, son of Talha, a chief of some note, and custodian of the Ka'aba. He had no doubt, in that capacity, attended with the keys of office to give the Holy Prophet admittance to the Holy House; and, perhaps, like many others who gazed from a respectful distance on that memorable scene, was won over by the devotion of the Holy Prophet to the Ka'aba and the elevation and beauty of the service then performed. The position of the Holy Prophet at Mecca was greatly strengthened by the accession of such leading men. There can be no doubt that the movement in his favour was not confined to those just mentioned, but was wide and general; and that the cause of Islam was gaining popularity in Mecca day by day.

During the spring and summer of the eighth year of the Hijra several military excursions were undertaken, with varied fortunes. A party of fifteen men was sent to Dhat Atlah, on the border of Syria. There they found a great multitude assembled who were called upon to embrace Islam. A shower of arrows was the answer. The Muslims fought desperately; one man alone survived to tell the tale. This disaster probably paved the way for the grand attack directed shortly after against the border-districts of Syria. The immediate cause was the murder by the Chieftain Shurahbil at Muta, of a messenger on his way with a despatch from the Holy Prophet to the Ghassanid prince at Bosra. It was immediately resolved to punish the offending chief. A general call of all the fighting men was made, and a camp of 3,000 soldiers was formed outside Medina. A white banner was mounted, and the Holy Prophet, placing it in the hands of Zaid, bade him march to the spot where the messenger had been slain, summon the inhabitants to embrace Islam, and, should they refuse, to draw the sword against them. In case Zaid was cut down, Jafar was to command; if Jafar, then Abdullah bin Rawaha; and if he too were disabled, the army should choose their own commander. Tidings of the coming army reached Shurahbil, who forthwith summoned to his aid the tribes of the vicinity. Thus, upon the alarm of invasion, there quickly rallied round Shurahbil a large well appointed army. Zaid received the startling intelligence on reaching Maan. The enemy, he heard, was encamped at Maab; his apprehension was increased by the rumour that Byzantine cohorts were with the host, and that the Emperor was at their head. He halted; a council of war was called; and for two days the Muslim chiefs discussed the difficulties of their position. Many advised that the Holy Prophet should be apprised of the new aspect of affairs and fresh instructions requested. Abdullah, on the contrary, urged an immediate advance in such passionate terms that everyone responded to it. So the camp advanced.

On entering the Belka by the southern shore of the Dead Sea, they suddenly found themselves confronted by an enemy in numbers and equipment surpassing anything they had ever seen before. Alarmed at the glittering array, they fell back on the village of Muta. There, finding advantageous ground, they halted and, forming front, resolved to offer battle. The Byzantine phalanx, with its cloud of Arabs on either flank, moved steadily down upon them. In the battle that ensued, Zaid, Jafar and Abdullah fell in that order. The leadership being now vacant, a council hastily called together fixed their choice on Khalid who forthwith assumed the command. But the chance of victory had passed away. It remained for Khalid but to save the dispersed columns from destruction, and even this taxed his skill and prowess to the utmost. By a series of ingenious rapid movements he drew off the remains of the army to a safe retreat. But he dared not linger longer in the dangerous vicinity and so, without further attempt to retrieve the day, he marched back straightway to Medina.

The loss of his cousin Jafar, and Zaid the faithful and beloved friend of five and thirty years, affected the Holy Prophet deeply. On the first intelligence of the reverse and of their death, which he received early in the day through a confidential messenger, he went to the house of Jafar. His widow, Asmaa, had just bathed and dressed her little ones when the Holy Prophet entered, embraced the children tenderly, and burst into tears. Asmaa guessed the truth and sobbed aloud. A crowd of women were gathering round her; the Holy Prophet silently left the place and, returning home, desired that provisions be sent to Jafar's house, observing, 'No food will be prepared there this day, for they are sunk in grief at the loss of their master.' He then went to the house of Zaid and Zaid's little daughter rushed into his arms, crying bitterly. The Holy Prophet was overcome and wept with her. A bystander, thinking to check his grief, said to him, 'Why thus, O Prophet?' 'This,' he replied, 'is not forbidden grief; it is but the fond yearning in the heart of friend for friend.'

About that time the Arab governor of Maan, Farwa, a Christian, sent a despatch to the Holy Prophet, announcing his adherence to Islam, with several presents – a white mule, a horse, an ass, and raiment inwrought with gold. The presents were graciously acknowledged in a letter from the Holy Prophet which contained directions for the spiritual guidance of the convert. The Byzantine government, hearing of his defection, sought, by offers of promotion, to secure his return to the Christian faith. He refused, and was put to death.

The repulse at Muta affected the prestige of the Holy Prophet among the northern tribes. There were rumours that the Bedouins of the neighbourhood had assembled in great force, and even threatened a descent upon Medina. Amr, recent adherent to Islam, was therefore placed at the head of 300 men, including 30 horse, with instructions to restore the prestige of Islam on the Syrian border. The selection of Amr was justified on the basis of his personal qualities, and also because he was connected with Bani Bali, a powerful tribe in the vicinity, and was possessed of personal influence which might aid in effecting the object of the campaign. In the event of serious opposition, he was to call upon the Arabs in that quarter who had already tendered their submission to come to his aid. After a ten days' march he encamped at a spring near the Syrian confines. There he found that the enemy were assembled in great numbers, and that he could look for little aid from the local tribes. He halted and despatched a messenger for reinforcements. The Holy Prophet at once sent 200 men, among whom were both Abu Bakr and Umar, under the command of Abu Obaida. Thus strengthened, Amr assumed command of the united troops, advanced, dispersed the hostile gatherings, and confirmed the friendly tribes. Having accomplished his objective, he returned to Medina.

Besides the Syrian tribes gained over by the success of Amr, several others, as Bani Abs, Murra, and Dhubyan now gave in their adhesion; and the Fezara with their chief, Oyeina, who had so long caused anxiety at Medina, at last tendered submission. Suleim also, who had taken part in the siege of Medina, joined the cause of Islam about this time. Most of the tribes in the vicinity of Medina had already recognised the supremacy of Islam.

Sir William Muir has commented (*The Life of Muhammad,* p. 399):

> The courteous treatment which the deputations which now
> began to come in from all directions experienced from the
> Prophet, his ready attention to their grievances, the wisdom
> with which he composed their disputes, and the politic assign-
> ments of territory by which he rewarded early declaration in
> favour of Islam, made his name to be popular, and his fame as a
> great and generous Prince to spread throughout the peninsula.

The Truce of Hudaibiyya had been now nearly two years in force.
Acting on the discretion allowed by the treaty, Khuzaa and Bani Bakr,
inhabiting Mecca and its neighbourhood, declared their adhesion, the
former to the Holy Prophet, the latter to Quraish. There had been
sanguinary feuds of old standing between them, and, though these
paled before the excitement of the war with the Muslims, the blood
which had been shed on either side caused hatred still to rankle in
their breasts. The Truce of Hudaibiyya allowed Bani Bakr again to
brood over their wrongs, and they sought opportunity to make
reprisals. Aided by a party of Quraish, they attacked by night an
unsuspecting encampment of Khuzaa, and slew several of them. A
deputation of forty men from the injured tribe, mounted on camels,
hastened to Medina, spread their wrongs before the Holy Prophet,
and pleaded that the treacherous murders be avenged.

Quraish, hearing of this deputation, were thrown into great alarm.
They despatched Abu Sufyan to Medina to procure a reconfirmation
of the compact of peace. On his way he met Budail, chief of Khuzaa,
returning from Medina after his interview with the Holy Prophet.
Abu Sufyan was not able to procure any reassurance from the Holy
Prophet. He departed home and reported his failure to Quraish, but
assured them that he had observed no hostile preparations in Medina.

In response to the appeal of Khuzaa, the Holy Prophet resolved to
march against Quraish, but the design was kept secret as long as it was
possible. Meanwhile, he summoned his allies from amongst the
Bedouins to join him at Medina, or at certain convenient points on the
road, but he did not disclose their destination. At the last moment he
ordered the Muslims in the city to arm themselves, announced his
project, and enjoined on all that no hint regarding it should, by any
possible way, reach Mecca. Notwithstanding this injunction, Hatib, a
devoted Muslim, secretly despatched a female messenger with a letter
to Mecca containing intimation of the intended project. Information
of this reaching the Holy Prophet, he sent Ali and Zubair in pursuit.
They overtook the messenger and recovered the letter from her. Hatib
excused himself by his natural desire to safeguard his unprotected
family in Mecca; and the plea, in view of his former services,

including his participation with the Muslims in the battle of Badr, was graciously accepted.

On 1 January 630 the army commenced its march. It was the largest force Medina had ever seen. The tents of the auxiliaries darkened the plain for miles around, and heavy contingents joined the Holy Prophet on the line of march. Two of these, Muzeina and Suleim, contributed as many as 1,000 men each. The Holy Prophet now found himself at the head of 10,000 men. Zubair with 200 men led the van. The march was made with such rapidity that within a week the army encamped at Marraz Zahran, but a single stage from Mecca. The Holy Prophet's uncle, Abbas, joined the Muslims on the road and was welcomed by the Holy Prophet with favour and affection.

The Holy Prophet commanded everyone to kindle a fire that night on the heights above the camp. No certain information of the march from Medina had yet reached Quraish, and uneasy at the portentous calm, broken only by vague reports, they sent forth Abu Sufyan to reconnoitre. In the evening, accompanied by Hakim bin Hizam, Khadija's nephew, and Budail, the Khuzaa chief, Abu Sufyan sallied forth on the Medina road. Ten thousand fires were by this time blazing on the mountain tops and appearing in full sight engaged their speculations, when suddenly in the dark Abu Sufyan was accosted by Abbas, who pointed out to him the wisdom of casting in his lot with the Muslims. 'Seat thee upon the mule behind me,' Abbas told him, 'and I will conduct thee to the Holy Prophet, and thou shalt seek quarter from him.' They were soon at the tent of the Holy Prophet, who, when Abbas apprised him of the arrival of Abu Sufyan, told him to take him to his tent, treat him well and to bring him up in the morning. At dawn Abu Sufyan was deeply impressed by the serried ranks of the Muslims following the Holy Prophet in Prayer. He realised that the Meccans had no means of withstanding such a formidable host. When he was received by the Holy Prophet, he enquired, 'If we do not oppose you by the sword, will you still employ the sword against us?' He was assured that if they did not resist with force, no force would be employed against them. The Holy Prophet then enquired from Abu Sufyan, 'Have you not yet discovered that there is no god but the Lord alone?' 'Had there been any god beside,' replied Abu Sufyan, 'surely, he would have been of some avail to us.' 'Then do you acknowledge,' enquired the Holy Prophet, 'that I am the Messenger of the Lord?' 'As to this,' countered Abu Sufyan, 'there is yet in my heart some hesitancy.' 'Woe is thee,' exclaimed Abbas, 'this is no time for hesitancy.' It was, indeed, no time for idle pride or scruple, and so Abu Sufyan, finding no alternative, repeated the formula of belief in God and in Muhammad as His Messenger. He then urged that as he was Chief of Quraish, some sign of honour may be appointed for him. He was told that whoever took refuge in his house would be safe. The Holy Prophet directed him to hasten back to the city and to announce that whoever closed the door of his house would be safe, and so also whoever entered the Holy House.

Before Abu Sufyan could quit the camp, the forces were already under arms, and were being marshalled in their respective columns. Standing by Abbas, he watched, in rising amazement, the various tribes, each defiling with its banner into its proper place. One by one, the different clans were pointed out by name and recognised. 'What is that black mass,' asked Abu Sufyan, 'with dark mail and shining lances?' 'It is the chivalry of Mecca and Medina,' replied Abbas, 'the honoured band that guards the person of the Holy Prophet.' 'Truly,' exclaimed the astonished chief, 'this kingdom of thy nephew is a mighty kingdom.' 'Nay, Abu Sufyan, he is more than a king, he is a mighty Prophet.' Abu Sufyan then hurried back to Mecca, and as he entered, shouted at the pitch of his voice, 'Ye Quraish, Muhammad is close upon us! He has an army which ye are not able to withstand. Whoever enters the house of Abu Sufyan shall be safe this day; and whoever shuts his door upon him shall be safe; and whoever enters the Holy House, he shall be safe.' So the people fled in all directions, to their homes and to the Ka'aba.

The army was now in full march on Mecca. The anxieties of a lifetime crowded into the moment. As the city was approached it was evident that there would be no opposition. Had any general opposition been organised it was here that a stand would have been made, yet no army appeared in sight. In token of his gratitude the Holy Prophet bowed his head low upon his camel and offered up thanksgiving to the Lord. The troops were told off in four divisions, and each was assigned a different road by which simultaneously to advance, with strict injunctions not to fight except in the last extremity, nor offer violence to anyone. Zubair, leading the left battalion, was to enter from the north, Khalid from the south, the men of Medina under S'ad bin Ubadah from the west, while the mild but vigilant Abu Obaida, commanding the Emigrants and followed by the Holy Prophet himself, took the nearest road skirting Jebel Hind. This disposition was wisely made; if opposition was offered anywhere, one of the other divisions would be at hand to take the enemy in the rear. As S'ad led on the citizens of Medina, he sang, 'Today is the day of slaughter; there is no safety this day for Mecca.' When this was reported to the Holy Prophet, he took the Medina banner from S'ad and gave it to his son Qais, a man of towering stature but of gentler disposition than his father.

Khalid's column encountered some violent opposition, in consequence of which a small number of Quraish and two of Khalid's men were killed, which saddened the Holy Prophet. He descended into the valley at a spot not far from the tombs of Abu Talib and Khadija. He was there joined by the division of Zubair and directed his tent to be pitched in the open space to the north of the city. 'Wilt thou not alight at thine own house?' inquired a follower. 'Not so,' he said, 'for have they yet left me any house in the city?' The great banner was planted at the door of his tent and he retired to repose therein but did not tarry for long. Again mounting Qaswa he proceeded to the Ka'aba and performed the circuits of the House. He then directed the demolition of the idols that were installed inside and around the Ka'aba. As each idol fell, he recited the verse: 'Truth has come and falsehood has vanished away. Falsehood does indeed vanish fast' (17:82). Thus was the Ka'aba restored to its true purpose, the worship of the One God, for which it was originally designed.

He then desired Bilal to make the Call for Prayer from the top of the Ka'aba, and worship was performed by the surrounding multitude, as it has been ever since, according to the ritual of the mosque of Medina. A crier was then sent through the city with the proclamation 'Whoever believeth in God, and in the Last Day, let him not leave in his house any image whatever that he doth not break in pieces.' He likewise deputed a party of Khuzaa to repair the boundary pillars around the sacred territory. Thus he gave practical proof that while determined to uproot idolatry from the land, he was equally resolved to uphold the sanctity of Mecca. He won the hearts of the inhabitants by his ardent declaration of attachment to the city. 'Thou art the choicest spot on earth unto me,' he said, 'and the most delectable. If thy people had not cast me forth, I would never have forsaken thee.' Ansar now began to express their fear that, as the Lord had given him victory over his native city, he would not return to Medina as his home. He overheard it and, calling them around him, assured them he would never quit Medina. 'God forbid it,' he said. 'Where ye live, there will I live, and there too shall I die.'

Having performed these immediate and necessary tasks, the Holy Prophet, peace be on him, sent for the leaders of Quraish and asked them how he should deal with them. They replied that they fully merited whatever punishment he might choose to inflict upon them, but that they knew he was a generous brother and would deal with them as such. The Holy Prophet pronounced judgment in the words addressed by Joseph to his brethren: 'No retribution shall be exacted from you this day' (12:93). He told them they were free.

All the scorn and ridicule poured on him by the Meccans; their implacable hatred and enmity; the long years of bitter, cruel and sustained persecution; all the fighting, the hardship and suffering; the loss of dear and devoted Companions, all – all was in the moment of triumph laid aside, banished from the mind and forgiven in the name

of the Lord On High, the Gracious, the Merciful, the Creator and
Master of all. God's glorious command was carried out to the
utmost (41:35, 36):

> Good and evil are not alike. Repel evil with that which is best
> and lo, he between whom and thyself was enmity is as though he
> were a warm friend. But none attains to it save those who are
> steadfast, and none attains to it save those who possess abundant
> good.

The gates of love and mercy were opened wide. Bitter enemies of
the morning became warm friends by midday. Some hearts were still
sullen; the humiliation, though softened by magnanimity, was hard to
endure, but even these could not long withstand the healing effect of
the balm so generously and beneficently applied by the Prophet of
God. History furnishes no parallel instance of such complete
forgiveness, such utter beneficence, on so large a scale.

A dozen individuals were exempted from this amnesty on account
of the atrocities of which they, individually, had been guilty, but of
these also all were eventually forgiven, except four who suffered the
extreme penalty.

Abu Jahl, commander of the Meccan army killed during the battle
of Badr, had been the Holy Prophet's bitterest enemy in Mecca. His
son, Ikramah, was one of the Meccan commanders in the battle of
Uhud who had spotted the inadequately guarded rear pass and had led
the attack which ended in near disaster for the Muslims. When Mecca
fell Ikramah left the town and proceeded to the coast, intending to
cross over to Abyssinia, being convinced that he could have no
security in Mecca or anywhere near it. His wife approached the Holy
Prophet and asked whether Ikramah could return to Mecca while
professing his idolatrous beliefs. He replied that faith was a matter of
conscience and conscience was free. If Ikramah returned to Mecca he
would not be molested, and could live there in security professing
whatever he chose to believe in. On this assurance, she followed
Ikramah and persuaded him to return to Mecca. On arrival there he
repaired to the Holy Prophet and received the assurance which he had
already given to his wife. Thereupon he announced his acceptance of
Islam and the Holy Prophet asked him if there was anything he
wished for. He replied that he could wish for no greater bounty than
God had already bestowed upon him in opening his heart to the
acceptance of Islam, but he did desire that the Holy Prophet should
pray to God to forgive him all the enmity that he had borne towards
the Prophet and the Muslims. The Holy Prophet prayed accordingly
and then bestowed his own mantle on Ikramah, saying, 'He who
comes to me believing in God can claim my house as his.' Ikramah

proved himself a sincere and zealous believer and set the seal on his faith by laying down his life in defence of it on one of the Syrian battlefields some years later.

At last the Holy Prophet bethought himself of procuring some nourishment. He went to the house of his cousin, Um Hany, daughter of Abu Talib, who was delighted to welcome him but was distressed that she had nothing in the house which she could offer him except a piece of very stale bread, too hard to be swallowed. When she mentioned this to the Holy Prophet, he smiled and said, 'Surely, Um Hany, it can be softened by being soaked in water. And have you anything which might make it more palatable?' She replied, 'There is a little of the dregs of some vinegar left from long ago.' The Holy Prophet observed, 'That would be excellent.' He then proceeded to soak the piece of bread in water and when it was softened he ate it with the few drops of black vinegar, first pronouncing the name of God over the meal and rendering thanks to Him when he finished, as if it had been a banquet. He thanked his cousin and observed, 'Um Hany, what a bounty bread and vinegar is!'

During the succeeding fortnight, while occupied in the arrangement of public affairs at Mecca, the Holy Prophet sent forth several armed parties to destroy the idolatrous shrines in the vicinity and secure the submission of the surrounding tribes. In the course of one of these operations Khalid put to death some members of a tribe who had tendered submission and laid down their arms. The Holy Prophet was grieved at the intelligence, raised his hands to heaven, and adjured, 'Lord, I am innocent in Thy sight of that which Khalid has done.' To prove the sincerity of his displeasure, he sent Ali with money to make compensation for the slain.

Mecca had fallen, but this did not bring peace. The Holy Prophet's march against Mecca had been so sudden that the first intimation of it that reached the surrounding tribes was the fall of the town. They were greatly agitated by the news, and felt that the time had come for the last effort to be put forth against Islam. The great Hawazin tribe occupied the ranges and slopes of the hilly country south-east of Mecca, and with their numerous branches and affiliated clans spread themselves over the wide steppes beyond Taif. That city inhabited by Bani Thaqeef of the same descent was their centre, and its inhabitants, devoted to idol-worship and closely connected with Mecca, feared the rapidly growing power of Islam. Accordingly they sent an urgent summons to all the branches of Hawazin stock to assemble, with a view to checking effectively the further spread of Islam. Having appointed a rendezvous at Autas, a valley in the mountain range north-east of Taif, they began rapidly to assemble there.

This movement compelled the Holy Prophet to cut short his stay at Mecca. Although the city had cheerfully accepted his authority, all its inhabitants had not yet embraced Islam. The Holy Prophet intended to leave their conversion to be accomplished gradually without compulsion. He left Muaz bin Jabal, well skilled in the Holy Quran and all questions of religious practice, to instruct the people of Mecca in the tenets and requirements of Islam, and appointed a Quraish youth, Attab, of the house of Abd Shams, over the secular administration of the city.

Four weeks had just elapsed since quitting Medina when the Holy Prophet marched forth from Mecca at the head of all his forces, swelled now by the addition of 2,000 auxiliaries from Quraish to the number of 12,000 men. Safwan, at his request, lent him 100 suits of mail and stands of arms complete, and as many camels. The array of tribes, each with a banner waving at its head, was impressive. In three or four marches the army arrived near the entrance of the valley of Hunain. On their side Hawazin, gathered in great force at Autas under their chief Malik, numbering at least 30,000, had meanwhile also been advancing upon the same valley. The women and children of the tribe with their herds and their flocks followed in the rear. Malik hoped thus to nerve his troops to victory. During the night of the arrival of the Muslims at Hunain Malik drew up his men in a masked recess commanding the steep and narrow defile which formed the entrance to the valley and awaited there in silence the enemy's approach.

At early dawn, while it was yet dark, the sky being overcast with clouds, the Muslim army was in motion. The Holy Prophet, mounted on his white mule, followed in the rear. The vanguard of Banu Suleim, led by Khalid, were defiling leisurely up the steep and narrow pass when on a sudden Hawazin sprang from their ambuscade and charged impetuously down upon them. Staggered by the unexpected onslaught, column after column fell back and choked the narrow pass. Aggravated by the obscurity of the hour and the straitness of the rugged road, panic seized the army and they turned and fled. The rallying calls of the Holy Prophet had no effect, except that a band of devoted followers, including Abbas, his son Fadhl, Ali, Abu Bakr, Umar, Usama and Aiman, gathered round him. The confusion increased, the multitude of camels jostling wildly one against the other; all was noise and clamour and the Holy Prophet's voice was lost amid the din. He bade Abbas, who held his mule, to call aloud, 'Ye Ansar! Ye men of the Pledge of the Tree!' Abbas forthwith shouted these words over and over again at the pitch of his stentorian voice, till they reached far and near. At once they touched a chord in the hearts of Ansar; arrested in their flight, they flew to the Holy Prophet, crying aloud, 'Here we are; here we are.' A hundred of these devoted followers, disengaged with difficulty from the camels that jammed the road, threw themselves across the gorge and stayed the downward rush. Relieved from the pressure from above, the army rallied and returned to the battle. The Holy Prophet spurred forward his mule, calling out, 'I am the Prophet, no impostor; I am the son of Abdul Muttalib.' The conflict was severe, and the issue, from the nature of the ground and the impetuosity of the foe, for some time doubtful. The moment was critical, but in the end, the steadiness of Ansar and the enthusiasm of the rest when once recalled, won the day. The enemy fled and the rout was complete.

Malik, taking his stand with the flower of his army at the upper end of the valley, covered the escape of his broken forces; but he was unable to rescue the women and children who fell into the hands of the Muslims, with the camp and all that it contained. The spoils included 24,000 camels, 40,000 sheep and goats, and 4,000 ounces of silver. The prisoners, 6,000 in number, with the booty, were removed to the neighbouring valley of Jirana, and sheltered there awaiting the return of the army from Taif. The Holy Prophet knew that Hawazin would seek to regain their families, and an opportunity was thus skilfully left open for negotiation. The fugitive army was pursued as far as Nakhla; from thence part fled back to Autas, and part to Taif. The former entrenched themselves in their previous camp. A strong detachment was sent to dislodge them, which was accomplished after severe fighting. The dispersed fragments took refuge in the surrounding hills. As soon as the detachment returned from Autas the Holy Prophet led the army by way of Nakhla and laid siege to Taif, which had been the centre of all the trouble. But the battlements were strong, the city well provisioned, and there was a plentiful supply of water within the walls. Despite all efforts, the siege was successfully withstood for half a month when the Holy Prophet decided to raise the siege and the army marched back to Jirana. Here it was brought to the notice of the Holy Prophet that his foster-sister, daughter of Halima of Bani S'ad, was among the prisoners. He sent for her, seated her affectionately beside him, and offered to take her to Medina. But as she preferred remaining with her tribe he let her return to them with a handsome present.

Encouraged by the kind treatment of their kinswoman, a deputation from the various tribes of Hawazin presented themselves before the Holy Prophet. They professed submission to him, recounted the calamities that had befallen them, and urged, 'In these huts among the prisoners, are thy foster-mothers and foster-sisters who have nursed thee and fondled thee in their bosoms. We have known thee a suckling, a weaned child, a youth generous and noble; and now thou hast risen to this dignity. Be gracious, therefore, unto us, even as the Lord has been gracious unto thee.' The Holy Prophet was deeply touched, and turning kindly to them told them that if they had approached him earlier he would have released all their prisoners without ransom. He then inquired, 'Which of the two, your families or

your properties, is the dearer to you?' 'Our women and our children,'
they replied, 'we would not take anything in exchange for them.'
'Then,' continued the Holy Prophet, 'whatsoever prisoners fall to my
portion and that of my family, I give them up unto you. With regard
to the rest, come again at the midday Prayer when the congregation is
assembled, and ask of me to make intercession with them for you.'
They appeared at the appointed time and made their petition. Ansar
and Emigrants cheerfully followed the example of the Holy Prophet,
but some of the allied tribes, as Fezara, with Oyeina at their head,
declined to do so. The Holy Prophet offered to recompense them at
the rate of six camels for every captive, to which they agreed, and the
prisoners were all released.

At the time of the division of the spoils, 44 camels and 40 sheep or
goats fell to the lot of each soldier, and three times that number to
every horseman. Out of the one-fifth that fell to the share of the Holy
Prophet he took the opportunity of gaining, by a princely liberality,
the hearts of the leading chiefs of Mecca and of the Bedouin tribes. To
the most powerful he presented each 100 camels. Among them were
Abu Sufyan, his two sons, Yazeed and Muawiya, Hakim bin Hizam,
Safwan, Suhail, Huweitib, Oyeina, and others who but a few weeks
before were his deadly enemies. To the lesser chiefs, he gave 50
camels each. So liberal was he that in some cases where discontent was
expressed the gift was without hesitation doubled. His merciful
dealing with the Meccans when the city fell had secured him their
submission; his large-hearted liberality towards them now won him
their hearts. It was an even greater victory than the fall of Mecca.
Even Malik, the chief who had led Hawazin and who was still at Taif,
came when sent for, made his submission and was treated with the
same generosity. He soon joined the Holy Prophet and became an
exemplary believer. Confirmed in his chiefship, he entered upon a
constant warfare with the citizens of Taif and reduced them to great
straits.

It was conveyed to the Holy Prophet that his unprecedented
liberality towards his erstwhile enemies had occasioned some mur-
murs of discontent among younger Ansar. He called Ansar together
and addressed them thus: 'Ansar, it has been reported to me that you
are disconcerted because I have given large portions to these chiefs
out of the one-fifth, and have given nothing to you.' Leading Ansar
assured him that the discontent had been given expression to by some
of their younger irresponsible men, and that the bulk of them had no
grievance whatever. The Holy Prophet said, 'Now tell me, did I not
come unto you whilst you were wandering, and the Lord gave you the
right direction; needy, and He enriched you; at enmity amongst
yourselves, and He filled your hearts with love and unity?' 'Indeed, it
is even as you say,' they answered, 'to the Lord and to His Prophet

belong benevolence and grace.' 'Nay,' continued the Holy Prophet, 'but ye might have answered, and answered truly – for I would have vouched for it myself – thou camest to Medina rejected, and we bore thee witness; a fugitive, and we took thee in; an outcast, and we gave thee asylum; destitute, and we fed thee. Why are you disturbed in mind because of the things of this life wherewith I have sought to incline these men unto the faith in which you are already established? Are you not satisfied that others should have the flocks and herds, while you carry back with you the Prophet of the Lord? Nay, I will never leave you. If all mankind went one way, and Ansar went another way, I would go the way of Ansar. The Lord be favourable unto them and bless them, and their sons and their sons' sons forever.' At these words they wept, till the tears ran down upon their beards, and they cried with one voice, 'Yea, we are well satisfied, O Prophet, with our good fortune.'

The Holy Prophet spent about a fortnight at Jirana, during which period the booty captured at Hunain was all distributed. When everything was ended he started for Mecca, where he performed the Umra, and returned to Jirana the same night; and thence, striking through the valleys, took the direct route homewards to Medina.

The youthful Attab was confirmed in the government of Mecca, and an allowance assigned him of one dirhem a day. He was content with this moderate allowance. He said, 'Let the Lord make hungry that man's liver, who is hungry upon a dirhem a day. The Prophet hath appointed that as my sustenance. I have no further claim upon anyone.' Muaz was left behind to complete the spiritual instruction of the city. The annual pilgrimage followed shortly afterwards; Attab presided.

Chapter 14

:Farewell:

In the ninth year of the Hijra, the Holy Prophet lost his daughter Zainab, who had never recovered from the ill-treatment that she had suffered on her escape from Mecca. Um Kulthum, whom Uthman married after Ruqayya's death, had also died, so that of his daughters Fatima alone was left. Shortly after his return from Taif his wife, Mary the Copt, bore him a son who was named Ibrahim. The Holy Prophet was delighted at his birth. He was able to visit him almost daily and fondle him in his arms.

The fall of Mecca opened a new era in Islam. It practically established its supremacy in Arabia. At the opening of the ninth year, on his return from Jirana, the Holy Prophet arranged for the recovery of Zakat from the tribes which had tendered their submission. Collectors were deputed in every direction to make the assessment, and bring it in to Medina. They were well received, and accomplished their mission without obstruction, excepting only one or two cases. A branch of Bani Temim chanced to be encamped close at hand when the collector arrived to make the collection from an adjoining tribe. While the herds and flocks of their neighbours were being collected for the assessment, Temim, anticipating a like demand, came forward with bows and swords and drove the collector away. The Holy Prophet despatched Oyeina with fifty horsemen, who fell unexpectedly on them, and making about fifty captives, men, women and children, carried them to Medina. Bani Temim, some of whom had fought by the side of the Holy Prophet at Hunain and been munificently rewarded at Jirana, lost no time in sending a deputation of eighty or ninety chief men to beg for their brethren's release. When they were received by the Holy Prophet they sought leave to contend for the palm of victory in rhetoric and poetry with the orators and poets of Medina. The Holy Prophet gave permission and the contest proceeded. By the Holy Prophet's direction Hassan bin Thabet was the last to recite his glowing and well measured verses. When he finished the strangers were astonished at the beauty of his poetry and observed, 'By the Lord, how rich is this man's fortune! His poet, as well as his orator, surpass ours in eloquence.' The Holy Prophet liberated the prisoners, and, having entertained his visitors hospitably, dismissed their chief with rich presents and provisions for the way. All the branches of the tribe which had not yet given in their adhesion now embraced Islam.

Among other expeditions, one was about this time despatched against Bani Tai under the command of Ali, who performed his mission effectively and returned with many prisoners. Amongst them was the daughter of Hatim, the Christian Arab chieftain, famous for his generosity but now for some time dead. His son Adi having fled to Syria, his sister, on disclosing her identity to the Holy Prophet, was at once released and presented with a change of raiment and a camel on which, joining the first Syrian caravan, she went in quest of her brother. At her solicitation Adi presented himself before the Holy Prophet, and having embraced Islam, and been confirmed in the chiefship of his tribe, distinguished himself thereafter in the service of Islam.

The Mosque of the Holy Prophet was now the scene of frequent embassies from all quarters of Arabia. His supremacy was everywhere recognised; and from the most distant parts of the peninsula, from Yemen and Hadramaut, from Mahra, Oman and Bahrain, from the borders of Syria and the outskirts of Persia, the tribes hastened to offer submission. They were uniformly treated with consideration and courtesy. Their representations were heard publicly in the court of the Mosque, which formed the hall of audience, and there whatever matters required the directions of the Holy Prophet were discussed and settled. Simple though its exterior, and unpretending its forms and usages, more power was exercised, and affairs of greater importance transacted, in the courtyard of the Mosque of the Holy Prophet than in many an Imperial Palace.

In the autumn of 631, intimation reached the Holy Prophet of the gathering of a large army on the borders of Syria, and he resolved to meet the danger with as large a force as could be collected. The journey in contemplation was so distant and the heat of the season so excessive that, contrary to his custom, the Holy Prophet gave timely warning of his objective so that the necessities of the way might be foreseen and provided for. Though some of the Bedouin tribes showed little alacrity in obeying the Holy Prophet's command to join the army, and some men of Medina were on various pleas excused, extraordinary eagerness pervaded the ranks of loyal and earnest Muslims. Offerings and contributions poured in from every quarter, and from these sources transportation and supplies were provided for the poorer soldiers, though some still had to be turned away. The numbers of those who finally assembled for the march have been variously estimated, and were probably in the neighbourhood of 30,000, of whom not less than 10,000 were cavalry. After a hot and thirsty march, the army arrived at Tebuk, where there was plenty of shade and water and a halt was made there. The rumours of invasion had by this time melted away. There was nothing at the moment to threaten the border. So the Holy Prophet contented himself with sending a strong detachment under Khalid to Duma, and with receiving the adhesion of the Jewish and Christian tribes on the shores of the Gulf, towards the east of which the army was encamped. To John, the Christian prince of Ayla, the Holy Prophet addressed a letter summoning him to submission. The prince arrived with presents, was received with kindness and was entertained hospitably. The following treaty was concluded with him: 'In the name of God, Most Gracious, Ever Merciful: A compact of peace from God, and from Muhammad the Prophet and Apostle of God, granted unto Yuhanna, son of Ru'ba, and unto the people of Ayla. For them who remain at home, and for those that travel by sea or by land, there is the guarantee of God and Muhammad the Apostle of God, and for all that are with them, whether of Syria or of Yemen or of the sea coast. It shall not be lawful to hinder the men of Ayla from any springs which they have been in the habit of frequenting, nor from any journey they desire to make, whether by sea or by land. The writing of Juheim and Shurahbil, by command of the Apostle of God.'

In token of approbation the Holy Prophet presented the Christian prince with a mantle of striped Yemen stuff and dismissed him honourably. The tribute was fixed at the yearly sum of a golden piece for every family or 300 for the whole town of Ayla.

At the same time deputations from the Jewish settlements of Maqna, Adhruh and Jarba presented themselves with a tender of submission to the Holy Prophet. To each was given a rescript specifying the amount of their tribute and enjoining them to afford refuge and aid to any Muslim travellers or merchants who might stand in need of their good offices.

Having concluded these matters the Holy Prophet left Tebuk after having halted there for twenty days and returned to Medina. Meanwhile Khalid had been travelling across the desert from Tebuk to Duma with 420 horse, the flower of the army. So rapidly did he march and so unexpectedly appear before Duma that Okeidir, the Christian chief, was surprised by him while hunting. Okeidir was taken captive and the city was ransomed in return for a large number of camels, sheep, suits of mail and stands of arms. With these, and carrying with him Okeidir and a brother, Khalid returned to Medina. The Christian chief, wearing a golden cross, and clad in brocade inwrought with gold, to the admiration of the simple inhabitants of Medina, was brought to the Holy Prophet who invited him to embrace Islam. Okeidir complied and was admitted to the terms of a favoured ally.

When the Holy Prophet returned to Medina many who had remained behind without permission came forward to exculpate themselves. They were suitably dealt with, under divine direction, according to the degree of their culpability.

About two months after the return of the army from Tebuk, Abdullah bin Ubayy, the leader of the disaffected party, died. With his death no one was left in the ranks of the disaffected possessing power or influence. The faction had died out. Those who had hitherto been lukewarm or disloyal soon embraced, heart and soul, the cause of Islam, and the authority of the Holy Prophet became fully and finally consolidated in Medina.

It was now ten months since the siege of Taif had been raised. Its inhabitants, still wedded to idolatry, maintained a sullen isolation. Urwah bin Masood, who had been one of the emissaries sent by Quraish to the Muslim camp at Hudaibiyya, was absent during the siege of his native city, having gone to Yemen to learn the use of warlike engines for its defence. On his return, finding that all Mecca and the surrounding tribes excepting Taif had submitted to the Holy Prophet, and being himself favourably impressed with what he had seen at Hudaibiyya, Urwah went to Medina and embraced Islam. His first generous impulse was to return to Taif and invite his fellow citizens to share in the blessings of the new faith. The Holy Prophet, well knowing their bigotry and ignorance, warned him of the danger he would incur, but, presuming on his popularity at Taif, he persisted in the design. Arriving in the evening he made public his conversion and called on the people to join him. They returned to consult upon the matter. In the morning, ascending his roof, he made the Call to Prayer, upon which the rabble surrounded his house and shot arrows at him by which he was mortally wounded. His family and friends rallied round him, but it was too late. He blessed God with his dying breath for the honour of martyrdom, and prayed his people to bury him by the side of the Muslims who had fallen at Hunain. When the tidings reached the Holy Prophet he lauded the memory of the martyr, observing, 'He may be compared to the Prophet Yasin, who summoned his people to believe in the Lord, and they slew him.'

The martyrdom of Urwah compromised the inhabitants of Taif, and forced them to continue the hostile course they had been pursuing. But they began to suffer severely from the attacks of Hawazin under Malik, who, according to his resolve, had maintained an unceasing warfare against them. 'We have not strength,' they said among themselves, 'to fight against the Arab tribes all round who have plighted their faith to Muhammad, and are bound to fight in his cause.' So they sent a deputation of six chiefs with some twenty followers who reached their destination a fortnight after the return of the army from Tebuk. Mughira, nephew of the martyr Urwah, meeting the embassy in the outskirts of the city, hastened to announce their approach to the Holy Prophet, who received them gladly and directed that a tent be pitched for their accommodation close by the Mosque. Every evening he visited and instructed them in the faith. They freely communicated their apprehensions to him. As for themselves, they were quite ready at once to destroy their great idol, Lat; but the ignorant amongst them, and especially the women, were devoted to the worship and would be alarmed at its demolition. If the matter were postponed but for three years, and the people meanwhile familiarised with the requirements of Islam, the wishes of the Holy Prophet might then without difficulty be carried into effect. But the Holy Prophet would not consent. Two years, one year, six months were asked successively, and successively refused. The grace of one month might surely be conceded, they begged, but the Holy Prophet was firm. Islam and the idol could not co-exist. The idol must fall without a single day's delay. They then begged to be excused performance of the daily prayers, and that someone else might be deputed to destroy the image. 'As for the demolition of the idol with your own hands,' replied the Holy Prophet, 'I will dispense with that; but prayer is indispensable. Without prayer religion were naught.' To this they submitted. They pleaded that the forest of Wajj, a famous preserve for the chase in the vicinity of Taif, might be declared inviolate, and to this the Holy Prophet acceded, and the embassy, having finally tendered their allegiance, left with a rescript to the effect that they had desired.

Abu Sufyan and Mughira, both friends of the tribe, were deputed by the Holy Prophet to accompany the envoys and destroy their idol. Mughira, wielding a pick-axe and surrounded by a guard of his relatives, attacked the great image, and, amid the cries and wailings of the women, with his own hand hewed it to the ground. Taif was the last stronghold that held out against the authority of the Holy Prophet. It was also the only place where the fate of an idol excited the sympathy of the people. Everywhere else the idols were destroyed by the people themselves without a pang.

The month of pilgrimage now drew near and the Holy Prophet appointed Abu Bakr to lead the caravan of pilgrims from Medina, which was limited to 300 men.

The Holy Prophet's little son, Ibrahim, was now fifteen or sixteen months old. He fell ill in the middle of summer and his illness soon became grave. Though carefully tended, he expired in the arms of the Holy Prophet, who expressed the poignancy of his grief in the words: 'The eye sheds tears and the heart grieves, yet we say not aught that would offend our Lord. Ibrahim, we grieve sorely over thy parting. To Allah we belong, and to Him we shall all return.' Then he comforted Mary and her sister Sireen and bade them to be silent and resigned. The obsequies, prayers and burial were carried through by the Holy Prophet, assisted by his uncle Abbas and his son Fadhl. He lingered at the grave after it was filled up and, calling for a skin of water, caused it to be sprinkled over the spot.

An eclipse of the sun occurred on the same day, and the people spoke of it as a tribute to the death of the Holy Prophet's son. Sir William Muir has observed (*Life of Muhammad*, p. 430):

A vulgar impostor would have accepted and confirmed the delusion; but Muhammad rejected the idea. The sun and the moon, he taught them, are amongst the signs appointed by the Lord. They are not eclipsed on the death of anyone. Whensoever you see an eclipse, then betake yourselves to prayer until it passeth away.

The adhesion of Taif and the destruction of its famous idol had enhanced the Holy Prophet's fame throughout the south and east of the peninsula. A stream of submissive embassies from all quarters now flowed uninterruptedly towards Medina.

Among the embassies there was one from Bani Haneefa, a Christian branch of Bani Bakr, inhabiting Yamamah. One of the Bani Haneefa party was Musailamah, who, probably from what he then saw, conceived the idea that he might successfully set up a claim to prophethood. When the customary presents were distributed among them, the deputies solicited a share for him, saying he had been left behind in charge of the baggage. The Holy Prophet directed that he should have the same as the rest, as his position was none the worse among them because of his duty. Bani Haneefa, before their departure, embraced Islam and abandoned Christianity without compunction.

Sometime later, a deputation of fourteen chief men from Najran, in the centre of Arabia, repaired to Medina; among them was Abdul Masih of Bani Kinda, their chief, and Abdul Harith, Bishop of Bani Harith. On reaching Medina, they were permitted by the Holy Prophet to enter the Mosque and to perform their service, which they did turning towards the east. After some discussion, a treaty was made with them, which provided: 'The Pledge of God and His Prophet is given that no Bishop shall be removed from his bishopric, nor any monk from his monastery, nor any priest from his priesthood; their authority and rights shall not be interfered with, nor anything that is customary amongst them; so long as they conduct themselves peaceably and uprightly. They shall not be oppressed, neither shall they oppress.' With this they returned to Najran. Sir William Muir's comment on the religious aspect of the discussion between the Holy Prophet and the Christian embassy from Najran is (*Life of Muhammad*, p. 460):

We cannot but see throughout the earnestness of Muhammad's belief, and his conviction that a spiritual illumination had been vouchsafed to him, bringing with it knowledge and certainty, where to the Christian, as he conceived, all was speculation and conjecture.

A year later, Khalid was directed to lead a delegation to that section of Bani Harith of Najran who were not parties to the treaty and to call on them to embrace Islam. They all responded to his invitation and professed their belief in Islam. On receiving his report, the Holy Prophet summoned Khalid to return along with a deputation from the tribe, which accordingly visited Medina and were kindly and courteously received.

The supremacy of Islam being thus widely recognised in the south of Arabia, the Holy Prophet sent forth a band of officers charged with the instruction of the people and the collection of the public dues. Over them, he placed Muaz bin Jabal, who had by this time fulfilled his mission at Mecca. The Holy Prophet instructed them, 'Deal gently with people and be not harsh; put them not in fear, but rather cheer them.' This was the key-note of the instructions that he always gave to public functionaries.

The pilgrimage came round again. Five days before the commencement of the Month of Pilgrimage the Holy Prophet, followed by a vast multitude, set out on the journey to Mecca. All his wives accompanied him. One hundred camels, marked by his own hand for sacrifice, were led in solemn order. A stop was made at Dhul Haleefah where the whole company assumed the pilgrim's garb, the *Ihram.* The Holy Prophet mounted Qaswa and pronounced Talbeeh:

Here am I, O Allah, here am I;
Here am I. Thou hast no associate, here am I;
All praise and bounty are Thine, and Thine the Kingdom;
Thou hast no associate.

When his mount stood up and stepped out he repeated the Talbeeh, and again when it negotiated the first rise in the track, and thereafter on every change of position and posture, throughout; the multitude in his company following his example. Thus has it since been down the ages, and thus will it continue till the end of time.

As indicated in the opening words of his address on the Day of Arafat, the Holy Prophet knew that this was to be his only pilgrimage, and this consciousness added to his eagerness to leave no part of his task undone. A Muslim's knowledge that the Holy Prophet knew that what he esteemed as his greatest and final pilgrimage was not to be long delayed makes the memory of all that he did and said in the course of this pilgrimage poignant and precious.

On the tenth day of his journey the Holy Prophet reached Saif, an easy stage from Mecca; there he rested for the night, and on the morning, having bathed and mounted Qaswa, proceeded towards Mecca. He entered the upper suburbs by the same route which he had taken two years before and, passing down the main street, approached the Ka'aba. As he passed through the Bani Shaiba Gate, with the Holy House full in view, he raised his hands to heaven, and invoked a blessing on it: 'O Lord, add unto this House in the dignity and glory, the honour and the reverence, which already Thou hast bestowed upon it. They that for the pilgrimage, and the Umra, frequent this House, increase them much in honour and dignity, in piety, goodness and renown.' Then, mounted as he was on his camel, he performed the prescribed circuits with other preliminary rites, and afterwards retired to a tent pitched for him in the valley.

On the seventh of the month, after the midday Prayer, the Holy Prophet preached to the concourse assembled around the Ka'aba. Next day, followed by myriads of devotees, he set out for Mina where he performed the ordinary prayers and slept in a tent. On the second morning at sunrise he moved to Arafat, where he arrived shortly after noon. The plain of Arafat, in which 100,000 eager pilgrims were gathered, was humming with Takbir, Talbeeh, Tasbih, Tahmeed and calling down blessings on the Holy Prophet. He proceeded through the throngs to Jabal Rahmat (Mount of Mercy).

Muhammad, the Chosen of Allah; rejected by Quraish; persecuted; penned in with his family and a few Companions for thirty months in Shi'b Abi Talib and denied all provisions and contact; hounded out of Taif; forced out of Mecca with a price of one hundred camels proclaimed for his person, dead or alive; pursued by the hatred of Quraish even in Medina; challenged by force, besieged, plotted against; faithful, loyal, steadfast, humble, obedient servant of Allah; His Messenger par excellence; in rejection and in acceptance, in trial and in triumph proclaiming as his stand: 'Sufficient unto me is Allah, there is no god but He, in Him is my trust, the Lord of the Glorious Throne' (9:129); Muhammad was now surrounded by an ocean of faithful, devoted hearts, all proclaiming the glory of Allah, celebrating His praise, affirming His Unity, supplicating Him for forgiveness, mercy, compassion, invoking His blessings upon Muhammad. Arrived at the Mount, the Holy Prophet stood on the back of Qaswa and made his address:

'I bear witness that there is none worthy of worship save Allah, the One, without associate, and I bear witness that Muhammad is His Servant and His Messenger.

'I do not think, O people, that we shall be gathered together here again. Your belongings, your honour, and your lives are sanctified and made inviolate like the sanctity of this day, this month and this city. You will soon appear before your Lord and He will call you to account for all your doings. Take heed that you do not go astray, after I am gone, and start slaying one another.

'Take note, that I trample underfoot all un-Islamic customs and traditions. All blood-feuds are utterly wiped out. I hereby remit everything owed to any member of my family on that account.

'Riba [interest] has been declared unlawful and is no longer due. I hereby remit any interest due to any member of my family; for instance, all interest due to my uncle, Abbas bin Abdul Muttalib, is remitted altogether.

'Be ever mindful of the duty you owe to Allah in respect of your wives. You have married them with the guarantee of Allah's name, and you have made them lawful for yourselves in accordance with Allah's word. So be mindful of your covenant. They owe you fidelity; for any default on their part you may correct them gently. You owe them suitable maintenance. As regards those under your authority, see that you feed them with such food as you eat yourselves; and clothe them with the stuff you wear. If they commit a fault which you are not inclined to forgive, then sell them, for they are the servants of the Lord, and are not to be tormented.

'Allah has made you brethren one to another, so be not divided. An Arab has no preference over a non-Arab, nor a non-Arab over an Arab; nor is a white one to be preferred to a dark one, nor a dark one to a white one.

'I am leaving something with you that will safeguard you against all error, if you hold fast to it. That is Allah's Book.

'There is no new prophet after me, nor any new law. Worship your Lord, observe Prayer, observe the fast during Ramadhan, pay the Zakat cheerfully, perform the Pilgrimage to the House of Allah, and obey those in authority among you; Allah will admit you to His Paradise.

'You will be questioned concerning me also on the Day of Judgment. Tell me, then, what will you answer?'

There was a tremendous response: 'We bear witness that you have conveyed all Allah's commands to us.' The Holy Prophet raised his finger to heaven and then pointed it at the people, and voiced the adjuration, 'Hear, O Allah.'

The people affirmed, 'You have discharged in full your obligations as Prophet and Messenger.'

In the same manner again, the Holy Prophet begged, 'Bear witness, O Allah.'

A third time came the response, 'You have made clear to us that which is right and that which is wrong.'

Again the entreaty went up from the Holy Prophet, 'Hear, O Lord.'

He then charged those present to convey the substance of his address to those absent, observing that perchance he who hears at second hand may retain it better than one who is present.

As soon as he concluded, the revelation came: 'This day have I completed My commandments for you, and have brought to its fullness the favour that I have bestowed upon you, and have chosen Islam as your religion' (5:4).

The Holy Prophet descended from the back of Qaswa and directed Bilal to call the Azan. The whole concourse was hushed and the call went forth:

> Allah is Great, Allah is Great;
> Allah is Great, Allah is Great;
> I bear witness that there is no god save Allah,
> I bear witness that there is no god save Allah;
> I bear witness that Muhammad is Allah's Messenger,
> I bear witness that Muhammad is Allah's Messenger;
> Come to Prayer, come to Prayer;
> Come to Prosperity, come to Prosperity;
> Allah is Great, Allah is Great;
> There is no god save Allah.

The Holy Prophet led the combined noon and afternoon prayer services. Thereafter he remounted Qaswa and returning to the vicinity of the Mount of Mercy, among the boulders, stood on the back of Qaswa, facing in the direction of the Ka'aba, and raising his arms became absorbed in entreaty and supplication, in the attitude of one who, sore troubled and distressed, humbly begs for mercy. Long did he continue thus occupied with passionate entreaty before his Lord.

After sunset, the Holy Prophet proceeded to Muzdalifah, a distance of three or four miles, where, after leading the combined sunset and evening services, he spent the night in supplication, under the open sky, like all his fellow pilgrims. After sunrise, he returned to Mina and sacrificed the camels that had been brought for the purpose. After three days spent at Mina he proceeded to Mecca and on arrival there he performed the circuits of the Ka'aba and drank from Zam zam. Three more days were spent at Mecca and then the Holy Prophet returned to Medina with his followers.

The final year of the Holy Prophet's residence at Medina opened peacefully. The greater part of the peninsula acknowledged his authority. His days were now chiefly occupied with the reception of embassies, the issue of rescripts to his various delegates scattered over the land and the consolidation of the Islamic state.

Badhan, the Persian governor, who had early submitted himself to the Holy Prophet, died about this time. His son Shehr was continued in the government of San'a and the surrounding district. But the other provinces hitherto combined under his authority, as Ma'reb, Najran and Hamdan were divided among different governors.

A new cause of danger suddenly arose, in the emergence of three false claimants to the Prophetic office in different quarters of the peninsula. Their pretentions were not, however, developed till near the close of the life of the Holy Prophet, and the tidings which he received were hardly of so grave a nature as to raise serious uneasiness. The least important of the three impostors was Tulaiha, chief of Bani Asad, and a warrior of note and influence in Nejd. When the news of his imposture reached the Holy Prophet he sought, by aid of the faithful converts in his tribe, to put down the pretender. However, subsequent to the Holy Prophet's death he broke out into open rebellion, and was defeated, after a severe engagement, by Khalid, whereupon he retired into Syria. On Umar's summoning, he returned to his tribe and submitted to Umar's authority, and thereafter fought bravely on the side of Islam.

It has already been noticed that Musailamah had accompanied the deputation of Bani Haneefa to Medina. He was a man of small stature, in presence insignificant, but ready and powerful in speech. He claimed that he was the recipient of divine revelation and pretended also to work miracles. The Holy Prophet, hearing the rumour of his insolent pretentions, sent him a summons to submit to Islam. Musailamah returned the reply that he too was a Prophet like Muhammad himself. 'I demand, therefore,' he said, 'that thou divide the land with me; as for Quraish, they are a people that have no respect for justice.' The Holy Prophet's reply was, 'The earth is the Lord's, and He causeth such of His servants as He pleaseth to inherit the same. Peace be on him that follows the guidance.' Musailamah went on consolidating his authority and in the time of Abu Bakr constituted a menace for the Islamic state. He was fought in the battle of Yamamah and was killed by Wahshi, now a Muslim, who had killed Hamzah, the uncle of the Holy Prophet, on the day of Uhud.

The third false claimant was Aswad Ansi of Yemen, who abjured Islam during the Holy Prophet's lifetime. A prince of wealth and influence in the south, he assumed the garb of a magician, and gave out that he was in communication with the unseen world. He prosecuted his claims at first secretly, and gained over the chieftains in the neighbourhood who were dissatisfied with the distribution of power upon the death of Badhan. About the close of the tenth year of the Hijra, he openly raised the standard of rebellion, and drove out the officers of the Holy Prophet. Advancing on Najran, which rose in his favour, he suddenly fell on San'a, where, having killed Shehr the son of Badhan, he put his army to flight, married his widow, and established himself in undisputed authority. The insurrection, fanned by this sudden success, spread quickly, and the greater part of the country lying between Bahrain, Taif and the coast, was reduced to his authority. On intimation of this rebellion reaching the Holy Prophet, he contented himself with despatching letters to his officers on the spot to deal with the rebel according to the means at their disposal. Aswad, in the pride of conquest, had already begun to slight the commanders to whose bravery he was indebted for success. The officers of the Holy Prophet opened up secret negotiations with them, and, favoured by the tyrant's wife, who detested him and burned to avenge her late husband's death, soon put an end to the usurper, just before the death of the Holy Prophet.

After his return from the Farewell Pilgrimage, the Holy Prophet, receiving intimation of unrest among the tribes on the Syrian border, gave orders for an expedition to the Syrian frontier. On the day following the command it was announced that Usama, son of Zaid, the beloved friend of the Holy Prophet slain at Muta, was, notwithstanding his extreme youth (he was not yet twenty years of age), appointed to lead the army. There was some criticism of the appointment, but the Holy Prophet put it down by observing, 'Some of you criticized the appointment of his father Zaid to various commands. But he was entirely competent and I loved him. I also love his son and I am sure that he will prove competent.'

On the following day the Holy Prophet was seized with a violent headache and fever, but they passed off. The next morning he found himself sufficiently recovered to bind with his own hands the banner for the army, and presented it to Usama, saying, 'Fight thou beneath this banner in the name of the Lord, and for His cause.' The camp was then formed at Jurf; and the whole body of the fighting men, including Abu Bakr and Umar, were summoned to join it.

About this time the Holy Prophet received the revelation (110:2-4):

> Now that Allah's succour has become manifest and victory has been achieved, and thou hast seen people join the religion of Allah in large numbers, then glorify thy Lord, with His praise, and seek forgiveness of Him for their frailties. Surely, He is Oft-Returning with compassion.

He interpreted this as meaning that the task assigned to him by his Lord had been fulfilled and that his end, which had been intimated to him in the revelation vouchsafed to him on the conclusion of his address on the Mount of Mercy on the day of the pilgrimage, was now approaching. When he announced this revelation he observed, 'A servant of the Lord was granted the choice to stay on a little longer upon the earth or to return to Him forthwith, and he preferred the latter.' On hearing this, Abu Bakr, who was of the company, was overcome by emotion and exclaimed, 'Fain would we ransom thee with the sacrifice of our fathers, our mothers and ourselves,' upon which the Holy Prophet said, 'Were it permissible to take a human being as a devoted friend, I would have chosen Abu Bakr; but such love is permissible only for Allah.' Umar has related that when Abu Bakr exhibited deep emotion on hearing the latest revelation of the Holy Prophet and expressed his devotion to him in the words that have just been cited, he felt that Abu Bakr had been deeply affected without cause as the Holy Prophet had only cited the case of a devoted servant of God, who, on being granted the choice between a little longer life on earth and immediate return to his Lord, preferred the latter. 'But Abu Bakr,' he said, 'was blessed with greater spiritual penetration than we were, because he perceived that the Holy Prophet had mentioned his own case and not that of some other devoted servant of God.'

For a day or two the Holy Prophet continued to lead the Prayer services and to visit the apartments of his wives in rotation. One night he arose softly, and, followed only by a servant, walked to the burial ground in the outskirts of the city. There he rested long, absorbed in meditation. At last winding up his thoughts, he prayed aloud for those who were buried there, supplicating thus: 'Verily, both ye and I have received fulfilment of that which our Lord did promise us. Blessed are ye, for your lot is better than the lot of those that are left behind. Temptation and trial approach like portions of a dark night that follow one upon another, each darker than that preceding it. Lord, have mercy upon them that lie buried here.' With these words, he turned and went back to his apartment.

His sickness returned upon him with increasing violence, but it did not confine him entirely to his apartment. He was able to move into the Mosque and lead the public Prayers, till it became difficult for him to do so. He then directed that Abu Bakr should conduct the Prayers in his stead, upon which Aisha urged, 'Messenger of Allah, truly Abu Bakr is a man of a tender heart, and weepeth readily. He will not be able to stand in your place and to lead the Prayers.' 'Command that he lead the Prayers,' repeated the Holy Prophet, and Aisha still urging her pleas, he observed, 'Truly, ye resemble the foolish women in the story of Joseph; give command forthwith as I desire.' The command was given, and Abu Bakr conducted the public Prayers during the remaining period of the Holy Prophet's illness. There can be little doubt that by nominating Abu Bakr to this duty the Holy Prophet intended the delegation of his authority to him. This was further confirmed by his direction that all doors opening into the courtyard of the Mosque be closed, except the door of Abu Bakr's apartment.

With the consent of his other wives, he decided to remain in Aisha's apartment during the rest of his illness. He was now too weak to attend to any public business, yet the Syrian expedition occupied his mind and he kept saying to those around him, 'Send off quickly the army of Usama.' He also inquired about the embassies daily arriving at Medina, and enjoined for them the same hospitable treatment and gift of similar largesses as he had been wont to bestow.

His sickness had lasted nearly a fortnight when, on the night of Saturday, it began to assume a serious aspect. The fever rose to such a pitch that a hand could hardly be kept upon him from the burning heat. Observing his suffering, one of his wives exclaimed, 'You would surely have great reward.' 'Yea,' he answered, 'I swear by Him in Whose hands is my life, that there is not upon the earth a believer, sore afflicted with calamity or disease, but the Lord thereby causeth his sins to fall off from him, even as the leaves from a tree in autumn.' At another time he said, 'Suffering is an expiation for sin. If a believer suffer but the scratch of a thorn, the Lord raiseth his rank thereby, and wipeth away from him a sin.' And again, 'Believers are tried according to their faith. If a man's faith be strong, so are his sufferings; if he be weak, they are proportioned thereunto.' Umar, approaching the bed, placed his hand on his forehead, and suddenly withdrew it from the great heat. 'Messenger of Allah,' said he, 'how fierce is the fever upon you.' 'Yea, verily,' replied the Holy Prophet, 'but I have been during the night repeating in praise of the Lord, seventy Suras, among them the seven long ones.' Umar answered, 'Why not rest and take your ease, for has not the Lord suppressed all your weaknesses?' 'Nay,' replied the Holy Prophet, 'wherefore should I not yet be a faithful servant unto Him?' An attendant, while the Holy Prophet lay covered up, put his hand below the sheet and, feeling the excessive heat, made a remark like that of Umar. On which the Holy Prophet said, 'Just as this affliction prevaileth now against me, even so shall my reward hereafter be.' 'Who are they,' asked another, 'that suffer the severest trials?' 'The Prophets and the righteous,' answered the Holy Prophet, 'yet each of them rejoiceth exceedingly in his affliction.'

All Sunday the Holy Prophet lay in a helpless and, at times, delirious state. Usama, who had delayed his march waiting to see what the issue might be, came in from Jurf to visit him. Removing the covering he stooped down and kissed the beloved face. The Holy Prophet raised his hands in the attitude of blessing and then placed them on the young commander's head, who then returned to the camp.

At one time, Um Salama and Um Habeebah, who had both been exiles in Abyssinia, spoke of the beauty of the Cathedral of Mary there, and of the wonderful pictures on its walls. Overhearing them, the Holy Prophet said, 'These are the people who, when a saint among them dieth, build over his tomb a place of worship, and adorn it with their pictures. Let the anger of the Lord be kindled against those that turn the tombs of their Prophets into objects of worship. Lord, let not my tomb be ever an object of worship.' In the course of the day he recalled that there was some gold in the house, and directed that it should be divided amongst certain indigent families and observed, 'Now I am at peace. It would not have become me to meet my Lord, and this gold still in my hands.'

All Sunday night the illness lay heavy upon him, but the morning brought relief. The fever and the pain abated and there was some return of strength. The dangerous accession of fever on the previous night having become known, the Mosque was crowded in the morning at the hour of Prayer with anxious worshippers. Abu Bakr led the devotions; as Imam he stood in the place of the Holy Prophet before the congregation, his back turned towards them. He had ended the first *raka'a* and the congregation had just stood up for the second when the curtain of Aisha's door slowly moved aside and the Holy Prophet himself appeared. As he entered the assembly he whispered in the ear of Fadhl, son of Abbas, who with a servant supported him, 'The Lord hath granted unto me great joy,' and he looked around him with a gladsome smile remarked by such as at the moment caught a glimpse of his countenance.

Having paused thus for a moment, he walked softly to the front where Abu Bakr stood. The people made way for him, opening their ranks as he advanced. Abu Bakr heard the rustle and, guessing the cause, stepped backwards to vacate the leader's place. But the Holy Prophet motioned him to go on and moved forward towards the pulpit. There, on the ground, he sat by the side of Abu Bakr, who resumed the service and completed it in due form. Abu Bakr then entered into conversation with the Holy Prophet and expressed his joy at finding him, to all appearance, convalescent. He then asked his permission to go and visit at her house at the Sunh, a suburb of the upper city, his wife whose turn it was that day. On permission being granted, he departed.

The Holy Prophet then sat down in the courtyard of the Mosque near the door of Aisha's apartment and addressed the people who, overjoyed to find him again amongst them, crowded round. He spoke with emotion, and with a voice still so powerful as to reach beyond the outer doors of the Mosque. He inquired whether anyone had any claim against him. One or two who preferred a trifling claim were immediately compensated. The Holy Prophet proceeded: 'I have not made lawful anything excepting that which God has made lawful; nor have I prohibited aught but that which God in His Book hath prohibited.' Usama coming up to bid farewell, he said to him, 'Go forward with the army; and the blessings of the Lord be with ye.' Then turning to the women who sat close by, he admonished them: 'O

Fatima, my daughter, and thou Safiya, my aunt, work ye that which shall gain acceptance for you with the Lord; for I verily have no power with Him to save you in anywise.' He then rose and was helped back into Aisha's chamber.

Exhausted, he lay down upon the pallet stretched upon the floor and Aisha, seeing him very weak, raised his head from the pillow and, as she sat by him on the ground, laid it tenderly on her bosom. His strength now rapidly sank, and after a little he repeated in a whisper, 'To the blessed Companionship On High; to the blessed Companionship on High.' He stretched himself gently, and then all was still. The Holy Prophet had breathed his last.

The news of his death, spreading rapidly over Medina, soon reached Abu Bakr in the suburb of the Sunh. He immediately mounted his horse and rode back to the Mosque in haste. Meanwhile a strange scene was being enacted there. Shortly after the Holy Prophet had expired, Umar entered the apartment of Aisha and, lifting up the sheet which covered the body, gazed wistfully at the features of his beloved master. All was so placid, so natural, so unlike death, that Umar could not believe the mournful truth. Starting up, he exclaimed wildly, 'The Prophet is not dead; he hath but swooned away.' Mughira, standing by, vainly sought to convince him that he was mistaken. As, quitting the chamber of death, they entered the courtyard of the Mosque, Umar cried, 'The Apostle of God is not dead.' The crowd, attracted by the loud and passionate tone of Umar, flocked around him, and he went on haranguing them in similar strain: 'The hypocrites would persuade you that Muhammad is dead. Nay, but he hath gone to His Lord, even as Moses who remained absent for forty days, and then returned, after his followers had said he was dead. So, by the Lord, the Prophet shall return, and confound those that say that he is dead.' Umar found a willing audience. It was but a little while before that the Holy Prophet had been amongst them, had joined with them in Prayer on that very spot, and had gladdened their hearts by hope of speedy convalescence. The echo of his voice was hardly yet silent in the courts of the Mosque. The events of the day had produced such effect upon the people that, carried away by Umar's fervour, they gladly persuaded themselves that he might be in the right.

Just then appeared Abu Bakr. Passing through the Mosque he listened for a moment to the frenzied words of Umar and, without pausing further, walked onwards to the door of Aisha's chamber. Drawing the curtain softly aside he asked leave to enter. 'Come,' came the reply from within, 'for this day no permission needs to be asked.' He entered and, raising the striped sheet which covered the bed, stooped down and kissed the face of his departed friend, saying, 'Sweet wast thou in life, and sweet thou art in death.' After a moment he took the head between his hands and, slightly lifting it, gazed on the well known features, and exclaimed, 'Yes, thou art dead! Alas, my friend, my chosen one! Dearer than father or mother to me! Thou hast tasted the bitter pain of death; and thou art too precious with the Lord, that He should give thee the bitter cup to drink a second time!' Gently putting down the head upon its pillow, he stooped again and kissed the face, then replaced the covering and withdrew.

Leaving the room, Abu Bakr went at once to the spot without where Umar, in the same excited state, was haranguing the people. 'Sit ye down Umar, and be quiet,' cried Abu Bakr. But Umar went on, not heeding the remonstrance. So Abu Bakr, turning from him, began himself to address the assembly. No sooner did they hear his voice than they quitted Umar and gave attention to the words of Abu Bakr. He recited from the Holy Quran: 'Thou wilt die and they will die' (39:31), and 'Muhammad is but a Messenger; of a surety, all Messengers before him have passed away. If then, he die or be slain, will you turn back on your heels?' (3:145) He proceeded: 'Whosoever worshippeth Muhammad, let him then know that Muhammad indeed is dead; but whoso worshippeth God, let him know that the Lord liveth and doth not die.' The words of the Holy Quran fell like a knell on the ears of Umar and all those who had buoyed themselves up with the delusive hope of the Holy Prophet's return to life. The truth now bursting upon them, they sobbed aloud. Umar himself would relate, 'By the Lord, it was so that, when I heard Abu Bakr reciting those verses, I was horror-struck, my knees trembled, I dropped down, and I knew of a certainty that the Prophet was indeed dead.'

It was now towards the afternoon, when someone came running hastily towards the Mosque to say that the chief men of Ansar, with S'ad bin Ubadah at their head, had assembled in one of the halls of the city and were proceeding to choose S'ad for their leader. On hearing this report, Abu Bakr, after arranging that the family of the Holy Prophet should not be disturbed while they washed the corpse and laid it out, hurried, in company with Umar and Abu Obaida, to the hall where the people had assembled. There was urgent necessity for their presence. 'Let them have their own chief,' was the general cry of Ansar, 'but as for us, we shall have a chief for ourselves.' S'ad, who lay sick and covered over in a corner of the hall, had already been proposed for the chiefship of Ansar, when Abu Bakr and his party entered. Umar, still in a state of excitement, was about to speak, when Abu Bakr, afraid of his impetuosity, held him back, and himself addressed the people. 'Ye Ansar,' he said, 'all that ye speak of your own excellence is true. There is no people upon earth deserving all this praise more than ye do. But the Arabs will not recognise the chief command elsewhere than in Quraish. We are the Ameers; ye are our Wazeers.' 'Not so,' shouted Ansar, 'but there shall be an Ameer from

amongst us, and an Ameer from amongst you.' 'That can never be,'
said Abu Bakr; and repeating his previous formula in a firm
commanding voice he added, 'We are the noblest of the Arabs by
descent; and the foremost in the glory of our City. Choose ye whom
ye will of these two [pointing to Umar and Abu Obaida] and do
allegiance to him.' 'Nay,' cried Umar, in words which rose high and
clear above the growing tumult of the assembly, 'did not the Prophet
himself command that thou, O Abu Bakr, shouldst lead the Prayer?
Thou art our master, and to thee we pledge our allegiance, thou whom
the Prophet loved the best amongst us all.' So saying, he seized the
hand of Abu Bakr and, striking it, pledged faith to him. The words
touched a chord that vibrated in every believer's heart and Abu Bakr
was saluted Successor of the Holy Prophet.

Meanwhile, Ali, Usama and Fadhl son of Abbas, with one or two of
the Holy Prophet's servants, had been busily employed in the chamber
of Aisha. There on the spot on which he breathed his last, they washed
the body and laid it out. The garment in which he died was left upon
him; two sheets of fine white linen were wound around it; and overall
was cast a covering of striped Yemen stuff. Thus the body remained
during the night, until the time of burial.

On the morrow, when the people had assembled in the Mosque,
Abu Bakr and Umar came forth to meet them. Umar first addressed
the great assemblage: 'O ye people, that which I spoke unto you
yesterday was not the truth. Verily, I find that it is not borne out by
the Book which the Lord hath revealed, nor by the covenant which
you made with His Apostle. As for me, verily I hoped that the Apostle
of the Lord would continue yet awhile amongst us, and speak in our
ears a word such as might seem good unto him and be a perpetual
guide unto us. But the Lord hath chosen for His Apostle the portion
which is with Himself, in preference to that which is with you. Truly,
the Word, that same Word which directed the Prophet, is with us still.
Take it, therefore, for your guide and ye shall never go astray. Now,
verily, hath the Lord placed your affairs in the hands of him that is the
best amongst us; the Companion of His Prophet, the second of the
two when they were in the cave alone. Arise, and swear fealty to him.'
Forthwith, the people crowded round, and one by one, they swore
allegiance upon the hand of Abu Bakr.

The ceremony ended, Abu Bakr arose and said: 'Ye people, now,
verily, I have become your Chief over you although I am not the best
amongst you. If I do well, support me; if I err, then set me right. In
truth and sincerity is faithfulness, and in falsehood perfidy. The weak
and oppressed among you in my sight shall be strong, until I restore
his right unto him, if the Lord will; and the strong oppressor shall be
weak, until I wrest from him that which he hath taken. Now hearken
to me; when a people leaveth off striving in the ways of the Lord,

verily, He casteth them in disgrace. Know also that wickedness never aboundeth in any nation, but the Lord visiteth that nation with calamity. Wherefore, obey me, even as I shall obey the Lord and His Apostle. Whensoever I disobey them, obedience is no longer binding upon you. Arise to Prayers, and the Lord have mercy on you.'

When Abu Bakr had ended his address preparations were made for the burial. There was a difference regarding the place most fitting for the grave, but Abu Bakr said, 'I have heard it from the lips of the Prophet himself, that in whatsoever spot a Prophet dieth, there also should he be buried.' He therefore gave command that the grave should be dug where the body was still lying within the chamber of Aisha. It remained there from the afternoon of Monday to the same hour on the following day. On Tuesday, it was visited by all inhabitants of the city. They entered in companies by the door which opened into the Mosque; and, after gazing once more on the countenance of the Holy Prophet and praying over his remains, retired by the opposite entrance. The room was crowded to the utmost at the time when Abu Bakr and Umar entered together. They prayed as follows: 'Peace be upon thee, O Prophet of God; and mercy from the Lord and His blessing. We bear testimony that the Prophet of God has delivered the Message revealed to him; has fought in the ways of the Lord until God brought forth his religion unto victory; has fulfilled His words, commanding that He alone in His unity is to be worshipped; has drawn us to himself, and been kind and tender-hearted towards the believers; has sought no recompense for delivering to us the Faith, neither has he sold it for a price at any time.' All the people said, 'Amen.' When the men departed, the women followed in company, and then even the children crowded round for a last look on the Holy Prophet's face. In the evening, the final rites were performed. A red mantle, worn by him, was first spread as a soft covering at the bottom of the grave; then the body was lowered into its last resting-place by the same loving hands that had washed and laid it out. The vault was built over with unbaked bricks, and the grave filled up.

Aisha continued to live in her chamber thus honoured as the Holy Prophet's cemetery. She occupied a room adjoining that which contained the grave, but partitioned off from it. When her father died he was buried close by the Holy Prophet in the same chamber and, in due time, Umar also. Thus was fulfilled her dream that three moons fell from heaven, one after the other, into her chamber.

The first concern of Abu Bakr on assuming the office of Khalifa was to despatch the Syrian army and thus fulfil the dying wish of the Holy Prophet. But the horizon was lowering all around, and many urged that the force should not be sent just yet upon this distant expedition. Even Umar joined in the cry: 'Scatter not the believers; rather keep the army here; we may have need of it yet to defend the city.' 'Never,' replied Abu Bakr, 'the command of the Holy Prophet shall be carried out, even if I be left here in the city all alone, prey to the wolves and the beasts of the desert.' Then they besought that a more experienced warrior might be appointed to the chief command, but Abu Bakr would have none of it. He would admit of no excuse and no delay; the force was soon marshalled again at Jurf. Abu Bakr bade Usama be mounted and accompanied him on foot to the camp, treating him with the profound respect due to a commander appointed by the Holy Prophet himself, and begged permission that Umar might be left behind at Medina as his counsellor. The request was granted. He then bade Usama farewell, and exhorted him to go forward in the name of the Lord, and fulfil the commission received by him at the Holy Prophet's hands. The army marched, and the Khalifa, with Umar alone, returned to Medina. Having fulfilled the Holy Prophet's last command, in a matter of three weeks the army retraced their steps. It was a triumphal procession as they approached Medina; Usama rode upon his father's horse and the banner, bound so lately by the Holy Prophet's own hands, floated before him. Abu Bakr and the citizens went forth to meet him, and received the army with acclamations of joy. Attended by the Khalifa and the chief Companions, Usama proceeded to the Mosque and offered up Prayer in thanksgiving for the success which had richly crowned his arms.

Sir William Muir has summed up (*Life of Muhammad*, p. 509):

I will merely add that the simplicity and earnestness of Abu Bakr, and of Umar also, the first two Caliphs, are strong evidence of their belief in the sincerity of Muhammad; and the belief of these men must carry undeniable weight in the formation of our own estimate of his character, since the opportunities they enjoyed for testing the grounds of their conviction were both close and long-continued. It is enough that I allude to this consideration, as strengthening generally the view of Muhammad's character, which throughout I have sought to support.

Chapter 15

:Excellent Exemplar:

Muhammad was a Lawbearing Prophet. He was not a novelty, as there had been such prophets before him, for instance Moses, through whom God had foretold the advent of another Lawbearing Prophet like unto him (Deuteronomy 18:18). He was directed to proclaim: 'I am no innovation among Messengers' (46:10). This means that Muhammad had been prepared by God as a fit and appropriate channel for conveying divine law and guidance to mankind; and implied that his personality had been moulded to that end and that he illustrated conformity to that law and guidance in his own conduct. Though he lived in a region which had slight contacts with the rest of the world, and at a time when the art of history was still in its infancy, his was a truly historical personality. He lived his life in the full light of day. Enough is known of his early life to enable one to form a fair idea of his qualities and character. After he received the Divine Call his every word, act, and gesture were observed, and a complete record of them has been preserved. That was necessary, for otherwise not only would there be lack of certainty and confidence, but his life could not furnish us with an example of what he taught.

Muhammad was a human being – no more, no less – and therefore he could serve as an example for mankind. He possessed no supernatural powers, nor did he claim any. He was subject to the same conditions and limitations as his contemporaries. He suffered more than most and achieved outstanding success in his lifetime. His life had many facets and passed through many phases. Like other men, he was a son, a husband and a father. He had been a servant employed by a master, and was a citizen subject to the authorities of his town. God appointed him a teacher and a guide. He immediately became an object of scorn and derision, and soon of bitter persecution. He was a loving and watchful shepherd of his little flock. Through bitter persecution and hard fighting he gave proof of the highest courage, endurance and perseverance.

During the last ten years of his life he was called upon to discharge the duties of Chief Executive and Chief Magistrate of a heterogeneous community, divided into sections in conflict with each other. He thus became the head of a state fraught with internal frictions and beset with external dangers of every description. In addition to the heavy duties and responsibilities pertaining to his prophetic office, he was called upon to display qualities of administration and statesmanship which taxed him to the utmost. He was a man of peace. The due discharge of the trust and responsibility which God had been pleased to place upon him demanded the establishment and preservation of peace. His enemies would let him have no peace. They forced him to take up arms in defence of the most fundamental human right: freedom of conscience. He hated war and conflict, but when war was forced upon him, he strove to render it humane. He abolished all savage and barbarous practices. He commanded in battle, but scrupulously refrained from personally shedding blood. His strategy was faultless and was always designed to reduce loss of life and human suffering to the minimum. During eight years of fighting, punctuated with pitched battles and numerous pre-emptive expeditions, the total loss of life suffered by his enemies was 759, and that suffered by his own people was 259. Binding obligations and demands of justice imposed upon him the duty of avenging wrong and punishing evil in a harsh world, but his judgments were always tempered with mercy. He did not fail to exercise sternness when the occasion demanded it, for any such lack would have been a failure in the discharge of his obligations. He would not tolerate treason or treachery, but was never vindictive. He was most forgiving and forbearing in respect of personal wrongs suffered by him.

The following description of his person and character is taken from Sir William Muir (*Life of Muhammad*, pp. 510-13):

His form, though little above mean height, was stately and commanding. The depth of feeling in his dark black eyes, and the winning expression of a face otherwise attractive, gained the confidence and love of strangers, even at first sight. His features often unbended into a smile full of grace and condescension. He was, says an admiring follower, the handsomest and bravest, the brightest-faced and most generous of men. It was as though the sunlight beamed in his countenance. His gait has been likened to that of one descending a hill rapidly. When he made haste, it was with difficulty that one kept pace with him. He never turned, even if his mantle caught in a thorny bush; so that his attendants talked and laughed freely behind him secure of being unobserved.

Thorough and complete in all his actions, he took in hand no work without bringing it to a close. The same habit pervaded his manner in social intercourse. If he turned in a conversation towards a friend, he turned not partially, but with his full face and his whole body. In shaking hands, he was not the first to withdraw his own; nor was he the first to break off in converse with a stranger, nor to turn away his ear. A patriarchal simplicity pervaded his life. His custom was to do everything for himself. If he gave an alms he would place it with his own hands in that of the petitioner. He aided his wives in their household duties, mended his clothes, tied up the goats, and even cobbled his sandals. His ordinary dress was of plain white cotton stuff, made like his neighbours'. He never reclined at meals.

Muhammad, with his wives, lived, as we have seen, in a row of low and homely cottages built of unbaked bricks, the apartments separated by walls of palm-branches rudely daubed with mud, while curtains of leather, or of black haircloth, supplied the place of doors and windows. He was to all of easy access – even as the river's bank to him that draweth water from it. Embassies and deputations were received with the utmost courtesy and consideration. In the issue of rescripts bearing on their representations, or in other matters of state, Muhammad displayed all the qualifications of an able and experienced ruler. What renders this the more strange is that he was never known himself to write.

A remarkable feature was the urbanity and consideration with which Muhammad treated even the most insignificant of his followers. Modesty and kindliness, patience, self-denial, and generosity, pervaded his conduct, and riveted the affections of all around him. He disliked to say No. If unable to answer a petitioner in the affirmative, he preferred silence. He was not known ever to refuse an invitation to the house even of the meanest, nor to decline a proffered present however small. He possessed the rare faculty of making each individual in a company think that he was the favoured guest. If he met anyone rejoicing at success he would seize him eagerly and cordially by the hand. With the bereaved and afflicted he sympathised tenderly. Gentle and unbending towards little children, he would not disdain to accost a group of them at play with the salutation of peace. He shared his food, even in times of scarcity, with others, and was sedulously solicitous for the personal comfort of everyone about him. A kindly and benevolent disposition pervaded all those illustrations of his character.

Muhammad was a faithful friend. He loved Abu Bakr with the close affection of a brother; Ali, with the fond partiality of a father. Zaid, the freedman, was so strongly attached by the kindness of the Prophet, that he preferred to remain at Mecca rather than return home with his own father. 'I will not leave thee,' he said, clinging to his patron, 'for thou hast been a father and mother to me.' The friendship of Muhammad survived the death of Zaid, and his son Usama was treated by him with distinguished favour for the father's sake. Uthman and Umar were also the objects of a special attachment; and the enthusiasm with which, at Hudaibiyya, the Prophet entered into the Pledge of the Tree and swore that he would defend his beleaguered son-in-law even to the death, was a signal proof of faithful friendship. Numerous other instances of Muhammad's ardent and unwavering regard might be adduced. His affections were in no instance misplaced; they were ever reciprocated by a warm and self-sacrificing love.

In the exercise of a power absolutely dictatorial, Muhammad was just and temperate. Nor was he wanting in moderation towards his enemies, when once they had cheerfully submitted to his claims. The long and obstinate struggle against his pretentions maintained by the inhabitants of Mecca might have induced its conqueror to mark his indignation in indelible traces of fire and blood. But Muhammad, excepting a few criminals, granted a universal pardon; and, nobly casting into oblivion the memory of the past, with all its mockery, its affronts and persecution, he treated even the foremost of his opponents with a gracious and even friendly consideration. Not less marked was the forbearance shown to Abdullah and the disaffected citizens of Medina, who for so many years persistently thwarted his designs and resisted his authority, nor the clemency with which he received submissive advances of tribes that before had been the most hostile, even in the hour of victory.

Such is the testimony of a biographer who was not too favourably disposed towards the Holy Prophet. The testimony of Khadija, his most intimate companion for fifteen years before the Divine Call came to him, with regard to his character and qualities, has been noted earlier. Her devoted comradeship during the first ten years of his ministry till her death shortly after the lifting of the blockade, is further confirmation of the estimation that she had formed of his character earlier. Aisha, daughter of Abu Bakr, whom he married two years after the Emigration, when asked about his character replied, 'His character was the Quran,' than which there could be no higher praise.

During the period of persecution in Mecca, the Holy Prophet endured everything without complaint and proved himself a good and law-abiding citizen. Yet he was never afraid and was not deterred from doing all that he considered was due from him. He had, in association with some others, undertaken the obligation to go to the assistance of any person who might have been wronged and to procure justice for him. He never failed or faltered in the discharge of that obligation, even after he himself became the object of persecution. On one occasion, an outsider sought help from the Meccans in respect of the recovery of a sum of money owed to him by Abu Jahl. Those whom he approached directed him cynically to the Holy Prophet, who immediately accompanied the man to Abu Jahl's house and knocked at his door. Abu Jahl, amazed at seeing Muhammad before him, admitted the claim. The Holy Prophet then asked him to discharge his obligation, which he promptly did. When Abu Jahl later appeared before his fellows, they jeered at him and taunted him with having submitted meekly to Muhammad's demand. He said he had been so awed that he could not help himself.

Even during the Meccan period the widow, the orphan, the needy, the wayfarer, the slave and the distressed were the objects of the persecuted Prophet's special care and concern. At Medina he continued his simple ways and austere habits. For days together his hearth remained unlit. He and his subsisted on a meagre diet of dates or parched ground barley. Sometimes water alone sufficed. He had but one change of clothes. His dwelling was of the simplest and barest. He slept on a leather sack filled with twigs and branches of trees. He never slept in a bed; never ate bread made out of ground flour; never ate his fill.

At night, between the prescribed services, he spent long hours in prayer. He stood so long in the course of these prayers that sometimes his feet became swollen. On one occasion Aisha was moved to venture a mild protest against such prolonged devotion. The Holy Prophet answered, 'Aisha, God has been so profuse in bestowing His bounties upon me that it behoves me to be the most grateful of His servants.' The character of his domestic life may be gathered from one of his own well-known sayings: 'The best of you is he who behaves best towards the members of his family.'

He constantly exhorted his people towards moderation in all respects. Noticing that some were inclined to carry austerity to the extreme, and to occupy themselves so much with prayer and fasting that they were apt to neglect their normal obligations, and to injure their health, he admonished them: 'I fear God more than any of you fear Him, yet I fast and I eat; I pray and I discharge all my obligations towards my family and my people. It is not right to carry any matter to the extreme. God loves best those acts of worship and piety which, though moderate, are carried out without being felt a burden. Having performed that which is prescribed, pray and fast and worship God while you may do so cheerfully; stop when your spirit or your body begins to feel the strain.'

He did not disdain humour and with all his grave occupations did not altogether neglect the lighter side of life. On one occasion, when he was sitting at home with Aisha, an old woman came to visit her. Thinking that it was a good opportunity to ask a favour of the Holy

Prophet, the visitor begged him to pray that she might be admitted to heaven when her time came to depart this life. The Holy Prophet replied, 'There will be no old women in heaven.' Distressed, the old lady began to bewail her fate. The Holy Prophet hastened to explain that what he had meant was that there would be no question of age, of old or young, in heaven; all would be alike. He comforted her till she was restored to cheerfulness. On one occasion he challenged Aisha to a race, which she won. A year or two later he challenged her again and this time he won. He laughed, saying, 'Aisha, we have come out even.'

Aisha once confessed to him that she had suspected him of an unfairness, but had soon found out that she was mistaken. He remarked, 'Aisha, there is a Satan in everyone of us, of whose promptings we should beware.' 'Is there a Satan inside you also?' she inquired. 'Yes,' he replied, 'but he has accepted submission.'

One day he happened to pass near a date-palm garden in which some people were engaged in carrying out grafting. He enquired what they were doing, and when they explained the process he asked them why they did not do it another way. The following year they complained that they had adopted his suggestion but the trees had yielded less fruit than normal. He observed, 'I had merely made an enquiry from you. You know more about these things than I do. You should have followed the method which experience had taught you was best.'

He was often called upon to decide disputes and give judgment. He warned, however, that he had no means of discovering the truth except through what was stated before him. It was quite possible that one party to a dispute might, by plausible arguments, succeed in persuading him that it was in the right, when in fact the other party was in the right, and he might give judgment in favour of the first. Even so, the party in whose favour judgment was given must remember that it was answerable to God. The mere fact that it had obtained judgment from him would not serve to absolve it if it were not in fact in the right.

The Holy Prophet's clemency and compassion were well-known. A poor man confessed to him publicly that he had been guilty of a certain wrong. The Holy Prophet imposed a mild penalty by way of a fine, which would be distributed in charity; but the man pleaded that he was unable to pay. Just then someone brought a basket of dates to the Holy Prophet to be distributed in charity. He bade the wrongdoer to take the dates and distribute them among the poor. Said the man, 'Messenger of Allah, I know of no one more deserving of charity than myself.' The Holy Prophet laughed and replied, 'Well, then, take them yourself and that will suffice as your penalty.'

On another occasion someone confessed having committed a wrong, but the Holy Prophet paid no attention to him and, as it was

Prayer time, stood up to lead the Prayer. After the Prayer, the man again confessed his wrong. The Holy Prophet inquired, 'Did you not join us in the Prayer service?' On the man replying in the affirmative, the Holy Prophet observed, 'Well then, your Prayer has wiped out your offence.'

During the course of a journey, the Holy Prophet and his party rested among a grove of trees to escape the noon-day heat. The Holy Prophet hung up his sword by the branch of a tree and lay down to rest under its shade. An enemy who had been on the prowl for an opportunity to kill him stole into the camp, and, finding the Holy Prophet sleeping unguarded, approached him, secured his sword, and, drawing it, sat down on his chest. The Holy Prophet woke up in surprise as the man, brandishing the sword, said, 'Who can save thee now?' The Holy Prophet gently uttered the single word 'Allah,' moved away from under the man, raised himself and took hold of his assailant, wresting the sword from him. The position was now reversed. 'Who can save thee now?' inquired the Holy Prophet. 'No one!' exclaimed the man in terror. 'Why do you not say "Allah"?' asked the Holy Prophet as he released the man.

To the Companions who had now gathered round them, the Holy Prophet explained what had happened, and inquired from the man, 'Will you bear witness that there is no one worthy of worship save Allah, and that I am His Messenger?' The man said he could not do that, but he would promise that he would not fight against him. The Holy Prophet let him go free.

This incident is a testimony to the Holy Prophet's presence of mind in situations of extreme danger and his complete trust in God. It will be recalled that on the occasion of his flight from Mecca when Quraish had tracked him to the mouth of the cave in which Abu Bakr and he had taken refuge, and Abu Bakr became apprehensive lest they might be discovered and the Holy Prophet might be exposed to serious danger, he reassured Abu Bakr with, 'Have no fear. We are not only two, there is a third with us, even God.'

In his early days in Medina, there was an alarm one night and the Muslims began to gather in the mosque as they had been directed to do on such occasions. They were awaiting the Holy Prophet when they observed him appear through the gloom riding a pony, returning from the plain. He reassured them that he had ridden out to investigate, and that there was no cause for alarm and that they should go back to sleep. He proved himself the most alert of them all.

At the commencement of the battle of Hunain when the Muslim forces fell into confusion and the Holy Prophet was left only with a dozen or so followers, he asked his uncle, Abbas, to call out the Muslims to rally to the standard and, himself spurring his mule, despite Abu Bakr's efforts to restrain him, went forward towards the enemy calling out, 'I am God's true Prophet, no impostor; I am the grandson of Abdul Muttalib.'

'The Holy Prophet had been sent as a manifestation of God's mercy to mankind' (21:108). His mercy was all-embracing, without limit, and without discrimination, from which even the animals and birds were not excluded. He was not niggardly about it, as lesser men might have been (17:101). He had to be stern in dealing with grave offences, treason and treachery, but that too was a manifestation of mercy, as a wolf has to be destroyed out of mercy to the sheep. That which inspired him first and last was his duty to God. His beneficence towards all human beings was only one aspect of the performance of the duty which he owed to his Maker. No consideration could stand in the way of the performance of that duty. When the Meccans gave his uncle, Abu Talib, the choice between adhering to Muhammad or retaining the chieftainship of the tribe, Abu Talib put the matter to the Holy Prophet. The Holy Prophet told him that he could withdraw his protection, but that as for himself, he must continue till the end to do what God commanded him. He would not desist even if the Meccans placed the sun on his right and the moon on his left. That stand he maintained without the least swerving till the last. With him God always came first. So much was this so that even his enemies in Mecca were wont to say of him 'Muhammad is intoxicated with the love of his Lord.'

God had, of His grace and wisdom, commanded the Holy Prophet to shoulder the responsibility of conveying His message to mankind and of leading them back to Him. His enemies did not believe in his mission, nor that what he proclaimed as revelation was received by him from God, so God posed a challenge to them, which they never took up and to which they had no answer. He was commanded to proclaim, 'If God had so willed, I would not have recited the Quran to you, nor would He have made it known to you. I have lived among you a whole lifetime before this. Will you not then understand?' (10:17) Thus God put forward the purity and righteousness of the Holy Prophet's life, which those who opposed him so bitterly had observed at close quarters, as proof that he was not capable of uttering a lie against God. Faced squarely with this challenge, not one of them attempted to assert that Muhammad had on any occasion been guilty of saying or doing that which was not utterly true, completely righteous. The exemplary life that he had led, before their very eyes, up to the moment that the Divine Call came to him, was a guarantee of the truth of his claim.

Yet, all the time he had to stress that he was but a man like the rest, lest, observing the security that he enjoyed in the midst of constant danger, the success that he extracted even from persecution and defeat, and the ultimate triumph of his cause to which the whole of

Arabia had progressively become witness, some might be tempted to ascribe to him supernatural capacities and powers of superhuman status. He was commanded to proclaim, 'I am but a man like yourselves. I have received revelation that your God is only One God. So let him who hopes to meet his Lord act righteously, and let him associate no one in the worship of his Lord' (18:111).

When challenged by his opponents to show them a sign, like causing a spring to gush forth from the earth, or causing the heavens to fall upon them in pieces, or ascending to heaven and bringing down with him a book which they could read, he was commanded to reply, 'Holy is my Lord. I am but a man sent as a Messenger' (17:91-4).

It was necessary to stress this both in view of what had happened in the case of some previous prophets who were exalted as divinities by their followers, and also for the simple reason that only a man can be an exemplar for men. An angel or a god cannot set an example which men can follow. The dimensions would be utterly disparate. It is a curious inversion that a prophet's opponents often seek to justify their rejection of him on the ground that he is but a man like them, a single individual from among themselves (54:25). Yet, as the Quran points out, it is only a man who can serve as God's Messenger to men. 'An angel would be sent as a Prophet if the earth were peopled with angels' (17:95-6).

The Holy Prophet's disclaimer of any supernatural powers or capacities is repeatedly emphasised in the Quran. For instance, he is commanded to say that he does not possess knowledge of the unseen, save only that much as God reveals to him (2:256; 72:27-8). Had he possessed such knowledge, he would have collected abundant good for himself, and no evil could have touched him (7:189). It is true that the Holy Prophet had full faith in God's promises of help and the ultimate triumph of his cause, but he set a clear example that faith in God and in His promises entailed the putting forth of the utmost effort towards the achievement of the purpose and goal which God Himself had appointed. For instance, he had been assured of God's protection against his enemies (5:68); of his victorious return to Mecca (28:86); of the ultimate success and triumph of his cause (58:22-3); but he did not for one moment slacken his vigilance or his effort in respect of the complete discharge of his own duties and of exhorting his followers to do the same (3:140, 201).

He was not only kindly and affectionate towards those who came in contact with him, praying for them and exhorting them constantly to order their lives in accordance with divine commandments and guidance, but also exerted himself to the utmost to train them in every aspect of life, so as to prepare and equip them for the due discharge of the responsibilities that lay upon them and much heavier ones that were about to be placed upon their shoulders (3:150). He was commanded to exhort his followers to pray for even those who persecuted them and paid no heed to the warnings of God, and overlook and forgive their trespasses (45:15).

He was a mercy for mankind. God called him such and he did indeed prove himself so in every respect. It was grievously painful for him that his people should be distressed, and he was ardently desirous of promoting their welfare – tender and compassionate at all times and anxious to apply balm to their much harassed and wounded spirits (9:128). When persecution became unbearable in Mecca, the Holy Prophet directed those of his followers who could do so to migrate across the Red Sea to seek shelter and peace in the dominions of the Emperor of Abyssinia. Later, when life was made impossible for him and for the Muslims in Mecca, the Migration to Medina was decided upon, but the Holy Prophet himself stayed on in Mecca till all those who could be the objects of the resentment of the Meccans, and were free to do so, had departed from Mecca. Of the free male adults, only Abu Bakr, Ali and himself were left. Abu Bakr accompanied him and Ali, who had been entrusted with the return of money and articles which some Meccans had left with the Holy Prophet for safekeeping, soon followed him.

The Holy Prophet was always on the easiest terms with everyone. All had free access to him. A party of Muslims who had no home, nor possessions of any kind, eked out an austere livelihood during part of the day and spent the greater part of their time in the company of the Holy Prophet in the mosque, spending their nights on a platform in the courtyard of the mosque. They were known as the Company of the Platform. The Holy Prophet was most affectionate towards them and, every morning, after the dawn Prayer service, sat down among them and shared his frugal breakfast with them. He often invited them to take part with him in his other meals.

A poor freedman by the name of Zahir made his living out of a small patch of ground some distance out of Medina, which he tended and cultivated as a market gardener. Two or three times a week he would carry the sparse produce into Medina where he set up a stall in an open space. He would take some of it as a present to the Holy Prophet, who in return would present him with articles procurable in the town which might be of use to him or which he might be in need of. The Holy Prophet was wont to say, 'Zahir is our country, and we are his town.' On one occasion, during the noon-day heat, the Holy Prophet happened to pass near Zahir's stall where he was hawking his produce. He was exposed to the fierce heat of the sun, his torso glistening with perspiration. The Holy Prophet approached him quietly from behind and, putting out his arms on both sides of his face, covered his eyes with his hands as children sometimes do in sport. Zahir put up his hands to his eyes and from the softness of the hands covering them concluded that this intimate and affectionate gesture could come only from the Holy Prophet. Taking advantage of the situation, he extended his own arms backwards and, encircling the Holy Prophet between them, he pulled him close to himself and began to rub his sweating body against the Holy Prophet. The Holy Prophet began to laugh and removed his hands from Zahir's eyes. This was his way of administering comfort to one who might have considered himself lonely and friendless, and might have been weary of his task.

It was his simple and unaffected humanity which earned for the Holy Prophet God's affirmation that he possessed the highest moral excellences (68:5), and that God's grace had been bestowed upon him in abundance (17:88).

The highest yearning of the human soul is to win the love of God through its own devotion to, and love of, Him. The Holy Quran succinctly points the way for the satisfaction of that yearning. The Holy Prophet was commanded to say, 'If you love God, follow me; then will God love you and forgive you your faults. Surely, God is Most Forgiving, Merciful' (3:32). When Aisha said that the character of the Holy Prophet was the Quran, she meant that the Holy Prophet illustrated in his own person to the fullest degree the excellences that the Quran teaches. It was because he had become a living example and illustration of the highest excellences that man is capable of achieving, that God's testimony affirmed, 'Verily, you have in the Messenger of Allah an excellent exemplar, for him who fears Allah and the Last Day, and who remembers Allah much' (33:22).

In short, the whole of the Holy Prophet's life – his every thought, every movement, every action, his very being – was devoted to God in the effort to seek closer communion with Him. This is also clearly affirmed by divine testimony. He was commanded to say, 'My Prayer and my sacrifices and my life and my death are all for Allah, the Lord of the worlds. He has no associate. So am I commanded, and I am the first of those who submit wholly to Him' (6:163-4).

The West has, with a few honourable exceptions, through fourteen centuries consistently ignored all that was patently good and beneficent in the life of the Holy Prophet and in Islam and, when confronted by his example and his doctrine, has taken shelter behind flimsy and untenable excuses. Its favourite objection has been that Islam was spread by the sword. By whose sword? The Holy Prophet was but one man against the whole world. Through thirteen long years of his ministry at Mecca, under the severest persecution and the gravest provocation, he and his small band of followers set the example of steadfast law-abiding citizens, who offered no violence against violence. Finally, some of them having left for Abyssinia, the greater part of them migrated to Medina and the Holy Prophet followed them later. His Meccan enemies should have then left him alone, calling it a good riddance. But they would not leave him and his in peace. It was they who unsheathed the sword against him and his followers. It was then that he was, under divine command, compelled to take up the sword in defence of freedom of conscience, which is proclaimed in positive and emphatic terms by the Holy Quran. It was the persistence of Quraish in the use of force against the Muslims, much inferior to them in numbers and equipment of every type, that brought ruin upon Quraish; the same happened after the fall of Mecca to other tribes.

The facts speak eloquently in this, as in all other, contexts. During the Meccan period of his ministry the Holy Prophet did not employ the sword on any occasion, even in defence. There could be no question of anyone being forced or coerced in any way to accept his message. His wife Khadija, his cousin Ali, still only a boy, his freedman Zaid and his closest friend Abu Bakr accepted him without the slightest hesitation; the last, when told of Muhammad's claim of Prophethood, at once exclaimed, 'That mouth is not capable of uttering a falsehood.' Slowly others followed: Uthman, Zubair, Talha, Mus'ab bin Umair, Suhaib, Bilal, and some time later Umar and Hamzah, all of whom played distinguished roles in the early history of Islam. Was any of them forced or coerced into believing in the truth of the Holy Prophet? The number of such outstanding personalities who joined the ranks of the Muslims in Mecca, despite the severest persecution, continued to grow steadily. Was there any suspicion in respect of any of them that they had been forced to declare faith in the Holy Prophet by force or coercion? Was the delegation from Medina, composed of seventy men and two women, who swore the pledge of allegiance to the Holy Prophet, and, despite the warning of Abbas, uncle of Muhammad, affirmed that if the Holy Prophet decided to move to Medina, they would safeguard him with their very lives, actuated to undertake that fearful responsibility by anything save the sincerity of their faith and the depth of their devotion?

It is airily argued that the Holy Prophet did not employ force in Mecca as he possessed little strength there. But if the faith to which he invited steadily gained strength in Mecca under the most adverse conditions, what need had he to employ force for its propagation after he had migrated to Medina? Even before his arrival there, Islam was making rapid progress among Aus and Khazraj and all that the Holy Prophet and the Muslims needed was to be left alone to lead their individual and collective lives in accordance with the teachings of their faith. But they were not left in peace. Did the Holy Prophet lead his ragged force of just over 300 men, half-starved, ill-equipped and ill-armed, against 1,000 experienced warriors of Quraish, well-fed, well-equipped, well-armed and well-mounted, in the field of Badr, in order to convert Quraish by the sword to Islam? In the eyes of the worldly the Holy Prophet's project was a suicidal adventure. He was compelled to embark upon it in defence of the freedom of conscience, trusting wholly in divine support. Of the 70 Quraish taken prisoners in the battle of Badr, was a single one forced to accept Islam on the point of the sword? A year later at Uhud, were 750 Muslims pitted against 3,000 Quraish for the purpose of forcing them to accept Islam at the point of the sword? Two years later, did a Confederate force of 20,000 besiege Medina because the Muslims under the command of the Holy Prophet had been forcing them to accept Islam at the point of the sword? Later, at Hudaibiyya, was it the Holy Prophet who was anxious to secure a truce with Quraish and to put an end to fighting, or was it Quraish who sought an end to the use of the sword? The Holy Prophet was so keen that the sword be sheathed between him and Quraish that, in order to secure his purpose, he accepted every reasonable and unreasonable condition proposed on behalf of Quraish, so much so that the Muslims felt that the terms of the treaty were humiliating. Is it or is it not a fact that once fighting was ended between Quraish and the Muslims, Islam began to make much faster progress than it had made during the years of conflict? At Hudaibiyya, the Holy Prophet was accompanied by 1,500 Muslims; in less than two years when a flagrant breach by Quraish of the treaty forced the Holy Prophet to march on Mecca, he was followed by 10,000 devoted Muslims. What is it then on the basis of which the West has persisted in charging the Holy Prophet with having spread his faith by the sword?

Sir Thomas W. Arnold, a well-known and highly respected orientalist, at one time Professor of Arabic in the University of London, made a thorough research into this question and in his outstanding work, *The Preaching of Islam,* first published in 1896, established beyond a doubt that the sword had nothing to do with the spread of Islam.

De L. O'Leary has affirmed (*Islam at the Crossroads,* p. 8):

> History makes it clear, however, that the legend of fanatical Muslims sweeping through the world and forcing Islam at the point of the sword upon conquered races is one of the most absurd myths that historians have ever repeated.

For nearly two centuries the Muslims have been deprived of the sword. Most Muslim countries, one after the other, passed under the domination of Christian colonial powers and have regained their independence only during the last thirty years. During this period political power rested in the hands of Western countries and Christian missionaries spread all over the world, including Muslim lands, with unlimited resources at their disposal for the purpose of propagating Christianity and winning the world for it. What has been the result?

Islam and the Muslims are in a much stronger position today than they were 150 years ago. In several countries of Africa during the last fifty years Islam has been steadily gaining ground against Christianity. Where is the sword at the point of which Islam is winning the hearts of increasing numbers of people almost everywhere today? Even in the countries of the West latterly small communities of indigenous Muslims have been established who uphold moral and spiritual values above the material values that dominate the West. Their number is increasing.

Some Western critics have been anxious to make out that the Holy Prophet's personality was a bundle of inconsistencies. They acknowledge that up to the time of his Migration from Mecca to Medina his life was a model of virtue, purity, uprightness, gentleness, compassion, human sympathy and of all that is good and beneficent; but that after he had acquired power in Medina all these excellent qualities, though not abandoned altogether, were marred by cruelty, vindictiveness, self-indulgence and licentiousness. Any intelligent person who has made even a cursory study of human nature must indignantly reject such a caricature as an utter impossibility. What these critics forget is that once the Holy Prophet was accepted in Medina as Chief Executive and Chief Magistrate, the scope of his responsibilities was enormously extended, and that many of them called for the exercise of sterner qualities than had been needed during his Meccan life. His positive and beneficent qualities were not affected adversely in the least degree. Outstanding examples of every one of them continued to be exhibited throughout. His character shone even more brilliantly in Medina than it had in Mecca for the very reason that many of his qualities had had no scope for coming into play during his Meccan life. For instance, take forgiveness. While he was in Mecca, he was sorely persecuted and was grievously ill-used. He bore everything with patience and steadfastness. It cannot, however, be said that he exercised forgiveness in any striking manner. He had no opportunity to forgive. Forgiveness predicates that the person who has suffered a wrong should have power to exact retribution and should forbear and forgive. In Mecca the Holy Prophet had no such power. Therefore if he had never gained power it would have been a mere academic speculation that the person who possessed all his beneficent qualities would have exercised his quality of forgiveness also at the highest level if he had been in a position to exact retribution for the wrongs done to him. In the case of the Holy Prophet, however, there are several instances of the exercise of the quality of forgiveness at the highest level and on the largest scale in the hour of triumph, of which there is no matching instance in human history. On the day that Mecca fell, he forgave all, but even more, after the battle of Hunain, he bestowed generous largesses upon those who, only a matter of weeks earlier, had been his bitterest and most implacable enemies.

In Medina he was responsible for the maintenance of public order and for the security of the whole population of the city, Muslim and non-Muslim alike. He had to punish crime, but his justice was always tempered with mercy. In the course of the safeguarding of the security of Medina he had, unfortunately, to deal sometimes with extreme cases of treason and treachery. He had to act sternly and even harshly, but that was a duty that he could not honestly evade.

His critics cite his treatment of Banu Quraidha as an example of his cruelty. Attention may be drawn to Stanley Lane-Poole's summing of the case. He has said that a fearful example was made of this clan, not by Muhammad but by an arbiter appointed by themselves. When Quraish and their allies were besieging Medina and well-nigh stormed the defences, this Jewish tribe entered into negotiations with the enemy which were only circumvented by the diplomacy of the Holy Prophet. When the besiegers had retired Muhammad naturally demanded an explanation of the Jews. They resisted in their dogged way and were themselves besieged and were compelled to surrender at discretion. Muhammad, however, consented to the appointing of a chief of a tribe allied to the Jews as the judge who should pronounce sentence upon them. His sentence was harsh, bloody; but it must be remembered that the crime of these men was high treason against the state and one need not be surprised at the summary execution of a traitorous clan (*Studies in a Mosque,* p. 68).

It may be added that the Holy Prophet, in carrying out the sentence, accepted every recommendation for mercy that was made to him. It was objected that as he had in advance agreed to carry out the sentence, whatever it might be, there was no room for mercy left. But the Holy Prophet pointed out that mercy was his prerogative, of the exercise of which he could not be deprived. In one instance, he not only accepted the recommendation made to him to spare the life of the offender, but as the result of further intercession he also directed the release of the members of his family and the restoration to him of his property; yet the person concerned refused to take advantage of the Holy Prophet's clemency.

Frithjof Schuon has observed (*Understanding Islam,* p. 89):

> Another reproach often levelled at him [Muhammad] is that of cruelty; but it is rather sternness that should be spoken of here, and it was directed, not at enemies as such, but only at traitors, whatever their origin; if there was hardness here, it was that of God himself through participation of Divine Justice which rejects and consumes. To accuse Muhammad of having a vindictive nature would involve, not only a serious misjudgment of his spiritual state and a distortion of the facts, but also by the

same token a condemnation of most of the Jewish Prophets and of the Bible itself; in the decisive phase of his earthly mission, at the time of the taking of Mecca, the Messenger of Allah showed a superhuman gentleness in face of a unanimous feeling to the contrary in his victorious army.

Professor Laura Veccia Vaglieri, at one time Professor of Arabic and Islamic Culture in the University of Naples, has observed (*An Interpretation of Islam*, p.28):

> Against the accusation of cruelty, the answer is easy. Muhammad, Head of a State, defender of the life and freedom of his people, in the exercise of justice, punished severely individuals guilty of crimes, and this attitude of his has to be considered in the light of his times and also in the light of the wild and barbarian society in which he lived. Muhammad, as a preacher of the religion of God, was gentle and merciful even towards his personal enemies. In him were blended justice and mercy, two of the noblest qualities which a human mind can conceive. It is not difficult to support this with many examples that are to be found in his biographies.

Another calumny that is persistently levelled at the Holy Prophet is that in his later life he became licentious. That is an enormity that has only to be contemplated to be immediately rejected as utterly incompatible with his life and character. Let us first consider the question of polygamy in general, and whether a plurality of wives negates high spirituality. In this context it should be remembered that in none of the great religious systems has polygamy been forbidden in the scriptures of a religion. All the Jewish Prophets, including the great lawgiver Moses, had a plurality of wives. No one has ever alleged that because of this they could not be accounted as leading virtuous lives.

All through human history it has been recognised that in certain circumstances and under certain conditions polygamy is not only permissible but is fully justified. It appears to be forgotten that licentiousness does not consist in a plurality of wives, but in the character of the relationship between men and women even inside marriage, and certainly when a relationship is established between a couple outside marriage. From the moral and spiritual points of view, the main purpose of marriage is the safeguarding of chastity. That very purpose might make polygamy desirable and even necessary in certain cases. There are several other contingencies of a social and sometimes of a political character that might justify recourse to the permission accorded by Islam in that behalf. It must be remembered that polygamy is not compulsory in Islam, far from it. It is permissible under very strict limitations, the principal one being the maintenance of complete equality between the wives, as is said: 'But if you should apprehend that you may not be able to deal justly between your wives, then marry only one' (4:4). A permission may be abused by persons who lack moral strength, but that does not mean that the permission itself is not justified and even wise.

Let us now consider the case of the Holy Prophet himself. Sir William Muir has observed (*Life of Muhammad*, p. 514):

> In domestic life the conduct of Muhammad is exemplary. As a husband his fondness and devotion were entire. As a father he was loving and tender. In his youth he lived a virtuous life; and at the age of twenty-five he married a widow forty years old, during whose lifetime for five and twenty years he was a faithful husband to her alone.

Professor Vaglieri has observed (*An Interpretation of Islam*, pp. 67, 68):

> Enemies of Islam have insisted in depicting Muhammad as a sensual individual and a dissolute man, trying to find in his marriages evidence of a weak character not consistent with his mission. They refuse to take into consideration the fact that during those years of his life when by nature the sexual urge is strongest, although he lived in a society like that of the Arabs, where the institution of marriage was almost non-existent, where polygamy was the rule, and where divorce was very easy indeed, he was married to one woman alone, Khadija, who was much older than himself, and that for twenty-five years he was her faithful, loving husband. Only when she died and when he was already more than fifty years old did he marry again and more than once. Each of these marriages had a social or political reason, for he wanted through the women he married to honour pious women, or to establish marriage relations with other clans and tribes for the purpose of opening the way for the propagation of Islam. With the sole exception of Aisha, he married women who were neither virgins, nor young nor beautiful. Was this sensuality?

The motive behind such marriages in the estimation of the Holy Prophet is well illustrated by his direction to Abdul Rahman bin Auf who was appointed to command an expedition to Dumatul Jandal and who was given the direction by the Holy Prophet that if he came to terms with the tribe concerned he might marry the daughter of their chief, which he did and from whom he had a son who became a renowned jurist in Islam, as has already been noticed. The Holy Prophet did not direct that Abdul Rahman bin Auf should bring the daughter of the chief to Medina so that the Prophet might marry her.

The Holy Prophet married Aisha, the daughter of his closest friend, Abu Bakr; and Hafsa, daughter of Umar, who had become a widow and for whom her father was anxious to arrange a marriage; and Um Salamah, widow of a loved Companion, who had been left with several children; and Um Habeebah, daughter of his then bitterest enemy, Abu Sufyan, who had been widowed in Abyssinia; and his first cousin, Zainab bint Jahsh, who had been divorced by Zaid, his freedman; and Safiyah, also a widow, daughter of his most implacable enemy, Huyay bin Akhtab, who had been executed on account of his treachery after the siege of Medina; and Jawairiyyah, the widowed daughter of a chief who had embraced Islam along with his tribe. He also married Mary the Copt who had been sent to him as a gesture of goodwill by the Christian Viceroy of Egypt. The motive in all these cases is clear.

But one has not to be apologetic on behalf of the Holy Prophet, peace be on him, in this matter of a plurality of wives, or indeed in respect of any other aspect of his life. The crucial question in the context of his domestic life is what was the character of his relationship with his wives. Looked at from that point of view, he also proved an excellent exemplar.

Frithjof Schuon has observed (*Understanding Islam*, pp. 88, 89):

> There was in his life a superhuman grandeur of soul; there were also marriages and through them a deliberate entry into the earthly and social spheres – we do not say into the worldly and profane spheres – and *ipso facto* an integration of collective human life into the spiritual realm in view of the Prophet's avataric nature. On the plane of piety attention must be drawn to the love of poverty, the fasting and the vigils; some people will no doubt object that marriage, and especially polygamy, are opposed to asceticism, but that is to forget, first, that married life does not remove the rigour of poverty, vigils and fasts, nor render them easy and agreeable, and secondly, that in the case of the Prophet marriage had a spiritualised or tantric character, as has indeed everything in the life of such a being because of the metaphysical transparency phenomena they assume. Looked at from outside, most of the Prophet's marriages had, moreover, a political aspect – politics having here a sacred significance connected with the establishing on earth of a reflection of the City of God – and, finally, Muhammad gave enough examples of long abstinences, particularly in his youth, when passion is

considered to be most strong, to be exempt from superficial judgments on this account.

Except for his marriage to Sudah, a pious, aged, indigent widow, all the Holy Prophet's subsequent marriages took place after his migration to Medina. How was he occupied in Medina and what was the type of life that he led there? Even the most casual reader, from the circumstances of his life in Medina which have been set out earlier, would be deeply impressed with his heavy responsibilities, his diligent discharge of them, his preoccupation with the teaching of the faith to his followers, ministering to them as their spiritual preceptor, leading the five daily Prayer services, administering the affairs of the heterogeneous population of Medina, spending the greater part of his night in voluntary Prayer; and would wonder how much of his time was spent in the company of his wives, and how that time was employed by him. It must also be remembered that the faith that he preached had forbidden altogether the use of alcohol and all intoxicants, looked unfavourably on comforts and luxuries, and that the Holy Prophet's own life was a model not only of simplicity, but even of rigorous asceticism. He permitted no indulgence of any kind to himself or to his wives.

The Holy Quran has inculcated the spirit that should inspire the relationship between husband and wife. It says, 'Of His Signs it is that He has created mates for you of your own species that you may find peace of mind through them, and He has put love and tenderness between you. In that surely are Signs for a people who reflect' (30:22). Then there is the admonition, 'Consort with them graciously. Should you dislike them, it may be that you dislike something in which Allah has placed much good' (4:20).

The Holy Prophet summed it up in, 'The best of you is he who behaves best towards his wife.' When he consorted with a wife he supplicated, 'Lord, safeguard us against Satan, and keep Satan away from that which Thou mightest bestow upon us.'

Aisha is reported to have said that the Holy Prophet was more modest than a virgin. Would that be the description of a person who was consumed with carnal passion and sought every opportunity for the satisfaction of his sensual desires through marrying a large number of women? It would also be instructive to reflect upon the standard of life that was prescribed in the Holy Quran for the wives of the Holy Prophet. He was commanded (33:29-35):

Say, O Prophet, to thy wives: If you desire the life of this world and its adornment, come then, I shall make provision for you and send you away in a handsome manner. But if you desire Allah and His Messenger and the home of the hereafter, then

Allah has prepared for those of you who carry out their obligations fully a great reward. Wives of the Prophet, if any of you should act in an unbecoming manner, her punishment will be doubled. That is easy for Allah. But whoever of you is completely obedient to Allah and His Messenger and acts righteously, We shall double her reward; and We have prepared an honourable provision for her. Wives of the Prophet, if you safeguard your dignity, you are not like any other women. So speak in a simple straightforward manner, lest he whose mind is diseased should form an ill design; and always say a good word. Stay at home and do not show off in the manner of the women of the days of ignorance, and observe Prayer, and pay the Zakat, and obey Allah and His Messenger. Allah desires to remove from you all uncleanness, members of the Household, and to purify you completely. Remember that which is rehearsed in your homes of the Signs of Allah, and of wisdom. Verily, Allah is the Knower of the minutest things, All-Aware.

There is no indication at all that any of them fell short in any respect of that which was prescribed for them, either during the life of the Holy Prophet or after his death. The period of widowhood in the case of some of them was quite prolonged. They spent it with great dignity, in beneficence and in the fear of God. That again is proof that their association with the Holy Prophet was at the highest moral and spiritual level.

We may sum up the character of the Holy Prophet in the words of two Western scholars, one German, the other British. Tor Andrae has recorded (*Muhammad: The Man and his Faith*, pp. 11, 12):

That Muhammad really lived cannot be disputed. The development of Islam – at least when compared with the other world religions – is open to the clear light of history, and presents us with yet another proof that the Prophetic personality is the original source of the new religious creation. Truly: 'My Prayers and my worship and my life and my death are unto God, Lord of the worlds. He hath no associate. This am I commanded, and I am the first of the Muslims' (6:163,164). The first of the Muslims! Muhammad is absolutely justified in so designating himself. He is the first representative of a new and independent religious type. Even today, after a period of development of thirteen centuries, one may clearly discern in genuine Islamic piety the uniqueness which is ultimately derived from its founder's personal experience of God.

W. Montgomery Watt, the well-known Orientalist, has said *(Muhammad at Medina,* pp. 334-5):

We may distinguish three great gifts Muhammad had, each of which was indispensable to his total achievement.

First, there is what may be called his gift as a seer. Through him – or on the orthodox Muslim view, through the revelations made through him – the Arab world was given an ideological framework within which the resolution of its social tensions became possible. The provision of such a framework involved both insight into the fundamental causes of the social malaise of the time, and the genius to express this insight in a form which would stir the hearer to the depths of his being. The European reader may be put off by the Quran, but it was admirably suited to the needs and conditions of the day.

Secondly, there is Muhammad's wisdom as a statesman. The conceptual structure found in the Quran was merely a framework. The framework had to support a building of concrete policies and concrete institutions. In the course of this book, much has been said of Muhammad's far-sighted political strategy and his social reforms. His wisdom in these matters is shown by the rapid expansion of a small state to a world empire, and by the adaption of his social institutions to many different environments and their continuance for thirteen centuries.

Thirdly, there is his skill and tact as an administrator and his wisdom in the choice of men to whom to delegate administrative details. Sound institutions and a sound policy will not go far if the execution of affairs is faulty and fumbling. When Muhammad died, the state he had founded was a going concern, able to withstand the shock of his removal and, once it had recovered from this shock, it expanded at prodigious speed.

The more one reflects on the history of Muhammad and of early Islam, the more one is amazed at the vastness of his achievement. Circumstances presented him with an opportunity such as few men have had, but the man was fully matched with the hour. Had it not been for his gifts as a seer, statesman, and administrator and, behind these, his trust in God and firm belief that God had sent him, a notable chapter in the history of mankind would have remained unwritten. It is my hope that this study of his life may contribute to a fresh appraisal and appreciation of one of the greatest of the sons of Adam.

Muhammad left an enduring impress upon a large mass of mankind. He indeed proved himself an excellent exemplar, as God has described him in the Holy Quran (33:22). That is why God ordained:

'Allah sends down His blessings on the Prophet, and His angels constantly invoke blessings on him. Do you, O believers, also invoke Allah's blessings on him and offer him the salutation of peace' (33:57). In obedience to this divine command, all through the centuries, Muslims have constantly prayed for, and invoked Allah's blessings upon the Holy Prophet. There are, today, more than 750 million Muslims spread in different parts of the world, and their number is daily increasing. An average Muslim invokes God's blessings on the Holy Prophet at least forty times during the course of each day, and many of them do it much oftener. Every time the Holy Prophet is referred to in conversation by name or by his Prophetic office, Allah's blessings are invoked upon him and Allah's peace is called down upon him. Thus every moment of the night and day, millions of devoted hearts supplicate the Almighty for His blessings on His Prophet. Has there been in the history of man any other who has been so richly blessed; and it is right that it should be so. One who devoted his life so utterly to the service of God and His creatures, as did the Holy Prophet, is deserving of the deepest gratitude on the part of the whole of mankind. By constantly invoking the blessings of God upon him, those who do so seek to repay a fraction of the great debt that humanity owes him.

Our last word is: All praise belongs to Allah, Lord of the worlds.

Bibliography

Bodley, R. V. C., *The Messenger,* New York, Robert Hale, 1946.

Denison, J. H., *Emotion as the Basis of Civilisation,* New York and London, Charles Scribner's Sons, 1928.

Dermenghem, E., *Life of Mahomet,* English translation, London, Routledge & Sons, 1930.

Draycott, G. M., *Mahamet, Founder of Islam,* New York, Dodd Mead, 1916.

Kennedy, Pringle, *Arabian Society at the Time of Muhammad,* Calcutta, Spink, 1926.

Lamartine, De Prat, *History of Turkey,* English translation, 3 vols, New York, D. Appleton, 1855-7.

Lane-Poole, S., *Studies in a Mosque,* London, Eden Remington, 1893.

Montgomery Watt, W., *Muhammad at Medina,* Oxford, Clarendon Press, 1958.

Muir, Sir William, *Life of Mahomet,* 4 vols, London, 1858-61.

O'Leary, De Lacy, *Islam at the Crossroads,* London, Kegan Paul, 1923.

Schuon, Frithjof, *Understanding Islam,* trans. D. M. Matthew, London, Allen & Unwin, 1963.

Scott, S. P., *History of the Moorish Empire in Europe,* 3 vols, London, Lippincott, 1904.

Vaglieri, L. V., *An Interpretation of Islam,* Washington DC, The American Fazl Mosque, 1957.

Index